by Susannah Gardner
and Shane Birley

Wiley Publishing, Inc.

Blogging For Dummies®, 3rd Edition

Published by
Wiley Publishing, Inc.
111 River Street
Hoboken, NJ 07030-5774

www.wiley.com

Published by Wiley Publishing, Inc., Indianapolis, Indiana

Published simultaneously in Canada

For general information on our other products and services, please contact our Customer Care Department within the U.S. at 877-762-2974, outside the U.S. at 317-572-3993, or fax 317-572-4002.

For technical support, please visit www.wiley.com/techsupport.

Wiley also publishes its books in a variety of electronic formats. Some content that appears in print may not be available in electronic books.

Library of Congress Control Number:

ISBN: 978-0-470-56556-8

Manufactured in the United States of America

10 9 8 7 6 5 4 3

About the Authors

Susannah Gardner is the co-founder and creative director of Hop Studios Internet Consultants (`www.hopstudios.com`), a Web design company specializing in custom Web solutions for content publishers.

Hop Studios brings an insightful concern for community building and editorial workflow to bear on each project backed by solid design and interface interaction skills. The company builds many types of sites, but specializes in those with copious, rapidly changing content or with a strong journalism, education, or editorial component (like blogs!).

Susannah is also a freelance writer and author; she is the author of *Blogging For Dummies, 2nd Edition*, *Buzz Marketing with Blogs For Dummies*, co-author of *BitTorrent For Dummies*, *Dreamweaver MX 2004 For Dummies*, and *Teach Yourself Visually: Dreamweaver MX 2004*, all from Wiley Publishing.

Prior to running Hop Studios, Susannah worked in the Online Journalism and Communication Program at the University of Southern California, writing curriculum, teaching, and conducting research at the intersection of technology and journalism. She was a senior editor of the Online Journalism Review, the media industry's only Internet-focused journalism publication. Susannah also spent four years at *The Los Angeles Times*, one of six editors responsible for launching that newspaper's Web site. During her time at LATimes.com she established the site's multimedia lab, which produced ground-breaking Web audio, video, and animation. She also launched and edited MetaHollywood, an online-only publication that covered new Hollywood technology and was LATimes.com's single largest revenue source in 1998.

Susannah earned bachelor's degrees in Print Journalism and American literature at USC. To learn more about her Web design company, visit `www.hopstudios.com`.

Shane Birley is a Vancouver-based Web developer, creative writer, and blog consultant with more than 15 years of experience in developing Web sites. In January 2006, he cofounded Left Right Minds Initiatives with his partner Allyson McGrane.

Left Right Minds is a creative solutions company for nonprofit societies, charities, and businesses. The business evolved from Shane's work with developing Web sites (through his previous company, Vicious Bunny Creative) and Allyson's ongoing work with nonprofit arts groups. Both partners have experience giving workshops about their areas of expertise and in training others to use new technology and business skills. In addition to Web development, the company manages and represents performing artists with the support of the Canada Council for The Arts.

As a partner in Left Right Minds, Shane is now working to develop Web sites using content management systems that enable his clients to edit and update their own Web content. He regularly gives workshops on blogging and did extensive research for *BitTorrent For Dummies*. Shane has a background in improvisational theatre and a B.A. in English — these qualifications enable him to translate difficult computing concepts into easy, plain language. To learn more about his Web company, visit `www.leftrightminds.com`. He also writes a personal blog at `www.shanesworld.ca`.

Acknowledgments

Susannah: As with every book I have worked on, I find it unfair that my name is on the cover when so many people played such an important role in getting this book finished.

Many grateful thanks go to Shane Birley, a good friend, who is my coauthor on this book. He met deadlines, turned in screenshots, and kept himself on top of both the technology he was writing about and the book production schedule as well. It has been wonderful to collaborate with him again. Thanks are due also to Shane's life and business partner Allyson McGrane, who kept him fed and functioning during deadlines.

As always, I send a special shout out to Janine Warner, the long-time *For Dummies* author who gave me my start in the technical book business.

Rebecca Huehls, my editor, and acquisition editor Amy Fandrei at Wiley both deserve more credit than me for making this possible; without their behind-the-stages work there would literally be no book. Of course, there are many more folks at Wiley Publishing that I should be thanking — and do. Someday I hope to meet some of you people in person and buy you a well-deserved beverage.

My technical editor, once again, is Paul Chaney. Paul is the Internet marketing director at Bizzuka, Inc., and an all-around nice guy. You couldn't ask for a more conscientious, helpful and funny person to point out all your niggling little technical errors.

Friends, family, colleagues and clients all cut me some slack while I was meeting deadlines for this book. Special thanks go to Matt, Debbie, Jan, and Phil Gardner, Pat and Virginia Smith, and Degan Beley. Thanks for making me the person I am today.

My coworkers Rachael Ashe and Justin Crawford at Hop Studios picked up slack, held phone calls, made tea, and fielded the occasional technical emergency at deadline time, and I'm so appreciative of them and of the opportunity I get each day to work with them.

That leaves my husband Travis Smith to thank, and there are neither words nor time enough to tell you what a gem he is. You'll just have to trust me: no Travis, no book.

No acknowledgements in a book of mine would be complete without a few words about you, dear reader. You make this whole business worth doing. Thank you.

Shane: Since the previous edition of *Blogging For Dummies* was released, it is amazing how the landscape of the blogosphere has changed and yet how much of it has remained the same. I have to send out a huge thanks to Susannah for allowing me the opportunity to collaborate with her on this edition. She is an incredibly amazing person, and I am very thankful to count her as a good friend.

Thanks to everyone who helped me on this edition or, at the very least, tolerated me when deadlines were approaching. Ken Driediger, who still keeps me sane even though he doesn't know it, Robin Thompson who is always there to keep me grounded in my creative life. I also need to thank Kirstie McCallum and Victor Terzis — two of the coolest people I know and work with daily. They know me far too well.

As always, I appreciate the love and support of my family. To my mother — who bought me my first TRS-80 computer, when I really wanted a Coleco video game console. To my father who taught me everything about life, love, and the pursuit of great beer. And to my sister, Kristen, who may be taller than me, still knows I am the bigger and older brother and I will always know more than her.

My biggest thanks goes to Allyson McGrane, my partner in crime, life, and just about everything else. She was incredibly supportive in helping to proofread, listening to me report on all the latest blog technologies, and most of all walking our pugs Serendipity and Faith when I was focused on getting the next paragraph down on paper.

I am sure I have forgotten some people but you know who you are and I thank you.

Publisher's Acknowledgments

We're proud of this book; please send us your comments at http://dummies.custhelp.com. For other comments, please contact our Customer Care Department within the U.S. at 877-762-2974, outside the U.S. at 317-572-3993, or fax 317-572-4002.

Some of the people who helped bring this book to market include the following:

Acquisitions and Editorial

Project Editor: Rebecca Huehls

Acquisitions Editor: Amy Fandrei

Copy Editor: Laura Miller

Technical Editor: Paul Chaney

Editorial Manager: Leah Cameron

Editorial Assistant: Amanda Graham

Sr. Editorial Assistant: Cherie Case

Cartoons: Rich Tennant (www.the5thwave.com)

Composition Services

Project Coordinator: Katherine Crocker

Layout and Graphics: Samantha Cherolis, Melissa K. Jester, Christine Williams

Proofreaders: Rebecca Denoncour, Cynthia Fields

Indexer: BIM Indexing & Proofreading Services

Publishing and Editorial for Technology Dummies

Richard Swadley, Vice President and Executive Group Publisher

Andy Cummings, Vice President and Publisher

Mary Bednarek, Executive Acquisitions Director

Mary C. Corder, Editorial Director

Publishing for Consumer Dummies

Diane Graves Steele, Vice President and Publisher

Composition Services

Debbie Stailey, Director of Composition Services

Contents at a Glance

Table of Contents

Introduction

Allow me to be the first to welcome you to the blogosphere, an exciting and energetic space online that people are using to reach out, build communities, and express themselves. *Blogging For Dummies*, 3rd Edition, is designed to help you through the process of starting a blog quickly, and it gives you the tools you need to make the most of your experience in the blogosphere. I've added a lot of new material since the last version of this book — keeping pace with the World Wide Web is a challenge!

This book is designed to be useful for all kinds of bloggers, whether you're the CEO of a major corporation or a hobbyist with a passion for communicating. I focus on what makes a blog work — and how a blog can work for you. Also, I realize that not everyone has the technical skills necessary to start a blog themselves, so I provide options for all levels of experience.

This book is useful to you, whether you're taking part in the conversations in the world of blogs or becoming a blogger yourself. I cover everything from technology to legal issues, so you can go forward knowing you have a resource that covers every aspect of this exciting medium.

About This Book

Whether you're building a blog as a rank beginner or redesigning an existing blog to make it better, you can find everything you need in these pages. The fact that you're holding this book very likely means you have some ideas about starting a blog — and I want to get you started right away!

The first part of the book gets you blogging quickly and safely. Chapter 1 introduces you to blogging, Chapter 2 walks you through the world that is the blogosphere, and Chapter 3 helps you choose the software and tools you need to get started. In Chapter 4, I show you the fastest and easiest way to get started immediately with your very own blog.

However, you don't have to memorize this book or even read it in order. Feel free to skip straight to the chapter with the information you need and come back to the beginning later. Each chapter is designed to give you easy answers and guidance, accompanied by step-by-step instructions for specific tasks.

I include sidebars that give you more information, but you don't need to read those sidebars if you're short on time. Technical Stuff icons also indicate helpful extras that you can come back to when you have more time.

Conventions Used in This Book

Keeping things consistent makes them easier to understand. In this book, those consistent elements are *conventions.* Notice how the word *conventions* is in italics? That's a convention I use frequently. I put new terms in italics and then define them so that you know what they mean.

URLs (Web addresses) or e-mail addresses in text look like this: `www.bloggingfordummiesbook.com`. Sometimes, however, I use the full URL, like this: `http://traction.tractionsoftware.com/traction` because the URL is unusual or lacks the `www` prefix.

Most Web browsers today don't require the introductory `http://` for Web addresses, though, so you don't have to type it in.

Foolish Assumptions

Just because blogs have a funny name doesn't mean they have to be written by funny people — or even humorous ones! If you can write an e-mail, you can write a blog. Have confidence in yourself and realize that blogs are an informal medium that forgives mistakes unless you try to hide them. In keeping with the philosophy behind the *For Dummies* series, this book is an easy-to-use guide designed for readers with a wide range of experience. Being interested in blogs is all that I expect from you.

If you're new to blogs, this book gets you started and walks you step by step through all the skills and elements you need to create a successful Web log. If you've been reading and using blogs for some time now, this book is an ideal reference that can help you ensure that you're doing the best job possible with any blog that you start or manage.

I do expect that you aren't tackling starting a blog without having some basic computer knowledge under your belt, not to mention a computer on your desk. If you're still figuring out how to use your computer or don't have access to an Internet connection, keep this book for a time when you're more able to put your computer and the Internet to work for you.

Having said that, you don't need to know much more than how to use a Web browser, open and create files on your computer, and get connected to the Internet, so you don't need to be a computer genius, either.

How This Book Is Organized

To ease you through the process of building a blog, I organized this book to be a handy reference. The following sections provide a breakdown of the parts of the book and what you can find in each one. Each chapter walks you through a different aspect of blogging, providing tips and helping you understand the vocabulary of Web logs.

Part I: Getting Started with Blogs

This part introduces you to the general concepts of blogging, including actually starting a blog today. In Chapter 1, I show you some good blogs and give you background about this young industry. You can find out what's involved in creating a blog and take a quick tour of what works in a blog and what doesn't.

While reading Chapter 2, you find guidance on how your friends, family, and business colleagues might react to your new blog. If you're interested in blogging frankly, you might want to read this chapter before you start criticizing your boss or writing about your personal life online.

In Chapter 3, you make a big decision: what blogging software you want to use. I explain what your options are and how to find blog software that has the features and extras you need. Also, choose a domain name and a Web host so that you can install your own blog software and control every aspect of the blogging experience.

Part II: Setting Up Your Blog

In Chapter 4, you can jump right in to a real blog and start a hosted Blogger blog. Sign up in ten minutes and have fun putting up text, links, and images. It really is that easy.

Chapters 5 and 6 are devoted to helping you start blogging in two other formats. Chapter 5 covers setting up and blogging with WordPress, a software application that you install on your own server. And Chapter 6 is all about the latest craze in the blogosphere: micro blogs.

Together, these chapters give you step-by-step instructions for both starting up a new blog and adding blog posts, images, and other fun stuff to the blog you start. If you read no other chapters in this book, read these!

Part III: Fitting In and Feeling Good

Part III is dedicated to making sure you know how to get the most out of your blog while meeting the needs of your audience. In Chapter 7, you can work on figuring out just what your topic is and how best to produce content around your subject. I even give you tips on dealing with writer's block.

In Chapter 8, you can define your audience and work on targeting your blog to reach that group most effectively — and keep readers coming back for more.

Chapter 9 helps you avoid a common blog problem: spam. Discover the tricks every blogger must know to keep Viagra ads from dominating their comment areas. More than that, however, Chapter 9 tells you how to cultivate a community of interaction and conversation on your blog.

Part IV: Going Beyond Words

In Part IV, you find a series of chapters that help you dress up your blog with style and neat technological tools. In Chapter 10, you can find out how to make the most of photos and other graphics in your blog. Did you know that adding a photo to your blog post makes more people read it? It's true!

If you can't say it with a photo, say it with your mouth by creating a podcast in Chapter 11. Everyone, from the newest blogger to the seasoned professional, uses this exciting area of the blogosphere to make themselves heard.

Words and photos aren't the whole story. A lot of bloggers are taking advantage of better bandwidth and more powerful computers to create video blog posts. Find out more about working with video in Chapter 12.

Part V: Marketing and Promoting Your Blog

Make your blog and yourself known on the Internet and in the blogosphere by using the tools described in Part V. In Chapter 13, you can find out what the heck RSS is and how you can use it to build traffic to your blog. Not only that, you can use RSS yourself to read other blogs quickly and find out what others are saying about you.

Twitter is showing up everywhere, even in sitcoms. In Chapter 14, get familiar with this fun new tool for keeping in touch with friends, family, and even your colleagues. You can dive into the depths of social networking in Chapter 15. You may find more going on with Facebook than you think!

Chapter 16 helps you use statistics and traffic-tracking tools to discover more about your audience members and how they're using your blog.

Part VI: Getting Business-y with It

If you've ever thought that you ought to be able to make a little money with your blog, then Chapter 17 is for you. Find out how to put ads on your blog, form relationships with sponsors, and use affiliate programs to make a buck.

If you're a corporate CEO or small business owner, then Chapter 18 is a must-read. In this chapter, I show you how businesses, nonprofit groups, and other organizations are making use of blogs to form relationships with clients and customers.

Part VII: The Part of Tens

In The Part of Tens, you can discover ten ways to increase the community interaction on your blog, ten cool tools that can make your blog even snazzier, and best of all, ten outstanding blogs that make the most of technology and the Internet.

Glossary

Blogs, sidebars, blogrolls, RSS — this medium has more jargon that you can shake a stick at. I define new terms in a chapter so that you know what's going on when you start blogging, and you can always consult the glossary at the back of this book for definitions of all those weird blog terms that have sprung up in recent years. Don't let a few acronyms keep you from enjoying the blogosphere!

HTML Guide

Get the goods on writing your own HTML code — happily, you don't need to do much of that on a blog (unless you want to)!

Icons Used in This Book

Here's a rundown of the icons I use in this book:

The Remember icon reminds you of an important concept or procedure to store away in your memory bank for future use.

The Technical Stuff icon signals technical stuff that you might find informative and interesting, but that you don't need to know to develop the Web sites described in this book. Feel free to skip over these sections if you don't like the techy stuff.

Tips indicate a trick or technique that can save you time and money — or possibly a headache.

The Warning icon warns you of any potential pitfalls — and gives you the all-important information about how to avoid them.

Where to Go from Here

Turn to Chapter 1 to dive in and get started with an intro to blogs and an overview of why this new medium is so exciting for so many people. If you just want to get started blogging today, read over Chapter 4. Otherwise, spend some time thinking about the best blog software solution for your situation — which you can read more about in Chapter 3. Already have a blog, but want to do more with it? I think Chapter 8's coverage of great content might be a great place to dive in. Don't forget to send me your efforts — I can't wait to see your blog! Drop me an e-mail at `susie@hopstudios.com`.

Part I
Getting Started with Blogs

In this part . . .

Part I is your crash course in blogging, from finding out what the heck blogs are all about and why people are bothering with them at all. It's an exciting section, and you won't want to miss a word! In Chapter 1, you find out why people are posting their most personal thoughts on the Web and why even businesses are getting involved. In Chapter 2, it's all about the ethics — how you can start a blog and keep your job at the same time. Chapter 3 shows you the ins and outs of several blogging software applications and guides you through picking the right solution.

Chapter 1
Discovering Blog Basics

In This Chapter

- Recognizing the hallmarks of a blog
- Getting started with your own blog
- Deciding what to blog about
- Blogging successfully

By now, you've probably heard the word *blog* tossed around by all kinds of people, seen it show up in news stories or cited on TV news broadcasts, or heck, you may even have a child, friend, or coworker who has a blog. Bloggers are showing up inside businesses, and businesses are even using blogs to reach out to their customers. But what exactly do all these people mean when they say they have a blog? And what does a blog written by a teenager have in common with one written by a CEO?

Don't be too hard on yourself if you aren't exactly sure what a blog is. The word *blog* is actually a mash-up of two other words — Web and log — so if it sounds made up, that's because it is. At its most basic level, a *blog* is a chronologically ordered series of Web site updates, written and organized much like a traditional diary, right down to the informal style of writing that characterizes personal communication.

In this chapter, you can find out just what makes a blog bloggy and why so many people are outfitting themselves with one like it's the latest celebrity fashion trend. (Hint: It's not just that we're all narcissists!) You can get some ideas that you can use to start your own blog and become part of the *blogosphere* (the community of blogs and bloggers around the world).

No matter what your teenager tells you, the blogosphere has absolutely no requirement that you must write your blog while wearing your pajamas. Also, you're allowed to use a spellchecker.

Making Yourself Comfortable with Blogs

I talk to a lot of people about blogs, many of whom know that you can find a blog on the World Wide Web, but who also have the impression that all blogs are written by navel-gazing cranks with an axe to grind or by 12-year-old girls. Some blogs really are diaries in which the blogger records the minutiae of day-to-day life — but blogs can be much more than that, and all kinds of people write them.

One of my favorite blogs falls into the personal diary category: Mimi Smarty pants (`http://mimismartypants.com`). A woman living in Chicago writes this blog, which records her thoughts and activities with such hilarious prose that I often find myself laughing out loud.

For contrast, visit Mäni's Bakery Blog Café (`www.manisbakery.com/blogcafe`), shown in Figure 1-1, a blog that the staff of Mäni's Bakery in Los Angeles writes for the bakery's customers. Mäni's uses the blog to announce menu changes and weekly specials, offer coupons, and talk about the bakery products, such as vegan cake.

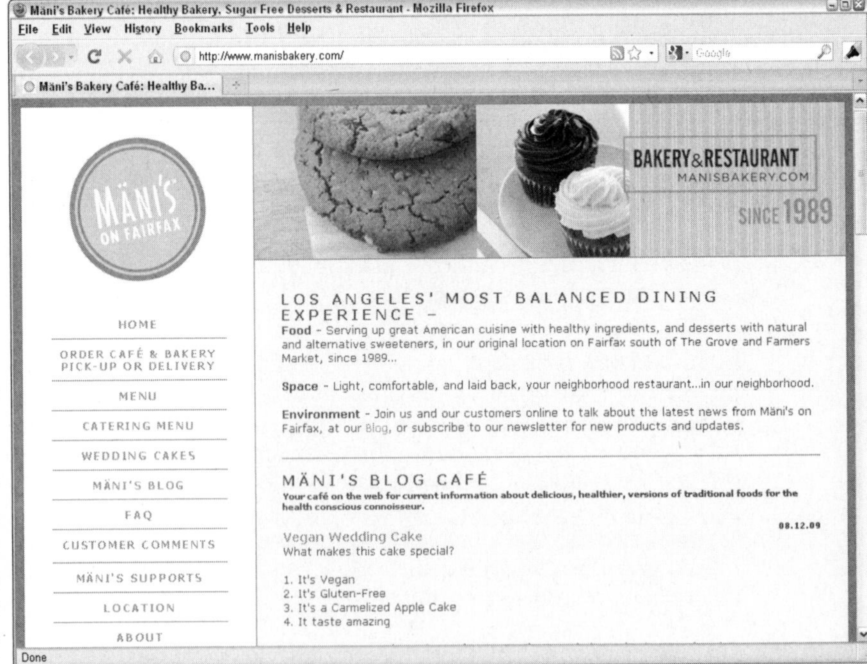

Figure 1-1: The Mäni's Bakery blog does a great job of keeping customers updated.

Think of a blog this way: It's a kind of Web site. All blogs are Web sites (the opposite isn't true, though), and neither the content nor the creator makes a blog a blog — the presentation does. A blog can be many things: a diary, a news source, a photo gallery, or even a corporate marketing tool. Blog content can include text, photos, audio, and even video, and bloggers talk about nearly any subject that you can imagine.

One of the reasons blogs have become such a popular way of publishing a Web site is because they're particularly good at generating high search-engine rankings. If you have a blog, it's more likely than a standard Web site to come up high in lists of search results for the topics you discuss because your posts are fresh and current. Search engines give an extra boost to Web pages that have the most recently updated or created content related to the keywords that someone is searching for. And better search-engine listings mean more visitors, more readers, more comments, and a more vibrant community. Individuals and companies have taken advantage of the blog medium to reach out to Web users.

How people use blogs

With millions of blogs in the world — the blog search engine Technorati (`http://technorati.com`) has tracked more than 133 million blogs since 2002 — it's obvious that blogging is a popular and successful format for publishing a Web site. But just what are people doing with blogs? They can't all be talking about their cats!

And they aren't. Bloggers are using the blog format to communicate effectively in all kinds of information spheres, from the personal to the professional. In fact, many blogs serve multiple purposes at the same time, mixing posts about activities at home with news pertaining to work. Your blog can serve many purposes in your life.

Documenting your life

A lot of folks use blogs for the same reason they might keep a diary — to chronicle their lives and activities. This urge to communicate appears in all kinds of mediums, from scrapbooking to taking digital photographs, and if you're interested in sharing these personal details with others, a blog gives you a fast, efficient way to do so.

If you send holiday newsletters every year or e-mail a group of friends and family to let them know about exciting events in your life, you can have a lot of fun with a blog. You can blog as often as you want, and your readers visit when they're ready to get more information. Best of all, each blog post gives your friends and family a quick way to respond to you without having to find the stamps; they only have to leave a comment on your blog post. You might find you're talking more with your family than ever before!

You don't have to find the postage stamps either, so keeping in touch through your blog is inexpensive and less time-consuming than snail mail. And no more envelopes to lick.

Of course, not all lives come up roses every day; they can't all be wedding and travel blogs. Personal blogs can be intense when they document rough times. Derek Miller (`www.penmachine.com`), a Vancouver-based writer, has used his blog, shown in Figure 1-2, to document his experiences with cancer. He posted this blog entry on June 8, 2009:

> "Sometimes, for a few days, it's easy to forget how sick I am. But I found out I have cancer two and a half years ago, and I've been under some sort of treatment — chemotherapy, radiation, surgery, or recovering from those things — the whole time. Tomorrow I'll hear the results of my latest CT scan, good or bad. That will help determine what comes next."

In your eagerness to let your friends know about what you're up to, don't forget that anyone in the world can access a blog (unlike a real diary or scrapbook), now and in the future. Don't publish anything that you might find embarrassing in the future, and have the same consideration when you talk about others or use photographs.

Figure 1-2: Derek Miller blogs about everything in his life, from chemotherapy to Apple's new operating system.

Exploring a hobby or passion

If you have a passion or hobby that you just love to talk about, consider doing so in a blog. Anyone who shares your interest is a potential reader and is bound to be looking for more information wherever he or she can find it.

You can detail your own experiences, offer advice to others, drum up support for whatever you like to do, or just talk about what you love. Best of all, you might be able to make connections with others who share your infatuation, making friends and finding ways to get involved with your hobby more deeply.

Cybele May runs a blog about something she loves: candy. Candy Blog (`www.candyblog.net`) is her personal labor of love and a great excuse to buy a lot of candy! Cybele reviews candies, writing extensive descriptions of taste, texture, and ingredients for fellow sugar enthusiasts. And they respond! Nearly every review garners comments from fans and critics of the candies that Cybele samples. Check out Candy Blog in Figure 1-3.

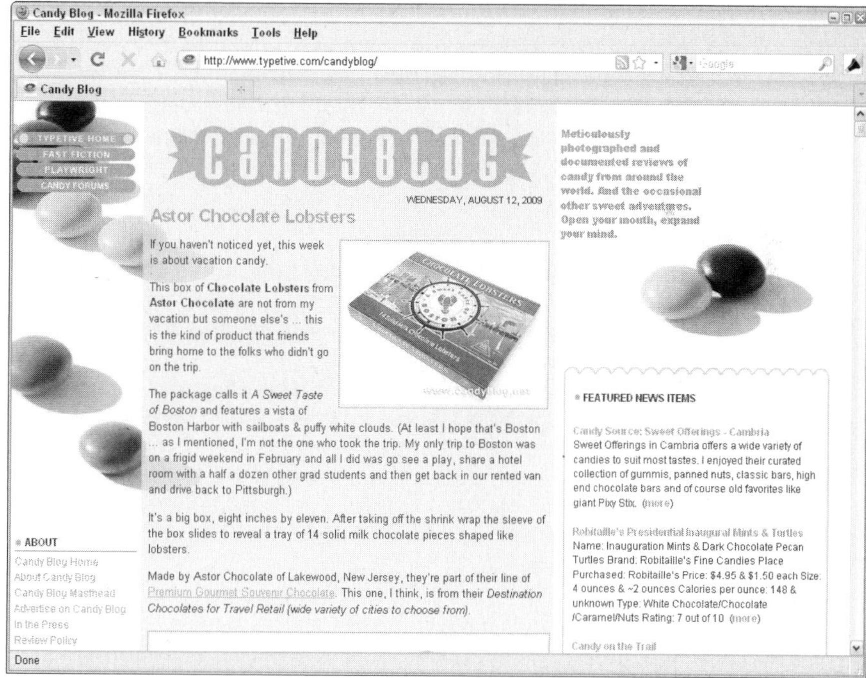

Figure 1-3: Candy Blog is a sweet labor of love for Cybele May.

Sharing information

Sometimes, a blog is all about sharing information. Journalists use blogs to report on local, national, and international news; critics and commentators use the medium to state their opinions and predictions. Educators keep parents and students abreast of classroom happenings and dates. Coworkers let colleagues in geographically distant offices know what's going on in relation to collaborative projects. The uses of the informational blog are really limitless.

The popular blog Boing Boing (`www.boingboing.net`) is a great example of an information-sharing blog. Self-described as a "directory of wonderful things," Boing Boing's several contributors are dedicated to keeping you up to date on all the weird and wonderful Web sites in the world. A selection of posts from August 2009 described the Nano Air Vehicle (it has wings, like insects do), a mouse who had made its home in an Oregon ATM, and a link to creating your own "Achingly Self-Referential Virtual Commodity Fetish Objects." This site is truly a random collection of news and links, perfect for the eclectic consumer of trivia.

Another popular information blog is TechCrunch (`www.techcrunch.com`). This guide to everything Internet covers everything from new companies to the latest geek gadgets and, of course, offers a lot of information about software. You might not find every post useful, but if you're trying to keep up with the breakneck pace of technological innovation on the Internet, you can find TechCrunch (shown in Figure 1-4) and blogs like it an invaluable resource.

Making money

You spend a lot of time producing your blog, and a lot of people read it. Why not turn those eyes into dollars? That's a question many a popular blogger has asked, and you can make it happen in several ways.

The most common technique involves including advertisements on your blog pages. For example, Google AdSense (`www.google.com/adsense`) provides in-page advertising that's designed to match the content of your blog and therefore be of interest to your readers. Each time a visitor to your blog clicks one of these advertising links, you earn money from Google. I talk more about making money from advertising programs, affiliate links, sponsorships, and more in Chapter 17.

Of course, companies haven't missed out on the fact that blogs can help them drum up interest in their products and services, or inform and connect with consumers. Many companies, small and large, have added blogs to their Web sites, and they use the blogs to start conversations with their customers and potential customers. In many cases, taking on the informal voice of the blog medium has helped customers understand that real people work in these organizations. This personal connection gives the company better credibility and often adds to customers' recognition of that company and its values in the marketplace.

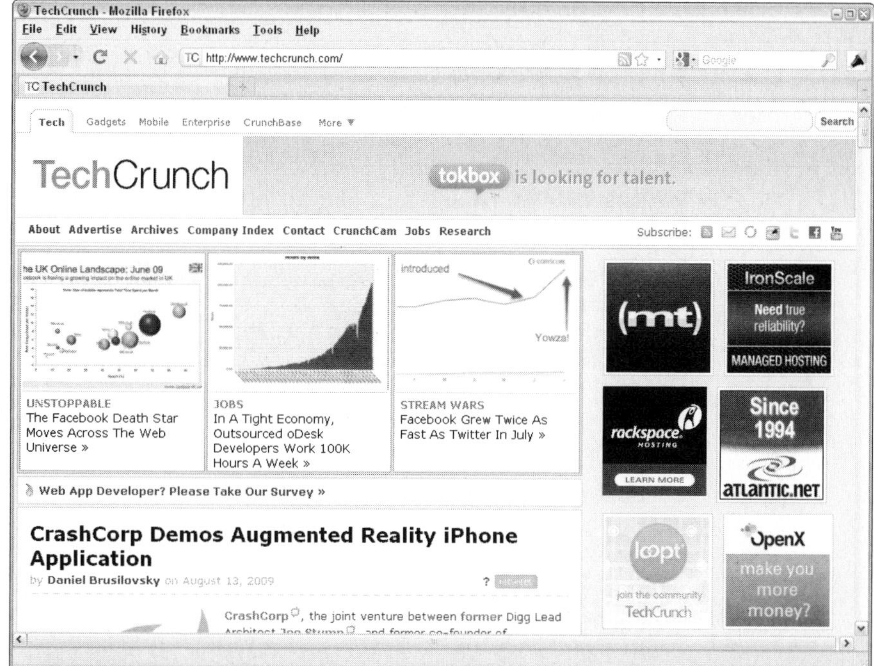

Figure 1-4: TechCrunch is your source for satisfying your gadget news appetite.

General Motors, Google, and Sun Microsystems all have company blogs, giving readers a peek inside the corporate culture of what might otherwise be fairly faceless monoliths.

Southwest has taken this approach (`www.blogsouthwest.com`). On the blog's About page, Southwest says, "Our goal with the new Nuts About Southwest remains to give our readers the opportunity to take a look inside Southwest Airlines and to interact with us." Southwest tries to make sure that the blog represents a lot of voices inside the company, from managers to captains — even the president of the company. Like with personal blogs, the tone is light and conversational, making the company seem friendly and accessible.

Recognizing a blog

You've probably seen a blog online already. Because the blogger isn't required to put a big This Is a Blog! sticker at the top of the page, you might not have realized that you were looking at a blog. With a little practice and familiarity with standard blog elements, though, you can identify any blog in a snap.

Regardless of what the blog is about or who writes it, every blog features

- **Frequent updates:** Most bloggers update their blogs a few times a week; some bloggers even update them a few times a day. Blogs don't have a schedule for publishing; the blogger simply updates the blog when it seems appropriate.
- **Posts or entries:** Each time a blogger updates the blog, he or she creates a blog *post,* or entry, that he or she then adds to the blog.
- **Permalinks:** Each time a blogger adds a post to his or her blog, that post appears on the blog's home page. At the same time, blog software creates a *permalink* page to contain only that blog post and its comments. (The word *permalink* is short for "permanent link.") Permalink pages are a big part of why blogs do so well with search engines — every post adds a new page to your Web site and provides another opportunity for your blog to come up as a search result.
- **Chronological order:** When a blogger writes a new blog post, that post appears at the top of the blog's first page. The next time the blogger writes a post, it shows up at the top, and the older posts move down the page.
- **Comments:** Most (though not all) blogs allow readers to leave comments — short text messages — in response to blog posts. Comments really differentiate a blog from most Web sites by encouraging interaction and conversation.
- **Archives:** Because blogs are updated so frequently, bloggers often sort their blogs into a date-based archive so that readers can find older information easily.
- **Categories:** Bloggers can also sort posts by subjects, or categories, which allows a blogger to blog about a number of different topics and lets readers focus in on the topics that most interest them.

Blog anatomy: Dissecting a typical blog

In this section, I give you a tour of the usual blog elements by using baker Rose Levy Beranbaum's blog, Real Baking with Rose Levy Beranbaum (`www.realbakingwithrose.com`). This blog is unusual because although Rose writes it herself, it's sponsored by Gold Medal Flour, which paid for the blog to be built and handles any maintenance costs associated with running it. It still has all the usual features that I discuss in this section, as shown in Figure 1-5.

Rose's sponsorship is unusual, but the format of her blog isn't. In fact, most blogs — no matter what topic they cover — look quite similar because the elements of one blog are common to all blogs.

Figure 1-5: Real Baking with Rose Levy Beranbaum is a sponsored blog written by a cookbook author.

Courtesy of Rose Levy Beranbaum, author of The Cake Bible (William Morrow).

Blogging through the ages

The concept behind a blog isn't new; after all, people have been keeping diaries and journals since the invention of the written word. Even on the Web, diary Web sites existed long before anyone used the word *blog.*

No one really knows when the first true blog was created, but estimates put the date around 1994. The term *weblog* came into existence in 1997, and it was quickly shortened to the more colloquial *blog.* If you want to read more about the history of blogging, read author Rebecca Blood's essay on the early days of blogging at `www.rebeccablood.net/essays/weblog_history.html`.

No one can really measure the number of blogs in the world, for a number of technical reasons and because blogs can be short-lived (accidentally or deliberately), but all studies of numbers indicate that the number of blogs increases dramatically every month. For example, in May 2007, the blog search engine Technorati (`www.technorati.com`) was tracking 75 million blogs; by July 2007, that number was up to 94 million.

Those common elements are:

- **Branding/logo header:** A *header* at the top of the blog displays the name of the blog, often including a logo or other visual element. This header is visible on every page of the blog, identifying it, even to a visitor who visits one of the interior pages without first going to the home page. In Figure 1-5, the header contains the name of the blog, a caricature of Rose, and the Gold Medal logo (indicating the blog's sponsorship).
- **Most recent posts:** At the top of the blog's home page, the most recent post appears. While you scroll down the home page, you see the next most recent post, and the next most recent post, and so on. New posts are always at the top, making it easy to find the latest, freshest information when you visit. Most blogs display around a dozen recent blog posts on the first page of the blog, and to read older posts, you can visit the archives.
- **Post information:** Along with each entry, blog software displays information *about* the post. This sort of post information typically appears — but a blogger doesn't have to include it. A blog might be missing an element or two that I list or have others that I don't mention:
  - The date and time the post was published.
  - The name of the post's author. On blogs that have multiple authors, the visitor may find this info especially important.
  - The number of comments on the post. In Figure 1-5, you can see the first post hasn't yet received any comments.
  - A link to the permalink page, usually labeled Permalink. Sometimes, as in Figure 1-5, the link to the permalink page is labeled Post/Read Comments because you can both read and write comments on the permalink page.
  - The category in which the blogger has placed the post. In Figure 1-5, the category of the top post is Announcements.
  - Other links to bells and whistles unique to the blog, such as the links to Send to a Friend (which allows you to quickly e-mail the post to a friend) or Print, shown in Figure 1-5.
- **Sidebar material:** Most blogs are laid out in two or three columns, with the most real estate given to the column that contains the blog posts themselves. The second and/or third columns display organizational material for the blog and peripheral information. Some blogs don't have sidebars at all, and on some blogs, you may see elements that I don't mention in the following list of typical sidebar components:
  - *Date-based archives:* Nearly every blog archives a post when the blogger publishes that post, both by date and by category. In the

sidebar of a blog, you can usually access both archive methods. Figure 1-6 shows the date-based archives of Rose's blog, broken down by month. Date-based archives can also show weeks and years.

- *Categorized archives:* Figure 1-7 shows the category archives of Real Baking with Rose Levy Beranbaum. By sorting each post into a category at the time that she publishes it, Rose creates an archive organized by subject, making it easy for you to find the posts that most interest you. Clicking a category link displays only the posts in that subject area, organized in reverse chronological order.
- *Blogroll:* A *blogroll* is a list of other blogs that the blogger finds interesting or useful. By including the blogs and Web sites that Rose likes to read on her blog, she can direct her readers to other interesting Web sites (see Figure 1-8). And who knows, those sites may return the favor, sending their visitors to her site.

Figure 1-6: A date-based archive.

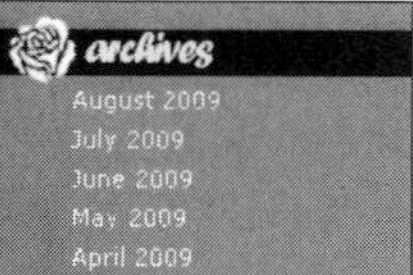

Courtesy of Rose Levy Beranbaum, author of The Cake Bible *(William Morrow).*

Figure 1-7: A categorized archive.

Courtesy of Rose Levy Beranbaum, author of The Cake Bible *(William Morrow).*

Figure 1-8: A blogroll.

sites i like
> Heavenly Cake Place
> Baking 911
> Baking Bites
> Becoming a Chef (Andrew Dornenburg and Karen Page)
> Better Baking
> BitterSweet Vegan Blog

Courtesy of Rose Levy Beranbaum, author of The Cake Bible (William Morrow).

- *Information about the author:* Because blogs are so personal, sometimes you want to know more about who's writing them. Many bloggers know their readers are curious, and those bloggers put together short bios and other information for readers. Bloggers sometimes display this information in the sidebar or link to it, like in Figure 1-9.
- *RSS feed link:* Readers can use RSS, or Really Simple Syndication, to subscribe to your blog by using a newsreader, such as Google Reader. After a reader subscribes via RSS, he or she can read the latest updates via the newsreader instead of visiting your blog. So, your readers don't have to visit your blog several times a day to see whether you've updated it. A blog often includes an RSS link (identified by a small orange icon, as shown in Figure 1-10) near the bottom of the sidebar. I talk more about RSS in Chapter 13.

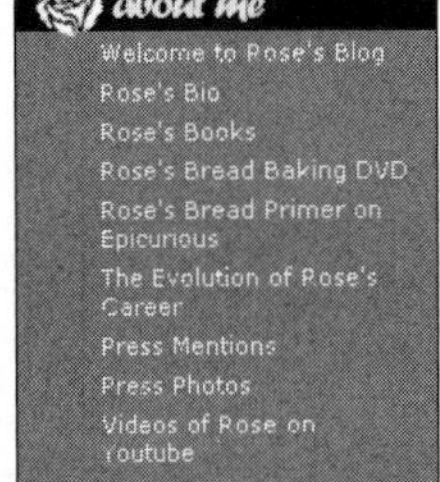

Figure 1-9: An About the Author section.

Courtesy of Rose Levy Beranbaum, author of The Cake Bible (William Morrow).

Figure 1-10: A link to an RSS feed.

Courtesy of Rose Levy Beranbaum, author of The Cake Bible (William Morrow).

Getting a Blog Started

One of the reasons that so many blogs exist is that you can set them up and publish them so easily. The early days of the Internet were full of heady talk about the democratization of publishing; people discussed how absolutely anyone would have the power to publish because of the prevalence of personal computers. In fact, that idea wasn't strictly true. A writer no longer needed a printing press and a distribution method to get his or her work to people, but he or she still needed specialized skills and technology.

Unless the would-be publisher spent time figuring out how to use HTML, owned a computer that had an Internet connection, and understood how to put files onto a Web server, he or she was still pretty much in the same can't-get-published boat. You could acquire those skills and the tools to publish, but you couldn't do so terribly easily.

The answer, as it turns out, comes down to technology — specifically, software. I believe blogging goes a long way toward making that initial promise of the Web come true. If you can write an e-mail, you can figure out how to use the simple interfaces of blogging software without any of the muss of dealing with HTML, FTP, or any of those other awful Web acronyms everyone's supposed to understand these days.

Figure 1-11 shows the publishing interface of Blogger (`www.blogger.com`), a great blogging software tool. To write a new post, you simply log in to Blogger, fill in the blanks for a new post, and click the Publish Post button to put the entry on your blog.

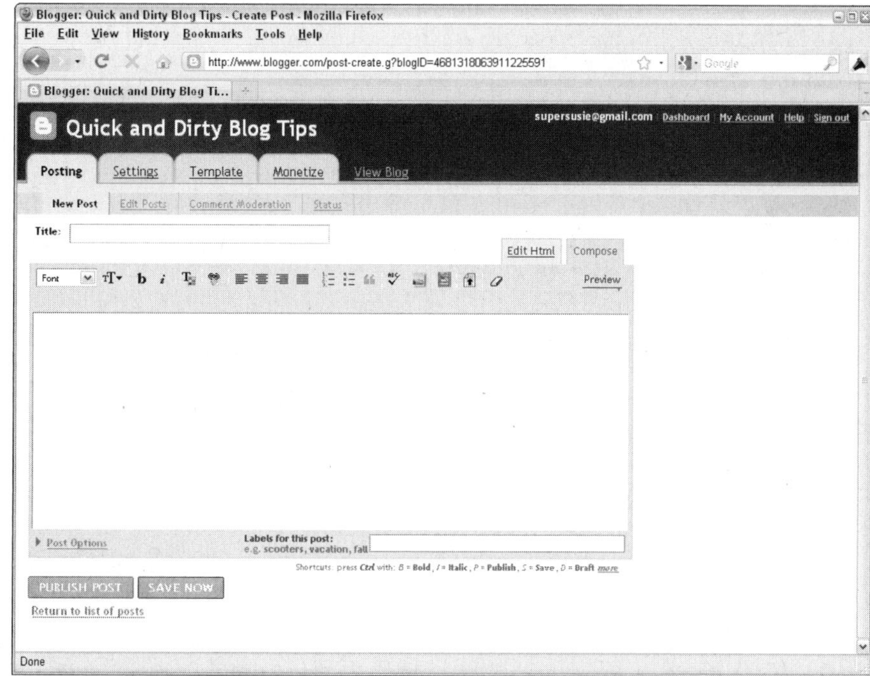

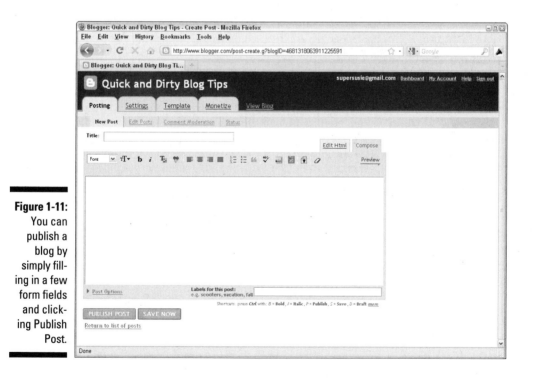

Figure 1-11: You can publish a blog by simply filling in a few form fields and clicking Publish Post.

Different blog software offer different feature sets. Like with all software, the tricky part is finding the right one to use for your situation and needs, but I can assure you, blogging software comes in all shapes, sizes, and price ranges. In Chapter 3, I talk extensively about choosing the right software solution for your blog. Chapter 4 shows you how to start a blog in about ten minutes by using Blogger, and Chapter 5 walks you through the details of using WordPress.

Choosing What to Blog About

You can find blog topics all over the map. If you haven't already read a blog, follow these simple steps to find one and read it, which is the best possible way to become familiar with the medium:

1. **Open your Web browser and go to `www.technorati.com`.**
2. **Type any search term that you're interested in reading about into the search box at the top of the page.**

   For example, you might enjoy reading a blog written by someone with whom you share a hobby, such as knitting or parasailing. Or try a search term that describes what you do for a living; if you're an accountant, for example, you might search for **tax regulations**. You can also search for something that can help you accomplish a task, such as buying a house or finding out how to paint.
3. **Click Search (the magnifying glass button to the right of the search box).**

   Technorati returns a list of recent blog posts that used your search term. When I searched for **knitting,** for example, Technorati showed me a blog post by someone who just bought some new yarn for making socks, one about a recipe for a knitting-themed birthday cake, and another post by someone who was frustrated with a pattern.
4. **Find a blog post that looks interesting and click the URL to visit the blog and read more.**
5. **Repeat Steps 1 through 4, as needed, until you find a blog that you enjoy!**

You can find blogs on so many topics that you can't keep from finding something interesting, whether it engages you professionally or personally. I read blogs on all kinds of topics that interest me, from (surprise) knitting to the arts to real estate.

The blog format is exceptionally well-suited to letting you explore an idea, a hobby, or a project — but don't let that stop you from using it for other things. People have created blogs to pass along marketing expertise, sell shoes, cover the latest celebrity gossip, raise funds for bike rides, and even write books. The topic or topics that you write about should excite you and hold your interest, and they can be about absolutely anything.

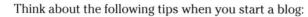

Having that much freedom can be a little scary and, if you're like me, can leave you with an absolute blank in your mind. No problem; you can start a blog today about one topic, and when you actually figure out what you want to write about, change directions and go down another road. It's a very flexible format!

Think about the following tips when you start a blog:

- **Choose a subject that genuinely interests you.** Don't choose a topic because you think being interested in it makes you look good or you think that it'll attract a lot of readers. You're the one who has to do the writing for the blog, and you can do that writing a lot more easily if you're enthusiastic about your subject. Your passion shines through to your readers and keeps them coming back.
- **Decide whether any topics are off limits.** Bloggers who keep personal diaries for their friends and families might decide to keep certain subjects out of the public forum of the Internet. For example, do you really want your significant other reading a frank account of last night's make-out session? How about your mom or your boss?
- **Think about your potential readers.** Who are they? How can you appeal to them and get them to keep reading your blog? Do you even care about how many readers you have? If you do, what do you want to show, explain, or ask them?

Creating a Successful Blog

Blogs are so quick and easy to set up that you can start one without having much of a plan in place for what you want to blog about, why you're blogging, or what you're trying to accomplish. Some people thrive on this kind of wide-open playing field, but others quickly become bored (or boring!).

To get your blog started on the right foot, think seriously about why you're blogging and then make a commitment to attaining your goals. Don't get me wrong — this isn't a job! But, just as you wouldn't expect good results from a dinner prepared without paying any attention to ingredients, you can't start your blog without having a recipe for success.

Here's my recipe for a good blog:

1. Preheat the oven by setting goals.
2. Measure out several cups of good writing.
3. Mix well with frequent updates.
4. Sprinkle in a lot of interaction with your readers.

Watching how someone else blogs is a great way of finding out how to be successful yourself! Keep track of how the blogs you enjoy are keeping you interested: Take note of how often the blogger updates his or her blog, the writing style, and which posts you find most engaging and get you to leave a comment.

Setting goals

Just like you have many different reasons to blog, you have many ways to create a successful blog. *Don't* forget that your goals and plans might not be the same as another blogger's. *Do* think about what your goals are and keep those goals in mind when you start your blog.

The following are ways that you might define a successful blog:

- **Numbers:** Many bloggers are eager to attract readers to their blogs, and they define success by the number people who visit every day.
- **Comments:** Some bloggers find the interaction with readers in the comment area of the blog very gratifying. For these bloggers, getting a comment every day or on every post might mean they're successful.
- **Results:** Many bloggers start their blog in order to accomplish a task (such as raising money for a charity), to sell a product, or even to get a book contract (blogs have done all these things). When these bloggers meet their goal, they know they've succeeded!

When you start your blog, take time to think about how you define success. Do you want to help your entire family keep in touch? Do you want to let your friends back home know more about your college experience? Are you starting a company and trying to get attention in the media? Consider writing your goals into your very first blog post and then returning to that post every few months to see whether your goals have changed and to remind yourself of what you're trying to accomplish.

Writing well

Many people think that blogs are poorly written, misspelled, and full of grammatical no-no's such as incomplete sentences. Most criticism has at least some basis in reality, and this case is no different. Many bloggers *do* write their blogs very casually, paying only cursory attention to spelling and grammar.

For many, this informality is part of the charm of the format. Readers find the colloquial, conversational tone accessible and easy to read, and bloggers who write informally seem approachable and friendly.

I'm not making an excuse, however, for ignoring all the rules of writing. Well-written and correctly spelled blogs attract readers just as often (perhaps more often) as those that aren't. You can develop a friendly, personal way of writing without losing touch with the dictionary. I encourage the use of spell-checking, even for very informal blogs intended for friends and family.

For a professional blog, don't even consider writing without paying attention to spelling and grammar. Your readers will run the other way, and your competitors will get a good snicker out of it.

Most importantly, however, think through your writing and consider your reader. Take the time to practice and develop a voice that sounds personal and conversational while still qualifying as good, engaging writing. Don't let the chatty style of a blog fool you — the best bloggers spend just as much time writing a casual blog post as they would a work memo.

You can find tips on how to develop your voice in Chapter 7.

Posting frequently

Commit yourself to writing new posts on your blog frequently. Ah, *frequently* is such a deceptive little word — because really, what does it mean?

For some people, frequently means every day. For others, it means three times a day. If you want a blog that doesn't eat up every spare moment in your life but that you still update enough to keep people interested, define the word *frequently* as at least two or three times a week. (If you want to blog more often than that, go to town.) This number of updates strikes a good balance for most blogs.

Many bloggers use a little trick to account for periods of writers block or for when they go on vacation: They write posts ahead of time and then save them for later. Using your blog software, you can schedule a date and time for a post to go live, making it possible for you keep your readers entertained, even while you're having your appendix removed or sitting on a beach in Hawaii.

You also need to pace yourself. In the first heady days of having a blog, the posts flow freely and easily, but after a few months, you might find it difficult to be creative.

Interacting with comments

Comments make blogs really different from a Web site; the opportunity to interact and converse with the creator of a Web site and with other readers is almost unique to blogs. (Forums, also called bulletin boards, offer one way to engage in online conversation on the Web, but they aren't as directed by regular posts as blogs. Everyone in the forum community is free to chime in with a topic or question.)

Visitors to a blog have the opportunity to leave a comment on each post. Sometimes, readers leave comments in reaction to what they read; other times, they might offer a suggestion or pose a question. Because any reader can leave a comment, readers may leave comments about other comments!

Blog posts often include a link directly below each post, indicating how many comments readers have left. Clicking this link takes you to a page that displays the post, any comments that readers have left about that post, and a form that you can use to leave your own comment.

After someone makes a comment, it appears in the Comments area of the blog, usually labeled with the comment writer's name, along with the date and time that he or she left the comment. On some popular blogs, readers compete to see who can leave the first comment on a new blog post.

In Rose Levy Beranbaum's blog Real Baking with Rose Levy Beranbaum (`www.realbakingwithrose.com`), Rose often responds to questions that readers ask by putting the answer in her blog post's comments area. Rose's comments have a shaded background that other comments don't have (see Figure 1-12) and feature her personal avatar image.

Not every blog allows comments. Many popular bloggers find that they're overwhelmed by the sheer volume of responses that they get and must turn off comments because they can't keep up with them. We should all be so lucky to have that problem. For most bloggers, comments are an important way to develop a dialogue with readers.

I recommend you keep comments turned on in your blog. They're an easy way to involve your audience in your topic and to get valuable feedback about what you're doing with your blog.

Unfortunately, spammers can take advantage of comments as easily as they can send you unwanted e-mail. If you keep comments turned on, you get unwanted comments that have commercial messages, unless you take preventative measures (which is becoming easier to do). You or your readers might even find some spam comments offensive, just like some kinds of spam e-mail. If you decide to allow comments on your blog, be sure to read them and delete inappropriate messages. Your readers will thank you. In Chapter 9, I talk at length about encouraging comments — and dealing with those comments that you don't want.

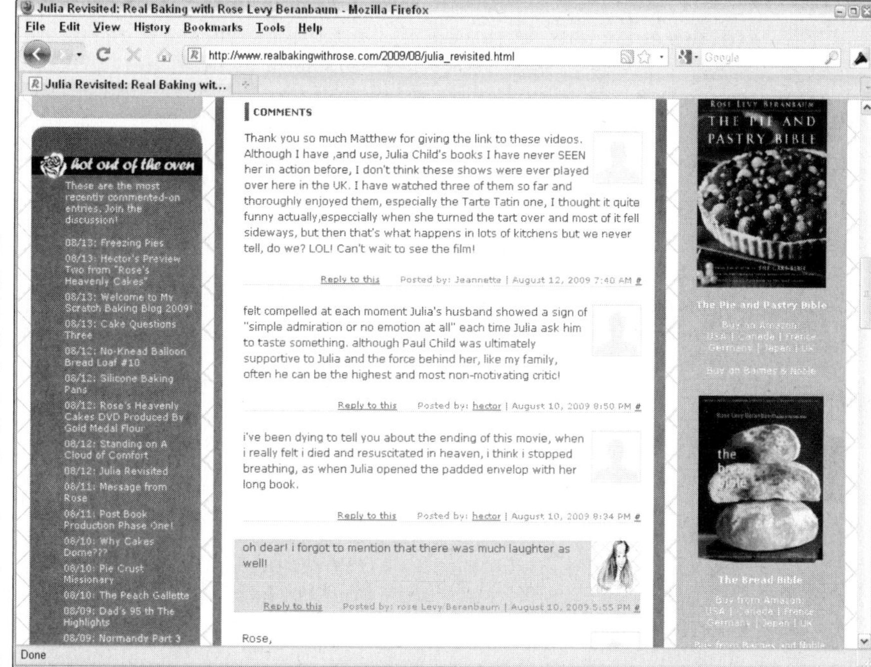

Figure 1-12: The Real Baking with Rose Levy Beranbaum blog allows readers to leave comments and questions for the blog's author.

Courtesy of Rose Levy Beranbaum, author of The Cake Bible (William Morrow).

Designing for Success

Blog design is a very personal experience. The decisions you make about how your blog looks are just as important as the technology that you choose to run your blog and what you choose to put on it. Because the Web is an ever-evolving medium, no solid rules exist that tell you what you should or shouldn't do with your blog. But you can follow guidelines to keep your best foot forward.

The blog that you're starting is a reflection of you and your professional life. Even if your blog is for personal expression, it represents who you are. So, make sure that you have a good handle on how you want to present yourself to the world. If pink bunnies say everything you need, you should have pink bunnies. And if you need to look more corporate, you should avoid the pink bunnies — unless you sell Easter baskets and egg dye.

If you're blogging for business reasons, either on behalf of a company or to promote yourself, make sure that both the writing and design demonstrate the proper tone. Seek advice from bloggers like you and find out from friends and family just how they think your blog should look. Check out other blogs, especially blogs that reflect the same goals or tone you want to create. What does the design of those blogs say about the blogger and the blog content?

Whether you hire a designer for your blog, use a blog template, or try to make the design yourself, seek ways to make your blog stand out from the rest. If you're a business, make sure that your logo appears on your blog. If you're creating a personal blog, add your own photos. Even if you use a default template, you can often add an identifying graphic or element on the site that differentiates your blog from others.

Don't be afraid to start small and plan to redesign later. You can grow into your big ideas when you're sure that you know what you want, so take the time to look at what other blogs are doing while you make your plans.

Let your readers be your guide: If your mom visits your site and says that she can't read it, find out why. If your friends start talking more about the annoying background color than your latest blog post, you have a problem. Just like you do with your content, keep the design focused on the readers to keep them coming back for more.

The average blog has four very distinct areas in which to place and customize content: logos, headers, sidebars, and footers. In a blog, each of these areas has a specific purpose. As more blogs have come into existence, these areas have developed in specific ways that can help you organize your content.

Here's some detail about each of these customizable areas:

- **Logos:** Getting a visitor's attention on the Internet is a science in itself, and clean, crisp logos can hold a visitor's interest long enough to get him or her to read some of your blog. Typically, a logo appears near the top of each blog page. Many logos include an illustrated element and a special font treatment of the blog name.
- **Headers:** The header of any blog contains a few elements. The first element should be, of course, the name of your blog. The title should explain what your blog talks about or who you are as the main writer. You can also throw into the header some form of navigation that can help your visitors find their way around and provide them with quick links to special areas that you want highlighted on your site. On many blogs, the logo also appears in the header. Like the name suggests, headers appear at the top of blog pages.

- **Sidebars:** Sidebars usually become a major focus for a blog site. *Sidebars* are columns to the right or left (or both) of the main content area, and they contain elements such as navigational links, special highlighting graphics that point to social networking sites, lists of blogs that you read *(blogrolls),* archive links, or anything that you want to share with your visitors outside the context of a blog post. Sidebars usually appear on every page of your blog and look consistent from page to page. I cover customizing your sidebars with fun applications and features in Chapter 20.
- **Footers:** Footers live at the bottom of each blog page, and sometimes they do nothing more than feature a copyright message. More advanced bloggers have expanded the use of footers to include a significant series of links to content within their sites. These links might lead to comments on the blog, recent posts, or posts that you particularly want to highlight. The footer can feature parts of your blog that you want visitors to find easily.

Chapter 2

Entering the Blogosphere

In This Chapter

- Knowing what you're getting into
- Realizing what happens when you publish
- Blogging with standards
- Keeping your job while blogging
- Staying out of hot water with Mom
- Protecting your own identity online

If you put something on your blog, *anyone* can read it. Blogs, like all Web sites, are accessible anywhere in the world at any time, and anyone who can access a computer and understand the language the blog is written in can read it. (Some blog software does allow privacy settings or password protection — and if you use these options, you have more assurance of privacy.)

And, like with all Web sites, people can print, duplicate, and fax blog posts, tape them to lamp posts, distribute them to a class, or post them on social networking Web sites such as Facebook. A reader of your blog can even copy and paste the text of your blog posts into a text editor or e-mail message, sending that text buzzing around the world in the blink of an eye.

You can't know who's reading your blog, why they're reading it, or what they might do with what you post. I often talk to bloggers who say, "Well, my only readers are my friends and family, so I don't worry too much about what I write." Your friends and family may very well be reading (in fact, I hope they do!), but they may not be the only readers. Don't make the mistake of assuming that you know who is and isn't reading your blog! I'm not saying that your readers *aren't* only your friends and family, but you can't know that for sure.

Some blog-hosting sites require you to register in order to use them, such as MySpace, and so they offer you a smaller potential audience. Not just anyone who has a computer and an Internet connection can read those blogs; anyone with a computer, an Internet connection, and an account on that service can read them. Those blogs might offer you more privacy, but generally the barriers to registering for a service such as MySpace are very low: You just need an e-mail address. The blogs might as well be public.

In rare instances, an entire blog is password-protected and therefore readable only by visitors who know the login information for the site. As long as that login information stays private, the blog is private. All the points about people being able to copy and paste or print the post still apply, however.

In this chapter, I drive home the point that you shouldn't post anything to your blog that you don't want anyone in the world to read — and yes, that includes your best friend, your significant other, your mother, your co-workers, your boss, your landlord, your neighbor . . . you get the idea.

Assessing Your Involvement

Any productivity guru will tell you that individuals who are looking for advice think with their short-term brains. When you start a new project, you rarely think beyond the end of the calendar year — and even that could be a somewhat generous assumption. New bloggers aren't any different.

Think about where you want the blog to be in five years. Will you still actively blog, or will this blogging thing last a few days, weeks, or months? Recognizing your level of commitment helps establish a clear vision about the resources that you should put into the blog.

Making decisions about the future of a blog can be a tricky business, but here are a few questions to answer (maybe in your new blog!) about where your blog will take you:

- **What level of commitment are you willing to put toward your blog?** Take a moment to visualize your level of commitment. If you're wondering why the heck you thought you might want to blog in the first place, maybe blogging isn't for you. On the other hand, if you're thinking about how many ways you can use your blog to enhance your business visibility or to keep your family up to date about what you're doing, you might want to try blogging.

  The best starting point in determining your commitment is how many posts you're planning to write per day or week. Many popular blogs tend to post more than once per day, but at that stage, the blogs are usually making a little money, or the bloggers already have an established business (so the blog provides mainly a supplemental outlet for them). Posting once per week works for most personal blogs.

- **Do you like writing? How's your typing?** Being able to write is one skill, but being able to write and make your writing interesting and fun is entirely different. You can't pick up blogging overnight; you must figure out how to do it by practicing. A good way to do this would be to create a test blog on a free blogging service like Blogger.com and try posting for a period of time. If you have any distaste for writing or don't know whether the writing on a regular basis will work for you, you don't need to invest a lot of time and money until you know the answers to these questions.

Knowing how to type is an important skill that some new bloggers might not be very good at. If you don't like to write (or type!), consider a podcast or a videoblog. I talk about those formats in Chapters 11 and 12.

- **What will the blog be about? Is your blog personal or professional?** If you think of your blog as a personal space, that purpose suggests an appropriate level of time and money for your individual financial situation. You can choose a design solution and write content to suit your budget and time.

  However, if you want the blog to serve a business purpose or promote your professional acumen, keep in mind that company or consultancy needs to present a polished, professional image online with a professional-looking design — ideally, one that's integrated with any existing branding and logos. Also rather than squeeze in time for writing the blog, designate time for blogging just as you would for a meeting, project task, or other work-related responsibility.

- **Do you think that your new blog might grow into a new career, lead to new clients and business, or help build connections with peers and colleagues?** Web sites can really help you make connections (just like joining social networks and finding old classmates), and I presume that, in part, you're starting a blog to reach out to a community. If the community is a professional one or a group whose respect you must earn, your blog can send unspoken messages about who you are and what you stand for. But you don't need to get all corporate!

  Most popular bloggers have developed careers based on their blogs unintentionally, all thanks to the quality of the blog. Bloggers have used blogs as starting points for book deals, television shows, and even direct sources of revenue. Think about the needs of your audience members and how to appeal to them, even when you consider what software to use. If you want to build an empire, choose the software that has the bells and whistles necessary to make that empire possible. You find out more about software in Chapter 3.

- **How comfortable are you with sharing information about yourself or about your business or industry?** The Internet is a public space. Don't forget that anyone can read what you reveal about yourself on your blog, not just the people you're trying to reach. (See the next section for details.) Occasionally, bloggers find themselves the recipients of unwanted attention and discover that they need to blog more anonymously than they'd planned.

What Happens When You Publish?

Blogging is a very immediate medium — when you publish a post, it goes live on your blog right away. In fact, several things happen the moment you click the Publish button:

- The post appears at the top of your blog's home page.
- The blogging software adds the post to your blog's archive, usually by both date and subject, and to your RSS feed, which gets updated in newsreaders.
- Anyone who signed up for e-mail notifications receives an e-mail about your post.
- If your blog software pings blog search engines and services, those search engines and services receive a notice from your blog software that you've updated your blog. (A *ping* is simply an electronic notification.)
- A search-engine crawler indexes the post the next time it visits your blog.

All these changes happen whether or not you think about them. The fact that blog posts are quickly distributed with a minimum of effort on the part of the blogger is part of the beauty and effectiveness of this format. Blog software and services are designed to deliver your content quickly.

Of course, you can edit your blog posts after you post them, and many bloggers make changes when necessary (see the "Making mistakes" section, later in this chapter, for some suggestions about changing your blog posts appropriately). However, editing after you post gives you a pretty ineffective way to control your message, because visitors might read or e-mail the original post before you make your edits.

The content you publish on a blog or Web page can live on in other unintended ways as well:

- Other bloggers might quote your post and expand on it on their blogs, creating partial copies of your deathless prose.
- Blog services might point to, and even partially excerpt, your blog post.
- Search engines might cache or otherwise archive the content temporarily or permanently.
- An Internet archive, such as the Wayback Machine (`www.archive.org/web/web.php`), might add your blog post to its database.

You can see these effects demonstrated in Figure 2-1; a Google search (`www.google.com`) for the phrase **what happens when you drink coke** turns up not only a blog post, but several references to that same post on other blogs and Web sites, and on the news-sharing site Digg (`http://digg.com`). Google links to the original blog post, and you can also access a cached version archived by Google.

I don't want to scare you — after all, publishing to your blog is a good thing! You want each of these processes to happen because they bring readers to your blog and present your content to potential readers. But be sure about what you're posting before you do start the ball rolling.

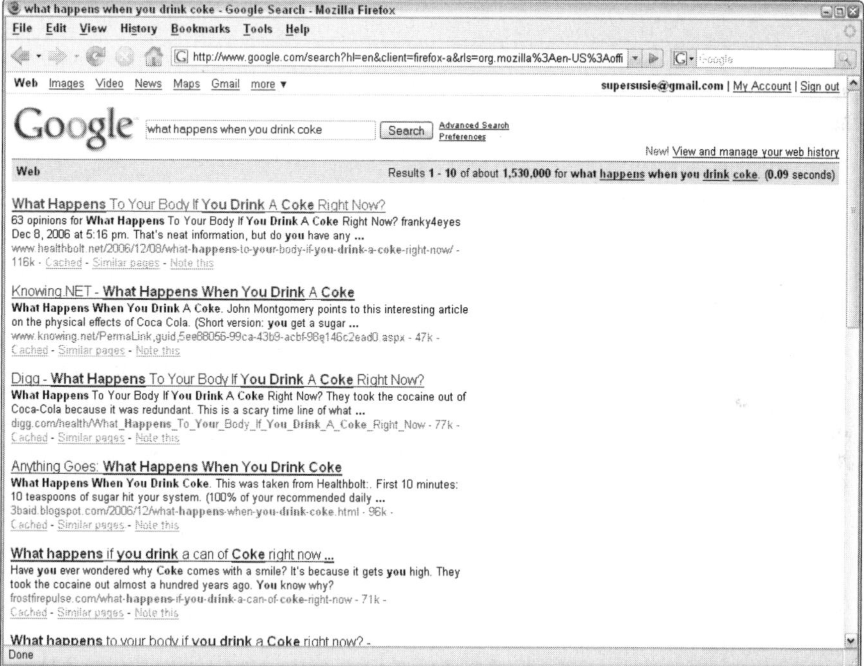

Figure 2-1: Searching for the topic of a post turns up the post, references to it, and links to the search engine's cached version.

Blogging Ethically

The best defense, as they say, is a good offense. As a blogger, you should think about what you write before you publish it, as well as afterwards.

What I'm about to say might shock you, so prepare yourself: Bloggers have a code of ethics.

Okay, what I really mean is that *some* bloggers have a code of ethics. This loose set of ethics and standards, to which many serious bloggers adhere, developed as blogs matured from a new medium into a more established one. For most old-school bloggers, the word to think about is *transparency,* which represents a whole range of ideas. I introduce transparency here and explain in more detail in the following sections:

- **Truth-telling and honesty:** In keeping with the diary format of a blog, being transparent on your blog has a lot to do with telling the truth about who you are, why you're blogging, and what you want to accomplish with your blog. You want to communicate openly and honestly on a blog, dealing straightforwardly with your topics and ideas, and with your readers.

  This idea of honesty doesn't mean you need to reveal information that you're not comfortable disclosing online — quite the contrary. But it does mean you don't intentionally mislead your readers, as I explain in the upcoming section, "Telling the truth."
- **Admitting mistakes:** No one's perfect, and you'll eventually make a mistake. Whether you post something that you heard, which turns out not to be true, or you blog angry, the real test is how you respond to making a mistake. In the blogosphere, you need to own up to your words, apologizing if you need to and making corrections when they're necessary.
- **Maintaining a dialogue:** A good blogger is aware of, and responsive to, his or her readers via the comments that those readers leave on blog posts. A blog isn't created in a vacuum. In fact, many bloggers feel that you can use a blog to build real relationships with people.

The idea that you can use a blog for meaningful interaction is revolutionary. At the core, blogging is about real people talking with each other and sharing real knowledge and experiences.

Of course, a blog isn't necessarily great literature — and that's fine. But transparency comprises worthy ideas, especially if you plan to blog about personal and sensitive topics. Read on for more details.

Telling the truth

Honesty in blogging is different from honesty in real-life relationships or even journalism or advertising, because knowing who someone is or what they represent online is complex. Consider the following:

- **Blogging anonymously:** Blogging under a pen name is okay. For many bloggers, telling the truth is first about emotional honesty and second — or perhaps not at all — about revealing who you are. For example, a personal blogger may connect with a community over a sensitive topic and thus want to use a pen name.

The blogosphere doesn't like poseurs. If you choose to blog about your life and do so anonymously, be prepared for readers to challenge whether you're a real person. Know that your true identity may be revealed, either publicly or among people who know you in real life. Be prepared to defend your writing as your own, especially if your anonymous blog could create conflict in your offline life or career.

A famous incident from 2001 concerning the blog of Kaycee Nicole, a young teenager who had just died of leukemia, demonstrates the kind of thing I'm talking about. People all over the world followed her blog, chatted with her online, even spoke with her on the phone during her illness. In fact, the life and death of Kaycee was the product of imagination. After some suspicious anomalies surfaced, several savvy bloggers tracked down real-world evidence that she not only hadn't died, but didn't even exist.

- **Blogging about products and services at the behest of the product or service provider:** The online community has slammed bloggers for blogging about products and services for money without revealing that they were paid to do so. A blog scandal in 2003 put Dr Pepper into the public eye for soliciting blog posts from a group of teenagers about a new product called Raging Cow. The teens received trips, samples of the product, and gift certificates, and the company asked them to promote the drink on their personal blogs. Many of the teens did so without revealing that they basically received compensation for promoting the product, and when the arrangement became public, a blogosphere boycott of the company and a lot of anger against the bloggers ensued.
- **Blogging as a fictional character:** Interestingly, Dr Pepper also started a blog for the product that, ostensibly, the Raging Cow herself wrote during her travels around the country, as shown in Figure 2-2. Bloggers roundly criticized this blog at the time (for being fake, of course). But the idea of creating fictional characters that write blogs has stuck around, and many bloggers have used it successfully since then. The format is still controversial, but it's also highly effective!

In general, I recommend following these rules about honesty in your blogging:

- Explain who you are and why you're blogging.
- If you need to hide your identity or those of people you mention, indicate that you're doing so and why.
- If you start a fake blog, make sure that you disclose somewhere on the site that it is, in fact, fake. (You'd think that a blog written by a cow is obviously fake, but it doesn't hurt to say so.)

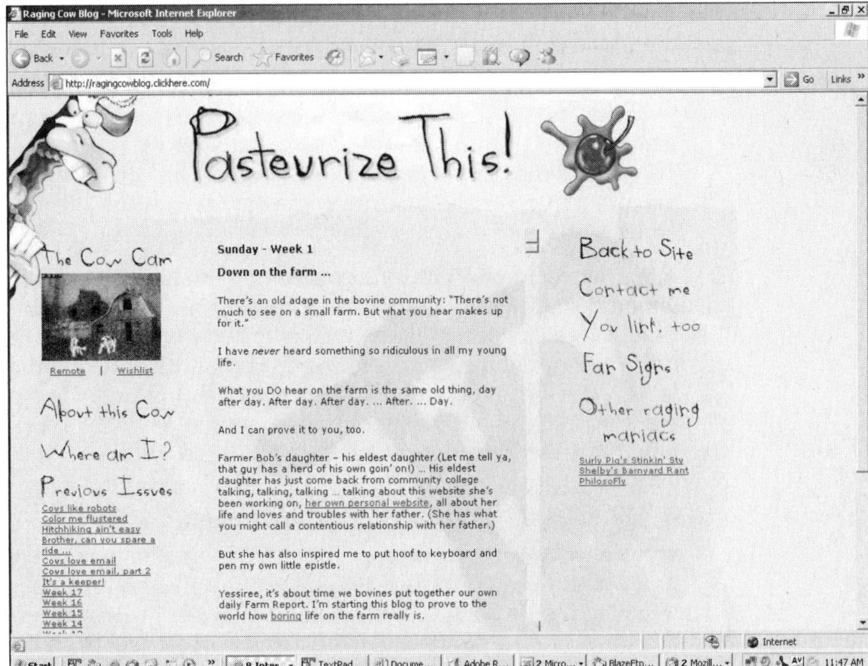

Figure 2-2: The Raging Cow blog was an early example of a fake blog written by a fictional character.

- If you're making money from your blog posts, explain the arrangement and how you're allowing it to influence (or not influence) what you write.
- If you mention a fact or story that you got from someone else, explain who. If you can link to the source, do.
- Take responsibility for what's on your blog, no matter where else you might have heard or read about what you write.

Making mistakes

If you make a mistake on your blog, admit it. Apologize, if necessary. Above all, don't try to deny it or hide it.

Mistakes, big and little, are inevitable and upset people, but you can do a great deal to help yourself and your credibility by how you handle the mistake after you or your readers discover it.

In general, most bloggers try to avoid editing posts after they publish those posts, which is part of the transparency I discuss earlier in the section

"Blogging Ethically." Sometimes, however, you need to correct the original post when you make a factual or grammatical error. Fortunately, bloggers have evolved ways to indicate corrections in blog posts, such as using strikethrough text on the original error and following it with the correction, like this:

```
President Bill Clinton played his ~~trumpet~~ saxophone on The
        Arsenio Hall Show.
```

Blogger Darren Barefoot uses this technique on his blog (`www.darrenbarefoot.com`). In Figure 2-3, he corrects a grammatical error that changes the meaning of a sentence. Other bloggers use italics or bold, or make notes at the top or bottom of the blog post, to make these kinds of corrections. The strikethrough style, however, has the advantage of letting you indicate the original error clearly.

Making a correction while retaining the error is best (unless the error was libelous or is causing legal trouble). Try to avoid simply changing the text like the mistake never existed.

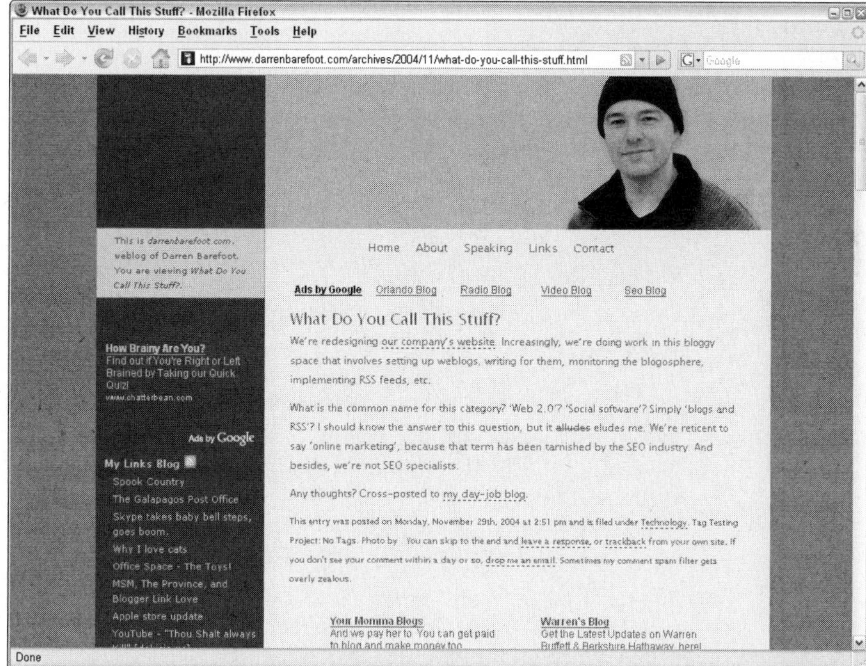

Figure 2-3: On his blog, Darren Barefoot uses strike-through text to cross out an error.

You can handle updates that you want to make to a blog post in two ways:

- **Expand on your original post:** If you change your mind about something, or simply need to expand on what you first said, you may want to do so in the original blog post, instead of starting a new post. Updating the original blog post ensures that readers see your original post at the same time as the update.

  For very important updates that change the intention or meaning of a post, Darren Barefoot (`www.darrenbarefoot.com`) posts the update at the end of the original post labeled `UPDATE`, as shown in Figure 2-4. In this case, the update expands on the original post by pointing out new resources. Some bloggers preface the new content with the acronym `ETA` (which stands for Edited to Add).

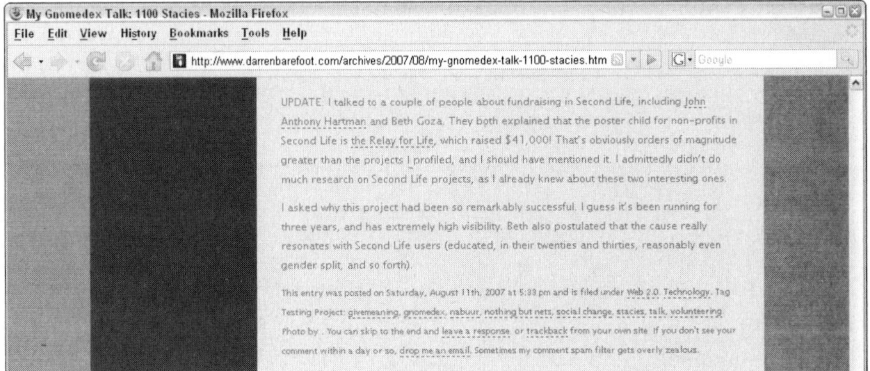

Figure 2-4: When he has new information to add to a blog post, Darren Barefoot adds an update to the bottom of the original post.

- **Start a new post:** When you really mess up, you might also choose to add a new blog post that explains what went wrong and how you might be able to avoid similar mistakes in the future (assuming that's possible!) or that just clarifies the whole situation. You don't always need to go this far, but if it helps clear the air, why not? Plus, you can use the extra post to apologize if you need to.

If you start a new post to explain a mistake, link to the old post and also go into the old post to create a link to the new one, just so all your readers get a chance to see all the details.

Handling dialogue

You write your blog in hopes that people read it and (usually) respond and interact with you, as well. The mechanism for interacting with your readers involves blog post comments. Comments are both a boon and a bane for bloggers — they provide a source of much interesting dialogue, but they can also likely provide an area for people to post spam and other unwanted material.

A blogger who neglects to read comments and respond to them quickly loses the community of people who write those comments because they can get frustrated and leave. On the flip side, reading and replying to those same folks generally earns a blogger a larger and more engaged audience.

You don't need to keep all the comments on a blog, however. Be sure to pay attention to the conversation others generate on your blog, and when necessary, exercise your judgment about removing personal attacks, libel, obscenity, spam, or other undesirable content.

In Chapter 9, I cover building a strong community dialogue by using the comments on your blog.

Keeping Your Job While Blogging

You can blog about anything you want. And you spend a lot of time at work. So maybe you're blogging about work. Work can certainly provide you with a great source of stories and jokes. In fact, at my office the other day, my partner did the stupidest thing. . . .

Ahem.

Anyway, blogging about work can get you in trouble. Your colleagues and your boss might not appreciate that you repeat water-cooler gossip on your blog, complain about the most boring meeting ever, or talk about how you photocopied inappropriate body parts when you were "working" late on Thursday.

If you choose to discuss people you work with on your blog and someone may be able to identify them (even if you don't include your coworkers' names), you can get yourself in hot water with both your coworkers and your boss.

And all that trouble comes before you reveal trade secrets or stock information!

Some bloggers identify both themselves and their employers on their personal blogs. Doing so is certainly transparent — after all, work is a big part of your life — but it isn't necessarily wise. For one thing, if you blog about your work place and you name your employer, readers might think that you're blogging on *behalf* of your employer.

This perception isn't fair, but a lot of readers have it. After all, if you blog on your own time (and you do blog on your own time, right?) and don't use company blogging software, who can consider you a spokesperson for your company? Honestly, most people won't think you're a mouthpiece for your company, but they might associate your thoughts and opinions with your employer. Generally speaking, employers don't want people to identify them by the political agendas, family relationships, or dating habits of their employees.

Most employers today know that blogs exist, and they're fully capable of typing your name, their name, or the company name into a search engine and finding blogs that talk about them or their company. Blogging anonymously — although a good idea if you want to criticize your employer — doesn't really guarantee that you won't get caught, particularly if other people in your office know about your blog.

Employers who regard their employees as representatives of their businesses might even institute a company blogging policy that dictates whether you can identify your employer on your personal blog. This policy might even request that you not blog at all, especially if you are the visible face of the organization or speak for the company in other situations.

I encourage you to blog about whatever floats your boat, but if you want to blog about work, you need to do so safely. Here are a few tips that you can use to stay on your employer's good side:

- **Regardless of what you blog about, don't blog at work.** Using company time and resources to write a personal blog is a clear violation of most employment contracts and can get you disciplined or fired, even if all you do on your blog is sing your boss's praises.
- **Find out whether your workplace has a blogging policy.** If your boss doesn't know, consult with the HR department. In some cases, a policy might be in place that makes certain requests of your blogging behavior, and you can choose whether to comply with them. Give some thought to complying with them and have good reasons if you choose not to.
- **Ask questions about your employer's blogging policy if it's unclear or incomplete.** Find out whether you can't discuss certain subjects and whether you can identify yourself as an employee.

- **Be smart about what you choose to say about your work and your colleagues.** If you wouldn't feel comfortable saying what you write in public, don't put it on your blog. (Go back to the beginning of this chapter if you're unclear on the idea that the Web is a public place.)
- **Don't reveal trade secrets.** Trade secrets include confidential information about how your employer does business that can impact revenue or reputation. If you aren't sure whether you can blog about something, run it by your boss first.
- **Review other rules and regulations that might impact what you can blog about.** For example, some employers have policies about taking photographs of the workplace, or revealing addresses or buildings. Those policies seem unrelated to blogging — until you put those photos or information on your blog.
- **Consider including a disclosure statement on your blog that says you're blogging for personal expression and not as a representative of your employer.** Thomas Duff makes his blogging position clear in his very thorough disclosure statement on Duffbert's Random Musings (`www.duffbert.com/duffbert/blog.nsf/htdocs/TDUF63Z2TS.htm`), which is shown in Figure 2-5.

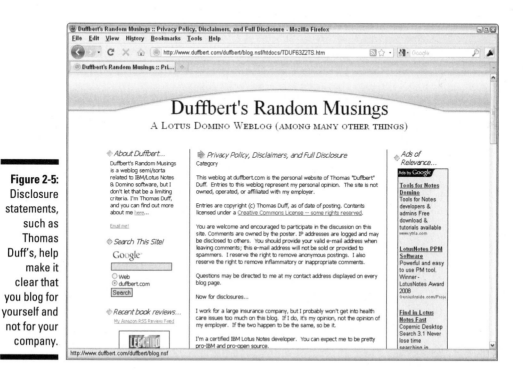

Figure 2-5: Disclosure statements, such as Thomas Duff's, help make it clear that you blog for yourself and not for your company.

Blogging without Embarrassing Your Mother or Losing Friends

You might think it goes without saying that if you can lose your job over opinions that you express on your blog, you can also damage your personal relationships with friends and family. I'm saying it anyway.

Many bloggers get caught up in the confessional mood and post content that they later regret — though perhaps not as much as a friend or relative regrets it.

Understanding what's at stake

Successful blogger Heather Armstrong alienated her family early in her blogging career when she posted her views on the religion in which she was raised. Her parents, who were still firm believers in that religion, read the post, which also hurt her extended family and the community in which they lived. (I'm sure she received plenty of e-mails from people outside of family who also felt strongly about their religion.) Heather calls herself a poster child for what not to do on a blog, though in fact, the process has resulted in Dooce (`www.dooce.com`), a blog that's both well-known and profitable online today.

In an interview with Rebecca Blood (who studies blogs), Heather cautions that criticizing others might make great posts, but the chances are good that the person you criticize will read what you've written and feel hurt. You can read the full interview on Rebecca Blood's Web site at `www.rebeccablood.net/bloggerson/heatherarmstrong.html`.

Even if you never criticize others, you might possibly reveal information about others — their conversations with you, the date you had last night, the disappointing sexual encounter — that your friends and family may find disturbing.

Protecting others in your life

Call it the Mom test: Can your blog post get you in trouble with your mom? Sure, you're an adult, and so is she — but she's the most likely person to call you on an inappropriate blog post. Your coworkers might be appalled when they read about your love life, but they probably won't ever tell you that your blog is a problem. Your mom will.

In some ways, all this advice is common sense:

- Don't blog about topics that you think might hurt others.
- Don't blog about others without their permission, even about topics that you consider inconsequential. Don't identify friends and lovers by name without their permission.
- Remember that your blog software archives your blog posts, so someone might read what you say today at a later time. For instance, if you write a report on an unsuccessful relationship, the next person you want to date might read it.

Before you hit the Publish button, stop for a second and put yourself in the shoes of your reader: Are you writing for the reader, or are you writing for yourself? If your answer is the latter, you might be better off keeping a real diary in a format that the entire world can't publicly access.

Protecting Your Privacy and Reputation

Your blog might not reflect your employer's viewpoints or your family's, but it certainly reflects your own. Don't forget that what you put on your blog today might stick around for a long time to come and that the reader might not always have your best interests at heart.

Never put any personal identifying information online that exposes you to possible identity theft or physical confrontation: Don't post your Social Security number, home address, birthdate or place, mother's maiden name, passwords, bank account numbers, or any information that you use as password reminders or identifying information with financial institutions. Most bloggers prefer to keep phone numbers private, as well. Don't reveal this information about the people you blog about, either.

Many bloggers solve the issues discussed in this chapter by choosing to blog anonymously or by using a *handle* — a phrase or moniker that doesn't personally identify the writer.

Don't forget that many of your online identities are linked. For example, if you use a nickname when you leave comments on other blogs, and then use that same nickname on a bulletin board or when you sign up for a social-networking service, people can easily connect the dots. In fact, many of these services already work together.

For example, on one of my blogs, I display my Flickr photo stream, my blogroll maintained with Bloglines, and my latest Twitter messages. My Facebook profile pulls in my Amazon wish list, my music playlists, and my horoscope.

Here's my point: If you identify yourself on any of these sites or tools, and then tie them together in some way, others can easily follow the trail to figure out who you are.

Anonymity gives you a great way to protect yourself on your own blog, but it doesn't keep you from showing up in other people's blogs or Flickr photo streams. If your friends and family have blogs, consider setting ground rules with them about situations and topics that you want excluded as subjects on their blogs. Be willing to accept the same kinds of requests about your own blog writing.

One of the best ways to take charge of your own online identity is to start a Web site or blog yourself. If other people are mentioning you online, having an official Web site that contains accurate information can help supplant or downplay less desirable material.

If you want to find out more about controlling your online identity or protecting your privacy, review some of these great online resources:

- Visit the Electronic Frontier Foundation's (EFF) guide "How to Blog Safely (About Work or Anything Else)" at `www.eff.org/wp/blog-safely` for advice on blogging anonymously.
- The EFF's "Legal Guide for Bloggers" is a great resource on a number of issues, including defamation, privacy rights, and legal liability: `www.eff.org/issues/bloggers/legal`.
- Anil Dash, an early and well- respected blogger and a vice president at Six Apart (which makes blog software), has written about this issue. Find Anil Dash's take on taking control of your own digital identity at `www.dashes.com/anil/2002/12/privacy-through.html`.

Chapter 3

Choosing and Hosting Blog Software

In This Chapter

- Choosing a domain name for your blog
- Identifying a good Web host
- Deciding between hosted and non-hosted software
- Getting your blog software in place

If you're serious about turning your blog into a visual masterpiece, you're likely to choose a blog software package that you install on your own Web server. Hosted solutions are great, but you run up against the limits of customization quite quickly.

In this chapter, you can find information about choosing the right software for your situation. If you pick blog software that you need to install, you also need to get yourself a domain name and Web hosting where you can install your software.

Prepare yourself for strange new technology jargon while you explore what makes blogging exciting, frustrating, confusing, and rewarding — blogging software.

Having Your Own Domain Name

Of course, you want a blog — that's why you're reading this book, right? — but before you get too much further, you need to deal with the single most important decision of your blogging career: the name of your blog!

That name should tie closely into the *domain name,* or Web address, that your visitors use to access your blog. And if you have a domain name, you obviously need Web hosting so that your blog software has a place to live on the Internet. In the following sections, I walk you through domain names and Web hosting.

A *domain* is the address (or main URL) that people type in their Web browsers to get to your Web site. Think of a domain like an address to your house. Each house on a street has an individual address. When someone looks for you in the phone book, he or she can find your address. If you search for a Web site by using your favorite search engine, you can find the Web site address.

Picking a domain name

You can use any word or phrase as your domain name (assuming no one else is using that domain name). You can make your domain name a company name, a nickname, or your favorite food group. For years, professional Web designers and developers have been saying that all the good domains are gone, which is far from the truth. After all, new Web sites and blogs are launched all the time, and many of them have great, memorable domains!

For an example of a great domain name, check out Vanessa Farquharson's blog Green as a Thistle (`www.greenasathistle.com`), which documents her effort to live a more sustainable lifestyle by doing something "green" every day (see Figure 3-1).

Figure 3-1: Think creatively to find a blog name and domain, like Green as a Thistle.

Think up a phrase or sentence that says something about you and your blog as a starting place. Write down your topic keywords onto sticky notes, and then move them around and see whether you can stumble on something great.

What exactly does a domain do for you? It has several plusses:

- Your readers can easily remember your site. Your mom can brag about you and send visitors to your blog.
- Having a domain of your own looks professional; it's a nice marketing benefit at a small cost.
- You can change Web hosts or hosted blog solutions with impunity because your address is actually a separate service. If — or when — you move your blog, your Web host can help you use the same domain to get to your new server on the Web.

Your domain should represent your blog's name and purpose, although at the end of the day, there are no hard and fast rules. Here are a few quick guidelines that you might want to follow. Try to choose a domain that

- Matches your blog name
- Is based on your topic keywords
- Is a play on words or slang based around your topic
- Is humorous or memorable

If you're having trouble coming up with a name idea, consider using your name. In fact, even if you ultimately want to use another domain for your blog address, owning the domain for your own name is a good idea. You can use several domain names to reach the same Web site or blog, too, so use your own name as a domain might help people find you in search engines.

Many online tools can help you choose a domain name if you're having trouble. Domain-name-choosing Web sites help by suggesting word combinations and coming up with randomly generated choices. One good site to use for this purpose is Bust a Name (`www.bustaname.com`), which is shown in Figure 3-2.

Even if you end up using a hosted blog solution and therefore don't need to get Web hosting, you can buy a domain and forward the address to your blog. This is handy to do because it makes your blog's address easier to remember. After you register your domain, check the Help text of the registrar to find out how to forward the domain to your blog's Web address (URL). Instructions vary by registrar.

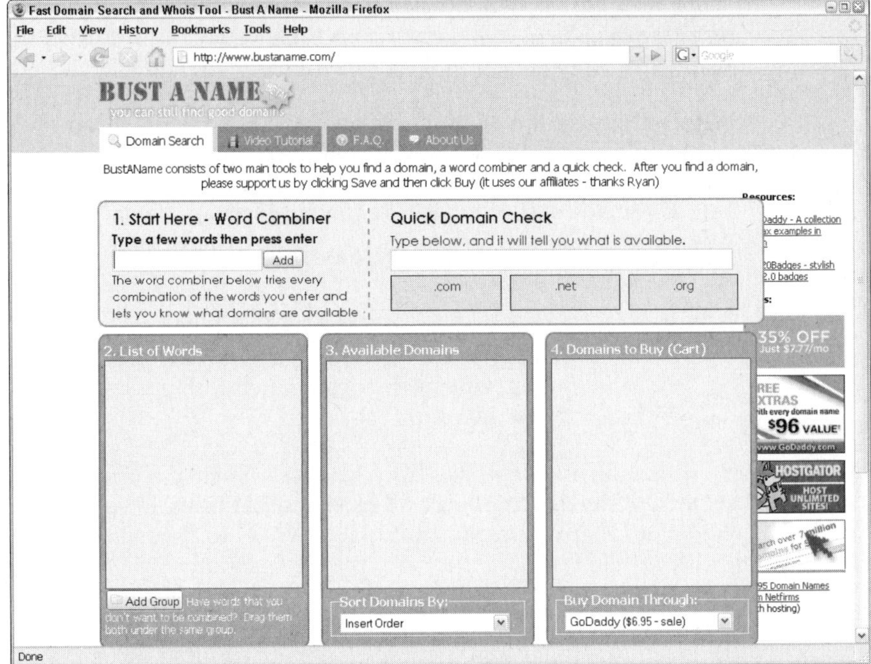

Figure 3-2: Bust a Name can help you brainstorm name possibilities for your domain.

Registering a domain

Registering a domain is a straightforward process. First, use a domain registrar to buy your name. After you own the name, you just need to point your new domain at your Web host. This process basically involves telling your domain registrar which Web server your Web site is on; your Web hosting company or domain registrar gives you the information and tools to make it all work.

You can use many domain registration services. The choice really comes down to the domain management interface — the tools that you get in order to manage your domain. Some management screens are incredibly difficult to work with. Finding a host that has a clean and easy-to-use interface makes a world of difference when you're updating or making changes to your Web domain. Be sure to shop around, as well. The annual fee for domain registration varies widely, and for the most part, the price differences don't equal a difference in what you're getting.

You can choose to register for your domain for a single year or for multiple years at a time. Typically, registering for multiple years earns you a small discount. If you choose to register for only a year, you need to renew the domain in a year (assuming that you want to keep your Web site going). Many domain registration companies also offer Web-hosting and e-mail packages.

Make sure that you keep your domain registration up to date. If you have any changes to your domain or contact information, including your e-mail address, update your domain information immediately. If your information isn't current, you could lose access to your domain or miss e-mail reminders to renew your domain. Make sure to print a copy of the login information and store it safely.

Visit any of the domain registrars in the following sections to check whether your domain is available, and then register it.

Go Daddy

`www.godaddy.com`

Go Daddy is a popular Web host and domain registrar that provides a long list of Web services, including domain hosting, Web hosting, and e-mail address hosting. It has a good reputation and is easy to contact if you require assistance. A `.com` domain is priced at $10.69 for a year's registration.

To register a domain with Go Daddy, follow these steps:

1. **Point your Web browser to `www.godaddy.com`.**
2. **Type the domain you're interested in into the Start a Domain Name Search text box.**
3. **Select the suffix that you want to use from the drop-down menu, as shown in Figure 3-3.**
4. **Click the Go button.**

   GoDaddy returns a page indicating whether your domain is available.
5. **If your domain is available and you want to complete your purchase, click the Add and Proceed to Checkout button to add it to your shopping cart.**

   If your domain is unavailable, scroll down the page to the Search for Another Domain text box and try a new name.
6. **Continue shopping for other domains on GoDaddy or follow the instructions for completing the credit card purchase of the domain you select.**

Figure 3-3: Choose a suffix to use with your desired domain name.

Network Solutions

`www.networksolutions.com`

Network Solutions is one of the grand-daddies of all registrars. At one time, it was one of the few places you could register a domain. Services are varied and flexible, but domains are a little pricey. A `.com` domain is priced at $34.99 for one year of registration.

Domainsatcost.ca

`www.domainsatcost.ca`

This domain registrar, located in Canada, provides registrations for all major domains, including `.com` and `.ca` domains. They have a support number (long distance applies), and they do answer the telephone — a rarity among domain hosts. Domainsatcost.ca is reasonably priced at $12.95 CDN (that's Canadian dollars!) a year.

Finding Web Hosting

With a domain in hand, you can turn your attention to Web hosting.

If the domain is your address, *Web hosting* is your actual house on the Web. Web hosting provides the Web server where your software, graphics, and other files live online. When people use your address — the domain — the Web server gives them the pages that they want.

Doing your research

Your primary concern is to find a Web host that has everything your blog software needs to run. Because you want to use a blog software package, you might have more specific needs than are on offer for a typical Web site.

Most blog software uses a LAMP (Linux/Apache/MySQL/PHP) Web server, a mix of several kinds of Web server technology that are ideal for running dynamic Web sites such as blogs:

- **Linux:** A very common Web server operating system. It's very stable and considered a standard for Web servers. As a blogger, you probably don't need to make too many changes to the operating system, as long as it's in place for you.
- **Apache:** Apache is *Web-page-serving software,* which means it looks at what Web page is requested and then feeds the browser the appropriate file. It does most of the hard work of serving Web pages to visitors coming to your Web site.
- **MySQL:** MySQL is the most popular database software for blogs. For any blogging package, you need some kind of database system to store all your blog posts and run the other functionality of the blog software, and MySQL is the standard database tool for most blog software.
- **PHP:** PHP is the programming language that a lot of blogging and content management systems use. It sits between the blogging software and the database, making sure all the parts work together.

The preceding four technologies are considered the bare minimum that most blogging packages need to function. But you should consider these requirements, as well:

- **Disk space:** For blogging, disk space is important if you decide to store a lot of images on your blog or upload audio and video files. Uploading images is relatively easy to do, but you need the space to store those images. For the average blog that has a few photos, you most likely want about 500 megabytes (MB). Blogs that have a lot of photos require several gigabytes (GB) of disk space. Video blogs need a whole lot more disk space (unless you use an online video-sharing service) than text or photo blogs, so you want more than 10GB — those files do take up a lot of space!

Running out of disk space is an easily solved problem: Most Web hosts allow you to add disk space when you need it for an additional cost. Check with your Web host to find out what they charge for additional storage.

- **E-mail management:** You probably want an e-mail address with your new domain. If you want to use your blog for business purposes, having an e-mail address that matches your domain looks more professional.
- **Backups:** Consider how you plan to back up your data (including your database content) and whether the Web host will also back up the files on your Web-hosting account. Knowing this information can save you from disaster and data loss in the future. Daily backups aren't a bad idea!
- **Bandwidth and CPU resources:** Computers and networks can take only so many visitors and downloads, and hosts usually set a quota on how much bandwidth you can use for the particular Web-hosting package that you buy. Ask about what happens if you exceed your monthly allowance of bandwidth. (Usually, you have to pay for the extra resources.) For most bloggers, this won't be an issue but if you develop a very popular blog with lots of visitors, or are serving very large files like videos, bandwidth can become an additional cost.

Buying Web hosting

After you purchase your domain, you *should* be able to pick a Web host just as easily. But the reality is that Web host offerings are all over the map, so you need to do your research, ask for recommendations from friends and colleagues who have Web sites, and compare the details of what different hosts offer.

When comparing Web hosts, always confirm the numbers provided in sales materials. Here are the top questions to ask a prospective Web host about its Web-hosting packages:

- What's your reliability and uptime guarantee? Most Web hosts will tell you the amount of time in a given month that they guarantee your Web site to be available given normal traffic loads — but none of them can absolutely guarantee 100% uptime.
- What's your data transfer limit, and how much do you charge for additional bandwidth? Bandwidth/data transfer is used as visitors visit your Web site and download pages from your site in order to view them. If

you have a lot of files being transferred, or a single file that thousands of visitors download, you may hit your limit and need to buy more.

- How much disk space does the package include, and what do you charge for additional space?
- What kind of technical support do you offer? What are your telephone hours? How do you handle e-mail support?

When you find a Web host that interests you, check out the packages on offer. Many Web hosts provide a handy comparison chart that you can use to quickly compare pricing and features, as Nexcess.net (`www.nexcess.net`) does in Figure 3-4.

The following sections help you get started with your Web-hosting search by discussing three top Web-hosting services.

Go Daddy

`www.godaddy.com`

Go Daddy is a popular Web host — and domain registrar — that provides a long list of Web services. Its smallest Web-hosting packages start at around $4.99 a month.

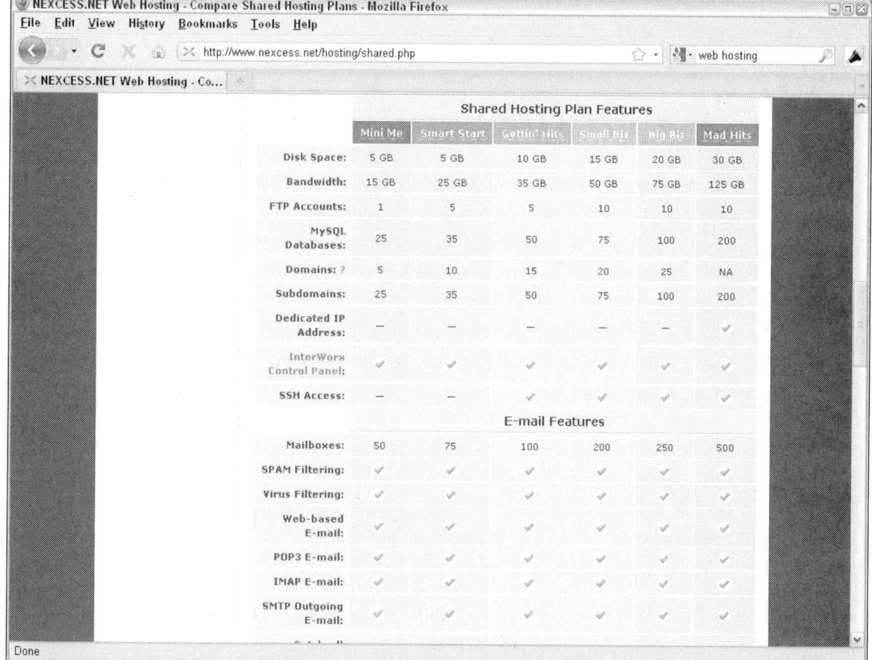

Shared Hosting Plan Features

	Mini Me	Smart Start	Gettin' Hits	Small Biz	Big Biz	Mad Hits
Disk Space:	5 GB	5 GB	10 GB	15 GB	20 GB	30 GB
Bandwidth:	15 GB	25 GB	35 GB	50 GB	75 GB	125 GB
FTP Accounts:	1	5	5	10	10	10
MySQL Databases:	25	35	50	75	100	200
Domains: ?	5	10	15	20	25	NA
Subdomains:	25	35	50	75	100	200
Dedicated IP Address:	—	—	—	—	—	✓
InterWorx Control Panel:	✓	✓	✓	✓	✓	✓
SSH Access:	—	—	✓	✓	✓	✓
E-mail Features						
Mailboxes:	50	75	100	200	250	500
SPAM Filtering:	✓	✓	✓	✓	✓	✓
Virus Filtering:	✓	✓	✓	✓	✓	✓
Web-based E-mail:	✓	✓	✓	✓	✓	✓
POP3 E-mail:	✓	✓	✓	✓	✓	✓
IMAP E-mail:	✓	✓	✓	✓	✓	✓
SMTP Outgoing E-mail:	✓	✓	✓	✓	✓	✓

Figure 3-4: Check the Web host for package comparison charts to help make your decision.

For a new blogger just starting out, I recommend the Economy Plan, which includes 10GB of disk space and 300GB of bandwidth, in addition to daily backups and 24-hour phone and e-mail technical support. You can receive discounts if you sign up for a year or more at a time.

Doteasy

`www.doteasy.com`

Doteasy offers a wide range of Web-hosting solutions for bloggers, including hosting. Doteasy offers 24-hour e-mail technical support. Blog-friendly Web-hosting options start at $7.95 a month — the cost of the Ultra Hosting package, which includes 1000MB of disk space and 20GB of bandwidth per month.

Nexcess.net

`www.nexcess.net`

Nexcess.net is a popular Web-hosting company located in Ann Arbor, Michigan. It has quite a few packages and displays them in an easy-to-compare format. Its e-mail support is extremely fast and effective. Web packages start at $9.95 a month.

The Mini Me package sets you up with 5GB of disk space and 15GB of bandwidth, and includes daily backups.

Deciding on the Right Blogging Software

No matter where you take your blog, it all starts with one crucial decision: what blog software you want to use. Choose wisely, grasshopper, and watch your blog software grow while you add more bells and whistles. Pick poorly, and be faced with the ultimate chore: migrating your blog from one blog software package to a better one. You can do this transfer, but you can't do it easily. Spend the time to find out about the available blogging tools and the functionality they provide now so that you can save yourself a lot of headaches later.

First, you need to recognize that all blogging platforms aren't created equal. Of course, blogging software packages, whether they're managed by you or by paid Web-hosting technical staff, all share the same or similar functionality that you need for a typical blog. But each software package was designed with very different goals in mind.

Unlike software that you install on a desktop or laptop computer, blogging software requires a server environment to function. What a challenge, for a non-technical blogger who just wants to start posting, to make a good decision about Web servers!

Bloggers can use either of two kinds of blogging platforms:

- **Hosted blogs:** *Hosted* blog services provide a unique situation in which you don't need to worry about the software technology at all. You can concentrate on worrying about what your next blog post will be about, rather than how to configure a Web server. To use hosted blogging software, you log in to the editing tool, write a post, click the Publish button, and log out.

  You don't need to think about *how* the software is managed, just as long as it's there the next time you want to post something. Many bloggers consider this setup the deal of the century. One popular hosted solution is Blogger.com, which I discuss in detail in Chapter 4.

  Extra bonus: If you choose hosted software, you don't have to worry about Web hosting — the software company is providing that service for you! See the section "Understanding Hosted Blog Software," later in this chapter, for a more in-depth discussion of this option.

  Social networks allow you to connect with current friends and make new ones while sharing photos, videos, and text. They've exploded in popularity in the last few years, and many of them have added a blogging tool. I cover how blogging fits into social networking in Chapter 15.

- **Non-hosted blogs:** You might want to run your own blogging system right from the beginning. This type of setup is known as *non-hosted* or *installable* blogging software. By installing blog software on your own Web server, you take on all responsibilities related to maintaining the blogging software and the data created when you blog. Strictly from a technical point of view, this type of setup for a new blog might be a little on the difficult side and cause more stress — especially for the nontechnical folks who are figuring things out while they go — but you ultimately get more flexibility when you use a non-hosted setup. For example, Serious Eats (`www.seriouseats.com`), a blog that covers food news from all over the blogosphere, uses Movable Type, a blogging solution that you install on your own server.

  Okay, I lied. Hosting your own blog is a *lot* more difficult than the point-and-click solution of hosted software. If you love a challenge or want all the bells and whistles, however, consider hosting your blog yourself. Later in this chapter, the section "Understanding Blog Software That You Install on Your Own Server" explains the details of how non-hosted blog software works.

Budgeting for software

Many of the hosted services available to new bloggers usually don't charge the user — at least, at the basic level of service. A great number of the non-hosted blogging software packages are also free, but the Web server that you need to install them on most definitely isn't. How much money you can commit to your new blog can help you figure out what platform you should acquire.

Consider how much financial commitment you want to dedicate to your new blogging life. Costs can be associated with

- **Blogging software:** Some packages are free; others aren't. In some cases, the blogging software might be free for personal use but can cost money if you use it for commercial purposes.
- **Upgrades:** When you choose a software package that has a price tag, be sure to note the costs for upgrading that software down the line. Blog software is in flux, and you'll need updates!
- **A domain name:** Regardless of whether you choose a hosted or non-hosted solution, you can buy a domain name (also called a *Web address*) and point it at your blog.
- **Web hosting:** If you choose a blogging software package that needs to be installed on a Web server, you need to find Web hosting.
- **Support costs:** If you have questions about your blog software or Web hosting, getting answers might cost you. Find out what the support policies are for both software and hosting before you buy.
- **Web designers:** If you need to hire a Web designer or developer to produce a design, install the software, and get your blog started, you have to pay those folks.
- **Special bells and whistles:** You might find that you can purchase and use extra add-ons with your blog, from cool functionality to exciting designs.

Making sure you get the basics

Each blogging package has a great number of options to choose from. Some options are designed to trick out your ride, making your blog into a thing of beauty and delight. Some options you absolutely need to have. Good blogging software *must* have the following features:

- **A usable publishing interface or control panel:** Check out how the control panel looks before you commit yourself. A good user interface is important, and if you can't make sense of what you see, chances are good that you won't enjoy using the software.

- **Comments:** A blog isn't a blog unless your readers can leave comments on your posts. You don't have to use the comments, but blogging software without comments takes away a vital element of blogging — allowing your readers to cultivate discussions.
- **Spam deterrents:** Spam comments are a part of every blog, but that doesn't mean you have to live with them. Like e-mail spam, comment spam tends to be an automated process that posts on your blog useless information and includes links to all kinds of other sites. Look for blogging software that has functionalities in place to help you moderate and block spam.
- **Pinging:** A blog software package that uses pinging services is a great idea. *Pinging* is an automated notification system for search engines and newsreaders, letting those services know that you've updated your blog. Because search engines tend to rank "fresh" content highly, letting them know when you have new content means that your blog may be more likely to appear, and appear higher, in search results.
- **RSS feeds:** If your blog software doesn't have an RSS feed, move on to different blog software. If you're at all interested in building traffic to your blog, an RSS feed is the single best built-in software feature that you can use to meet that goal. An *RSS feed* is a computer-readable version of your blog, standardized so that it can appear in newsreaders and on Web sites and blogs. For more information about RSS, read Chapter 13.

I highly recommend two other features, although not all bloggers use them:

- **Categories:** Blogs often jump from topic to topic, and categorizing your posts gives your readers a quick and easy way to sort through your content, focusing on what most interests them. The Modern & Contemporary Design Blog — MoCo Loco — at `www.mocoloco.com` uses categories to sort blog posts; Figure 3-5 shows the categories in the sidebar to the right.

  Categories are high-level organizational tools. For example, a food blog might have posts sorted into categories like Vegetarian, Dessert, Main Dish, and so on.
- **Tags:** A *tag* is a term associated with a blog post. (For example, when I write a blog post about my new cat Maggie, I tag that entry "kitten.") Tagging is a relatively new technology, but it has proven to be one of the best ways to sort through blog data quickly. The Cool Hunting blog (`www.coolhunting.com`) uses tags in the left column, shown in Figure 3-6.

  Tags are like keywords you might use when doing a search on a search engine Web site, and they tend to be more specific than categories. A blog post on a food blog might use categories as I describe in the preceding bullet, and then tag individual posts with more specific terms, like chocolate, hazelnut, and brownie. To differentiate between categories and tags, think of categories as describing a group of blog posts, and tags as describing individual posts.

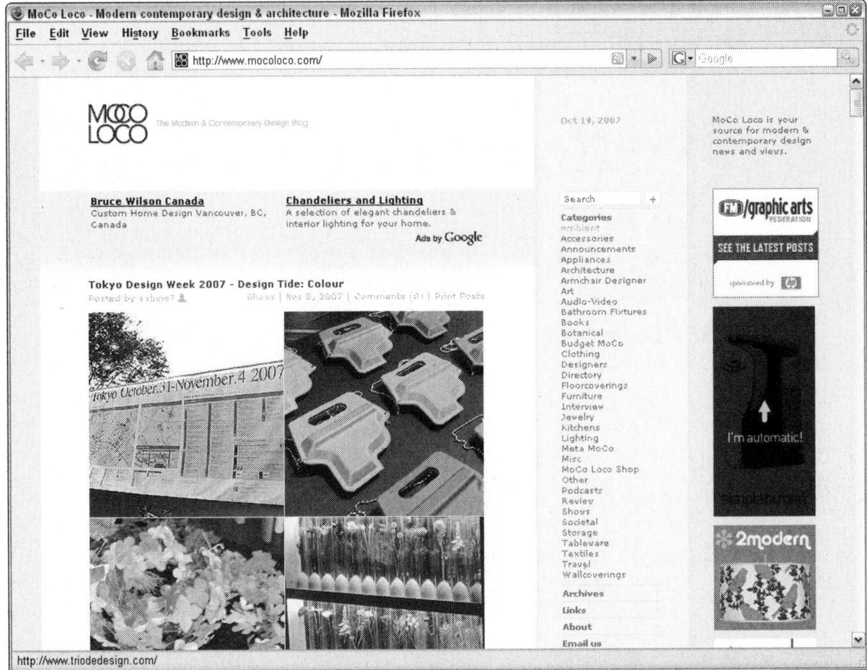

Figure 3-5: MoCo Loco sorts reviews of modern design by using categories.

Upgrading with bells and whistles

You can implement a number of cool toys on your blog:

- **Trackbacks:** *Trackbacks* are a useful technology that allows bloggers to link to blog posts on related topics. If your blog software is trackback-enabled, you can link to another blog simply by using the URL of the original posting. In this automatic process, your blog software lets another blogger's software know that your blog has referenced a post so that the software can create a link on the original post.

  Trackbacks can also be a source of spam, and as a result, they're not as important in the blogosphere as they used to be. So, although they're nice to have, if the blog software package that you want to use doesn't offer trackbacks, don't automatically eliminate that software from consideration.

- **News aggregation:** One of the handiest features of blogging software is the ability to aggregate news by using RSS feeds. Having a news aggregator included with your blog package allows your site to pull in information from other blogs. You can then provide this information to your readers, offering them content from other sources.

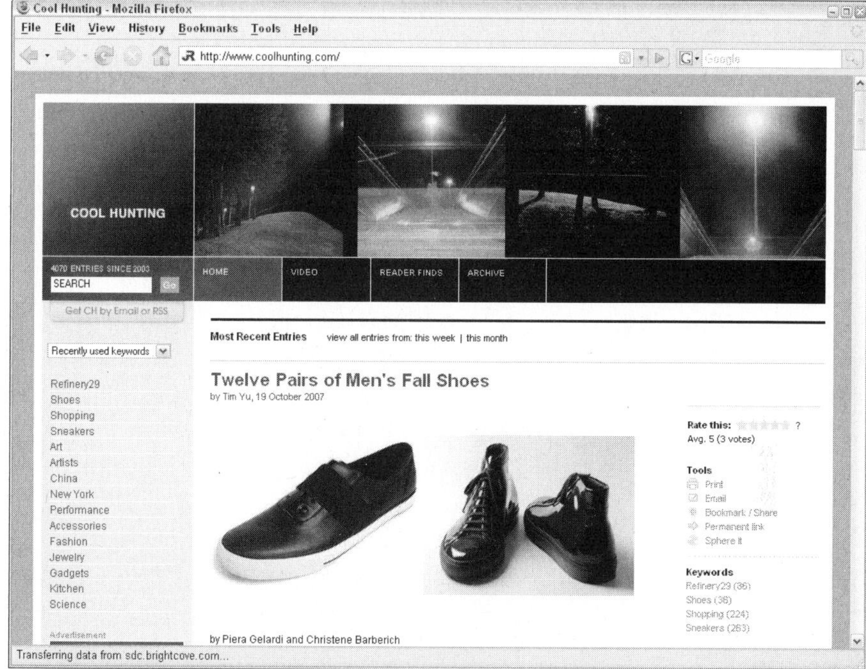

Figure 3-6: The Cool Hunting blog uses tags to label content — they appear in the left column.

Courtesy of Captain Lucas, Inc.

- **Spam blacklist:** Most blogging packages have some kind of blacklist protection against spam comments. These blacklists are often centralized lists of e-mail addresses, URLs, and IP addresses that spammers use, which the blog software prevents from commenting in any blog post on your blog. With an up-to-date blacklist, you can stop a lot of spam before it becomes a comment.
- **Spam whitelist:** Some blogging software includes the ability to use a whitelist, in which you preselect the users that can comment. Spam-filtering systems and blog user accounts are quickly replacing this type of system, however.
- **CAPTCHAs:** *CAPTCHAs* are images that display letters and/or numbers that a person can read but a machine can't. When someone wants to leave a comment on a post, he or she must correctly type these letter/number combinations into a comment field, which proves to the blog software that the commenter is indeed a human and not a computer spam system. This process blocks out the comment spam and lets through the valuable feedback. Variations on CAPTCHAs include simple math problems that a user needs to solve in order to post a comment. Jared Flood's Brooklyn Tweed blog (`http://brooklyntweed.blogspot.com`) uses CAPTCHAs, as shown in Figure 3-7.

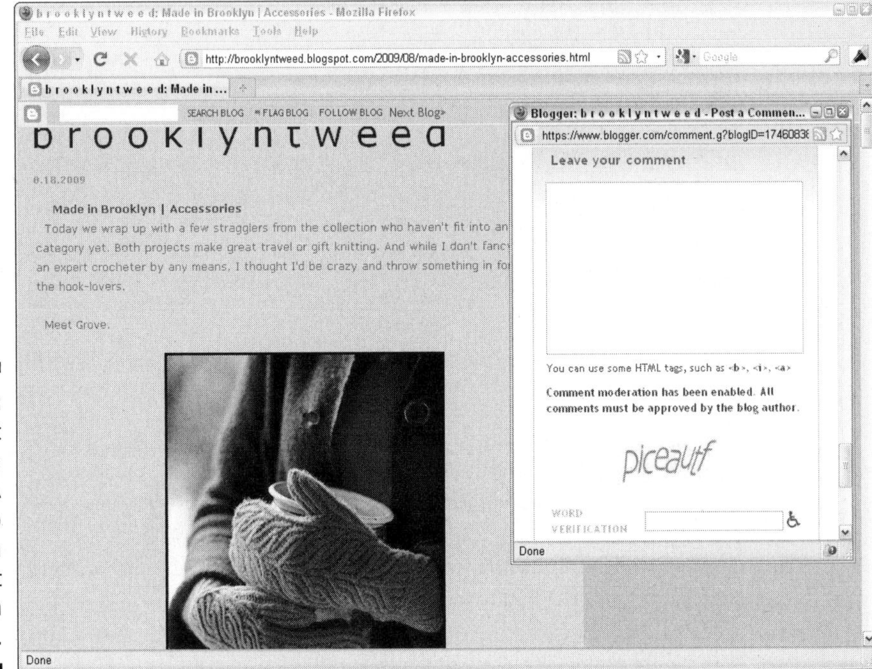

Figure 3-7: You must fill out a CAPTCHA form to leave a comment on Brooklyn Tweed.

You can tie together more and more Web services these days, from your photos on Flickr, to your Twitter updates, to your . . . well, you have a lot of possibilities. Some blog software allows you to automate those kinds of connections, so if that interests you, keep an eye out for software with these features. I walk you through some possibilities in Chapter 15.

Understanding Hosted Blog Software

Hosted services take a whole lot of responsibility off the blogger. The blog software company manages the data, software, and Web hosting; the blogger manages the content. Some services, such as Blogger, do it all for free, whereas other services, such as TypePad, charge a monthly fee to run your blog. Yet other services, such as WordPress, offer a level of free service with the option to upgrade when your blogging requires a little more power. Hosted blog software allows you to make someone responsible for the entire gauntlet of technical tasks that don't excite you.

Seasoned blogging veterans recommend that new bloggers start by using a hosted service that's free. The reason is simple: If you find the idea of having a blog appealing, but you haven't ever tried blogging or played with blogging software, you might not like it all that much in reality. So, an expert — say, the one writing this book — tells newbie bloggers to take a free blogging service for a test drive before committing a lot of time or money.

After all, actually sitting down and running a full- or part-time blog is a whole lot of work. If writing turns out not to be your cup of tea, using a free service for a while means that you haven't poured much money down the drain to find that out.

Reaping the benefits

An upfront cost of zero is very attractive to new bloggers. If you want access to blog technology and have a limited budget (not to mention all those other annoying budget commitments, such as food and rent), free looks just about perfect. Not all hosted software is free, but they generally have quite reasonable costs. A hosted blog that charges a monthly fee is still cheaper than most monthly cell phone plans, about on par with a newspaper subscription.

But free or inexpensive isn't the only upside to hosted blog services. They really take the complication out of starting a blog. For the technophobe, a hosted solution is ideal because you have very few technical issues to worry about. Hosted services take care of

- Web domains
- Software maintenance and updates
- Data storage and backup
- Template design and management

Hosted solutions are also generally quicker to set up than software you have to install on your own server, so you can start blogging sooner when you choose one of these solutions.

Updates are generally free, and the software is available to the enduser 24 hours a day and seven days a week. Sounds like a really good deal, huh?

Living with the limitations

Before you sign yourself up, be sure you understand the tradeoffs that come with using a hosted blog service. Ultimately, you don't control your own blog. If the company goes out of business, takes servers down for maintenance, or decides to change its offerings, you're pretty much stuck with the results.

A free hosted solution, for example, might suddenly decide it should start charging; one that already charges can always raise its rates.

Most hosted solutions let users make some modifications and tweaks, but you can't install your own plug-ins and extras; in many cases, the level of customization is quite limited. With hosted blog software, that ubiquitous WYSIWYG (what you see is what you get) acronym is a double-edged sword: You can't actually do more with less.

If you blog on behalf of a company or business, you might want to cross a hosted solution off your list for a couple of reasons:

- You probably need to make your blog part of an existing Web site, integrated into the look and feel of the company brand; hosted blogs don't allow this customization or integration.
- With a business blog, you need control of the data. Putting the blog on your own server removes any doubts about security or data ownership.

When you think about whether to use a hosted solution, be sure you understand the terms of service of that host. Some hosts reserve the right to cancel or remove your blog or blog posts.

Make sure to read all the fine print for the host that you want to use! You don't want to run into legal restrictions that mean you can't actually use your blog the way you want to, and you definitely don't want to suddenly find your blog missing if the hosted software company decides you're in violation of its rules.

Choosing hosted software

In the following sections, you can take a look at some of the most popular hosted platforms to see which might be the best fit for you and your new blog. These blogging software packages have been around for quite a while and are regarded as some of the best that the blogging community has to offer.

Blogger

`www.blogger.com`

Blogger is the quintessential hosted blogging platform. Started in 1999 at Pyra Labs, Blogger weathered the rough Internet waters at the turn of the century to become the most well-known hosted blogging platform. The Blogger service became incredibly popular, and eventually, Google purchased it. Since then, Blogger has introduced many new features and remained one of the premier blogging platforms. Blogger has many features that allow bloggers to publish multiple blogs:

- All blogs are free and hosted for you, with no hassles and no mess.
- Blogger offers a wide variety of free templates to get you going, which you can customize in a number of ways.

- The publishing tool now has Google AdSense (a blog advertising program) and other neat elements, such as polls and lists, integrated into it, allowing you to add functionality to your blog.
- If you don't want Blogger to host your files, you can save all your blogging files to another server.

I show you how to get Blogger set up in Chapter 4. Because you can use it so easily and set it up quickly (and because it's free), I encourage all new bloggers to use Blogger as a learning tool, even if you plan to use other blog software for your real blog.

WordPress.com

```
www.wordpress.com
```

In 2005, the popular WordPress blogging platform launched a hosted service, in addition to software that you can install on your own server. WordPress.com, as shown in Figure 3-8, offers a clean, easy-to-use interface, and bloggers tend to see it as more flexible than anything else on the market. Now that WordPress.com has added new functionality and additional themes, you can set it up very quickly.

In short, Wordpress.com

- Is free to use
- Has many options for design templates, letting you choose a look that suits your content
- Includes features such as tags and categories, permitting easy organization of your posts
- Offers spellchecking, rich-text editing, and photo uploading
- Lets you measure your site traffic and statistics to help gauge your popularity
- Integrates an excellent spam-fighting tool, Akismet

TypePad

```
www.typepad.com
```

TypePad was launched in 2003 to great fanfare. It allows you to do more than just blog; it was one of the first blogging platforms to offer the ability to create static content pages. TypePad pricing starts at $4.95 a month and ranges upward, depending on the services that you want to include.

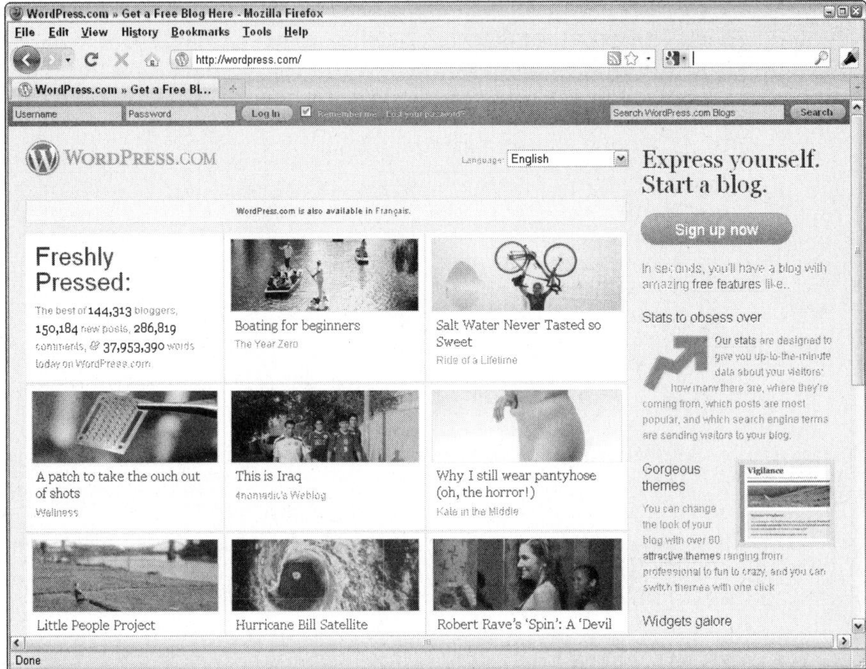

Figure 3-8: You can use WordPress.com to get a free but powerful blog.

TypePad offers

- WYSIWYG (what you see is what you get) posting and editing environment, which means you don't need to know HTML
- Tools that allow you to insert photos into your posts quickly, automatically resizing them and adding thumbnails to blog posts
- Tools that allow you to quickly place videos and podcasts into your blog posts

Understanding Blog Software That You Install on Your Own Server

If technology freaks you out, you can make life easier by using hosted solutions, but bloggers who require more flexibility than hosted solutions offer may choose non-hosted blogging packages. Configuring software to your own tastes and requirements can really improve the overall quality of your blog, making it more attractive to readers and ultimately more successful.

Flexibility can make or break your blog. If you have the money and the skills to install your own blog software, doing so can give you better tools and control over your blog, enabling you to do things like customize the design, add third-party widgets for serving ads, or dabble in customizing the publishing interface.

Choosing a non-hosted blog isn't a plug-and-play solution. Unfortunately, choosing to install blog software, rather than to use a hosted service, means that you need a whole bunch of other technical services to make it all work.

Reaping the benefits

If you use non-hosted blog software, you're in full control — you can do just about anything to the software after you install it:

- **Design personalization:** For those who have Web design skills, stand-alone blogs generally are very adaptable. Some blogs have incredibly diverse and clever designs, many created by the author of the blog to match the style and topic of the blog. Installing the software on your Web server gives you access to every part of the blog software's innards, from templates to graphics, so you can make your blog as pretty as a picture. Or tough. Very tough.
- **Customization:** A lot of the blogging software available is *open source* (meaning the code for the software package is available to developers so that they can manipulate it). Programmers can add, remove, update, and improve functionality for each package. Some packages offer many different options, and independent programmers might also offer additional functionality either for free or a low cost.
- **Looking smart:** The blogging world has social divisions, just like any other, and at the top of the blogging heap, you find geeks. If you want to play with the cool nerds, you need to install your own blog software. Technical bloggers will recognize your prowess and give you props.

Living with the limitations

The first stumbling block you discover when installing your own blogging software, is . . . installing your own blogging software. Somehow, you have to get the software files onto your server, run the scripts, modify the code, and generally muck about in the ugly innards of the software. This process can either be simple or a complete nightmare, depending on your technical savvy and the complexity of the blog software package that you choose.

You can shortcut this issue by choosing a Web-hosting company that offers blogging software. Most blogging software companies provide a list of Web hosts who have in-house expertise in handling their software; just browse around on the software company's Web site to find that list. You can also have the blogging software company install the software for you. For a fairly reasonable fee, you can put that job into the hands of an expert. This solution makes sense for one big reason: You need to install the software only once. If you don't already know how to do it yourself, you don't have to spend hours beating your head against a wall to obtain knowledge you'll probably never need again.

Of course, all software requires some level of maintenance, and most Web hosts don't handle software upgrades and tweaks; be prepared to handle those requirements when they come up by doing them yourself or finding an expert who can handle them for you.

Using non-hosted software has some other downsides, as well:

- **Design personalization and code customization:** Making your blog look pretty sounds great, but you need a cornucopia of associated skills to make that happen — everything from graphic design to HTML coding. If you don't have these skills yourself or access to someone who does, you don't actually have the ability to customize your blog, despite your software.
- **Domain registration and Web hosting:** Unlike the hosted systems, you can't avoid spending money to host your own blog software. Several costs automatically kick in, such as domain name registration and Web hosting (explained in the sections "Registering a Domain" and "Finding Web Hosting," earlier in this chapter).
- **Technical support:** Even if you pay to get the blog software installed for you or sign up with a Web host that does it automatically, if the software breaks (and doesn't all software break at some point?), many Web hosts can't or won't fix it.
- **Backing up:** If you install your own software, you're responsible for making sure that the software and data get backed up or for finding a Web host that includes backups as part of the hosting package.

Choosing non-hosted blogging software

If you're ready to make the leap into the deep end of the blogging pool, the following sections give you recommendations for a range of well-respected non-hosted blogging tools.

Movable Type

```
www.movabletype.com
```

Movable Type is the grandfather of all installable blogging platforms. Released in 2001, it quickly became one of the most popular blogging software packages, for geeks and pundits alike. Movable Type was the first blogging software that permitted contributions by multiple authors, and bloggers highly regard it for the many ways that you can leverage it to create easily updateable Web sites and blogs.

If you're serious about looking at hosting your own installation, Moveable Type is a strong contender. Movable Type offers

- A WYSIWYG (what you see is what you get) editing environment that saves you time and effort
- Easy tools for categorizing your posts, inserting photos and multimedia, and spellchecking
- Automatic generation of RSS feeds to give your blog longevity
- Searchable content, tags, and other cool tools
- A range of licensing options for personal, commercial, and educational use

Pricing varies, but the basic commercial installation is $395.95, and you may qualify to use the free Blogger license if you are an individual blogger and not setting up a blog for an organization or business.

WordPress

```
www.wordpress.org
```

Since 2003, WordPress has provided a solid platform for new and experienced bloggers who want the control of installing blog software on their own computer. Many bloggers say that WordPress is the easiest blogging platform (aside from hosted blogging software) to set up and configure. I cover installing and using WordPress in Chapter 5.

The interface acts exactly the way the hosted WordPress.com system works, so if you're considering using WordPress, sign up for a test blog on WordPress.com to get a good preview of how WordPress works.

Here are some of the highlights:

- WordPress is free!
- It offers many, many user-submitted and -prepared designs, ready for use.

- It includes tags and categories, allowing you to organize your posts easily.
- It has editing tools (such as spellchecking), offers common text styles, and gives you easy ways to include photos, videos, and other media.
- It displays statistics about your visitors to help you understand the traffic to your blog.
- It fights spam with a range of antispam tools.

ExpressionEngine

`www.expressionengine.com`

Back in 2001, a company called pMachine released a blogging software package called pMachine Pro. pMachine Pro quietly hatched a following based on pMachine's clean interface, solid performance, and flexibility in both design and layout. From that success, pMachine built the content management system and blogging software ExpressionEngine, an exceptionally powerful platform.

Today, pMachine (now known as EllisLab) supports all kinds of sites by using ExpressionEngine, which it offers in both commercial and personal flavors. Like Movable Type, ExpressionEngine is highly regarded by Web developers because it offers great blogging tools, but it's flexible enough to be used to develop all kinds of Web sites — not just blogs.

ExpressionEngine users have

- The ability to run multiple blogs that have many contributors
- A powerful templating engine
- Additional modules and community plug-ins, including mailing lists, forums, and photo galleries
- Strong comment moderation and prevention tools
- Different levels of user access, allowing administrators to control what blogs and templates users can edit

ExpressionEngine's commercial license runs you $249.95, the non-profit/personal version is $99.95, and you can use a free option if you forego technical support.

Installing blog software

After you purchase your domain and Web hosting, you can get into the nitty gritty technical tasks: installing your blog software. To get started, look for installation instructions on your blog software company's Web site. Each blogging package has a set of instructions for doing the job yourself and details about hiring company technical support to do the job for you.

Keep in mind that installing blog software is a one-time task! When you finish, you don't ever need to do it again, and you probably don't need the skills necessary to install the software in order to use your blog.

Unfortunately, the steps that you need to take to install a particular blog application vary dramatically from software to software, so I can't give you detailed step-by-step directions. Each blog software package has its own particular requirements for installation, but the general process follows these steps:

1. **Download the latest version of your blogging software.**
2. **Uncompress the package and upload it to your new Web host by using FTP (file transfer protocol).**
3. **Execute the installation application associated with your software.**

To make your installation experience as trouble-free as possible, watch out for the following common problems:

- **File location:** When you upload your blog package, make sure that you upload it to the correct location. All Web hosts tell you where to place your Web files and software so that visitors can find your blog. If you put your files in the wrong place, no one can access your blog.
- **Database requirements:** Sometimes, you need to create a database prior to installing your blog software. Each Web host has a different procedure for creating a database, so if your installation instructions mention this requirement, consult the Web host documentation or support materials to find out how to set things up properly.

Sound like gibberish? The truth is that almost anyone can use blogging software, but only quite technically advanced computer users can install it themselves. If you're a Web designer or developer, you may be able to install the software yourself. If you aren't technical but want to be, this project gives you the chance to really get your hands dirty.

However, if tech stuff makes you cringe, you can investigate having someone else install the software — my main advice is to find a professional:

- **Web designers:** Many people who build Web sites for a living can help would-be bloggers get blogging software installed and running. Of course, you need to pay these folks for their time, so shop around for several quotes to get the best deal.

- **Blogging software companies:** The best blogging software companies offer inexpensive solutions to this problem: They install the software for you on your own Web site. Check with the blogging software company to see whether it offers this service.
- **Web-hosting companies:** Some Web hosts install software for you if you ask (and pay them), and some even offer a one-click installation. These one-click installations can save bloggers from headaches, pain, and midnight crying sessions. You just click a button to install the desired blogging software on your Web server. If this option sounds appealing, check with the Web host you're eyeing before you sign up to see whether it offers one-click blog software installations.

Many of the blogging software companies have figured out that installing blog software creates a real barrier to the nontechnical customer. As a result, you can often go to a blogging software company's Web site and find a list of Web-hosting companies that offer one-click installation for a particular blogging platform.

Part II
Setting Up Your Blog

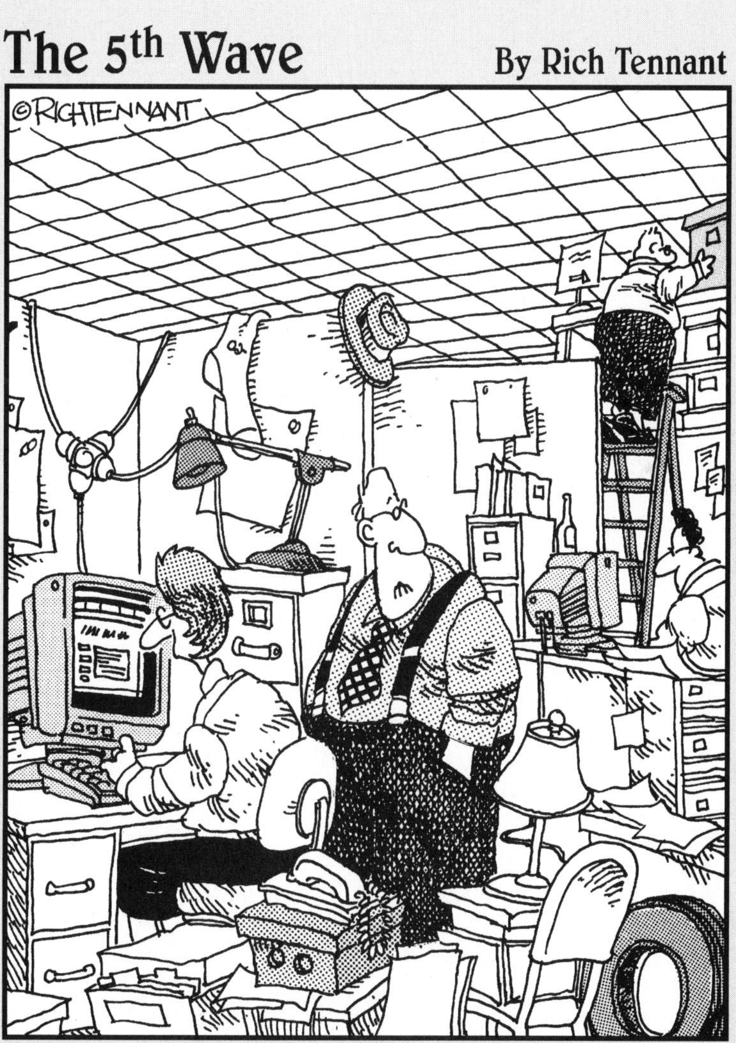

"Just how accurately should my blog reflect my place of business?"

In this part . . .

Enough chitchat? Ready to get going right now? I'm with you. Part II is all about getting your hands dirty, starting with Chapter 4, where I get you started with a tool called Blogger. I kid you not; you can set up a blog and start posting within about 10 minutes. Blogger isn't the only tool around, of course. Chapter 5 introduces you to a great piece of blog software you install on your own Web server: WordPress. And in Chapter 6 you have fun with micro blogs — if you really, really don't have much time to spend on a blog, this extremely short format style might be just the ticket.

Chapter 4

Starting a Blogger Blog

In This Chapter

- Signing up with Blogger to get started
- Writing, publishing, and viewing your first blog post
- Managing your blog settings
- Customizing your blog template to match your style

Part of the beauty of a blog is how quickly and easily you can get going. You can go from zero to blog in about ten minutes by using good blog software, especially if you go with hosted blog software, such as Blogger, which is the focus of this chapter. I show you how to set up a blog with Blogger, write and publish blog posts by using its interface, manage your settings, and customize your template to make your space on the Web unique.

If you're unfamiliar with hosted blog software versus server-based software, flip to Chapter 3 for an introduction to blog software. In Chapter 5, you can find an introduction to WordPress, which offers both hosted and server-based blogging software. And in Chapter 6 you can learn about micro blogging, a short format blog style.

Starting a Blog with Blogger

You can't find a better place to get introduced to blogging than Blogger (`www.blogger.com`). It's free, fast, and easy to use. Because you can get started so easily, you can use Blogger to play with code and discover how blogging works without having to invest a lot of time and energy in Web servers and complicated installation processes.

Blogger promises to get you blogging in three steps: Create an account, name your blog, and choose a template.

Each hosted blog software platform has a different process for getting started, but each one requires the same kind of information: your contact information and a name for your blog.

Creating an account

Before signing up with Blogger, you need login information (a username and password), which you can get in a couple of ways:

- **Through a Google account:** If you have an account with one of Google's services, such as Gmail, you can log in to Blogger by using that account information. (Blogger was acquired by the popular search engine company Google in 2002.)
- **Through Blogger:** If you don't have a Google account, you get one when you sign up with Blogger.

To sign up for Blogger when you don't have a Google account, follow these steps:

1. **Click the Create Your Blog Now button on the Blogger home page (`www.blogger.com`).**
2. **Type your e-mail address in the Email Address field.**
3. **Choose a password and type it in the Enter a Password field.**

   When you type your password, Blogger indicates whether you need to increase the password *strength* — meaning how difficult it would be for someone to guess your password. Click the Password Strength link for more information about creating a more secure password.
4. **Retype the password in the Retype Password field.**
5. **Type the name that you want to associate with your blog in the Display Name field.**
6. **Unselect the Email Notifications box if you don't want to receive e-mails from Blogger.**

   If you do want to receive these e-mails, leave the box checked.
7. **Type in the Word Verification field the word shown as an image.**
8. **Select the Acceptance of Terms check box.**

   You can read the Terms of Service to see what you're agreeing to by clicking the Terms of Service link.
9. **Click Continue and move on to the following section in this chapter.**

To sign up for Blogger by using an existing Google account, follow these steps:

1. **Type your Google account username and password into the appropriate fields on the Blogger home page (`www.blogger.com`).**

2. **Click Sign In.**

   The Blogger Dashboard appears.

3. **Click the Create a Blog link in the Dashboard, and then check out the following section in this chapter.**

Naming your blog

When you have a Blogger account set up, you can choose a name for your blog. If you're creating a blog that you really plan to use (rather than just test, a topic that I discuss in Chapter 3), give a lot of thought to the name that you choose. Your blog name needs to accurately portray your blog's tone and content. If you plan to use this blog as a test space, don't worry too much about choosing a name that has a lot of meaning, but be sure you choose something that you can remember!

To name your Blogger blog, follow these steps:

1. **Type the name of the blog in the Blog Title field.**

   You can type about 50 characters in this field.

2. **Decide what phrase you want to use in your URL and type it in the Blog Address field.**

   A *URL* (uniform resource locator) is better known as a Web address. To open your blog, visitors type this address into the address bar of their Web browsers. You can use any work or phrase that you want as a URL, as long as someone else isn't using it, but you probably want to keep it short, sweet, and memorable so that others can get to your blog quickly and easily. You can't use spaces or punctuation, except dashes, in your URL.

   You can type about 35 characters in this field.

3. **Click the Check Availability link to see whether the Web address you want to use is available. If it isn't, type a new phrase into the Blog Address field and try again.**

   You might have to make several tries to find an available blog address — Blogger is popular!

4. **Type in the Word Verification field the word shown as an image.**

5. **Click Continue.**

   You can now proceed to the Choose a Template phase of the setup, covered in the following section.

Choosing a template

One of the fun features of Blogger allows you to choose from a number of templates for your blog. The template determines both the look and feel of your blog, and also how the blog elements appear on the page. Blogger has fun templates to choose from, and don't forget that you can customize or change the template later if your first choice no longer looks as fresh in six months. (For more info, see the "Customizing Your Template" section, later in this chapter.)

To choose a template during the initial setup of your blog, follow these steps:

1. **Use the scrollbar to scroll through the available templates in the Choose a Template screen (see Figure 4-1).**

   These steps are a continuation from the preceding section. If you want to change your template without going through the preceding steps, you can pick a new template from the Layout area of the Blogger Dashboard.

   The previews on this page give you an idea of how your blog would look if you used the various templates.

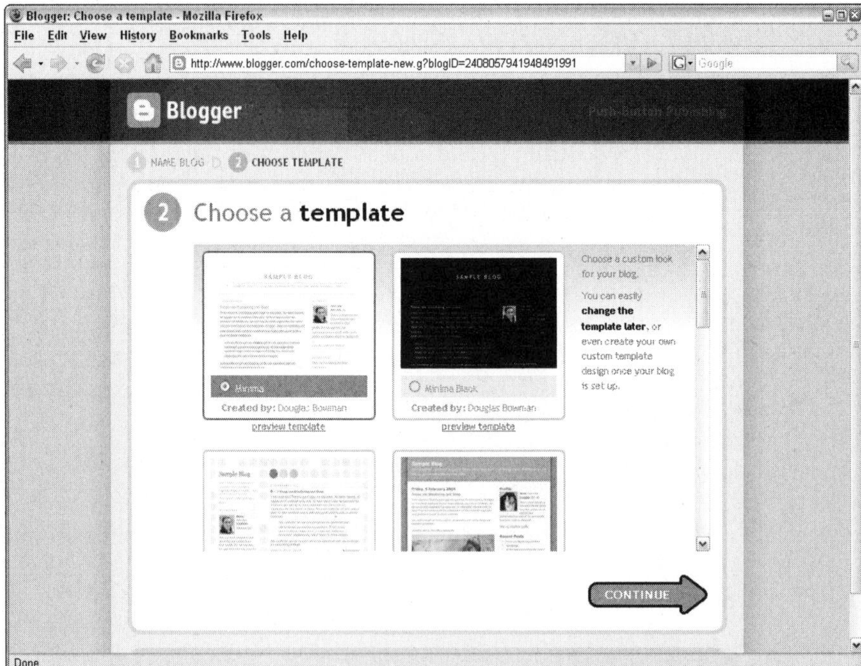

Figure 4-1: You can preview the Blogger templates when you start a new blog.

2. **When you find something intriguing, click the Preview Template link below the thumbnail.**

   A larger image of the template opens in a new browser window so that you can take a closer look. Close the preview window when you finish.

   You can preview as many or as few templates as you want by using the corresponding Preview Template links.

3. **After you decide on a template, select the radio button below the template of your choice.**

4. **Click Continue.**

   Blogger displays a screen confirming that it has created your blog, and it presents a Start Blogging link that you can click to add an entry to your blog.

After you complete this setup process, you don't need to repeat it when you want to add a post to your blog. The next time you come to Blogger, simply use the login boxes in the top-right corner of the home page to log in and get started posting to your blog.

Writing a Post

You officially join the blogosphere by writing your very first blog post, an *entry,* for your new blog. (The *blogosphere,* by the way, is the semi-ironic way that bloggers refer to themselves, their blogs, and the phenomena that is blogging today. You're a member of the blogosphere when you have a blog, regardless of whether you think it's the dumbest word you've heard this year.)

The mechanics of writing a blog post aren't much different from writing an e-mail. Bloggers usually make most posts quite short, and they write those posts directly and conversationally. Of course, you might decide to use your blog to write the next Great American Novel, in which case, your posts might be quite a bit longer than what's standard! That's fine, too. Every blog takes on a personality and life of its own. If you want to find your own narrative voice for your blog, go to Chapter 7.

If you've used a Web-based e-mail service such as Gmail, Hotmail, or Yahoo!, the Blogger software feels very familiar. To create the post, you simply have to fill in the appropriate fields in a form, format the text, and then send it off to its destination — in this case, to your blog, rather than a friend's e-mail inbox.

Follow these steps to write a blog post on Blogger:

1. **Go to the publishing screen.**

   If you just finished signing up for your blog, as described in the section "Starting a Blog with Blogger," earlier in this chapter, click the Start Blogging link to start a blog post; the publishing screen appears, as shown in Figure 4-2.

   If you took a break and are coming back to Blogger, log in. After you do, Blogger takes you to the Dashboard — a kind of control panel showing you the blogs that you have set up and giving you access to tools that let you post, find help resources, or even create another blog. Click the New Post link on the Dashboard to get to the Publishing screen shown in Figure 4-2.

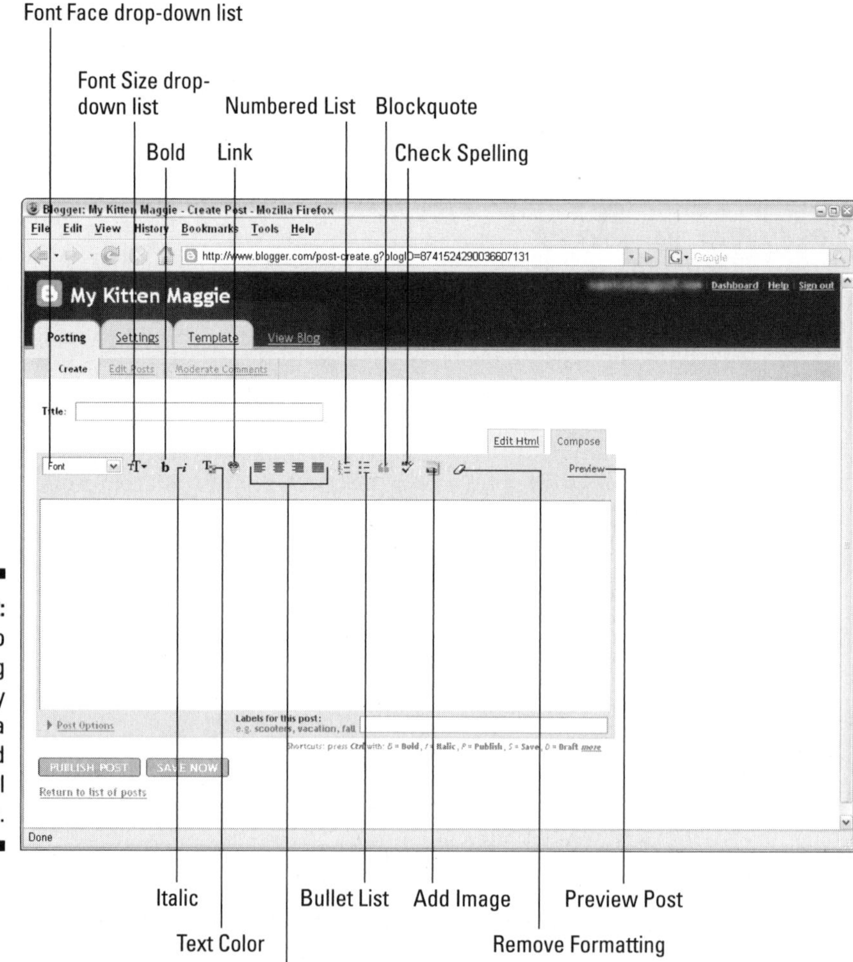

Figure 4-2: Posting to your blog is as easy as using a Web-based e-mail service.

2. **Enter a title for your post in the Title field.**

   Titles are a lot like newspaper headlines: They should be catchy and informative, and they should encourage visitors to your blog to continue reading the rest of the post.

3. **Write your post in the large field.**

   Consider writing your blog posts in a standard word-processing program, such as Notepad or Microsoft Word — and then saving that post. Too many bloggers have spent hours composing right in the entry field of their blog software, only to find that their Internet connection has failed or another technical problem has occurred — which results in a lost post. You don't want to lose all your carefully considered prose just because your cat pulled the cable modem out of the wall! Blogger does have an Auto Save feature installed, but it's still safer to compose offline, and then simply copy and paste the text into the blog software.

4. **Format your post.**

   Blogger's entry field includes icons across the top that let you change the font style and font size, apply bold and italic to text, and create common formatting styles, such as lists. To use these features, select the text in the field that you want to modify by clicking and dragging over the text; then, click the appropriate icon or select an option from the desired drop-down list.

If you know how to write HTML code, you can also try composing your post in the Edit HTML mode. Click the Edit HTML tab and include HTML tags in your text, as needed. If you want to find out more about coding HTML, I discuss common tags in Appendix B.

Adding a link

The Link icon — the small globe icon that has a link of chain on top of it (refer to Figure 4-2) — deserves special attention. You use this icon whenever you want to link to another blog, a news story, that embarrassing Web site that your best friend just created, or any other page on the Web.

When you want to create a clickable link in your blog post, follow these steps:

1. **Highlight the text that you want to make clickable by clicking and dragging.**

2. **Click the Link icon.**

   A pop-up window appears, as shown in Figure 4-3.

3. **Enter the URL of the Web site to which you want to link and click OK.**

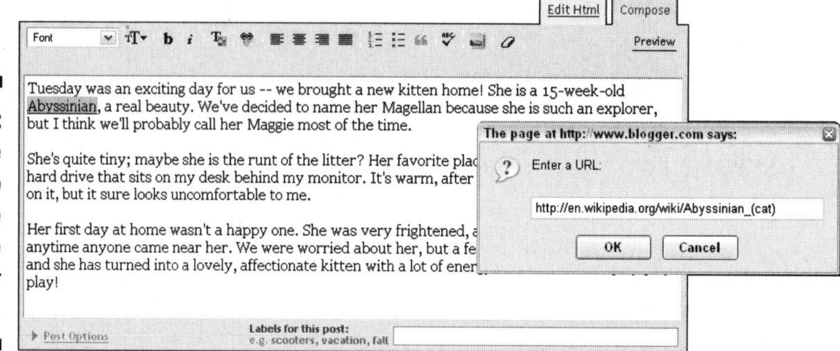

Edit Html
Compose
Font
Preview
Tuesday was an exciting day for us -- we brought a new kitten home! She is a 15-week-old Abyssinian, a real beauty. We've decided to name her Magellan because she is such an explorer, but I think we'll probably call her Maggie most of the time.
The page at http://www.blogger.com says:
Enter a URL:
http://en.wikipedia.org/wiki/Abyssinian_(cat)
OK
Cancel
Labels for this post:
e.g. scooters, vacation, fall
Post Options

Figure 4-3: Using the Link icon to create clickable text in your blog post.

Include the full URL of the Web page in this field. Don't delete the `http://` that's prefilled in the form for you. The URL you use should look like this:

```
http://en.wikipedia.org/wiki/Abyssinian_(cat)
```

And not this:

```
en.wikipedia.org/wiki/Abyssinian_(cat)
```

You can most easily make sure that you have the right link by going to the Web page to which you want to link, copy the URL from the address bar (press Ctrl+C to copy and then Ctrl+V to paste; on a Mac, use ⌘ rather than Ctrl).

After you click OK, the linked text appears as underlined blue text in your post. But it doesn't become clickable until you publish it.

Don't forget that if you know HTML and would prefer to create the link manually by using HTML code, you can do so from the Edit HTML tab.

Spellchecking your text

Blogger provides a handy tool for anyone who needs help with spelling (and who doesn't?). After you finish writing your post, click the Check Spelling icon. It's the icon that shows the letters ABC with a checkmark below them (refer to Figure 4-2).

Blogger highlights incorrectly spelled words in yellow. Click any misspelled word to see a list of suggested alternatives, as shown in Figure 4-4. Select any suggestion from the list or simply type your own correction.

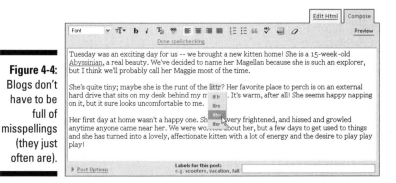

Figure 4-4: Blogs don't have to be full of misspellings (they just often are).

Including an image

You can make your blog post more appealing by including an image. Longtime bloggers can tell you that adding a photo or artwork encourages visitors to read more of the surrounding text. And, of course, everyone knows how many words that photo is worth!

Blogger has some good built-in tools that allow you to upload an image that's already the right size and format for displaying on the Web. If you need help formatting photographs from a digital camera or another source, Chapter 10 shows you how.

Follow these steps to upload an image from your computer and add it to your blog post:

1. **Click the Add Image icon.**

   It looks like a photograph (refer to Figure 4-2).

   The Upload Images window opens.

   Most Web browsers block pop-up browser windows from opening. If you click the Add Image icon and nothing happens, go into your browser settings to turn off this protection. In some browsers, you can block pop-ups from certain Web sites, rather than all sites, so you can choose to allow Blogger to open a particular pop-up window without subjecting yourself to other annoying pop-ups. Consult your browser's Help menu if you need assistance with its pop-up–blocking feature.

2. **Click the Browse button in the Add an Image from Your Computer section of the page.**

   A File Upload dialog box opens, as shown in Figure 4-5.

3. **Locate the image that you want to upload from your computer and select it.**

4. **Click Open.**

   The location of the image is inserted into the image field.

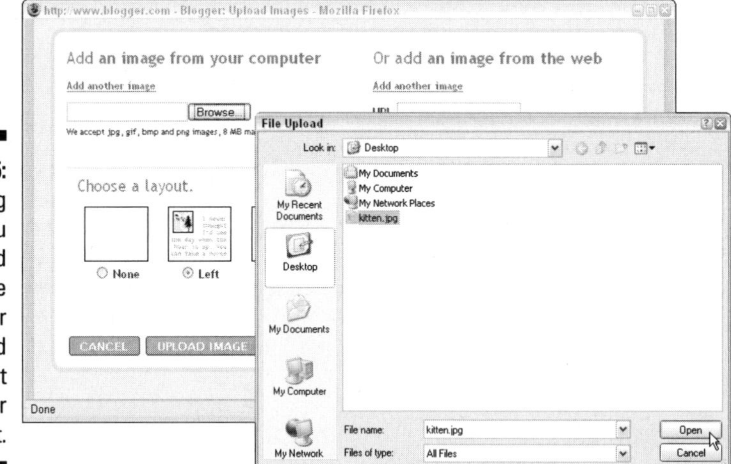

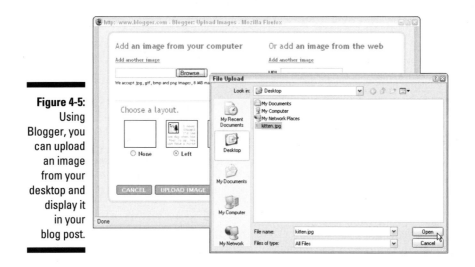

Figure 4-5: Using Blogger, you can upload an image from your desktop and display it in your blog post.

5. **Choose a layout and image size from the options provided.**

   Here are the options you get:

   - *Layout:* Determines how text wraps around the image. You can choose None, Left, Center, or Right.
   - *Image size:* Determines how large the display of the image is in your blog post, regardless of the dimensions of the source image. You can choose Small, Medium, or Large.

6. **Click the Upload Image button.**

   Blogger uploads your image and inserts it into your blog post; the Upload Images window closes.

You can also add an image to your post from another Web site, as long as you have permission to use the image or it's in the public domain. (Read more about copyright in Chapter 8.) You can add an image from a site easily by using Blogger. Just follow these steps:

1. **Find an image or photo on the Web that you want to use.**

   Make sure that you're allowed to use it by checking copyright permission or asking the creator.

2. **Right-click the image and select Copy Image Location from the menu that opens.**

   Phrasing of this option may differ in different browsers. If you don't see anything that looks right, choose Properties from the menu. A window opens that shows you the URL address, which you can then click and drag to highlight. Press Ctrl+C to copy the address (⌘+C on a Mac).

3. **Head back to Blogger and start a new post, or open one that you've already created.**

4. **Click the Add Image icon.**

   It looks like a photograph (refer to Figure 4-2).

   The Upload Images window opens.

5. **Press Ctrl+V (⌘+V on the Mac) to paste the image address into the URL field on the right of the window.**

6. **Choose a layout and image size from the options provided.**

   Here are the options you can choose from:

   - *Layout:* Determines how text wraps around the image. You can choose None, Left, Center, or Right.
   - *Image size:* Determines the dimensions of the image as it appears in your blog post, regardless of how big the source image is. You can choose Small, Medium, or Large.

7. **Click the Upload Image button.**

   Blogger uploads your image and inserts it into your blog post; the Upload Images window closes.

Publishing Your Post

When you're satisfied with your blog post, you can publish it so that the world can admire your erudition. Publishing a post isn't hard: Click the orange Publish Post button at the bottom of the page. Your post appears on your blog, making it available for others to read.

Before you publish, you can take advantage of three areas of the Blogger Publish page that I find very helpful: previewing, saving as a draft, and selecting post options.

Previewing your post

Before you publish, you can preview what you've created by clicking the Preview link (found on the far right of the editing icons). This preview is WYSIWYG (what you see is what you get), which means that it shows you the post exactly as you formatted it, including links, text colors, embedded images, and so on.

I like to preview my post before I publish because I can more easily read for meaning and content at this point. Think of the preview as a last chance to catch grammar problems or even to think twice about what you're posting if it's controversial. Of course, you can also see how the text and content flow around any images that you've added.

If you see changes that you want to make, simply click the Hide Preview link to go back to the editing screen.

Saving as a draft

Many bloggers like to create posts in advance of when they plan to publish them. For example, if you're planning a vacation, you can write several posts before you leave. When you put them into Blogger, click the Save as Draft button, rather than the Publish button. Clicking the Save as Draft button sets the status of the post to draft, and even though you can access it via the Blogger Dashboard, it doesn't appear on your blog until you go back into the post and click the Publish Post button.

When you create a post, Blogger automatically saves it once a minute, so you may not have to click Save as Draft if you want to keep a post as a draft. Clicking the Save as Draft button, however, ensures that the saved version is the latest one.

Setting post options

Below the entry text and just above the Publish Post button, you can see a Post Options link. Click this link to open a menu.

You can choose whether you want readers to be able to comment on your blog post by selecting the Allow or Don't Allow radio button. You can actually choose from two Don't Allow options: The first keeps already-posted comments visible, even though no one can add new comments; the second hides (but doesn't delete) already-posted comments.

You can make the decision to turn off comments at any time, so if you decide later that you don't want to receive further comments, you can always edit the entry and turn off this option then.

Most of the time, you want to allow comments; after all, part of what makes a blog exciting to read is the opportunity to interact with the blogger. Sometimes, though, you might write an entry that you don't want to read discussion about, perhaps because you don't want to start a long argument or because the entry has become a target of spammers. You can find more about interacting with your reading community and preventing spam in Chapter 9.

You can also set the publication date and time that appears on the post. By default, Blogger sets the publication date and time of the entry to the date and time that you began writing that entry. However, you have the power to alter the date and time.

You might choose to change the date or time for a number of reasons:

- **Social or professional reasons:**
  - Create a blog post for a friend's birthday and make the date match the time your friend was born.
  - If you're blogging at work, you might want to set your date and time to a period when you weren't supposed to also be at your desk (ahem) *working*. Chapter 2 discusses blogging and workplace issues in detail (and recommends that you don't blog at work, unless that's part of your job responsibility).
- **To work around your schedule:**
  - If you take a long time to write a post, by the time you're ready to publish it, you might need to put a more realistic time on the entry.
  - If you save your post as a draft and publish it later, you can update the date and time to accurately reflect the real publication date.

In Blogger, you can easily change the date and/or time by typing the new figures in the same format on the post publishing page.

If you're writing a post that you want to publish in the future, simply set the date and time for that future. Even after you click the Publish Post button, Blogger doesn't put the post on your blog until the date and time that you specified.

Viewing Your Blog Post

After you publish, you can see how your post looks on the blog. You may find this step rewarding — and you definitely don't want to skip it. Even if you preview your post before publishing, you haven't seen your post in the way that your readers see it. You can do that only by actually going to your blog as it appears to everyone on the Web and taking a look.

You need to view your post for another reason, too: Computers can still make errors or fail between the moment you click Publish and when the entry shows up on the blog. I like to look at my blog every time I post a new entry to make sure that it actually looks right on the page and that the blog software successfully processed it.

When you click Blogger's Publish button, the system provides you with a handy link to view your blog. Click View Blog to head over to your blog and see your handiwork.

Of course, if you prefer taking the long way, you can always type the Web address (the one that you chose when you set up your blog) into the Web browser to see your blog without going through the Blogger Dashboard.

While you look at your blog, make sure the formatting, images, and text look the way that you want them to and click any links that you created. If anything doesn't work quite properly, go back into Blogger and make changes to your entry.

Selecting the Dashboard Settings

Blog software, as a rule, is quite customizable. As the owner of the blog, you can decide a number of things about the way your blog looks and works, and you can control those elements from the control panel — called the Dashboard in Blogger — of your blog software.

Most blog software packages work quite similarly, and if you know how Blogger works, you can make the most of any other software.

Blogger divides its settings into several areas: Basic, Publishing, Formatting, Comments, Archiving, Site Feed, Email & Mobile, OpenID, and Permissions. I cover important highlights from the Settings in the following sections.

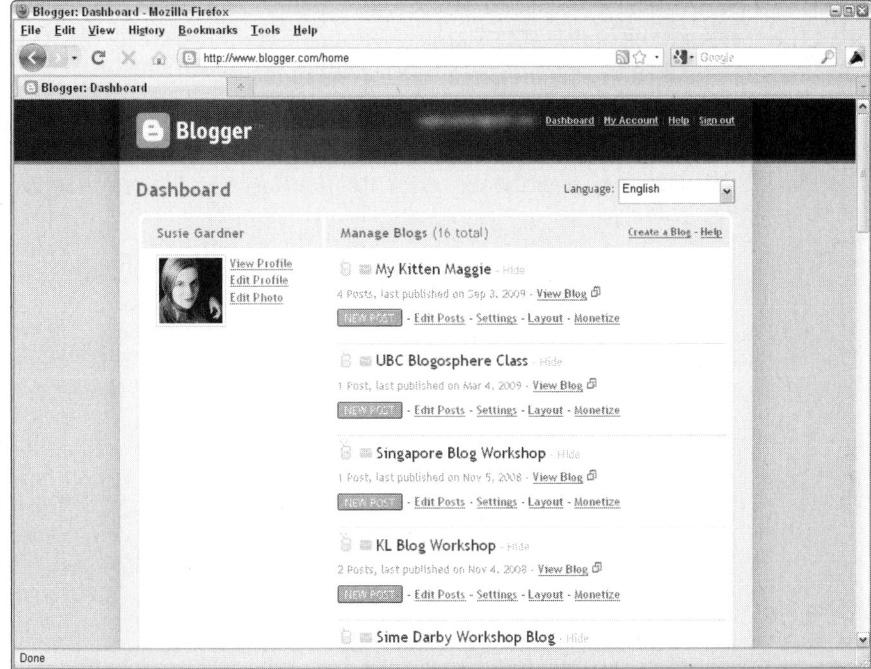

Figure 4-6: The Blogger Dashboard gives you quick access to layout and posting tools.

You access all the Blogger settings via the Blogger Dashboard. (In other blog software packages, this area is called the control panel, the admin panel, and so on.) To reach the Dashboard, just log in to the Blogger Web site. If you're already logged in, look for a link to the Dashboard in the upper-right corner of any page and click it. My Dashboard is shown in Figure 4-6.

The Dashboard shows all the blogs that you've started with Blogger. For each blog, you can quickly start a new post or jump into editing older posts. Also, a click takes you into the blog settings, or to the template or layout that you're using.

If you make changes to any of the Settings areas described in the following sections, be sure to click the Save Settings button at the bottom of each page to save your new settings.

Making basic changes

On the Basic Settings tab of the Dashboard, you can change the name of your blog (Blogger refers to this name as the blog title) and also give it a short description. Most of the Blogger templates display the description near the top of the page. If you change the title on your blog page, the URL that readers type into a browser to visit your blog stays the same.

Follow these steps to change your blog's name:

1. **From the Dashboard, click the Settings link for the blog that you want to edit.**

   The Basic Settings tab, shown in Figure 4-7, appears.

2. **Edit the Title and/or Description.**

3. **Scroll to the bottom of the screen and click Save Settings.**

   A Blogger page appears, displaying a confirmation message at the top that it saved your settings.

Figure 4-7: Use the Basic Settings tab to change the name of your blog or add a description.

The most interesting setting on the Basic Settings tab is Show Email Post Links. Setting this option to Yes adds a small e-mail icon to each post on your blog. This icon permits your blog visitors to e-mail the post to a friend or colleague who might find it interesting, which is a nice little service for your readers that might gain you a few more visitors.

At the top of the Basic Settings tab is a dangerous but important option: Delete Blog. If you ever decide to remove your words from the Web entirely, this button removes your blog — all your posts, images, and other files — from Blogger and from the Web. If you click it by mistake, don't panic; Blogger asks you to confirm the deletion before going ahead.

Making publishing changes

The Publishing tab of the Dashboard is small but mighty! If you aren't happy with the Web address for your blog, you can edit the address by changing the Blog*Spot Address setting. For instance, if you start a blog called My New Kitten Maggie and your cat grows up (they do that, I hear), you might want to edit both the name and the location of your blog. (You have to make the name change on the Basic Settings tab, which I describe in the preceding section.) Use the Publishing tab to change the URL. For example, you can change

```
http://mynewkittenmaggie.blogspot.com
```

into

```
http://mygrownupcatmaggie.blogspot.com
```

You can change your address only to one that another Blogger member isn't already using, so you may have to make several tries before you find one that's available. Although you can make changes to the URL of your blog, remember that doing so means that no one can access your blog from the previous address, so anyone who has bookmarked your blog or memorized the address can't reach you after you make the change.

Blogger has a great tool that allows you to export your blog as HTML pages to your own Web server. You can then display these HTML pages as part of a larger Web site. To configure Blogger to perform this function, look for information on the Publishing tab about how to get started.

Making formatting changes

On the Formatting tab of the Dashboard, you can customize how your blog appears, from the format of the date and time to the number of posts on your blog home page. You can also set the language of your blog.

One neat setting in this tab is the Post Template setting at the bottom of the page. Many blogs follow a standard format. For instance, if you start a movie-review blog, you might choose to follow a similar way of reviewing each movie, perhaps by giving the name of the movie, the director, the lead actors' names, a short review, and a numeric rating. No matter what movie you review, you provide the same information and use the same format each time your write a blog post.

The Post Template allows you to set up standard HTML code that formats your blog post. After you set up a Post Template, every time you start a blog post, that code automatically appears in the entry, and you can easily format your post by putting the information in the right spots.

I can't cover this feature in depth because I don't know just what kind of standard formatting you want to use, but the process of implementing a standard template works like this:

1. **From the Dashboard, click the Settings link for the blog that you want to edit.**

   The Basic Settings tab appears (refer to Figure 4-7).

2. **Click the Formatting option in the Settings area.**

   The Formatting tab opens.

3. **Scroll to the bottom of the screen and type or paste the text or HTML code that you want to use for every blog post into the Post Template field.**

4. **Click Save Settings.**

   A Blogger page appears, displaying a confirmation message at the top that it saved your settings.

Making comment changes

Comments are both a strength and a weakness of the blog medium. Both readers and bloggers find the ability to leave a comment, which lets you interact or converse with a blogger, very attractive.

Commenting has a downside: Spammers have discovered the comment technology, as well. Just as with e-mail, you can expect some commenters to tell you about fabulous mortgage opportunities, Mexican pharmaceuticals, and other less-than-savory possibilities — information neither you nor your readers want.

The Comments Settings tab of the Dashboard provides settings to help you reduce spam on your blog. One of the best ways to reduce spam is to specify who can comment on your blog. From the Comments Settings tab, select an option from the Who Can Comment drop-down menu:

- **Anyone:** This option allows the widest possible audience, with no limitations on who can comment. It provides no spam prevention, but it also imposes no barriers to leaving a comment to genuine commenters.
- **Registered Users:** Sets your blog to accept comments only from registered members of Blogger so that you can cut down on some spam. Don't forget that not everyone has a Blogger account — or wants one — so you might lose some real comments.

- **Users with Google Accounts:** Because Google validates the accounts it creates, letting users who have Google accounts leave comments can help ensure that you get comments from humans, rather than spammers.
- **Only Members of the Blog:** Prevents anyone who isn't a member of your blog from leaving a comment. No one you haven't personally authorized as a member can leave a comment. This option creates a lot of work for you because you have to maintain the list of authorized members, but you don't get any spam.

You can add members to your blog from the Permissions Settings tab.

You can implement two other important Comment settings if you have spam problems. On the Comments Settings tab, you can specify

- **Comment moderation:** Change the Enable Comment Moderation setting to Always. Turning on comment moderation prevents anyone from posting a comment that you haven't approved. When someone leaves a comment, you get an e-mail that lets you know about the comment. From the Dashboard, you can authorize or reject the publication of the comment. You can also moderate comments via e-mail.

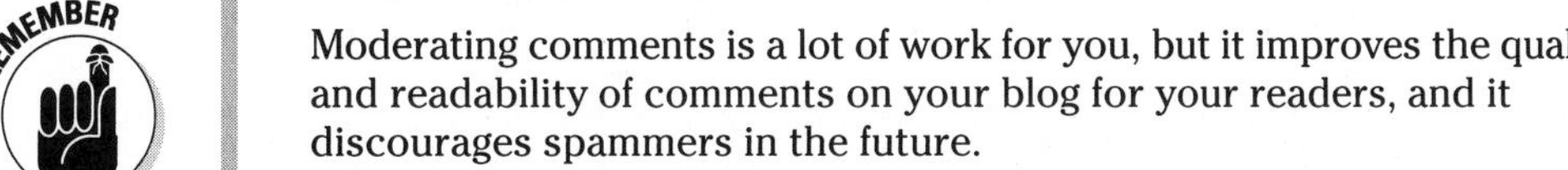

  Moderating comments is a lot of work for you, but it improves the quality and readability of comments on your blog for your readers, and it discourages spammers in the future.

- **Word verification:** Change the Show Word Verification for Comments setting to Yes. People who want to comment on blogs that have word verification turned on must type a word displayed in an image in order to submit a comment. Because many spammers use automated scripts to post spam on blogs, and only humans can read the text in an image, this verification cuts down significantly on the amount of spam.

At the bottom of the Comment Settings tab, you can enter an e-mail address in the Comment Notification Address field at which you want to receive notification when someone leaves a comment on your blog. This setting helps you keep track of comments left on your blog, especially when you have a lot of old posts on which you might not see comments when you view your blog.

Making e-mail changes

On the Email & Mobile Settings tab of the Dashboard, you can turn on a cool feature that allows you to post to your blog by sending an e-mail message. When configured, you can simply send an e-mail to the address from any device capable of sending e-mail (such as your phone!). The subject of the e-mail becomes the title of the blog post, and the text of the e-mail is the entry body. It's a very quick, easy way to publish to your blog, which makes it great for when you're traveling.

To set up a Mail2Blogger address, visit the Email & Mobile Settings tab and fill out the Email Posting Address field. Be sure to save the settings and test to make sure that it works!

Making permission changes

On the Permissions tab of the Dashboard, you can add authors to your blog — people who can also contribute blog posts, creating a group blog. To add someone as an author, you simply need that person's e-mail address. If the person you're adding has a Blogger or Google account, I recommend using that address so that all his or her Blogger and Google account services are tied together.

To add an author, follow these steps:

1. **From the Dashboard, click the Settings link for the blog that you want to edit.**

   The Basic Settings tab appears (refer to Figure 4-7).

2. **Click the Permissions option in the Settings area.**

   The Permissions tab opens.

3. **Click the Add Authors button.**

   A field for e-mail addresses appears.

4. **Type or paste the e-mail addresses of the authors you want to invite to post on your blog in the field.**

5. **Click Invite.**

   A Blogger page appears, displaying the address and invitation date for the invited author.

6. **Repeat Steps 3-5 to add additional authors.**

You can also decide to allow anyone to view the blog, or you can choose to restrict viewers to only people you invite or the authors of the blog. If you want to blog only for your family, use the Permissions tab to invite them as readers, which blocks anyone else from even seeing the blog (much less leaving a comment!).

Editing templates old-skool: Using code

If you're a Web designer or coder, and you want to sink your teeth into the Blogger template itself, you can still do so. To get to the code from the Blogger Dashboard, choose Layout⇨Edit HTML. You can edit the template in two ways:

- **Edit the HTML template directly within the Blogger Dashboard.** Preview and save the template while you go.
- **Download the template to your computer.** Edit it in your chosen HTML editor, and then upload the new template.

Both approaches require you to be proficient with HTML and CSS, and to know a certain amount of Blogger's own coding language, to successfully edit these files.

Customizing Your Template

The layout that you picked when you started your blog might look great to you, but many bloggers want to tweak and customize the look and feel of their blogs — I know I did when I started working on my blog. I was using personal words and pictures, and I wanted to make the rest of the site look more like my own Web site, rather than a Blogger design.

You can customize the design of a Blogger blog in three ways; you can accomplish all three by going to the Dashboard and clicking the Layout link underneath the name of the blog that you want to customize.

If you see the word Template, rather than Layout, underneath the name of your blog information in the Dashboard, you're probably using a blog that was set up before Blogger added the Layout features. You need to upgrade your blog in order to use the new features. To do so, read the "Upgrading to templates" sidebar in this chapter. You may find the distinction extra confusing because the Dashboard refers to Layout, but after you click into the Layout area, you see a tab that refers to templates.

In Blogger, a single template controls the layout and design of your blog, from the size of the text to the color of the background. Changing the template changes the design. In the past, changing the template required a fairly extensive knowledge of HTML and Blogger code, but now you can customize quite a bit without knowing code.

Editing page elements

When you click the Layout link, the Page Elements tab opens by default. The Page Elements tab of Blogger (see Figure 4-8) gives you, the blogger, a ground-breaking tool that allows you to have detailed control over the layout and look of your blog without requiring you to become an HTML guru and stay up late figuring out the intricacies of Web publishing. This kind of editing control reflects the growing do-it-yourself attitude found in the blogosphere: Bloggers want sites that reflect their own sensibilities, but not everyone has the time to become an expert or the budget to hire one.

This access also reflects the growing expertise of many computer users who can edit photographs and create graphics, and it gives them the ability to make the most of those skills.

In the Page Elements tab (see Figure 4-8), a wireframe of your blog template appears. A *wireframe* is a visual representation of the template layout that uses only outlines, or boxes, of the elements.

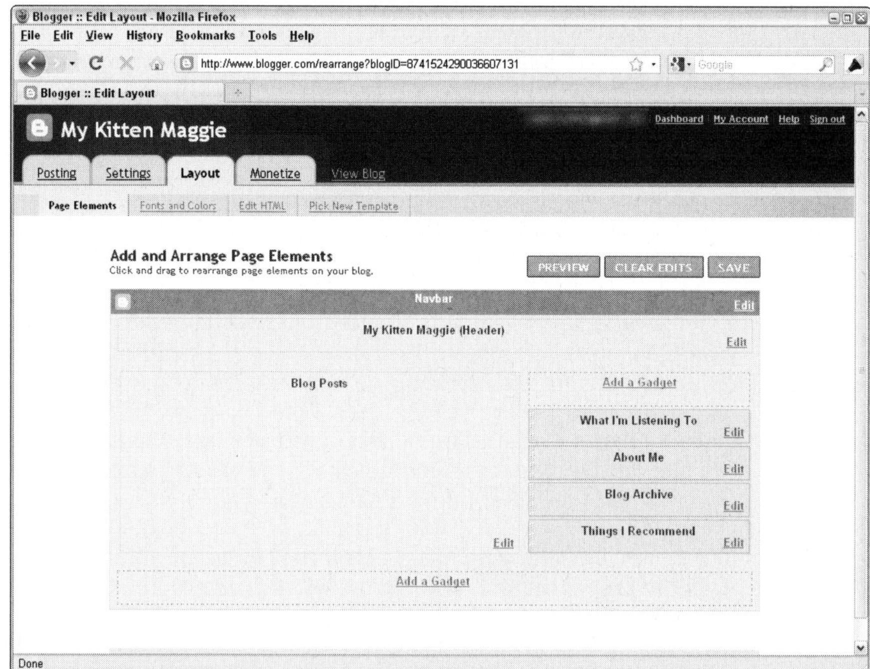

Figure 4-8: Use the Layout tab in Blogger to customize your blog layout.

The following list explains how you can use the wireframe features to customize your page:

- **Edit page elements.** Click the Edit link for any page element that is already being used to change its formatting. In most layouts, you can customize the navigation bar, blog header, blog posts, and sidebar elements, such as About Me and the Archive.
- **Add a gadget.** Click the Add a Gadget link to place in your sidebar polls, images, lists, advertising, and more from a library of Blogger-provided elements. You have many to choose from, but here's a quick list to give you a feel for the options:
  - Poll
  - List
  - Link List
  - Picture
  - Google AdSense (see Chapter 17)
  - Text
  - HTML/third-party functionality (see Chapter 20 for third-party tools that you might enjoy)
  - RSS or Atom feed (more about RSS in Chapter 13)
  - Video clips
  - Logos
  - Your profile
  - Headlines
- **Move page elements.** Click and drag them to a new position.
- **Preview edits that you've made.** See how your changes look before you save them to your blog by clicking the Preview button.
- **Revert to the original version of your template.** Click the Clear Edits button.

Editing fonts and colors

If you like the customization possibilities discussed in the preceding section, I think you'll like what you can do in the Fonts and Colors section of the Template tab, as well.

Upgrading to templates

If the first item on the Template tab isn't Page Elements, you might need to upgrade your template to the current format. Just follow these simple steps:

1. **Click the Customize Design tab.**

   The Upgrade Your Template page appears.

2. **Click Upgrade Your Template.**

   The Pick New Template page opens.

3. **Select a template to use.**

   If you're already using one of the existing Blogger designs, that design is preselected for you, so you can go to Step 4.

   To pick a new template, preview any template by clicking the Preview Template link below the corresponding thumbnail. A larger image of the template opens in a new browser window so that you can take a closer look. Close the preview window when you finish. After you find a template that you want to use, select it.

4. **Click the Save Template button.**

   Blogger implements the latest format of the template, which allows you to add or arrange layout elements in the Page Elements tab that becomes available after the upgrade.

The Fonts and Colors screen gives you fine control over the colors of the following blog elements:

- Text
- Page header
- Dates
- Blog entry titles and footers
- Sidebar background, text, and titles
- Link color

You can also edit the fonts and size of the text on your blog. If all the colors of the rainbow get to be too much, click the Revert to Template Default link and start over with the template designer's choices.

To edit a font color, follow these steps:

1. **Click the Fonts and Colors tab of the Layout area.**

   The fonts and colors palette and selection options appear.

2. **Select the item that you want to edit from the scrollable menu at the top-left of the page.**

   In Figure 4-9, I selected the Post Title Color.

3. **Click a color box in any of the palettes on the right to select a new color.**

   You can choose from these palettes:

   - *Colors from Your Blog:* This palette shows the other colors that you're using in your layout.
   - *Colors That Match Your Blog:* This palette shows colors that Blogger thinks fit well with the colors already in use.
   - *More Colors:* This palette shows a selection of other colors that you can play with.
   - *Edit Color Hex Code:* If you know the hexadecimal code for the color that you want to use, you can type it into this text box. *Hexadecimal code* is a code that contains letters and numbers which equate to a color. Primarily, graphic and Web designers use hexadecimal code.

   When you click a color, Blogger shows a preview of how it looks on your blog in the lower half of the screen.

4. **After you make your edits, click Save Changes.**

   A Blogger page opens, displaying a confirmation that it has saved your edits.

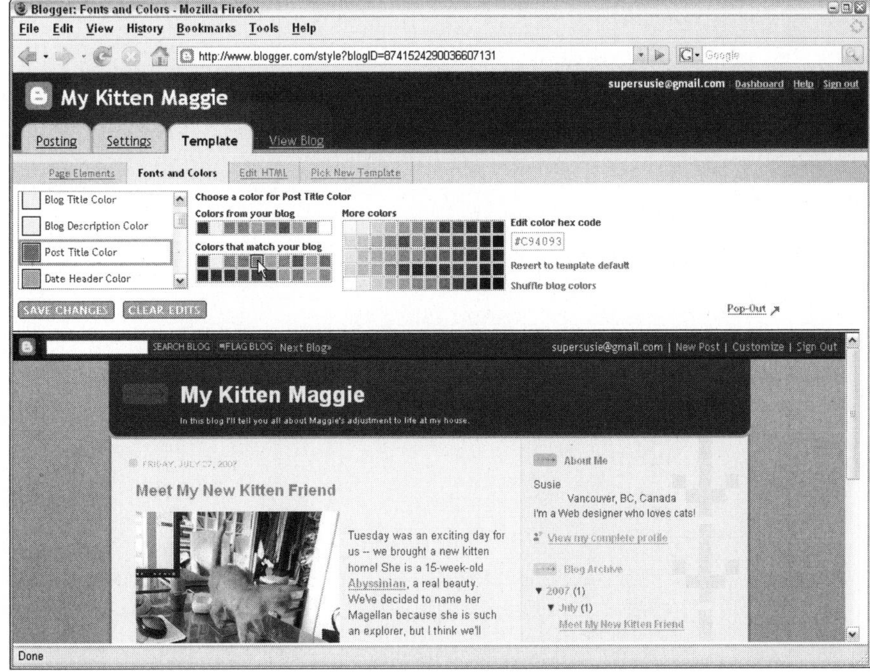

Figure 4-9: Use Fonts and Colors to change the text colors on your blog.

Choosing a new template

When you want a fresh new look, sometimes no amount of tweaking is enough — you need an entirely new template design to work with. At any time, you can visit the Pick New Template section on the Template tab and look through the available Blogger templates, preview them, and select a new one to use on your blog. Click the Save Template button after you select a new template.

If you customize your template by using the Fonts and Colors section and then pick a new template, you lose all your edits and tweaks. If you want to implement those tweaks sometime in the future, print a copy of your blog and make notes about what colors you used for each element. Then, put your paper template in a safe place!

Some of the available templates have multiple versions listed. The template designer has created variations on the main template that you might enjoy. To see a variation, simply select the radio button for one of the versions. The thumbnail loads, and when you preview the template, you can see a larger view.

Don't forget that you can customize your new template by using the Page Elements and the Fonts and Colors sections.

Chapter 5

Starting a WordPress Blog

In This Chapter

- Examining the different versions of WordPress
- Doing your WordPress install
- Kicking the Dashboard tires
- Writing your first post
- Customizing your blog
- Searching for all things WordPress

If you spend much time looking at blogs or talking to bloggers, you can't miss references to WordPress, one of the best-known and well-liked blogging software options available today. WordPress comes in two flavors — hosted and installable — and in this chapter, I focus on working with the installable version that you place on your own Web server.

This chapter runs through an overview of how to install WordPress on your server, use the administration panel, play with themes and widgets, and find out where to connect with other WordPress users in your local community and online.

I can cover only so much detail in a single chapter, so if you want to dive into greater detail about WordPress and find out how you can keep your software installation healthy for a long time to come, invest in a copy of *WordPress For Dummies,* by Lisa Sabin-Wilson.

Choosing between WordPress.com and WordPress.org

Some blog software is available as both a hosted service and a version that you can download and install. WordPress is one of those packages. (For a refresher on hosted versus server-based blogging software, see Chapter 3.)

References to WordPress (Figure 5-1) are uniformly about the version of the software that you download and install on your own server. You can check it out online at `www.wordpress.org`. However, the option at WordPress.com is a hosted version. Fortunately, you can use both types of WordPress for free.

When WordPress.com was launched, many bloggers rejoiced because WordPress had reached the blogging mainstream. Bloggers could now create blogs with ease and use the tools that they had come to love without having to tinker in the background or stress over how to maintain those blogs.

Table 5-1 breaks down the pros and cons of each version of WordPress.

Table 5-1 WordPress.com vs. WordPress

Flavor	*Pros*	*Cons*
WordPress.com	• A free and hosted service. The WordPress.com service deals with daily maintenance, such as backups and software updates. • Security is a little better than some hosting services: Your blogs are replicated in three different locations, thus keeping your blog posts safe. You also gain the benefits of the WordPress.com community's featured blog postings and shared content.	• You can't implement custom themes (you have to choose from about 70 themes). • You can't upload any custom widgets. • You can't customize the WordPress software.
WordPress	• Free. • You can fully customize the WordPress software. • You can use any theme you like or create your own.	• You must install and maintain the software yourself. • Needing your own domain and Web hosting adds to your costs.

Choosing a version of WordPress looks daunting, doesn't it? It really isn't. You just need to ask yourself these questions: How nerdy are you? Do you like fiddling with the dials? Jiggling the handle? If your answers are positive, then you should continue reading this chapter! If not, WordPress.com may be the WordPress for you.

Still stuck? You can find additional information about the two options at `http://support.wordpress.com/com-vs-org`.

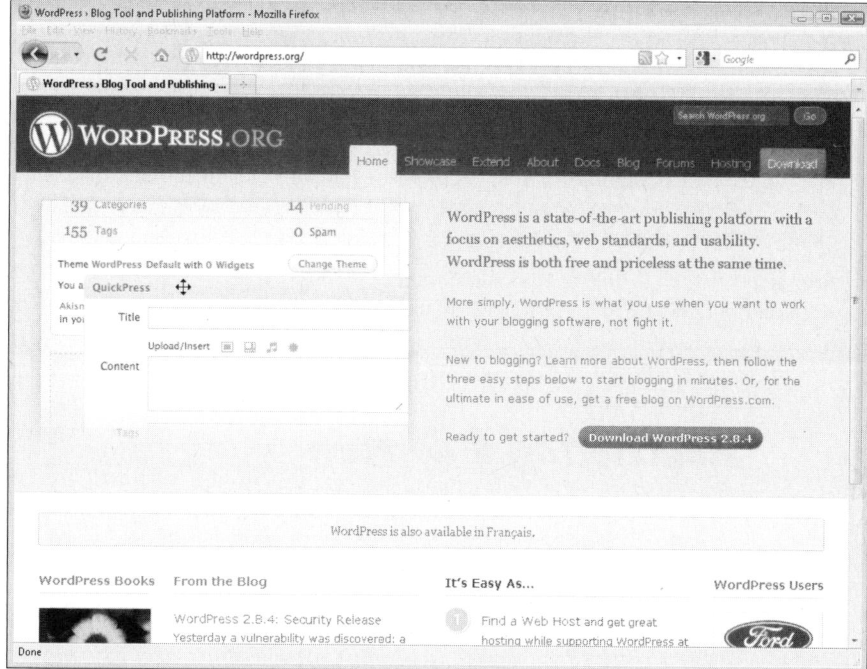

Figure 5-1: WordPress.org is the open source release of the WordPress platform.

You can find yet a third version of WordPress out there — WordPress MU (`http://mu.wordpress.org`). The MU stands for multiuser, and this flavor of WordPress can run thousands of blogs at the same time. Universities, newspapers, and blog networks usually use this version of WordPress.

Installing WordPress

In this chapter, I focus on installing and using WordPress on your own Web server. (If you think the hosted version is what you need, just point your Web browser to `www.wordpress.com` and follow the simple signup instructions to get started.)

You can get your WordPress installation up and running without a huge amount of difficulty, but in order to get your site going, you need to follow some very important steps.

Although this chapter walks you through the process, you can also follow along with WordPress's instructions, located at `http://codex.wordpress.org/Installing_WordPress`.

Open source software

WordPress is open source software, which means that its *source code* — the programming that runs the application — is freely accessible to developers who want to customize it or create new software from or for it.

Also, you can freely distribute open source software, and no one places restrictions on how you (or anyone else) can use it. In fact, one of the few terms of using open source software is that you can't place restrictions on the use or distribution of what you create from it.

Registering a domain

Do you know what you want to call your blog yet? Do you have a domain already? When you're itching to get your blog online and want to control every aspect, the domain is the first thing that you need.

A domain is the name and brand of your blog, and the Web address (or URL). It gives visitors an idea of what your blog is about and who you are. You can have some fun getting creative with your blog name! Before committing to a blog name, why not see what others have done? The following list gives you a few examples of some of the world's top blogs and their domains:

- **Engadget (`www.engadget.com`):** A technology blog that talks about gadgets
- **Tech Crunch (`www.techcrunch.com`):** A technology-industry blog
- **Boing Boing (`www.boingboing.net`):** A blog that talks about almost anything
- **Lifehacker (`www.lifehacker.com`):** A site that suggests ways that you can make your life better and more efficient
- **ReadWriteWeb (`www.readwriteweb.com`):** A site featuring several blogs that talk about Web technology

The domains in the preceding list make quite an impression, even if, at first glance, they don't necessarily tell the visitor what they write about. If you find and bookmark a blog that you like, you keep going back for the great content, not the domain name. In Chapter 3, I talk about acquiring domains in detail, if you need a refresher about them.

Selecting Web hosting

After you choose an appropriate domain for your blog, you need somewhere for your WordPress install to live. In Chapter 3, I tell you what to look for in Web hosting and make some recommendations. Don't forget that you can also ask other bloggers what host they use and what their experience has been.

If you've read Chapter 3 of this book, you already know that Web software such as WordPress has certain technical requirements. The requirements for WordPress are

- PHP 4.3 or greater
- MySQL 4.0 or greater
- The mod_rewrite Apache module

Most Web hosts have similar configurations and should be able to handle what you need, but you can review the official WordPress requirements page at `http://wordpress.org/about/requirements`. They also have a handy bit of text that you can copy and send to potential Web hosts to see whether their services can handle WordPress. How cool is that?

The WordPress community has already taken the question of Web hosting into its multitude of hands and come up with a list of recommended hosting companies. The community and WordPress developers voted these companies their top picks for providing everything that you need for WordPress:

- BlueHost (`www.bluehost.com`)
- DreamHost (`www.dreamhost.com`)
- Media Temple (`www.mediatemple.com`)
- Blogs About (`www.blogs-about.com`)
- Laughing Squid (`www.laughingsquid.com`)

Each of these companies offer well-known quality Web hosting, but if you want to continue looking, compare notes with other bloggers and make sure to refer back to Chapter 3 for good advice about choosing a Web host.

Getting the software

After you sort out your Web host and site domain, you next need to download and extract the WordPress files from WordPress.org and put them on your computer. Choose a place you'll remember, such as a documents or download directory. Follow these steps:

1. **Point your Web browser to `www.wordpress.org`.**

   The main WordPress page appears.

2. **Click the red Download tab in the top-right corner.**

   The site takes you to a short instructional page that has download information on it.

3. **Click the Download WordPress button.**

   Your Web browser may ask you to select a location to place the files that are downloading. If it does, choose a place on your computer that you will remember. Your Desktop or Documents folder are decent choices.

4. **After the compressed file downloads, double-click it to expand (or *unzip*) the files it contains on your computer.**

   The files are saved on your computer, as shown in Figure 5-2.

WordPress.org provides the downloadable file in two compressed formats: GZip (`.tar.gz`) and ZIP (`.zip`) format. These days, most computer systems recognize the ZIP format, and you should be able to open it without installing any additional software. After you expand the `.zip` file, you can delete it from your computer.

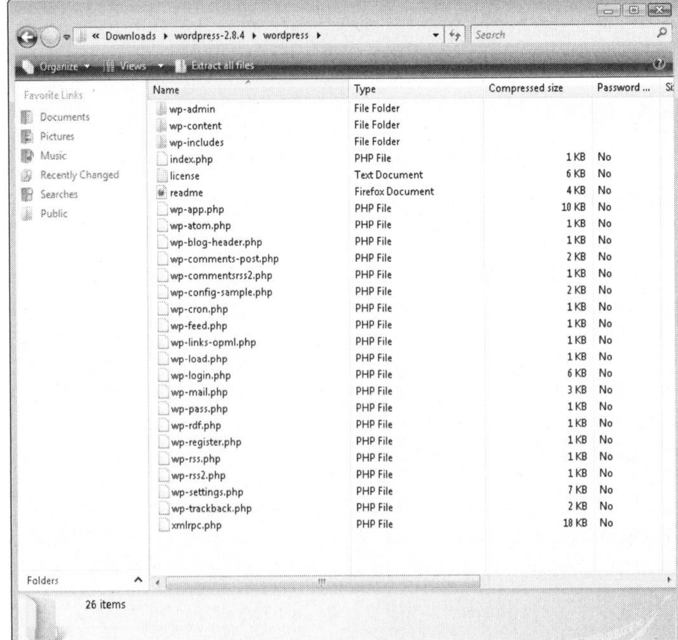

Figure 5-2: After you extract the WordPress files to your hard drive, you should see a folder structure similar to this.

What is FTP?

FTP is a technology used to copy files from one computer to another by using the file transfer protocol. Simply put, FTP allows computers that are running different operating systems (such as Windows or Mac) to move files across the Internet without experiencing format difficulties. It's an old technology that people still use every day to move Web site files.

Uploading the WordPress files

Do you have your files unzipped? Great! Now, the installation process gets a little more technical. You need to upload these unzipped files to your Web hosting space by using an FTP (file transfer protocol) client. If you don't have an FTP client installed on your computer, you have plenty of free options that you can download and install.

The following list gives you my favorite FTP clients:

- **FileZilla (`www.filezilla-project.org`):** Available for all computer platforms (see Figure 5-3)
- **Cyberduck (`www.cyberduck.ch`):** Available only for Macintosh computers

Both of these programs have the ability to connect and transfer files to your new Web host. To place the WordPress files on your Web host, follow these steps:

1. **Download and install the FTP client of your choice.**

   Look for installation instructions on the FTP software Web site.

2. **Start your FTP client.**
3. **Connect to your Web server by using the details that your Web host provided you for FTP access.**

   These details usually include a URL, username, and password.

   The directory in which you store the WordPress files is normally the main directory that you see when you connect via FTP. Check with your Web host if you're confused.

4. **Using the FTP software, upload the WordPress files from your computer to the server.**

   In some FTP clients, you can drag and drop the WordPress files to the location on the Web host. Others use arrow interfaces.

5. **When the files finish uploading, close your FTP client.**

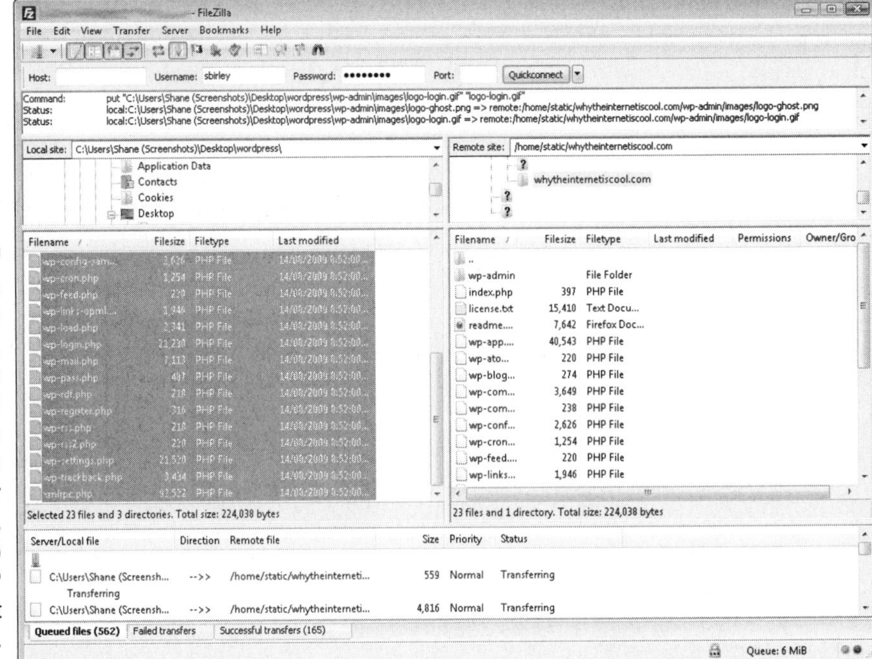

Figure 5-3: This FileZilla interface, which has the hard drive on the left and the Web server on the right, is similar to most FTP client interfaces.

At some point in the future, you may need to upload additional files (although WordPress is fairly good at doing most of its updates directly through the interface), so make sure to retain the information that you used to connect to your Web host.

Setting up the database

You're doing great! But don't rest on your laurels; this next step is probably the most technical. Take a deep breath and prepare to set up a database for your WordPress blog.

Arguably, setting up a database isn't actually terribly difficult. However, each Web host handles databases in different ways, so I can't give you straightforward instructions for accomplishing this task.

Your Web host is in the business of handling technical issues, and of course, they set up the environment in the first place. Don't hesitate to request assistance with your database setup.

The database system that you need to use is called MySQL. (Without MySQL, you can't use WordPress.) *MySQL* is a relational database management system. It can store all kinds of data for WordPress — from your blog posts to blogroll links, as well as all your WordPress settings. So, MySQL stores the blog posts that you write inside a database that's fast, efficient, and flexible.

If you want to know more about MySQL, pick up a copy of *PHP & MySQL For Dummies,* by Janet Valade. But take my word that after you set up your database, you won't need to know any more about it for the purposes of using WordPress.

After you know how to access your database setup tool, follow these steps:

1. **Log in to your Web host.**
2. **Create the database.**

   You need to name your database something that makes sense. If you have a blog called Joe Smith's Wondrous Adventures, you could name the database joesmith. The length of database names and database usernames are normally limited, and you can't include special characters in the names.
3. **Create a database user.**

   You can make the username anything, except the name that you used for your database. The same length and special character restrictions apply, though.

4. **Assign a password to that user.**

   Don't forget to write this information down so that you can use it when you run the WordPress install script.

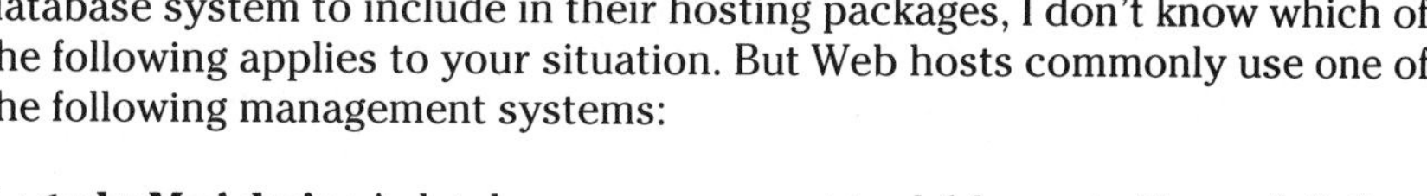

Because Web hosting companies can choose for themselves which MySQL database system to include in their hosting packages, I don't know which of the following applies to your situation. But Web hosts commonly use one of the following management systems:

- **phpMyAdmin:** A database management tool (shown in Figure 5-4) that a lot of Web hosts provide to their clients. You can create and delete databases, manage database users, and (depending on what permissions the Web host gives you) manipulate the data itself.
- **cPanel:** A common Web host interface that generally enables users to create and delete databases. You normally do any additional manipulation by using phpMyAdmin.
- **Plesk:** Yet another Web host interface that allows users to create and delete databases and manage database users. You do any data manipulation by using phpMyAdmin.

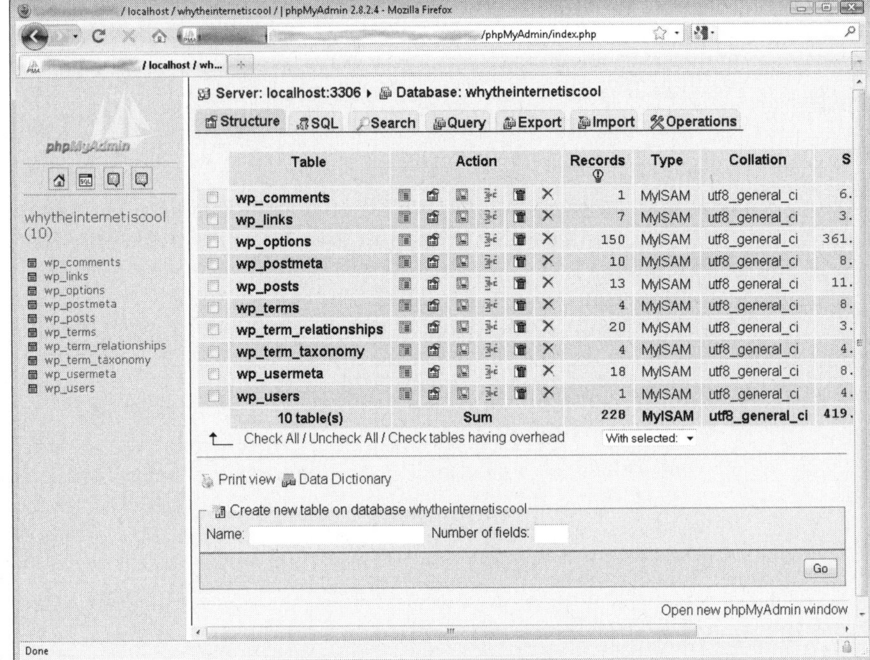

Figure 5-4: phpMyAdmin is a tool that you can use to manage and create databases.

The Web host that you choose probably uses one of the interfaces in the preceding list. You can figure them out and use them fairly easily. If you're running only one blog, you need only a single database. If you're thinking of running more than one, you need to find out how to keep your databases healthy and separate by using tools that your Web host provides.

Some Web hosts have automated WordPress installation and allow you to bypass all the installation instructions in this chapter — the Web host takes care of it all. Ask your Web host whether they offer packages that include WordPress installation as part of the setup.

Running the install script

After you put the WordPress files in the directory your Web host recommends and write down the database information, you only have to run the WordPress installer. The installer is super- simple. Things can go wrong, of course, but if the installer gets stuck, it does a very good job of letting you know exactly what you need to do.

Follow these steps to install WordPress:

1. **To run the installer, point your Internet browser to:**

   ```
   www.yourwebdomain.com/wp-admin/install.php
   ```

   Remember to replace `www.yourwebdomain.com` with your domain name!

   The installer checks to see whether you've created or edited the configuration file. If it doesn't find one, it will create it for you.

2. **Click Create a Configuration File.**

   This creates your WordPress configuration file. Now all you need to do is enter the information the configuration file needs.

3. **Make sure you have the database name, username, password, and hostname. If you do, click Let's Go!**

4. **Enter the database information (see Figure 5-5).**

   You can usually leave the database host as localhost because most Web hosting environments use that host without complaint. You don't have to change the table prefix, either.

5. **Click Submit.**

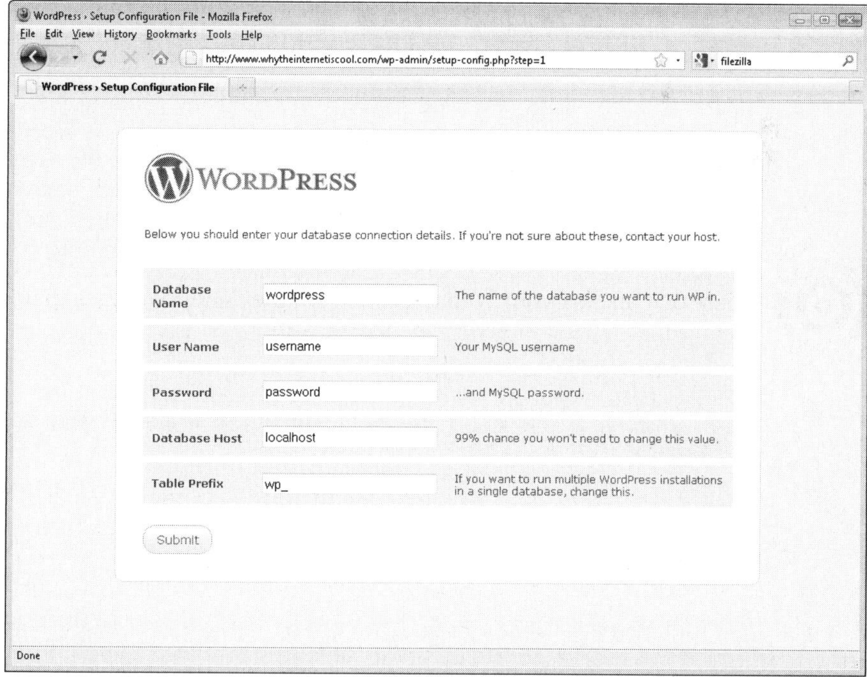

Figure 5-5: Provide the database information to the WordPress installer.

6. **Click Run the Install.**
7. **Enter a blog title and your e-mail address in the fields provided.**
8. **Click Install WordPress.**

   If everything goes well, the installer displays the word `Success` on the screen. The username and password of the administration user also appear on the screen. Keep a record of this information in a safe location because if your blog experiences any problems or you need to conduct any WordPress configuration or management you will need to log in using the admin account.
9. **Click Log In.**

   The log in page appears, where you can log in to your new installation.

   That's it! You've done it! You can now log in to your new WordPress installation and get busy publishing.

The configuration file is named `wp-config.php`. If your installer can't create the configuration file automatically, follow the instructions that WordPress provides at (`http://codex.wordpress.org/Installing_WordPress#Setup_configuration_file`) to create the file by hand.

Getting Familiar with Settings

After you have your new blog software installed and running, you can log in to your WordPress admin account and take a look around. The WordPress software does a lot right out of the box to make your blogging life as simple as possible. You have the ability to create blog posts; create static pages; add images and multimedia files; connect to social networking sites, such as Flickr and Facebook; and chat with blog visitors by using the commenting system.

Either these functions come with the WordPress install or you can add them by using a plug-in that you download and install. Each of these plug-ins typically has an administration page.

In the following sections, I introduce you to the administration section of the blog itself.

Logging in

Before you can start posting, you need to head on over to the Log In page and enter the username and password that was provided to you during the installation process.

In order to log in to your new Web site, you may want to bookmark the following link:

```
www.yourdomain.com/wp-admin/wp-login.php
```

Remember to replace `www.yourwebdomain.com` with your domain name!

Setting up an Editor account

WordPress allows you to set up and maintain several levels of user accounts in addition to the administrative account created during the setup process. These account types are called *roles.* They are:

- **Administrator:** Administrators have access to all features and areas of the blog software, from technical configuration to user accounts to content tools. This is the most powerful level of access on your blog; handle with care!
- **Editor:** This is a user that can publish posts, manage posts, and manage other account posts.
- **Author:** This is a user that can publish and manage his or her own posts.
- **Contributor:** This is a user role that allows someone to write and manage posts but not publish them live to the blog.
- **Subscriber:** This is a user that can read comments, post comments, and receive other private information.

If you are the only person blogging on your Web site, you should still go ahead and set up an Editor user account for creating blog posts. I recommend that you don't use the administrative account created during installation as the account you use when you author blog posts. It's a bit like driving a car by opening the hood and manipulating the engine directly; use the perfectly good steering wheel that comes with WordPress by setting up an Editor account.

Reserve the administrative account for administrative tasks like installing new themes, plugins, and any other general maintenance.

Set up your Editor account by following these steps:

1. **Log in to your WordPress installation.**
2. **From the Dashboard, click Users.**

   You see the full list of users and their roles.
3. **Click Add New.**

   WordPress loads the Add New User screen.

4. **Fill out the user fields.**

   You will see a listing of fields: username, first name, last name, e-mail, Web site, and password. Only three are required: username, password, and e-mail address. I also recommend filling in the first and last name.

5. **Select the Editor role.**

6. **Click Add User.**

   The user is created.

When you set up a new user, you can choose to send the account information to the new user's e-mail address. In our case, this account is for yourself so you don't need to select this checkbox. If you wish to have additional writers on your blog, consider setting them up as Authors — instead of Editors — and notifying them as you set up their accounts.

After you create your new Editor account, don't forget to log out of the administrative account, and then log in again as an Editor!

Using the Dashboard

Each time you log in to your WordPress blog, you end up on the Dashboard page. Get to know this page well because you spend most of your blogging time here. You can configure the front Dashboard to your liking by moving panels around and turning panels on or off. You can see the Dashboard in Figure 5-6.

On the left side of the Dashboard, a series of menus point you to the various sections of the administration panel. You likely visit some of these menus on a daily basis and some only once in a while:

- **Posts:** Includes links that allow you to edit posts, add new posts, and manage categories and tags.
- **Media:** Provides you with a link to upload new media files to your media library or manage previously uploaded media.
- **Links:** Manage lists of links on your Web site. For example, group links together into categories and post them in sidebars as blogrolls or other link lists.
- **Pages:** Clicking Pages takes you to the Page Administration section. Pages in WordPress are considered *static* pieces of content (pages that change only once in a while) and aren't blog posts. Use them for pretty much any section of your Web site, like a bio page or contact page. You can then link to these pages from a sidebar menu or via another blog post. Some themes may also provide you with menus that you can use to link to different sections of your blog.

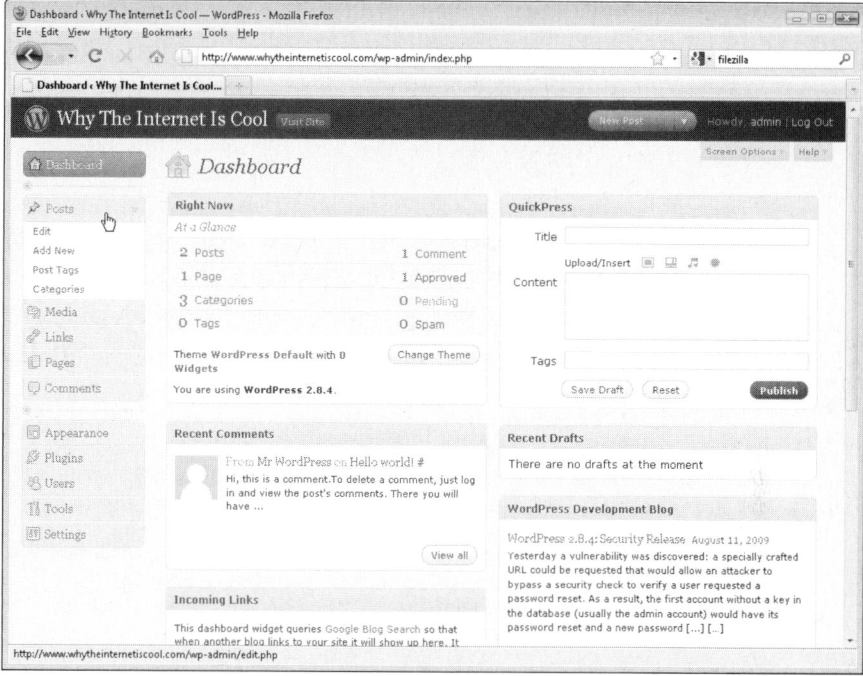

Figure 5-6: Prepare to spend a lot of time with the WordPress Dashboard.

- **Comments:** Post, delete, and respond to comments that readers have added to blog posts on your Web site.
- **Appearance:** View installed themes, activate new themes, edit existing themes, and search for additional themes from the online WordPress theme catalog.
- **Plugins:** View installed plug-ins, activate and deactivate plug-ins, search for new plug-ins from WordPress.org, and edit plug-in files right in the interface.
- **Users:** Manage the users for your blog, including readers and additional authors.
- **Tools:** Manage additional tools for improved speed by using Google Gears, import and export blog posts and comments, and conduct WordPress upgrades. Google Gears is an optional plugin for browsers like Firefox and Internet Explorer and adds functionality to your browser.
- **Settings:** Make all the general changes to the blog, such as the name of the site, your e-mail address, and the date and time-zone settings.
    - **Writing:** Contains settings for the editor interface, as well as default settings for categories, RSS, and tags. You can also access settings to set up remote e-mail.

- **Reading:** Choose the number of blog posts that appear on the front page of your blog and the number of postings available in your RSS feed.
- **Discussion Settings:** Control what kinds of communication your blog sends out. For example, you can get the blog to notify you by e-mail when someone adds a new comment.
- **Media:** Upload and manage any of your media files. You can add titles and descriptions, organize images and audio, add captions to images, and make minor changes to image sizes.
- **Privacy:** Set your blog so that search engines ignore it. Use this option only if you have a private blog that you want to share with a small number of people.
- **Permalinks:** *Permalinks* are the permanent links to your individual posts. You can configure the format of the post URLs so that they contain both date information and keywords, or keywords only. You can also set default categories for posts and tags.
- **Miscellaneous:** Settings for uploads, URL paths to files, settings for folder organization, and link update tracking.

Checking out the panels

On the right side of the Dashboard, you see a series of panels. Each panel gives you access to parts of the administrative interface for WordPress. The default panels are

- **Right Now:** Contains a quick overview of what's happening on your blog. The panel displays
  - The number of posts on the blog
  - The number of comments
  - The spam count
  - The number of categories and tags currently in use on the site
- **Recent Comments:** Lists the most recent comment activity on your blog and provides links that allow you to moderate and respond to comments without leaving the Dashboard.
- **Incoming Links:** Uses Google searches to show the sites that are sending visitors to your blog.
- **Plugins:** Gives you a quick list of the newest, the most popular, and the most recently updated plug-ins. A *plug-in* is a small piece of programming that you can attach to existing software to extend that software's functionality.

- **QuickPress:** Allows you to post a quick note on your blog right from the administration panel.
- **Recent Drafts:** Contains a listing of posts that you saved as drafts but haven't yet published.
- **WordPress Development Blog:** The latest postings from the WordPress development blog, which announces security patches and any other important updates.
- **Other WordPress News:** Contains a listing of blog posts from other WordPress blogs that talk about WordPress.

Creating a Post

I'm sure you're bursting at the seams to get your first blog post online. The process is quite simple in terms of using WordPress. The real challenge is coming up with good stuff to blog about! Jump to Chapter 8 for a lot of tips and ideas on writing for your blog.

To start a new blog post, follow these steps:

1. **Click the Posts menu in the Dashboard and select Add New.**

   WordPress opens the Add New Post page, shown in Figure 5-7.
2. **Give your post a title by entering it in the text box below Add New Post.**
3. **Add some text in the body text box.**

   Use the formatting buttons if you want to change the style of your text, create a list, or otherwise add elements.
4. **Use any of the other options that you want for this post.**

   WordPress gives you the following options:

   - **Excerpt:** If you want, you can write a short summary of your post for the Excerpt field.
   - **Post Tags:** *Tags* are keywords that describe the topic of your post. Tagging your posts lets search engines easily identify the subject material you discuss and means your post is likely to rank higher in search engine listings.
   - **Categories:** Use the Add New Category link in the Categories box if you need to create a new category for your post. Categories are general groups that you can sort you blog posts into so that readers can easily locate the content most interesting to them.

- **Discussion:** You can choose whether you want to allow readers to post comments on this posting and whether you want to permit trackbacks. I explain trackbacks in Chapter 3.
- **Custom Fields:** You can add custom fields to your posts, which you fully control. *Custom fields* are simply fields that appear in each blog post that you can display by altering the template for your blog. For example, if your blog is a restaurant-review blog, you might choose to add custom fields for the location or rating of each restaurant that you review.

5. **Click Publish to save your blog post and check out your blog to see how it looks!**

   If you're not ready to post your blog entry to the public, you can save your posting as a draft or preview it before you post it. Also, you can set a particular date if you want to schedule your post for publication in the future.

   Look for a Visit Site link at the top of the Dashboard; the link takes you right to your blog.

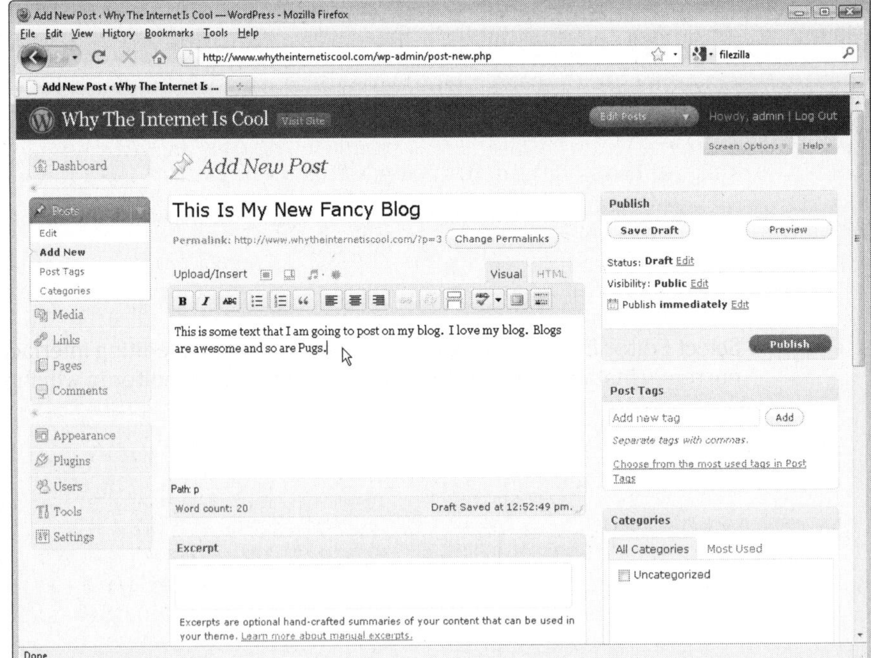

Figure 5-7: Adding a new post by using WordPress.

Customizing Your Design

After you play around with a few of the WordPress features, I know you're thinking, "How do I make this new blog pretty?" The answer is as simple as a menu click. Just follow these steps:

1. **From the menus on the left side of the Dashboard, click Appearance.**

   The Manage Themes page opens, displaying a list of themes that you can install.

2. **Search for themes based on color or keyword.**

   WordPress returns a list of themes based on your search query.

3. **Click Preview to see how a particular theme looks in a pop-up window. Close the pop-up to look at the list again.**
4. **After you find a theme that you like, click Install to load the theme onto your server.**
5. **Click Active to apply the theme to your blog.**

You can install several themes all at the same time, and then take time to test which theme best suits your blog.

Now, do you want to get into the code even more? If so, get ready to dive into HTML. Only the brave venture into this territory because it does require knowledge of HTML, CSS, PHP, and WordPress's own markup language. The code editing for WordPress includes a little more than just plain old HTML.

Some bloggers love playing with HTML code, and some run away as fast as they can. If you have the chops, however, the developers of WordPress have made accessing and modifying the theme files a fairly easy task.

Select Editor from the Appearance menu to get at the editing interface for the currently installed theme. The editor is simply a text editor in which you can manipulate the files in your theme without using any other technology to access the files (such as FTP). It's simple to use and doesn't have too many frills.

The drawback to using the editor is that you really need to know your stuff when it comes to HTML code, CSS, and a little PHP thrown in for good measure. If you don't know what these technologies do, I don't recommend touching your theme without a little practice beforehand. Make backups!

Finding Out More about WordPress

You could spend a lot of time figuring out WordPress, and I just can't fit it all into a single chapter. (I tried!) But you're far from alone in your search for a better understanding of your new WordPress blog. A great many Web sites and blogs can help you further your WordPress education. Here are a few handy resources:

- ***WordPress For Dummies:*** You knew that *For Dummies* had a book on this topic, right? Of course, you did! Why not pick up a copy? You can dig deeper into the ins and outs of WordPress code, themes, and widgets. This book can be your one-stop resource. Tell Lisa Sabin-Wilson that *Blogging For Dummies* sent you!

  `http://justagirlintheworld.com/wordpressfordummies`

- **WordPress Community:** The official WordPress documentation is available online and updated regularly. You can find out about the latest functionality and also see what's coming up in the future. The community offers a Frequently Asked Questions (FAQ) section, and you can get involved in this large and active Web community.

  `http://codex.wordpress.org/Installing_WordPress`

  `http://codex.WordPress.org/New_To_WordPress_-_Where_to_Start`

- **WordCamp:** Over the last couple of years, camps have been popping up everywhere. *Camps* (also known as *unconferences*) are informal gatherings of people who love to get together and talk about their interests. If you love WordPress, then you need to go to a WordCamp in your area soon because you can find out a lot of things not covered anywhere else. What could be better than a bunch of people getting together to talk about everything WordPress? Maybe a bunch of people getting together to talk about everything WordPress who also have cupcakes? Visit the Web site to see whether a WordCamp is coming to your community. If not, you could start one!

  `http://central.wordcamp.org`

Chapter 6

Starting a Micro Blog

In This Chapter

- Getting familiar with micro blogs
- Creating a Tumblr micro blog
- Posting to your micro blog on Tumblr
- Customizing the look and functionality of a Tumblr blog
- Taking a look at your micro blog

Do you think blogging might just be too much work? Before you dismiss my question as sarcastic, consider this: A 2008 study by Technorati indicated that most bloggers spend an average of ten hours a week on their blogs. That's not an insignificant amount of time, and not everyone has that kind of time to devote to blogging. (Interestingly, most of the bloggers Technorati surveyed for this study indicated that they blog for fun and without any financial reward. Check out the full study online at `www.technorati.com/blogging/feature/state-of-the-blogosphere-2008/`.)

So, if you're interested in blogging but worried about time, a micro blog might be an alternative you should consider. *Micro blogging* is pretty much what it sounds like — creating very short blog posts. But the micro blog may have all the other usual trappings of a blog, such as comments, RSS feeds, and so on.

In this chapter, I introduce you to micro blogging options and walk you through starting a micro blog of your own.

Introducing Micro Blogging

Micro blogging is characterized by very short blog posts, done quickly and frequently, and often from some nontraditional publishing tools, such as mobile phones, e-mail, instant messages, and text messages. However, you can still use a Web interface to produce a micro blog!

Some micro bloggers use their blog as a mechanism to collect and archive interesting tidbits of information that they come across while they surf the Web. Many micro blogs contain very little personal content in the form of writing, but a lot of photos, snippets of video, and links. In fact, many micro bloggers don't explain why they choose to include something in their blogs at all, and in this way, micro blogs can be much more idiosyncratic to the individual blogger than a regular blog.

We Are the Weirdos (`http://wearetheweirdos.tumblr.com`) is a micro blog produced with Tumblr (you can read more about Tumblr in the following sections). Created by Spencer, the blog (shown in Figure 6-1) is a motley collection of funny photos, screenshots, videos, audio files, and quotes.

Other micro blogging tools act a little differently. Facebook, LinkedIn, and MySpace — or any social network that allows you to post status updates — are technically micro blogging tools, as well. *Status updates* are very short text posts that are generally used to let others know what you're thinking or doing.

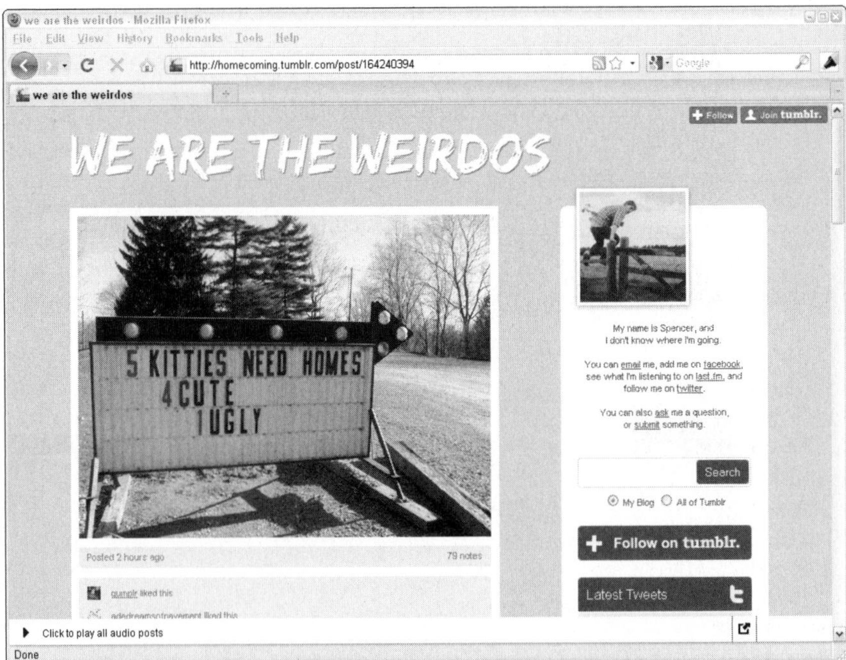

Figure 6-1: Spencer's We Are the Weirdos is a good example of a micro blog.

Twitter (`www.twitter.com`) is a micro blogging tool that broadcasts status updates. Degan Beley writes a restaurant review blog called Ethnic Eats (`www.ethniceats.ca`) and uses the micro blogging tool Twitter in combination with her regular blog to provide quick updates to her readers about where she's eating that night — a preview of reviews to come — as well as to cover topics that she might not put on the full blog. Her Twitter micro blog (www.twitter.com/ethniceats) is shown in Figure 6-2.

I spend more time covering the Twitter phenomenon in Chapter 14.

Some popular tools for micro blogging include

- Tumblr (www.tumblr.com)
- Posterous (www.posterous.com)
- Twitter (www.twitter.com)
- Plurk (www.plurk.com)
- Jaiku (www.jaiku.com)
- Identi.ca (www.identi.ca)

Figure 6-2: Degan Beley's Ethnic Eats Twitter feed keeps blog readers abreast of her food wanderings.

Starting a Micro Blog with Tumblr

In this section, I walk you through starting a micro blog by using Tumblr, one of the most popular micro blogging services out there.

Tumblr (`www.tumblr.com`) is hosted blog software, which means that you don't need to have Web hosting, a domain name, or anything more than the ability to access the Web site in order to get started.

I cover the differences between hosted and installable blog software in Chapter 3.

Signing up and getting started is a simple process. Just follow these steps:

1. **Point your Web browser to `www.tumblr.com`.**

   The main Tumblr page opens.

2. **Type your e-mail address into the Email Address text box.**
3. **Type a password of your choice into the Password text box.**
4. **Type a URL (usually the name of the blog you're creating) into the URL text box.**
5. **Click the Sign Up and Start Posting button, as shown in Figure 6-3.**

   Tumblr checks to see whether the URL you requested is available. If it isn't, go back to Step 4 and try again until you find an available URL.

   If the URL you want to use is available, Tumblr sets up your blog, and you're ready to starting posting!

Figure 6-3: You can sign up for Tumblr micro blog quickly and easily.

Creating a Text Post

Tumblr allows you to create blog posts by using text, photos, quotes, links, chat excerpts, audio files, and video. I show you how to post entries that include these different elements in the following sections. For more on including audio and video in your blog posts, jump to Chapters 11 and 12.

Create a quick text post in your Tumblr blog by following these steps:

1. **Click the Text Post icon (a capital T) on your Tumblr dashboard.**

   Tumblr displays the Add a Text Post page.

2. **(Optional) Give your blog post a title in the Title field.**
3. **Type the text of your blog post in the Post field.**

   Use as much or as little text as you want.

If you're ready, you can post to your blog right now by clicking Create post, or you can spend a little time making your post fancy. In the following section, you can find out about the options.

Formatting your blog post

Tumblr, like most blog software, gives you the ability to format your blog post while you create it. The icons just above the Post field, shown in Figure 6-4, enable you to format what you've written.

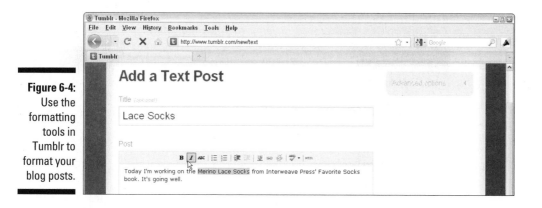

Figure 6-4: Use the formatting tools in Tumblr to format your blog posts.

Tumblr uses a WYSIWG (what you see is what you get) interface, which shows you the effect of a tool in your blog post right when you apply it. This list describes each of the available tools:

- **Bold:** Make any text in your blog post bold by clicking and dragging over the text that you want to affect, and then clicking the Bold icon. The selected text is made **bold.**
- **Italic:** Italicize any text in your blog post by clicking and dragging over the text that you want to affect, and then clicking the Italic icon. The selected text is then shown in *italics.*
- **Strikethrough:** This style is commonly applied to text that you need to correct. Click and drag over the text that you want to affect, and then click the Strikethrough icon. The selected text is then made `strikethrough`.
- **Unordered List:** In Web browsers, unordered lists are usually displayed as bulleted lists (like this list you're reading right now). You can most easily use this tool by typing each list item into your blog post on a separate line. Click and drag to select all the items, and then click the Unordered List icon.
- **Ordered List:** In Web browsers, ordered lists usually appear as numbered lists. You can most easily use this tool by typing each list item into your blog post on a separate line. Click and drag to select all the items, and then click the Ordered List icon.
- **Indent:** Indent a line or paragraph of text by clicking anywhere in the line or paragraph of text that you want to affect, and then selecting the Indent icon. Your text moves to the right.
- **Outdent:** You can outdent only text that you've previously indented. Click anywhere in the line of text from which you want to remove indenting, and then select the Outdent icon.
- **Insert/Edit Photo:** Add photos to your blog posts by linking to them on other Web sites. I give you step-by-step instructions for adding photos to your posts in the following section.
- **Insert/Edit Link:** Make any text or image in your blog a clickable link to any Web site. I give you step-by-step instructions for adding a link in the section "Adding links to your post," later in this chapter.
- **Unlink:** You can remove a link that you added by clicking the linked text or photo, and then clicking the Unlink icon.
- **Toggle Spellchecks:** Not a great speller? (You aren't alone.) Click the Spellcheck icon to run a spellchecker on your text. If you click the small arrow to the right of the icon, you can choose another language for the spellcheck default.

- **Edit HTML Source:** Are you an HTML guru? If you want to edit the source code of your blog post directly, click the Edit HTML Source icon and go to town.

Appendix B, at the end of this book, gives you some basic HTML editing code, if you're starting to explore this area.

Use the tools described in the preceding list to format your text, and when you're ready, move to the following section to add an image to your text blog post.

Adding an image to your post

Blog posts are more fun with photos! If you want to add an image to a text blog post on your Tumblr blog, you first need a photo on the Web. A lot of bloggers set up accounts with the photo-sharing site Flickr (`www.flickr.com`), post their photos there, and then include the ones they want to share via their blog by using Tumblr. On Flickr, you can also republish many photos by others, but be sure to check the licensing restrictions so that you don't inadvertently violate someone's copyright.

To find out more about copyright and photos, jump to Chapter 10. For now, feel free to experiment with a photo that I took, which you can view at `www.flickr.com/photos/supersusie/3815946553`.

Follow these steps to place an image from Flickr into your Tumblr text blog post:

1. **Use a Web browser to go to a photo on Flickr, such as `www.flickr.com/photos/supersusie/3815946553`.**
2. **Click the Add Sizes icon directly above the image.**

   Flickr takes you to a Download page for the image.
3. **Select whichever size you want to use from the Available Sizes row of links.**

   Flickr displays the image at the dimensions you chose. In my example, I selected Small.
4. **In the area labeled To Link to This Photo, click and drag to select the image URL in the photo URL box, as shown in Figure 6-5.**
5. **Press Ctrl+C (⌘+C on the Mac) or select Copy from the browser Edit menu to copy the image URL.**

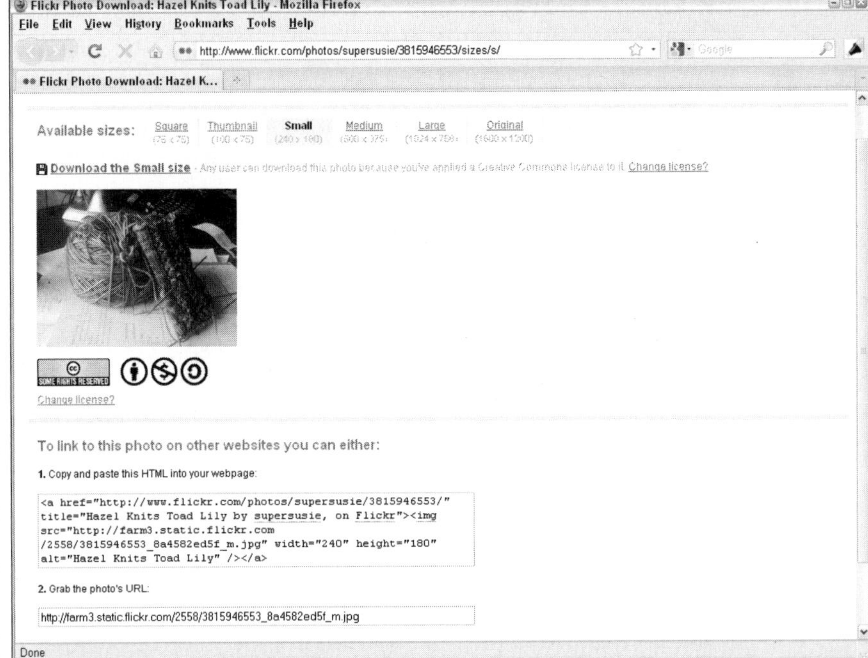

Figure 6-5: Flickr provides code that allows you to display an image on your blog.

6. **In your Tumblr text blog post, click where you want to put your photo.**
7. **Click the Insert/Edit Photo icon.**

   Tumblr opens the Insert/Edit Image window, shown in Figure 6-6.

Figure 6-6: Use the Insert/Edit Image window to place images on the Web into your blog post.

8. **Click in the Image URL field and press Ctrl+V (⌘+V on the Mac) to paste the URL into the field.**

   You can type a description into the Image Description field, but you don't have to.

   Tumblr calculates the dimensions of the image that you're using and places those values in the Dimensions fields after you provide the URL. Web images are measured in pixels.

9. **Select an option from the Alignment drop-down list.**

   I chose Right because I want to put the image on the right side of the text.

10. **Change the values in the Dimensions fields if you want to resize the image.**

11. **Click the Insert button to close the window and place the image in your blog post.**

    Tumblr displays the image in your blog post.

Adding links to your post

Links add a lot of value to a blog post by giving your readers the resources to explore a topic further or find more information about your discussion or idea. As long as you link to useful information, don't hesitate to add links to your posts.

You can add links to both text and images. Follow these steps:

1. **Select text or click an image in your blog post.**

2. **Click the Insert/Edit formatting tool (it's a small piece of chain).**

   Tumblr opens the Insert/Edit Link window.

3. **Type or paste a URL into the Link URL field.**

   In this example, I'm linking to the image featured in the preceding section, so I create a link back to Flickr by typing the following into the Link URL field: `www.flickr.com/photos/supersusie/3815946553`

   You can give a descriptive title to your link in the Title field, but you don't have to.

   If you want to open the link in a new Web browser window, select Open Link in a New Window from the Target drop-down list. If you don't select an option, the default behavior opens the link in the same window.

4. **Click the Insert button to add the link to the text or photo in your blog post (shown in Figure 6-7).**

   The image isn't clickable in the editing screen because you'd have trouble formatting or removing the link later if it was.

If you want to remove a link that you've created, you can easily do it. Simply click the text or photo on which you placed a link, and then click the Unlink tool.

Publishing your post

When you finish everything that you want to do to your blog post, it's time to publish! Simply click the Create Post button, shown in Figure 6-8, and your post appears on your blog for others to view.

Click on the Advanced Options box (it's in the upper-right of the Add a Text Post screen) to open the menu and type a date in the future for your blog post to publish if you want to plan ahead, instead of posting immediately.

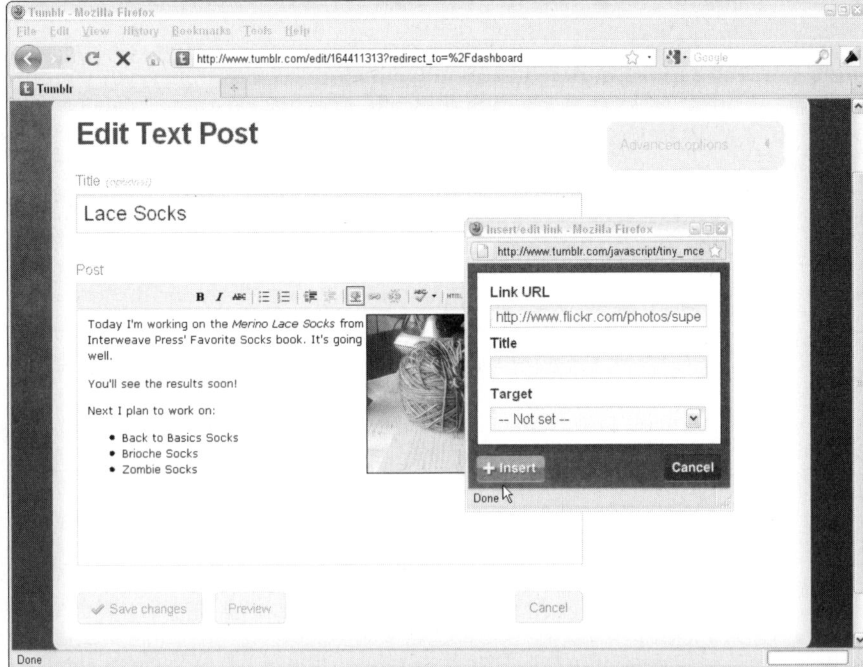

Figure 6-7: Quickly create a link in your blog post by using Tumblr.

Figure 6-8: Make your blog post available to the public by clicking Create Post.

Customizing Your Tumblr Blog

This section introduces you to the customization options for your Tumblr blog. You can change the look and feel of the blog, as well as some of the functionality. Adding your own touches really personalizes a blog and makes it feel more like home.

Get to the customization options by clicking the Customize link in the right column of your Tumblr Dashboard. A page that displays a preview of your blog opens, and the menu across the top enables you to adjust the following:

- **Info:** Update the following areas by using this option:
  - **Title:** Give your Tumblr blog a name.
  - **Description:** Some of the themes (discussed later in this list) display a short description text area. You can describe yourself, your blog, or whatever you think people might want to know about you and what you're doing.
  - **Portrait Photo:** Make your blog more your own by uploading a photo of yourself. Some themes display these images; some don't.

  - **URL:** If you want to change the URL of your blog at any point, you can take care of that here. Remember, you probably don't want to change the URL of a blog that already has visitors because then they can't find you easily anymore.
  - **Use a Custom Domain Name:** If you buy your own custom domain name, you can tell Tumblr about it, and then use that domain to access your Tumblr blog. You can find information on buying domain names in Chapter 3.

- **Theme:** Change the appearance of your blog by choosing one of the design themes provided by Tumblr. Tumblr offers nearly 200 different options to choose from. If you're good with HTML, you can also use this tab to create your own custom theme.
- **Appearance:** Even if you select a theme that you like, the Appearance tab allows you to further customize the colors. Clicking any color option displays a color picker, and from there, you can go crazy (or not).
- **Feeds:** If you have multiple blogs, or anything that provides an RSS feed, you can route those feeds into your Tumblr blog so that anything you post on those other blogs automatically becomes part of your Tumblr blog, too! Find more information on RSS in Chapter 13.
- **Advanced:** Anything you can customize that didn't fit in the other categories seems to be available in the Advanced tab:
  - **Timezone:** Set your time zone to match your geographic location (shown in Figure 6-9).
  - **Add Custom CSS:** Some themes available on the Theme tab include custom Cascading Style Sheets (CSS) styles. If you're not familiar with CSS, don't worry about it. Custom CSS is part of creating advanced layouts.

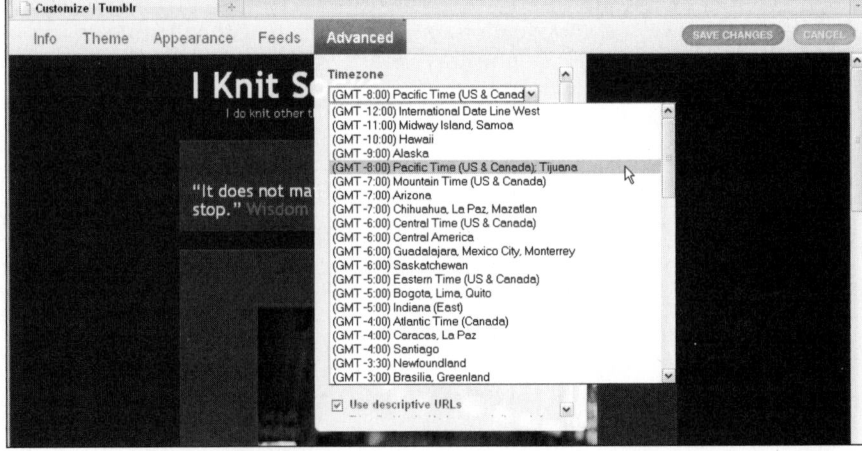

Figure 6-9: You can customize your Tumblr blog without knowing a lot of code or technical stuff.

- **Post Count:** Change the number of blog posts that appear on your blog's home page.
- **Options:** Extend the functionality of your blog by adding some neat features, including enabling high-resolution photos, opening links in new windows, shortening RSS feed posts, adding descriptive words to your URLs, enabling submissions from readers, and setting how you want search engines and Web site directories to handle your blog.
- **Allow Search Engines to Index Your Tumblelog:** Turning this option on means that your blog appears in the major search engines — a really good idea if you're trying to build an audience!
- **Ping the Blogosphere:** This option notifies the blog search engines (Technorati, My Yahoo!, and others) when you add a post to your blog.
- **Promote Me on Tumblr:** Checking this option means your blog shows up on some Tumblr directory pages, making it accessible to those who visit the Tumblr Web site.
- **Not Safe for Work (NSFW):** If you're blogging about sex-related or other workplace-sensitve topics, marking your blog NSFW alerts the directory and warns others.

- **Location:** Identify your geographic location so that people can discover your blog based on those coordinates in the Tumblr blog directory.

After you make updates in any of the customization tabs, be sure to click the Save Changes button at the top-right of the page. And then take a look at your blog so that you can be sure the changes were implemented correctly.

You can view your Tumblr blog at any time by pointing your Web browser to the URL that you chose when you signed up or by clicking the URL in the menu on the right side of the Dashboard, which you can see in Figure 6-10.

Figure 6-10: View your blog by clicking its URL in the Dashboard menu.

Exploring Tumblr Goodies

Tumblr offers fun extras for your blog on the Goodies page, accessible from the Account menu (see Figure 6-11).

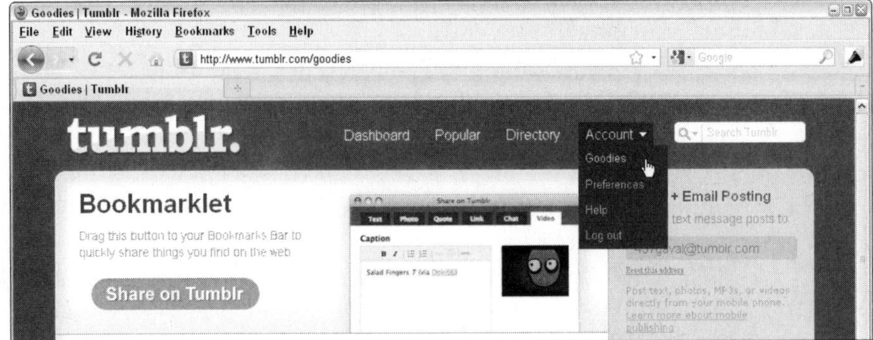

Figure 6-11: Select Goodies from the Account menu to play with a lot of fun posting extras.

On the Goodies page, you can find information about posting to your blog by using your phone, instant messages, or e-mail and a third-party-applications directory that you can use to find applications that let you post photos, videos, and other content quickly. The directory also has extras that you can install on your blog itself to add — among other things — the ability to play your audio posts via a menu on the page.

My favorite addition available in the Goodies area is Call in Audio. It's a really nice (and free) tool that you can use to call in and record audio posts by using a phone. You can create quick recordings on the go, and best of all, you don't need to buy any extra equipment or software!

Part III
Fitting In and Feeling Good

"Tell the boss you-know-who is talking smack in his blog again."

In this part . . .

Blog in hand, you're ready to join the ranks of the top bloggers in the world. This part helps you get there in style. Get to know your readers in detail, focusing on their likes and dislikes, and find out how to cultivate a following you can be proud of in Chapter 7. Even great bloggers have off days or need the occasional inspiration, so Chapter 8 walks you through developing great content and breaking through writer's block. Also, discover how to build community, keep your blog spam-free, and generate interaction in Chapter 9.

Chapter 7

Finding Your Niche

In This Chapter

- Discovering blog genres
- Creating appealing blog posts
- Making connections with other bloggers

If you're blogging only for your friends and family, you probably have a captive audience that stays interested, no matter what you choose to blog about on any given day. (Although, even your mom might get a little tired of hearing about what time you got up and what you had for lunch!)

Most bloggers, however, define blogging success as attracting, keeping, and growing an audience of interested readers who can't wait for the next pearl of wisdom to leave their fingertips . . . preferably an audience that leaves comments and interacts with the blogger and with other readers.

Creating this kind of blog is no small challenge: You're in competition with every other source of news, information, and entertainment in your audience members' lives (not to mention your own, if you have trouble finding time for blogging).

So, find a niche and exploit it fully. I have no way of knowing exactly what your niche is — that's something for you to figure out — but I can give you ideas and suggestions to help you start turning your mental gears. This chapter can help you find others blogging in your subject area, what they're doing right, and how you can make the most of your subject.

Deciding What Belongs on Your Blog

You may find picking a niche and sticking with it tough to do. Fortunately, blogging gives you a lot of leeway in how you handle a subject, in evolving your own style, and in what you blog about. The medium allows for a lot of experimentation, and your readers likely welcome new approaches and ideas while you go.

For your own peace of mind, however, you probably want to pick a broad theme and then explore within that theme. Do you like books? Why not blog about what you're reading and make recommendations? You can then take a natural leap to movies based on books, and to authors . . . even a simple idea can give you a lot of room to grow.

Some subject areas have worked as popular and successful blog topics already. You can take on the competition and start a blog about

- **Your kids:** Baby books might have gone out of style, but that doesn't mean you can't document your child's growth in detail on a blog. *Mommyblogging,* as it's called, is on the rise in a big way. Talk about a topic that has an infinite variety of discussions, products, problems, and cute photos!
- **Your hobby or interest:** Blogs are beautifully suited to help you make connections, so feel free to use yours to become part of a community of folks that shares your passion for knitting, sport fishing, geocaching, carpentry, or whatever your interest is.
- **Technology:** Many of the original bloggers chose technology as their focus — a great decision. People have a huge interest in technology and technology issues today. After all, more and more people have cell phones, personal computers, and MP3 players, and everyone has problems using them!
- **Politics:** Do I really need to point out that political commentary and criticism can make a good blog? A number of popular political bloggers have turned their online punditry into thriving careers in traditional media.
- **News of the weird:** Some very popular blogs make the most of the many strange Web sites by posting links and quick summaries of the sites on their blogs. These blogs cater to the lazy man's approach to surfing, and if you're interested in sharing the quirky oddities that you find, you can definitely get an audience for them.
- **Specialized news:** Offer a service for your busy readers by aggregating all the news on a particular topic, including quick tidbits and links to sources. You can create this kind of blog for both serious and comic topics — cranial surgery techniques to coverage of the latest teen sensation.
- **A personal diary:** If you have enough going on in your life to keep *you* interested in it, you can stick with the tried and true blog. If you have a unique voice and great writing, you can attract readers who can become friends.

The following sections look at each of these topics in a little more detail.

Mommyblogging

Generally speaking, *mommyblogging* is memoir-style blogging, detailing the trials, tribulations, and general hysteria of raising children.

Quite a few mommyblogs start before much mommying is going on — before or during pregnancy — and then proceed through infancy and upward. Don't let the fact that you're not quite a mommy yet deter you from starting a mommyblog.

They're often hilarious, often heartbreaking, and so easy to identify with. If you don't have children, you certainly were one once. Frankly, kids are *funny*.

You can find many great examples of mommyblogs out there; I had trouble picking just one to tell you about, but you can start exploring at the blog Woulda Coulda Shoulda (`www.wouldashoulda.com`). Mir, a mother of two, writes Woulda Coulda Shoulda, shown in Figure 7-1. Her blog has earned her coverage in *Parents Magazine, Redbook,* and *The Today Show;* inclusion in an anthology; and gigs speaking about mommyblogging at the BlogHer Conference (`www.blogher.com`).

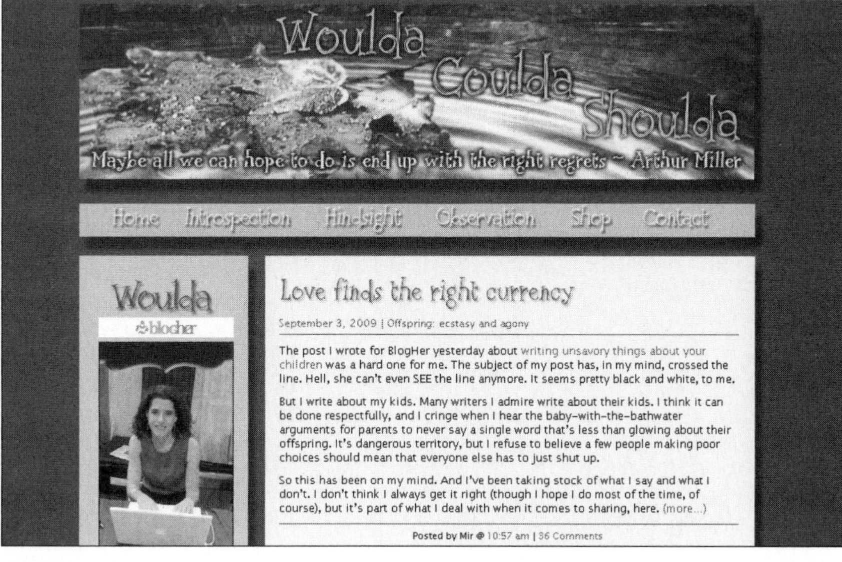

Figure 7-1: Mir's Woulda Coulda Shoulda is a memoir of a mother raising two children.

Turning your offline hobby into a blog

You probably already have offline hobbies that consume time and energy, and about which you have great passion. You also probably have plenty to say on the topic, but too few people are genuinely interested in hearing you expound about your hobby.

Find your compatriots online by starting a blog about your hobby and hooking into a community of people who share both your passion for the activity and also your passion for news and discussion about your hobby.

You can find many terrific hobby blogs out there; great blogs about everything from scrapbooking to jewelry-making to collecting airline safety cards.

One of my hobbies is knitting, and let me tell you, the knitters have caught onto blogging in a huge way! Bloggers who knit share stories about frustrating patterns, exciting yarns, sales, and more. I read knitting blogs because I can identify with what the blogger is describing, but also because I often find out something new.

One fun knitting blog is Yarn Harlot (`www.yarnharlot.ca`), written by a knitter living in Toronto named Stephanie Pearl-McPhee. Yarn Harlot (shown in Figure 7-2) is the online diary of a devoted knitter and author; Stephanie has also written six books of knitting humor. Her hilarious blog covers everything from knitting techniques to home renovations, and it never fails to entertain.

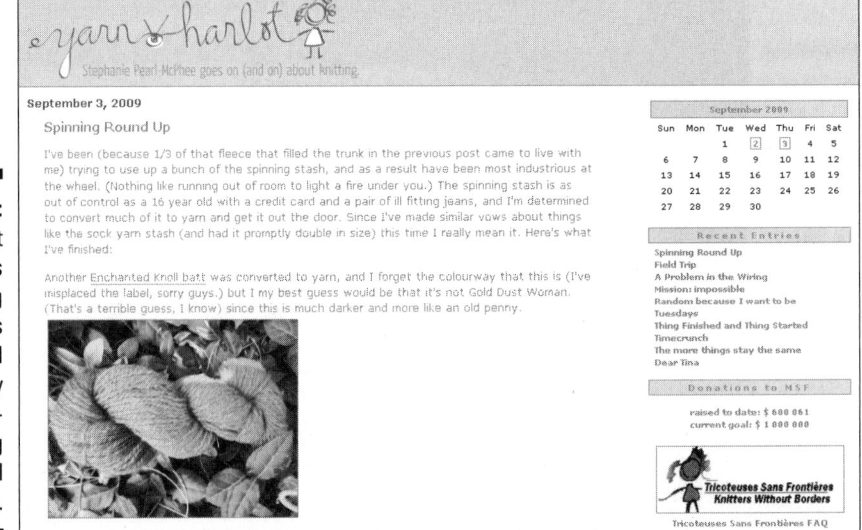

Figure 7-2: Yarn Harlot offers knitting techniques and engagingly self-deprecating personal stories.

Talking technology

Can anyone ever know enough about technology to make everything he or she owns function? At least for me, the answer is no. Just when I start to feel reasonably competent with computers, a hard drive fails. And how often have I brought home a new cell phone, ripped open the box with great excitement, and then failed utterly to figure out how to get my contacts imported? It's true — even I need technology help.

And I'm betting you do, too. Technology bloggers have figured this out, writing blogs that explain how to resolve common problems as well as blogs that whet your appetite for new gadgets. Don't you always think that a new and better device can solve your problems with the one you have now?

You can find a number of highly successful technology blogs around the Web, including some that have been in existence for years and years. Some of these blogs are specialized to a particular kind of tool or software; some are just about conveying the latest and greatest across the field.

If you work in technology or just have a passion for it, you can start a blog around your enthusiasm. That's what Dennis Lloyd did when he founded iLounge (`www.ilounge.com`).

iLounge, shown in Figure 7-3, covers anything and everything about Apple's iPod and iPhone devices. Started in 2001, shortly after Dennis Lloyd first laid eyes on an iPod, it has grown from being a blog into a true community site, including forums and photo galleries, in addition to the news blogs.

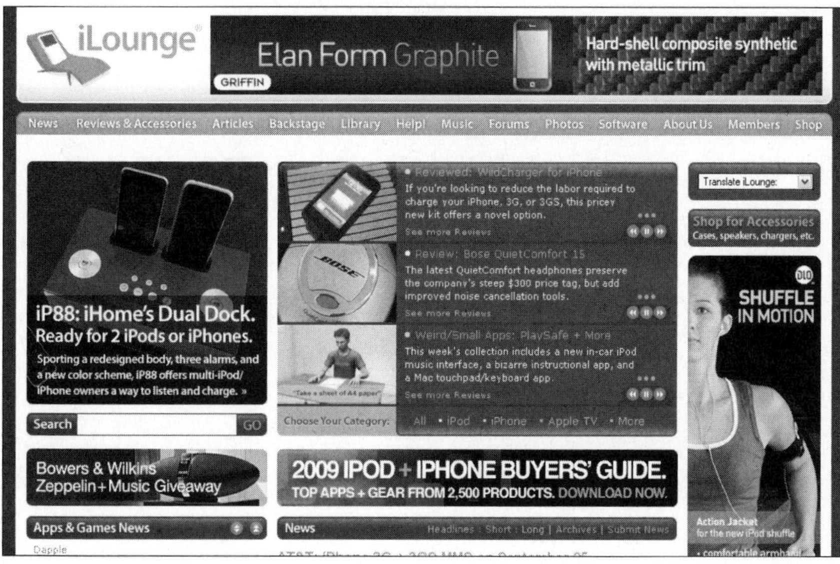

Figure 7-3: iLounge is the essential source for all news and issues for the Apple iPod and iPhone.

Getting political with it

No matter where you sit on the political spectrum, you live in interesting political times. You'll never be short of topics, from the latest political scandal to the next national election.

Some of the most popular political bloggers have turned their online musings into full-fledged careers in the media, from talk shows to newspaper columns. And some traditional journalists have bowed out of newspapers and television to move to a blog.

This niche has room for many kinds of blogs, from those criticizing national policy to those covering local school board and city elections. If you have a craving to get involved in politics but don't want to run for office, a blog might be a great way to develop an effective voice. And if you're a politician, you can follow the example of Barack Obama, who used a blog as part of his campaign strategy while running for the presidency of the United States (he won, by the way).

For some, the urge to sound off on politics has produced entirely new publications. Take, for example, Truthdig (`www.truthdig.com`), which won a 2007 Webby Award in the Political Blog category. (The Webbys are the Web's equivalent of the Oscars.) Shown in Figure 7-4, Truthdig was started by journalist Robert Scheer and publisher Zuade Kaufman to be a source for political commentary and news that challenges the "wisdom of the day."

Figure 7-4: Truthdig, winner of two Webby awards in 2007, challenges conventional political thinking.

Pointing out the strange

If it's bizarre, you can probably find a Web site about it. Many bloggers make a blogging career out of pointing blog readers to the strangest of the strange Web sites. These blogs are often called *link blogs,* which consist primarily of short descriptions and links off into the wild world of the Web. Today's blogger, in an attempt to cultivate the perverse, hilarious, and just weird, often adds more commentary, but the effect is the same: The reader gets a daily dose of random tidbits to enjoy.

A good example of a blog in this area is The Obscure Store & Reading Room (`www.obscurestore.typepad.com`), which focuses on news stories that seem just too bizarre to be true — but actually *are* true. Postings on the day this chapter was written ranged from stories about a boy who reported his own mother to 911 from the car for her bad driving and a social networking community called Enemybook (see Figure 7-5).

Figure 7-5: Get your daily dose of different at The Obscure Store.

Reporting news

The offline world is full of general news sources — the 200-page newspaper that struggles to appeal to all its readers or the broadcast news show that does local car chases and the weather well — and not much else. Specialized news sources are hard to come by.

Online, the situation is a little different. Quite a few news outlets have opted to offer news personalization features, letting you customize the news that you consume by topics. But many folks who have specialized interests still have to look through a lot of news sources to find truly pertinent stories.

If you're doing that kind of research for yourself, you can start a blog that shares your findings with others interested in the same topic. Are you an economist collecting stories about garbage production in North America? Or a marketing expert who keeps track of the latest guerilla marketing tactics in order to keep on your toes professionally? You can turn this research into a valuable blog for others who share your interest.

You can produce this format quite easily, as well, because posts are frequently just pointers to a news story or article on another Web site — the value for readers in a blog of this kind is that someone else (the blogger) has already done the work of finding the news, so sending them to another site is actually an important part of the service you're providing.

Quite a few bloggers have opted to develop blogs in a specialized news area and parlayed that success into a new revenue stream or sponsorship, so creating your own news blog might even prove to be a wise business move.

Even if you don't put advertising on your specialized news blog, keeping a blog of this kind demonstrates that you're on top of your field.

One journalist who left traditional media behind in order to serve as a clearinghouse of news about the media in Los Angeles is Kevin Roderick. His blog, LA Observed (`www.laobserved.com`), shown in Figure 7-6, is a must-read for journalists in Southern California and across the country. His blog is becoming quite a little empire while he expands into city hall and business coverage.

Revealing it all

If nothing in this chapter has appealed to you so far, perhaps you're looking for the blog classic: a personal diary. Part memoir and part confessional, personal diaries on the Web cover every topic that life can serve up.

Personal diaries can be real snooze-fests or tearjerkers nonpareil. Much depends, of course, on the quality of the writing. But much also depends on what happens in the life being documented. *Life bloggers,* as they're sometimes called, must deal with whatever comes up next for them, from weddings to being fired or hired to being diagnosed with cancer.

These blogs are usually easy to relate to and easy to read; they're also often humorous or heart-wrenching, and sometimes both. They take courage to write, whether read by millions or only five.

Figure 7-6: LA Observed covers the Los Angeles media space for journalists who don't have time to do it themselves.

For a great example of a personal diary blog, visit Penmachine (`www.penmachine.com`) for a journal written about a Vancouver-based writer's life, including his struggles with cancer (see Figure 7-7). Derek Miller tells the story like it is — his writing is full of emotional and gritty detail, and also the mundane circumstances of a full life lived despite health problems.

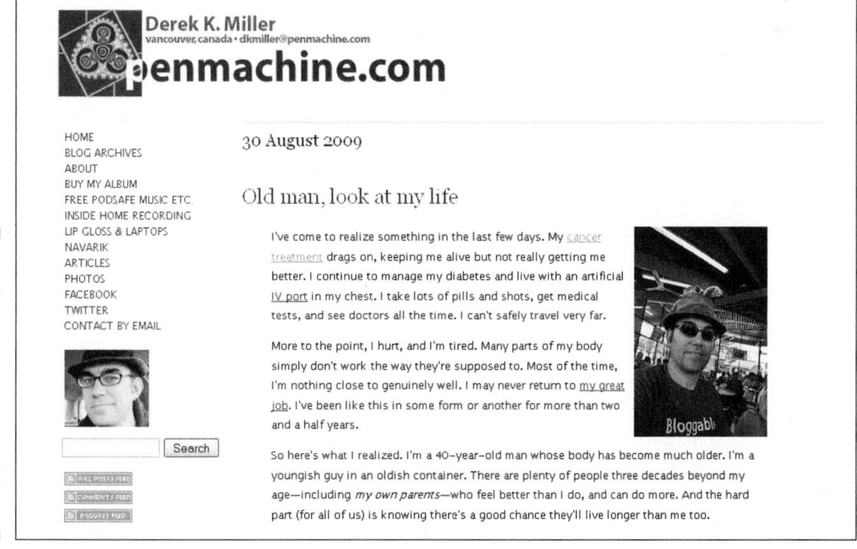

Figure 7-7: Derek Miller shares openly on Penmachine, a personal blog about his life.

Learning from the Pros

After you choose a topic, you can work on producing a readable blog that you can be proud of. In the following sections, you get ideas for setting up a blog successfully by cultivating your own talents and observing what others are doing right.

When you blog, much depends on the quality of your writing and your ability to make a connection with your readers. Work on developing a dialogue with your readers. Life bloggers often create this connection by revealing common experiences that many people can identify with. Businesses can choose to start a blog that gives typically silent members of a company (such as high-level executives or behind-the-scenes mechanics) a connection to customers.

Many blogs are maintained by more than one person; sometimes, contributions by several different people can enliven and enrich the conversation, as well as decrease the workload for any single blogger.

I cover creating great content in Chapter 8, and in that chapter, you can find out how to keep track of what's working for other bloggers.

Lurking on other blogs

You can best figure out what will work on your blog by seeing what's working on other blogs. If you aren't a regular blog reader, find some blogs and start reading!

The old, old Internet term *lurking* describes Web users who look at blogs, mailing lists, online discussions, and forums, but don't choose to participate in them. Lurking online doesn't have any negative connotations, though the word does sound kind of sinister.

In truth, lurking can help you find out about what kinds of communication and interaction are appropriate when you're new to a Web community or when you're planning to start one yourself. The vast majority of Web users are actually lurkers; most people don't do more than read or look at blogs.

Start your lurking career by finding a few blogs that you like, that you regard as competition, or that you find interesting for some reason. If you want to see a blog that has a very active, vocal audience, find one that has a lot of comments and make sure that you read them all. Many of the blogs mentioned in this chapter fall smack into this category, so why not start with them?

If you want to see how a blog evolves, find one that has been around awhile and look back through the site's archives to see how it got started. Most of all, pay attention to what you find interesting about the blog.

Here are some issues that you can figure out from lurking on a blog:

- **Posts:** Watch what the blogger (or bloggers) posts about, how often they post, and what days and times attract readers. See whether you can understand what prompts a blogger to post.
- **Interaction:** Pay attention to the posts that get a lot of comments and responses, and try to understand what gets people talking.
- **Resource use:** Look for instances when the blogger chooses to include a link, a quote, or other resource, and what it adds to the conversation.
- **Design:** Keep an eye out for blog designs and styles that you might want to imitate on your own blog.
- **Sidebar use:** Look at the blog sidebars for cool technologies and tools that the blogger uses (and that you might be able use on your own blog).

You want interaction with your blog readers, but some comments can cause problems because they're off topic or offensive, so you can use this opportunity to see how other bloggers handle bad comments. Pay attention to whether a blog comment policy is in place and how the blogger enforces that policy. When does the blogger choose to remove or edit comments? Do you agree with his or her choices? How do you want to handle problem comments on your own blog? I talk more about handling spam and bad comments in Chapter 9.

While you lurk, keep a list of notes and ideas for reference later, especially for items that you think are good ideas but that you aren't ready to implement quite yet. You can easily lose those first good ideas if you don't keep track of them somehow.

What works for someone else might not work for you, and it doesn't have to. The blogosphere is still young, and you have plenty of room and time to try new ideas. Rules and standards that others have adopted give you a good starting point, but you don't have to use them if they don't work for you.

Participating by commenting

When you're comfortable, you can start participating in your favorite blogs. Leaving comments can start your interactions on a blog. You don't have to take a long time to write comments, they help the blogger, and you might even further the conversation with your comment.

Leaving comments gives you experience with participating in a blog audience, and when you have a blog of your own, you can comment on someone else's blog to let others know about your own blog.

Many blog comment forms give you the chance to leave a URL when you post a comment, and the software often links your name to the URL. So, when you have a blog, leaving a comment that includes such a link is a bit like leaving a tiny, unobtrusive ad. When the blogger and other blog visitors read your comment, they might just choose to click the link and visit your blog, especially if they like what you had to say.

You might also get visitors who *didn't* like what you say! You invite disagreement any time you put your opinion out into the world, but don't let that stop you from doing it.

Some bloggers have made the mistake of abusing this little privilege, leaving comments that don't add to the topic or say much, simply to get the links to their blogs on the other bloggers' pages. Don't make this mistake. Be a genuine member of the blogosphere and leave comments only when you truly have something to say. "Nice site" is neither interesting to read nor particularly helpful to anyone.

Leave comments that distinguish you as a thoughtful contributor to the topic. If you can answer a question posed by the blog post or provide information that seems to be missing, you really contribute value with your comment. But you can also just leave your own opinion, even if you completely disagree with what the blogger is saying.

Reaching Out to Other Bloggers

Don't forget that other bloggers are your primary audience. These folks are online and already familiar with blogs, and you're likely to find other bloggers with whom you have things in common — maybe even the subject of your blog.

Meeting with bloggers in person and communicating with them online are terrific ways to network and market your blog. A lot of bloggers list the blogs that they read right beside their blog posts in the sidebar called a *blogroll,* so you might be able to generate some additional readership if you create relationships with bloggers.

Meeting in person

This is going to sound really old school, but you can turn online acquaintances into offline friends. In fact, it can be pretty fun.

For example, on a recent visit to Boston, I posted on the Rockin' Sock Club blog asking for yarn store recommendations, and I offered to meet with any knitters in town who wanted to get together. (The Rockin' Sock Club is a sock-knitting club put together by Blue Moon Fiber Arts. Only members of the sock club can post comments and blog posts.) As a result, I had a great afternoon with people I never would have met otherwise.

You don't have to knit socks to get together with bloggers, though. Most cities have an active community of bloggers that you can cultivate:

- Be sure to include your e-mail address or even a cell phone number on your blog, and let people know that you want to make new friends. Look for similar information on the blogs that you read if you're interested in getting in touch with a blogger.
- Look for bloggers who identify their location and get to know them on their blogs by posting comments.
- Visit Upcoming (`http://upcoming.yahoo.com`) or Meetup (`www.meetup.com`), and search for blogger get-togethers in your area. Many bloggers network with other nearby bloggers on a regular basis. You can even look up get-togethers when you're visiting a new place.
- Organize your own get-together and publicize it on your blog, Twitter, or on Upcoming or Meetup.

Using social networks

Social networking sites are designed to connect you with your current group of friends, and then extend those connections out to their friends. Each site that I mention in this section has a different mechanism for making that happen, and different types of community interaction occur. LinkedIn (`www.linkedin.com`), for example, is a professional networking site designed to showcase your work background and interests so that you can make connections to others in your field.

You can make friends in social-networking online communities, such as Twitter, Friendster, LinkedIn, MySpace, and Facebook. Social networking sites usually give bloggers a way to link to blogs, or even to notify others about new blog posts via profile pages, so if you're looking for online connections in the blogging community, these communities are a great place to start.

In fact, a lot of bloggers regard their blogs as a form of networking, and they're already looking to make these kinds of connections via social networking Web sites.

Facebook (www.facebook.com) is more about cementing your social friendships, even for tracking down old friends from high school with whom you might have lost touch. It has great additional applications and games that you can use to break the ice with a new friend.

Regardless of whether the folks in your social network have blogs, you can use the site to let them know about your blog, building up your audience and hopefully the participation on it by leveraging the goodwill of people you know and the people they know!

Chapter 8

Creating Great Content

In This Chapter

- Discovering who your audience is
- Getting words onto your blog
- Adding value by including links
- Planning for blogging dry spells

A lot of elements work together to make a blog work well, from a well-designed layout to fancy technical widgets, but none of those things can substitute for good content aimed at the right audience. In fact, if you write (or podcast or take photos) well and you're reaching readers who are engaged by your style and content, you can actually be successful without spending any time at all on how your blog looks. Good content can even make your readers forgive an awkward interface or missing bells and whistles, such as RSS feeds or categories.

So, if you do nothing else to make your blog succeed, focus on producing great writing, photos, audio, or videos. Know what your audience wants and deliver it. In fact, try slightly *under*-delivering it — keep your audience wanting more.

This chapter offers pointers on writing well for the Web and understanding what your audience expects from your blog.

In this chapter, I refer to competitors when I am describing other bloggers who are covering the same subject area as your blog, or trying to reach the same audience you want to attract. Remember that in the blogosphere the atmosphere is very collaborative; however, competitors can also be friends, contacts, occasional contributors to your blog, participants in your comments area, and good resources for information. So when I talk about competitors, I do so in the friendliest sense of the word!

Knowing Your Audience

First things first: How well do you know your audience? Are you hitting the right notes to attract the readers you want in the quantity you want them?

Not all bloggers care about the number of readers they get, but they do care about getting the right eyes on their words. Regardless of whether you're number-obsessed or just focused on your niche, you need to understand your audience and what your readers are looking for.

You can get an idea about your audience by

- Using statistics software to track the number of visitors to your blog and what links those visitors click
- Noting the content that elicits the biggest and best response from your readers (or the response that you want, even if it isn't the biggest)
- Looking at the blogs of others in your subject area to see what you can find out from their comment activity, search engine rankings, and other data

You might have to wait awhile for statistics and comments, but you can easily look at others' blogs, even if you're still developing your own blog. I talk in detail about measuring site traffic and statistics in Chapter 16, so jump there if you want to find out more about the readers you already have.

Finding your competitors

To find your competitors, you must first define your own niche. Your niche consists of what you're blogging about, the topics you cover, and what words you use most frequently in your posts. You use these keywords to describe yourself, and visitors use them to find you when they conduct a search on Google, Yahoo!, or another search engine.

Use these descriptive words (plus the word *blog*) to search for yourself on Google or another search engine. Investigate the results that come up and look for blogs that have content (never mind the look and feel of the blog for now) similar to the content you're creating or want to create.

You can also use one of the blog search engines, such as Technorati (`www.technorati.com`), Google Blogs search page (`http://blogsearch.google.com`), or Icerocket (`www.icerocket.com`). Figure 8-1 shows the results of a search on Technorati that used the terms *blogs, blogging, audience, niche,* and *success.* These results show posts from blogs that talk about these topics.

Figure 8-1: Use Technorati to find the blogs of your competitors.

You want to find other blogs that inhabit your niche, and then spend a week or two investigating these blogs. Your mission: Find the secret of their success, which I discuss in the following section. You want to know how those blogs get readers and how they keep those readers coming back for more.

Discovering the secrets of success

While you watch your competitors' blogs, you have a chance to figure out what topics they blog about, of course, but also how they reach out to their audience.

Your competitors might not be blogging in the most effective way. While you look at these blogs, decide whether your competitors are actually reaching their audience successfully or whether they're falling short. You can figure out as much from a failing blog as you can from a successful one.

While you visit these blogs, keep a journal of your impressions. Watch the following to investigate how these bloggers handle publishing and outreach:

- **How frequently the blogger puts new posts on the blog:** Frequency of blog posts is a big deal. Any blogger can tell you to post "frequently," but almost none can tell you want that really means. I talk more about how often you should post in the section "Writing Well and Frequently," later in this chapter, but you can explore this idea by noting how often your competitors choose to post to their blogs. Do they create new posts daily, or even multiple times a day? Or do they post a few times a week, or even once a week? When you become a reader of that blog, do you find yourself wanting more content or less?

- **When the blogger publishes blog posts:** Time of day can have a surprising impact on how readers receive a blog post. You need to reach your audience members when they're likely to be sitting at their computers. If your audience consists of stockbrokers, time your posts so that new content becomes available just before business hours start on the East Coast, not during dinner time on the West Coast. If you're targeting teens, try to publish before or after school hours, and not while they're sitting in homeroom.

  Sure, your readers can visit your blog anytime and pick up content that you posted in the middle of the night, but you can impress them with a blog that always seems to have fresh content just when they want it.

- **The length of posts on the blog:** You might be surprised to know that the ideal length of a blog post is a hotly debated topic among experienced bloggers. Some bloggers swear by the short-and-sweet recipe that guides most Web writing: Blog posts should get to the point quickly and allow readers to get back to their busy days with the information that they need. Others find that longer posts — even essays — do the job, keeping readers on the site longer and providing more thoughtful commentary. The topic of your blog, as well as your audience's appetite and available time, dictate the natural length of your blog posts. Looking at your competitors' blogs can tell you the number of words that they find optimal in a blog post, which you can use as a starting point for your blog.
- **When the blogger links to outside Web sites:** Linking to other blogs and Web sites is a great way to serve the reader. By pointing out other sources of information or even other blogs, you help them become more knowledgeable about your topic and keep them engaged with it. So, when do your competitors choose to link to other sites, and what sites do they link to? Are the links designed to entertain, educate, or inform? Are links included in the text of the post or broken out at the end? What makes you click a link yourself?

  I talk a lot more about linking other sites as a strategy for reaching your audience in the section "Linking to Serve the Reader," later in this chapter.

- **When the blogger addresses his or her audience directly:** A lot of bloggers use a very personal writing style that directly acknowledges the reader, kind of like this book. You might enjoy being addressed directly by a blogger because the conversation feels more personal. Or, depending on the topic of the blog, perhaps a more formal, almost academic approach is more appropriate. Either way, check out how your competition is handling this issue. When do they ask the readers for input or feedback, and how do they phrase those requests? Do readers actually respond, and if so, to what kinds of approaches?
- **Use of multimedia, such as photos, audio, and videos:** Although the majority of blogs are made up of a whole lot of words, you can still throw in the occasional (or even frequent) picture or video. In fact, bloggers

do it all the time to dress things up visually and keep readers interested. Take a look at how your competitors handle including multimedia in their blogs. Do they use photos to illustrate the ideas in the posts or just to attract the eye? What about animation or video? Do posts that have these extras get more comments or fewer? Do you like getting information in these other formats, or do you find it distracting?

- **Posts that get a lot of comments and posts that get very few:** A blog that gets a lot of comments signals that the blogger is resonating with his or her audience — even if just to make audience members mad. A blog that has no or few comments probably just leaves people flat (or maybe isn't even read). Not all bloggers get hundreds of comments every time they post. Some blog posts just get better response than others, and part of what makes a blogger successful is being able to know what makes those posts really work so that they can repeat the success. Watch your competitors' blogs to see when a post gets a big response and look at what kind of response it gets.

  Also, watch for the posts that don't get any response — you want to figure out why those posts didn't work so that you don't make the same mistake!

- **The writing style of the blogger:** Bloggers need to have good content, and for most bloggers, that comes down to having an accessible and readable writing style. For those blogs in your niche that attract participation and good press, what style does the blogger use? Personal? Professional? Humorous? What tone appeals to readers and makes them come back to the blog again and again? What approach do you find more readable and engaging?

You can use these same points of analysis on your own blog, too. After you have your blog up and running for awhile, take a look at your own content with the same critical eye that you use on your competitors. What are you doing right and wrong?

You may find this exercise hard to do. I'm sure you think everything on your blog is great — after all, no one sets out to write a bad blog post! Still, some of your posts are likely more popular with readers than others, and if you can figure out why certain posts work better than others, you can repeat that success again and again. In fact, developing a critical eye for your own content can really help you make your blog succeed: This medium doesn't hold still, and you need to be able to adapt your style and content while your audience grows and changes. Consider conducting this kind of survey of your content a couple of times a year to make sure that you stay on track and topical to the folks you want to attract, even if you're really aiming for just your immediate family.

Profiling your audience

When you finish your competitive analysis (which I explain how to do in the preceding section) and after you review your own content successes and failures, picture your audience in your mind's eye.

Create a clear picture for yourself of just who's in your audience. If you don't have the audience you're targeting at this point, you can try to develop a picture of who you want in your audience.

You don't actually have to draw a picture, though. You can create this profile in words that describe the characteristics of your ideal audience member. You can include anything that you want in this profile, from shoe size to personal hang-ups — any detail that helps you really know this person better and create content for this person on your blog.

Don't just say, "My ideal audience is anybody who is interested in *[insert your blog topic here]*." You already know that — otherwise, this person wouldn't be on your blog in the first place. You want to capture all the details that make this person different, unique, and interesting.

Take Gizmodo, as shown in Figure 8-2. Gizmodo (`www.gizmodo.com`) is a techie blog featuring information on gadgets and other nifty technical devices. The blog's tagline is "Gizmodo, the gadget guide. So much in love with shiny new toys, it's unnatural." Right away, you know that the audience for Gizmodo is more that just those interested in gadgets — Gizmodo readers adore gadgets, see them as playthings meant to entertain and amuse, and are perhaps unhealthily engaged by them (maybe at the expense of other hobbies and pursuits). And those audience members want their gadget news piping hot, fresh off the presses. Doesn't that tell you more about what kinds of posts will work best to attract and keep these kinds of readers?

Some of the concepts and facts that you might want to explore for your profile include

- Age
- Gender
- The nature of their interest in your topic (for example, familial, personal, emotional, or professional)
- Geographic location and proximity to you or to the topic of your blog
- Lifestyle (for example, workaholic, homebody, retired, world traveler, and so on)

- Occupation
- Education level
- Marital status
- Interests and hobbies
- Income
- Political leanings

Heck, you might even think about what your ideal audience member reads, eats, or wears; his or her sleeping habits and style of personal hygiene; and so on. If a specific detail seems like it might inform your writing and content, throw it into the mix.

When you have a reader profile in hand, you can be more targeted about what you choose to write about and how you address that audience.

Figure 8-2: Gizmodo focuses on the fanatical gadget enthusiast.

Writing Well and Frequently

I've said it before and I'll say it again: The primary ingredients for a successful blog are

- Good content
- Frequently updated content

But what do I really mean by *good* and *frequently?*

Good content compels, satisfying the readers' immediate interests but leaving them hungry for more. Think of a blog post like an appetizer: It should whet the appetite, pique the palette, and sustain the diner until the next course arrives. You don't want to give your readers Thanksgiving dinner — you want them to come back, and come back soon.

As a general rule, blogging has evolved into quite a personal, conversational medium, and textual blogs have a strong feel of the author and his or her personality. The first blogs were actually online diaries, and even today, most bloggers choose to use words such as *I* or *my* in their blog posts, creating an intimate and open feel — even on corporate blogs. This *first-person* writing differs dramatically from most corporate communication, which at best refers to the company as *our* and at worst only refers to the company by its full and official name.

Respecting copyright

Anything and everything you see on the Internet is protected by copyright. Copyright is just what it sounds like: "the right to copy" an original creation. Copyright law protects authors by giving that right solely to him or her.

Unless the creator of an image or photo specifically licenses his or her copyright to you, you can't reuse it, even if you give the author credit or link back to the original story. (This rule applies to text, photos, and videos, too.) But this rule has a few exceptions: You can quote a news story or a blog post on your blog if you use only part of it, and as long as you don't take credit for the work. Commentary and critique also allow you to excerpt a piece of text or other work. But don't think that just because you're the subject of a story or blog post that you have the right to repost the entire article on your blog or Web site. You don't. When in doubt, ask and get permission.

At `www.copyright.gov` get the goods on what you can use on your blog without running afoul of the law that protects other authors' text. You might particularly want to read the areas around fair use, especially if you plan to write reviews.

Take, for example, the McDonald's blog, Open for Discussion (`www.crmcdonalds.com/publish/csr/home/_blog.html`), written by McDonald's Vice President Bob Langert. In an August 20, 2007 post, Bob writes:

> "We all have one — a pet peeve that we just can't ditch. I was recently reminded of my #1 pet peeve while reading the latest account of McDonald's Moms' Quality Correspondents. They reported that McDonald's beef is 100% pure USDA-inspected beef. Frankly, I don't think this should be any kind of big 'Aha', and I am amazed that so many people question this established fact."

Figure 8-3 shows this post.

Writing in the first person isn't as easy as it looks (or reads); after all, most people spend years training to write more formally and commonly produce all kinds of documents in which first person writing is emphatically *not* suitable: memos, reports, new stories, invoices, and so on. You may have trouble finding an authentic, genuine voice that really feels comfortable. My best advice is to just practice, practice, practice.

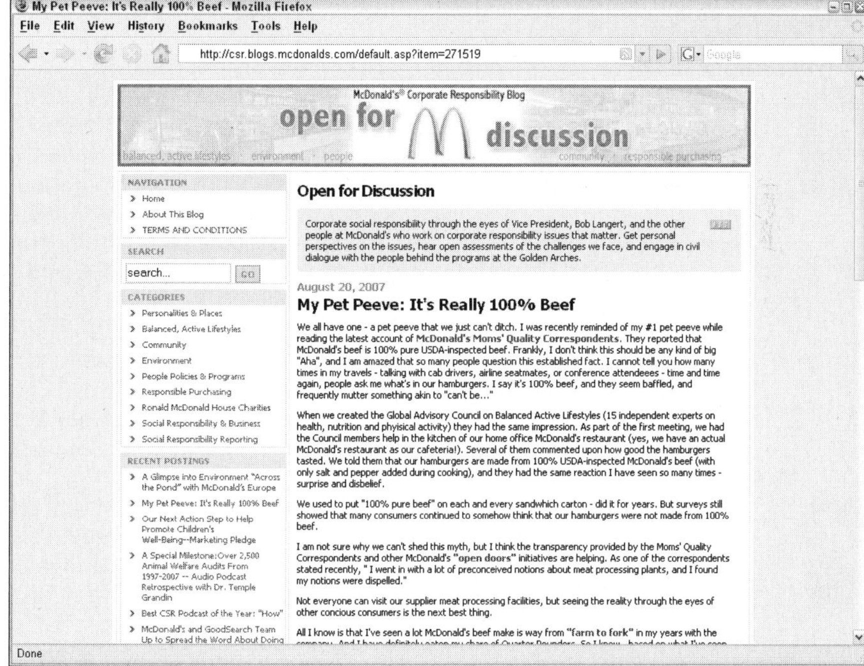

Figure 8-3: Even vice presidents are informal on blogs, as McDonald's VP Bob Langert is on Open for Discussion.

Think of your blog posts like letters or e-mails. Speak directly and simply, like you would in a personal note or letter. Try not to over-think your words, but don't go right into stream of consciousness (fun to write, hard to read).

One of my favorite techniques for making my blog posts readable is to close the door of my office and read my post out loud. If it sounds close to something I might actually say in conversation, it hits the right tone for a blog post — at least, on my blog.

When it seems appropriate, try using humor and jokes, especially if you can be self-deprecating. People just love self-deprecating bloggers. Here's an example from Stephanie Pearl-McPhee's Yarn Harlot blog (`www.yarnharlot.ca`):

> "I think that I can't be the only one who finds LA a little hard on the ol' self esteem. There is an alarmingly high ratio of tall, beautiful people compared to us ordinary souls, and it usually doesn't take long for me, the shabby and usually bra-less to feel out of place."

Sometimes I find it difficult to write to some anonymous audience member and get a conversational tone, so I imagine that I'm writing to a good friend. If I can be interesting enough to hold her attention, it ought to do the trick for my readers, too!

If you make your blog informal and conversational, you still can't completely ignore spelling, grammar, and sentence structure. Some bloggers do opt for a completely unedited approach, right down to not using capital letters, but keep in mind that people have more trouble reading poorly formulated writing, not less. If you have a business or professional blog, you definitely need to pay attention to spelling and grammar because these little details influence your credibility. Do your readers a favor — use the grammar and spellcheck functions of your word processor.

On the other hand, many blogs have made a reputation based on using incorrect spelling or grammar! An example is the funny blog I Can Has Cheezburger? (`www.icanhascheezburger.com`), which has built its popularity largely on bad spelling in hilariously captioned photos of cats.

Many bloggers like to quote news articles and blog posts, and then expand on them. If you take this approach, make sure that you understand the rules of copyright law when you use someone else's words — it's always best to ask permission! For more, read the sidebar "Respecting copyright," in this chapter.

Linking to Serve the Reader

Links — you need 'em. You may worry that by providing a link to a news story or online article, you're sending your readers away from your site into the black hole of the Internet, never to return. Your readers might, in fact, click the link and go read the article. But they probably won't forget where they found the link.

On a blog, links are just as much a resource as any other information that you provide. In fact, many blogs actually consist of collections of links around a topic or theme, pulled together to inform or entertain the blog's readers.

If you're providing good content and expanding on that content by using links, you're doing your readers a service that they won't forget — one they likely come back to you for.

Joey deVilla doesn't shy away from adding links to his blog posts on The Adventures of Accordion Guy in the 21st Century (`www.joeydevilla.com`), as shown in Figure 8-4.

This could make trade with the U.S., our largest trading partner (as we are theirs) a little more difficult, but on the personal scale, it's good — I've got a handful of trips down south scheduled in the next couple of months. Why, oh why wasn't it this way from 1999 through 2002, when I was flying to the U.S. at least once a month and my bank account was getting beaten up on the exchange?
The last time our currencies were at par was back during the Ford and Trudeau administrations, back when I was a still a landed immigrant and Wings' *Silly Love Songs* was the #1 song on the Billboard Top 100 for that year.
Related Reading
Chicago Tribune: CANADA DOLLAR HEADING FOR PARITY WITH U.S. FOR FIRST TIME SINCE 1976
Forbes: FOREX - CANADIAN DOLLAR ON THE VERGE OF PARITY VS US DOLLAR
The Globe and Mail: LOONIE TOPS 99 CENTS
AFP: CANADIAN DOLLAR HITS 1997 HIGH
This was written by Joey deVilla. Posted on Thursday, September 20, 2007, at 2:52 pm. Filed under Uncategorized. Bookmark the permalink. Follow comments here with the RSS feed. Post a comment or leave a trackback.

Figure 8-4: Joey deVilla adds a lot of links to his blog posts, helping his readers get more information.

In a September 20, 2007 post about the Canadian dollar's parity with the U.S. dollar, he included links to bios of the U.S. president and Canadian prime minister in office during the last time the currencies were equal, and he provided links to pop culture references current at that time. Also, he collected a list of news stories that cover the event.

Speaking of dollars, links are the currency of the blogosphere. A lot of bloggers point their readers to blog posts that they find especially interesting, even going so far as to quote the other blogger. In the sidebars of their blogs, bloggers regularly build lists of links to blogs that they read. These lists are called *blogrolls* (see Chapter 20).

In general, bloggers are generous about linking to other blogs and Web sites because the favor is frequently returned. As the saying goes, "You have to spend a little to make a little."

Adding links to your posts is a good thing . . . unless you're irresponsible about what you link to. Take your responsibility as a publisher seriously and don't send people to suspect resources or throw them into an adult-oriented site without warning.

When you link to a blog post, be sure you link to the permalink URL, not the blog's home page. A *permalink* is the unique Web address for an individual blog post — the permanent link to that page. You should use the permalink because the blogger might update the blog any time after you create the link, pushing the post that you mention down or even off the blog's home page.

The Web Style Guide (`www.webstyleguide.com`) covers everything from good Web design standards to graphics production, but you can probably benefit most from Chapter 6 of the guide, which covers links, titles, and common online styles.

Breaking Through a Blank Screen

At times, even outstanding bloggers hit dry spells and can't think of a word to write. You can safely anticipate a day sometime in the lifespan of your blog when you literally have nothing to say to your readers, no matter how much enthusiasm you have for your topic.

This phase will pass, but sometimes, you need a little help pushing back to a productive spot. Here are a few tips for making it through your dry spell:

- **Stockpile a few evergreen posts.** In newsrooms across the U.S., journalists regularly create *evergreen stories* (stories that can be printed or televised at any time and still be interesting). You can also put together a few evergreen blog posts that you can keep on hand against a day when your creative juices temporarily dry up. You can also use these kinds of posts for days when you're sick or on vacation, but still want to have something for your blog. A lot of blog software allows you to schedule a publication date for a blog post in the future, so you can even set these posts to go up automatically and take a well-deserved break.
- **Ask a friend to guest blog for a few days.** Bring some new perspective to your blog when you have none left yourself by asking a friend, colleague, fellow blogger, or even a critic to write some blog posts for you. Your readers might enjoy the change of style and tone (and if they don't, you

make them that much happier when you come back!). Be sure to return the favor when your guest blogger has a dry spell of his or her own.

- **Recycle an oldie but goodie.** When you can't think of exciting new content, bring out a great post from your archives. New readers appreciate seeing something they missed, and old readers might find new information in a second read. Professional blogger Darren Rowse points his readers to a list of best-of posts on ProBlogger (`www.problogger.net`). In fact, Darren pulls out the best posts of all time, for the month, for new readers, and just some of his favorites (see Figure 8-5).
- **Hold a contest.** When the well has run dry, you can hold a contest. Ask your readers to submit funny photos or write a caption for one of your funny photos. Show them a bottle of jellybeans and ask for guesses about how many pieces of candy are in the bottle. You get the idea: Distract them with shiny, happy prizes! But make sure you're fair and impartial in how you award prizes. If you say you plan to hold a raffle, be sure to actually do so!
- **Post a photo.** Rather than 1,000 words, put up a single photo. Take a picture of where you usually blog, show off your new laptop, or just take a walk in your neighborhood. You can dig out a photo of yourself as a kid or show that embarrassing haircut you had in the '80s.
- **Post about the books, movies, or television that you're consuming.** Tell folks about the other media you're enjoying. You can even hook up an Amazon Associates account and earn a little money from your recommendations. (You can find out how to set up this kind of account in Chapter 17.)
- **Give out your favorite recipe.** Dig out the cookbook and find your grandmother's fudge recipe or your mom's apple pie recipe, and share it with your readers. Better yet, take a break from the computer and make the recipe yourself so that you can put up a photo with your post.

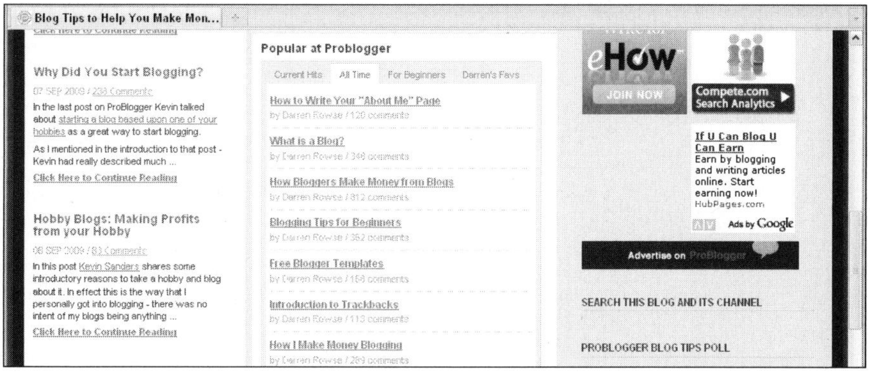

Figure 8-5: Darren Rowse points people to favorite posts from the past.

- **Blog from a new location.** Sometimes, breaking the routine can shake loose those recalcitrant brain cells. Try blogging from another room in your house, or head to the local Internet cafe or coffee shop.
- **Record an audio podcast.** If you can't write, talk! Give the gift of your voice to your readers — listeners — by trying something new and different. You might be pleasantly surprised and make podcasting a regular feature of your blog. Chapter 12 covers podcasting extensively.
- **Do an interview.** Ask a friend, colleague, neighbor, child, parent, boss, or public figure whether you can interview him or her for your blog. Type up a few questions, e-mail them off, and when the answers arrive in your inbox, a little copying and pasting should do the trick.
- **Take a quiz.** Let your readers know what superhero you are or what color your personality is by playing with some of the fun quizzes and polls online. The Superhero Quiz is at `www.thesuperheroquiz.com` (I'm Spider-Man), and you can find loads of others on blogthings (`www.blogthings.com`) and Quiz Meme (`www.quizmeme.com`).
- **Ask for suggestions from your readers.** Appeal to your readers for help finding new topics to post about. Also, look through your old posts and see whether you can expand on a post that worked well; check out comments and e-mails from readers, too!

Chapter 9

Building Community with Comments

In This Chapter

- Discovering what comments are and how to use them
- Maintaining and managing your blogging community
- Dealing with spammy comments on your blog
- Handling negative comments on other blogs

Every blog should have comments. Love them or hate them, they're an integral part of blogging. Comments provide the main source of interaction between you and your readership. Visitors to your blog can ask you questions, correct your writing, suggest your next blog topic, or leave a note to say hello.

Unfortunately, as interesting and thought-provoking as comment conversations can be, they're not without their challenges. Comment spam and negative commentary can take the joy out of blogging and make managing comments on your blog feel like a full-time job.

How you handle your blog community determines your level of stress and success. In this chapter, I talk about how you can set your own comment rules and monitor your community. I also give you some helpful hints about how to make your blog a positive place for conversation, as well as provide strategies for dealing with spammers and negativity.

Getting Interaction Going with Comments

Comments are an important part of a blog. When a blogger opts, through choice or necessity, to turn off commenting, the blogger loses some of what makes blogging such a dynamic, exciting medium: the interaction between blogger and readers. Not only the blogger loses out when he or she removes comments — most blog readers enjoy the comments left by others and often form a strong community feeling for fellow visitors.

A blogger may turn off comments when he or she simply doesn't have the time or desire to read and respond to comments, or when the tenor of the comments becomes a problem. Popular blogger Heather Armstrong only selectively allows comments on her blog Dooce (`www.dooce.com`) because her religious views and style of blogging generate a lot of negative interaction with readers in the comments. Political bloggers often have similar problems.

For other bloggers, their main issue with comments is related to time. A popular blogger can get hundreds of comments on a single blog post, and it takes time to read and respond to those comments, much less remove any inappropriate comments. Spam can also lead a blogger to restrict comments. Just as with e-mail, spammers have discovered that they can throw their unwanted commercial messages (anyone need a refinance?) into blogs, and even with the best blog software, some spam messages end up on the blog.

Still, the vast majority of blogs allow comments, and those blogs benefit hugely from the interaction and fun that comments can generate. On a blog such as Grey Matter (`www.greyswriters.com`), from the writers of the TV show *Grey's Anatomy,* readers really get involved with the show's writers. In the comments, readers share their thoughts on the show, offering feedback and suggestions.

Getting involved

If you want to have a dialogue with your readers, you need to allow comments on your blog, whether you're reaching out to your parents or to your customers.

Just because your blog posts have a comment form, though, people don't necessarily just jump in and start commenting. You need to tailor your posts to elicit dialogue and feedback, perhaps even by going so far as to ask specifically for responses.

If the comment areas of your blog look a little bare, ask some friends to help by reading and commenting for a few weeks. Comments tend to generate more comments, if you can get the ball rolling.

Of course, the problem might lie with your content or approach, so don't be afraid to experiment with your topic or style to try to get better results from your comment forms.

You want to be involved in your blogging community, right? If you don't, then turn that comment function off. Here's a quick checklist of tips for cultivating comments on your blog:

- **Make it easy for your readers to comment.** Sometimes, readers can have problems finding that Comment Now button or link. Keep your comment links visible to encourage people to comment.
- **Ask questions of your readers.** Get your readers to start participating by requesting advice, seeking out information, or asking for a recipe. The simple act of asking can do wonders for comments. Ask your visitors to tell you stories, answer questions, or give advice. For instance, if you're blogging about a frustrating travel experience, you might ask your readers for tips for the future. Or, if you're looking for a new laptop bag, ask your readers to recommend bags that they like.

  Specific, rather than general, questions work best to start a conversation.
- **Request topics or ideas.** Requesting ideas about your blog topics can generate an amazing response. You may also invite readers to send in blog posts they write that could benefit the community of your site. (If you make this invitation, make sure that you're clear about who owns the copyright! As the publisher of the content, you probably want to have the guest bloggers assign copyright to you.)
- **Communicate with your readers.** Make sure you're actively talking to your readers by responding to the comments that they leave on your blog.
- **Host comment-related contests.** Think of ways that you can turn comments into a contest. One common contest strategy involves asking people to leave a comment in order to enter a contest, and then drawing a winner randomly from those who participate.

Also, get involved with your blogging community. Visit other blogs and use their comment systems to get involved with their readers. In return, if you're active enough with your comments, those readers visit you, as well.

Enabling comments

Most modern blog software, regardless of whether it's hosted or installed on your own Web server (see Chapter 3), has tools that allow your visitors to comment and tools that allow you to handle the comments you receive. Check your documentation to figure out what functionality the software you're using offers — and don't forget that you may be able to customize the way in which your comment tools are configured to better suit your preferences and audience.

If you find yourself in a situation in which you use software that doesn't have that capability, and you can't change software, you can find third-party solutions. In fact, many bloggers who use top-of-the-line blog software opt to use another tool for comments because they want specific functionality.

One such tool is DISQUS (`www.disqus.com`), which offers a truly impressive range of functionality options — plus, it's free! You can use it to

- Allow visitors to track comments via e-mail or RSS.
- Allow visitors to rank comments on the site or reply to a comment directly.
- Allow visitors to flag comments as inappropriate or spam.
- Sort how the comments appear, either by date or popularity.
- Moderate comments to remove, edit, and screen out unwanted content.

Managing Comments

Like all good things, comments require care and feeding. Although I believe the resulting community dialogue makes that effort worthwhile, I can't deny that managing comments involves real work and time. In the following sections, I talk about ways you can set up your blog for comments, prevent possible problems, and deal with problems if they do crop up.

Establishing community guidelines

You want comments, but you want the *right* comments. Ideally, your visitors provide on-topic, interesting, and never ever profane feedback. Of course, we don't actually live in an ideal world, so setting some community guidelines for participation on your site can help clarify your expectations to your readers. Make those guidelines straightforward and clear. Your rules may exclude anything you want. Common blog rules outlaw comments that include

- Racist or bigoted speech
- Sexually explicit content
- Discussions or descriptions of violent or criminal acts
- Unlicensed copyrighted material
- Threats, harassment, or personal privacy violations

You have to enforce these rules, but simply having them in place can deter troublemakers from posting at all, particularly if you're scrupulous in enforcing your guidelines quickly.

The blogging software solution that you use might also have a set of standards in place with which both you and your visitors must comply. For example, Microsoft Windows Live Spaces (`http://home.spaces.live.com`), a hosted blogging solution, has a community code of conduct that you must enforce on your blog (shown in Figure 9-1). Every hosted blogging service has its own set of rules that you should be aware of. Don't get caught breaking the rules!

You may need to adapt any guidelines that you create over time, especially while your blog grows in popularity or changes its focus. Be sure to set a time every so often to review your own guidelines and make changes. You might include your visitors in the development of the community guidelines, checking with your readers about what you do to protect them. They'll love you for it.

Figure 9-2 shows the blog comment policy written by Kathryn Lord, who blogs about online dating and relationships on her Web site (`www.find-a-sweetheart.com`). For Kathryn, it all comes down to having common courtesy for her and for other readers — mud-slinging comments are history.

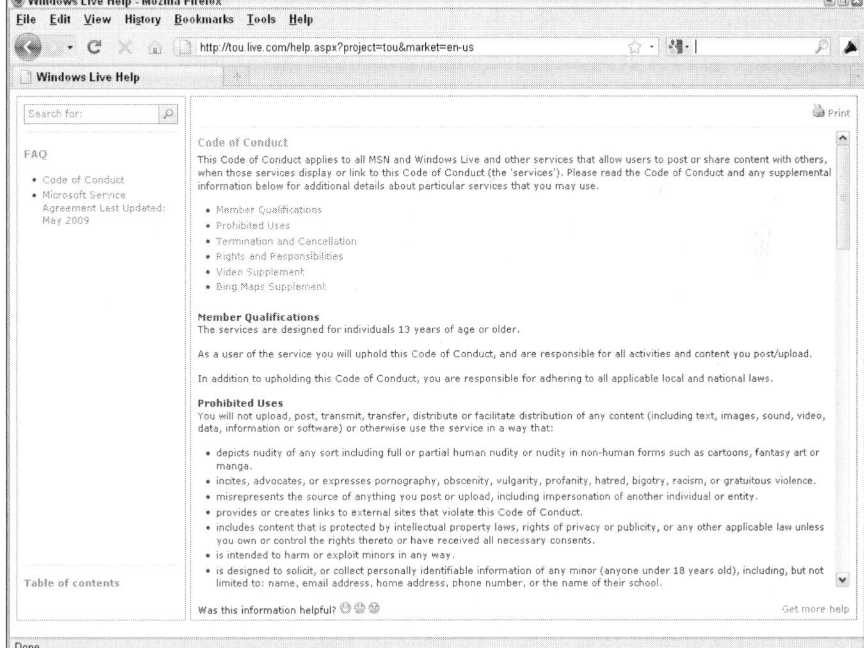

Figure 9-1: Microsoft Windows Live Spaces has a community code of conduct for its system.

Microsoft product screen shot(s) reprinted with permission from Microsoft Corporation

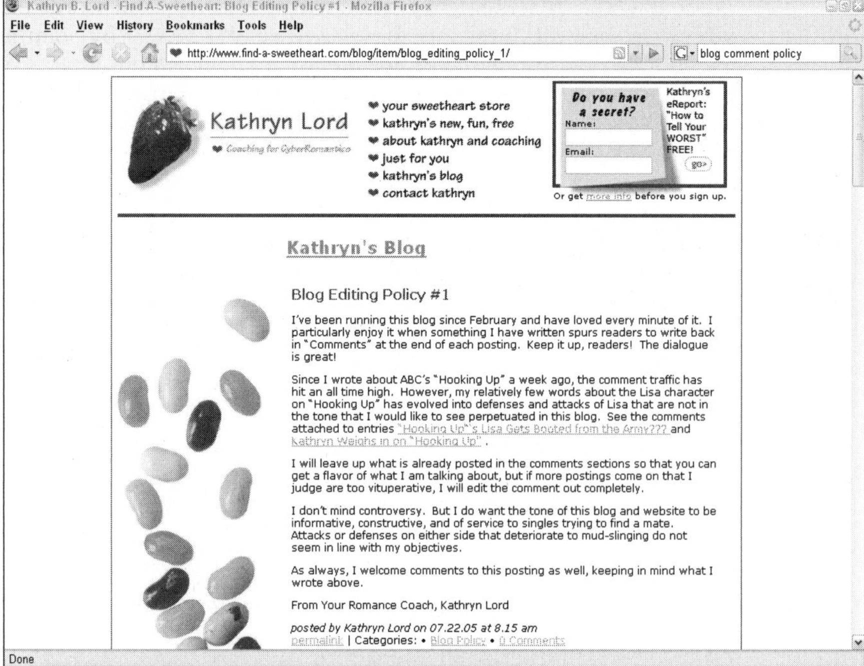

Figure 9-2: Kathryn Lord makes it clear in her blog policy that she maintains the appropriate level of courtesy.

On Greg Mankiw's blog for economics students, he asked his readers to simply treat each other with respect: "Please approach this blog with the civility you would bring to a college seminar. Don't post anything here that you wouldn't say to a fellow seminar participant face to face." You can read Greg's full blog comment policy at `http://gregmankiw.blogspot.com/2006/09/comments-policy.html`. Unfortunately, Greg Mankiw couldn't enforce his comments policy and decided to close comments entirely.

If you're thinking about writing a blog comment policy, take a look at what other bloggers have done. A quick search on Google for **blog comment policy** turns up some well-done policies that might give you ideas. And remember, you can add a blog comment policy at any time and amend your policy as needed.

Editing comments

Sometimes, a reader posts a legitimate comment that you need to alter in some way. For example, you might prefer to remove profanity from otherwise legit comments or edit a long Web link that's breaking a page layout. Whatever the situation, edit a reader's comments delicately.

Some of your readers might react poorly to having their words edited, and of course, the last thing you intend is to insult a reader by pointing out spelling or grammar issues. Use a sensitive hand, but remember that a comment on your blog is as much a part of the conversational give and take as your original blog posts. Not only that, you're also responsible for the words on your blog and may feel that you have a duty to remove hateful or offensive language, especially if young audiences read your blog.

Your blog is your domain, your kingdom, and your place in the world, so your word is final.

Of course, when you do choose to edit a comment, you might want to alert readers that you have done so and why, as I've done in comment #7 on my own blog, shown in Figure 9-3. You may also want to lay out in your blog comment policy circumstances in which you'll edit comments. Both these techniques can head off accusations of censorship.

An edited comment

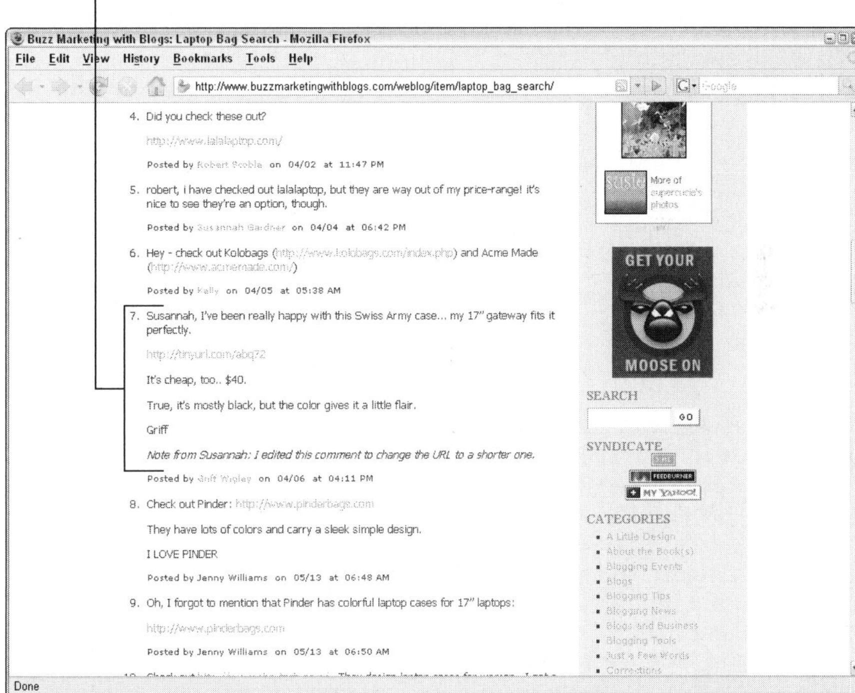

Figure 9-3: If you need to edit comments, let people know that you've done so and why.

Deleting comments

Unfortunately, not all the comments on your blog are fun to read, or are even remarks that should stay on your blog. When it comes right down to it, you control which comments appear on your blog, whether you moderate them ahead of time or afterward. You need to moderate comments because quite a few of your blog's comments probably come from spammers and add nothing to the conversation. But sometimes, you may need to delete comments from real people that are even on topic. Every blogger has to make a choice about what kinds of comments he or she needs to delete.

Bloggers choose to delete comments for these kinds of reasons:

- Comments that are off-topic for the post to which they're attached (a common issue with spam comments).
- Comments that make personal attacks on the blogger or other readers. For example, many bloggers draw the line at comments that contain racial slurs, name-calling, hate language, or speculation about things such as sexual orientation. People who leave these types of comments are often called *trolls.*
- Comments left anonymously or by using a fake name and e-mail address.
- Comments that feature a URL apparently included for marketing purposes.
- Comments that are libelous.
- Comments that are obscene.
- Comments that contain private information (which you don't want to make public).
- Comments that contain plagiarized material.

In blogging terms, a *troll* is an individual who posts irrelevant and often inflammatory things in blog comments. Trolls try to get an emotional response out of people and can be quite disruptive. Most blogs won't see any troll activity, but if you become popular, they will make an appearance from time to time.

Deleting comments is quite a personal decision, one that any good blogger runs into — after all, you want to get people talking, so you need to have opinions that can start dialogue. A milquetoast approach doesn't make an interesting blog, even if it does prevent offensive comments.

Most blog readers can accept that you get to make the decisions about which comments stay and which get the heave-ho on your own blog. Nobody likes to have their comments deleted, however, and readers often criticize bloggers when those bloggers delete comments, especially when the readers don't know why the bloggers deleted those comments. If you find yourself being questioned about deleted comments, you can always write a blog post about how you deal with comments and remind your readers about your blog's comment policy, or refer them to your comment policy if you have one.

Moderating comments

The single best solution for keeping spam off your blog is to read each and every comment left on your blog individually, removing the comments that are spam or inappropriate. Sifting through your blog's comments is called *moderating*. Moderating your blog comments can add overhead to your blogging time, but if you're dedicated to making your blog successful and useful to your readers, it's time well spent.

You have several options for how you manage the time that you spend looking through comment lists, but the method you choose as your primary line of defense depends on how your community grows.

You, your community, your software, or a combination of all three can moderate your blog. Table 9-1 covers the pros and cons of three approaches that you can try. Some bloggers have strong preferences at the outset, but you can experiment with the best setup for your blog and readers.

Table 9-1 Comment Moderation Options

Approach	*Pro*	*Con*
Review all comments *before* they're posted on your blog.	No spam ever appears on your blog unless you choose to allow it.	Comments are delayed before they're posted, making your blog not very spontaneous and rather slow-paced.
Review all comments *after* they're posted on your blog.	Comments appear on your blog more quickly, making conversation quick-paced.	You must review and remove unwanted comments frequently, probably daily.
Ask your readers to notify you of inappropriate comments.	Cuts down on your comment moderation hours by pointing you to problem comments quickly.	Turns your readers into police, a role that they might enjoy too much or not at all, changing the conversational tenor.

(continued)

Table 9-1 *(continued)*

Approach	*Pro*	*Con*
Let software weed out the bad stuff.	Using a combination of blacklists and whitelists (see more on these technologies in the section "Blacklists and whitelists," later in this chapter) means that you don't have to read through a lot of spam yourself.	You need to keep the software up to date because spammers always work out new ways to cheat the system, so budget time for behind-the-scenes technical work; ineffective against personal attacks or flames.

You can most easily maintain your sanity by using a combination of the methods in Table 9-1 to control spam. If your site becomes a popular location for online discussion, experiment with these methods to find one that suits you and your readers, while letting you keep enough time in your schedule for actually writing new blog posts!

Some blogs have communities that build quickly, whereas others take more time. You might need to change your spam prevention methods from time to time in order to take advantage of the community desire to help.

Recognizing Spam Comments

Spam! It's everywhere, lurking in your e-mail inbox, waiting to pounce on an unsuspecting click. It also hangs out on your blog, hiding in the comments — you might never escape it! Fortunately, you can slow the stream of spam messages, and even block most of them from appearing on your blog.

I don't recommend disabling comments just to keep out the spam. Blog comments are crucial for the life and health of your blog; if you want to make your blog more than just another Web site by having real conversations with your readers, you simply can't forego comments. You just have to take the good with the bad. And I won't lie about the bad: Fighting spam can consume valuable time and energy. If you're serious about blogging, you have to do it, no matter how unrewarding it feels. It's like taking out the trash: no fun, but if you don't do it, your house fills with garbage.

Any unwanted message that someone posts in the comment area of your blog is *spam,* especially those messages that include links to fabulous drug cocktails, unbelievable mortgage opportunities, and solutions to certain . . . ahem . . . anatomical size problems (which, naturally, you don't have).

The first time you see a spam comment on your blog, you might not recognize it. Long ago, you could easily pick out the spam posts on blogs: They consisted of incomprehensible text, inappropriate images, and links to pornographic Web sites. But, while the blogs evolved, so did the spammers, and today's spam comments might look like anything from a sincere compliment to a request for more information. Figure 9-4 shows a spam comment that was left on one of my blogs.

You — your brain and eyes — protect your blog from the outside world. If something looks suspicious to you, check it out so that you can protect yourself, your readers, and your search-engine ranking.

Because you're the first line of defense, you need to get a feel for the comments that are legitimately posted on your site. Take some time to see what your community is like. If your blog community needs time to grow, venture out onto other blogs and see what people are saying:

- Look at real comments and see how they're written.
- Get involved and add your own commentary to other blogs. The more experience you have at posting comments, the better you can identify the spam on your site.

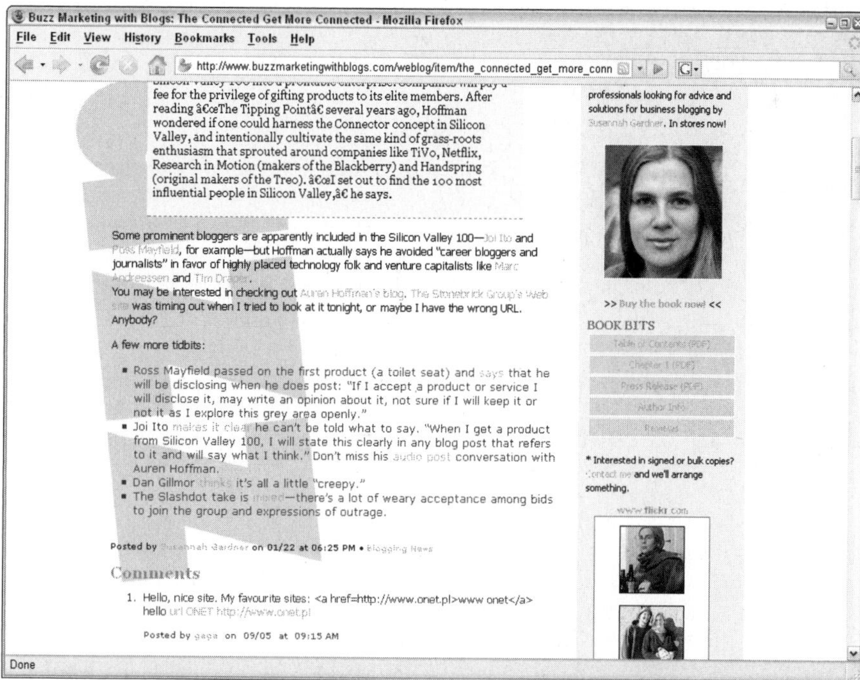

Figure 9-4: A spam comment, disguised as a real comment.

When you take the time to read real comments, you can more easily spot the spam.

Spam has certain styles. Spammers attempt to weasel into your site by looking like they have personal or generally harmless content. Sometimes, you can't tell a legitimate comment that has poor grammar and spelling from a spam comment that has similar attributes. Spammers count on this confusion. You may find sorting the wheat from the chaff a tricky bit of business, but by following a few tips, you can get through the spam onslaught with as little frustration as possible. Examine the following types of comments with skepticism:

- **Personalized and customized messages:** A real human being creates this type of spam, as opposed to an automated bit of programming. Usually a human being, paid by a spam company, visits your blog, reads a few posts and a few comments, and then customizes messages that fit in with the tone and style of the site. Often, the spammers even direct these messages to you by name. You can easily miss these messages when you're watching for spam comments.

  If the link that's included with a comment isn't related to the subject of the comment or the topics on your blog, the comment is probably a fake, no matter how on-topic it might seem.
- **Generic commentary or questions:** The generic message spam either requests that you do something or makes a very nonspecific remark. You often see comments such as, `You've got the same name as I do`, `Have you seen the new video?`, `Check out my blog?`, `Need you to do something for me`, or `Your blog is broken you need to see this.`
- **Flattery:** Finally, spammers use flattery. Spammers may send comments such as `Your blog is awesome` or `I like your blog, click to read mine`. As a general rule, regard these kinds of brief praise with suspicion (well, unless your blog really is awesome, of course!). Real fans usually elaborate more about what they like about your writing.

In general, a spam comment includes a link, usually to an advertising Web site or a site designed to look like a blog. The spammers hope that you or your blog visitors click the link, giving those spammers a traffic boost and potentially allowing them to collect a fee based on the number of times users visit the site or click a link. Look closely at comments that include links.

Many comment spammers are annoyingly ingenious about finding ways to disguise their messages. (Some aren't — you can easily recognize as spam the comments about Viagra or the ones that contain gibberish.) But the generic nature of comments gives them away. Keep your wits about you so that you can identify new trends and formats in comment spam techniques when they appear. The techniques described in this chapter can help you prevent or remove spam, but the human brain is endlessly inventive, which keeps the spammers a step ahead of any software solution to the problem.

Don't just leave comment spam on your blog and let your readers sort through the mess. Spam attracts spam: If you don't remove these kinds of comments, you actually end up with more spam on your site. And, when your readers click the spam links, spammers realize that you're not tending your blog, so they flock to it. Delete your spam. Your readers will thank you.

Unfortunately, spam isn't the only unwanted comment material you might deal with. Some of your legitimate commenters may use language that you don't want on your blog or post personal, offensive *flames* (or attacks) aimed at you or other readers. You're just as entitled to remove this kind of comment as you are to remove spam. In most cases, you can use the techniques described in the following section to handle flames and spam comments alike.

Understanding why spam exists

Junk snail mail, e-mail spam, and blog spam all exist for the same reason: because someone, somewhere, makes money on them. You may find this fact hard to believe if you just look at spam comments — a lot of them don't really make much sense, much less look like something you might click.

But spam comments aren't necessarily designed to make you or your readers click them. Blog spammers usually just want to raise the search engine profile of a site that they link to in their comments. Search engines use secret formulas to determine the result listings that you see when you do a search. The formula works to determine and display the most relevant results — the ones that best match your search terms — at the top of the list. One of the ingredients in this secret formula is the number of Web sites that link to a site, and another ingredient is the words used for that link.

So, when you write a blog post about a company that has a product you love and link to the company, you're really doing it two favors: You've praised it publicly, and you've given it a little boost in the search engine rankings, which helps it come up a little higher the next time someone searches for the product you reviewed. Aren't you nice? Now imagine that ten more customers do the same thing on their blogs. The company gets a lot of search engine love for all those different links.

Spammers are trying to scam this process by creating dozens, even hundreds, of links from many different Web pages to the Web site that they're attempting to boost in the search engine rankings. When a site appears high in the search engine rankings, you know what happens: More people visit it more often.

Ultimately, comment spam might simply want to get people to visit a particular Web site, but it takes a fairly indirect path to that result. After someone opens the Web site, the unfortunate visitor might get a chance to buy a product, click a link, provide information that he or she shouldn't about bank accounts, or view a page that has ads on it. And that's where the spammers make profit.

Don't avoid blogging just because of the amount of spam you're bound to get. After all, junk messages aren't anything new. You see spam in your e-mail all the time; heck, you even see it in your snail mail box, and you probably aren't about to stop getting mail delivered, right?

Fighting Spam with Software

Spam is a pain. But consider how much spam you really have to deal with: Do you get three spam messages every few weeks, or are you getting 500 an hour? If you're receiving only a few every month, you might not need to install any software because you can moderate the few problem comments yourself pretty easily. If your blog get dozens of comments every day, however, spam fighting can take up a lot of your time. The following sections explore some of the many blog software solutions available to make this task a little faster and easier.

Protecting your comment form

The tools described in the following sections are designed to give spammers trouble filling out the comment form on your blog. These tools try to prevent the spam from ever reaching your blog so that you don't need to deal with reading and deleting it.

These tools do that job fairly well, but they also present something of a barrier to people who want to leave a legitimate comment; remember, you want to cut down on spam, not real comments! Keep your audience's needs and abilities in mind when you implement any spam-fighting tools.

CAPTCHAs

A *CAPTCHA* (an acronym for something really long and boring) is a challenge-response test, meaning it's a question that your reader must answer correctly in order to post a comment. On a blog, CAPTCHAs are most commonly implemented in such a way that humans can complete them but computers can't. A CAPTCHA on the World Hum travel site (`www.worldhum.com`) requires the would-be commenter to duplicate the letters and numbers shown in an image in order to submit a comment, as shown in Figure 9-5.

CAPTCHAs were created to stop spammers from adding comments to blogs by using automated scripts that try to fill out any Web form that they find, especially blog comment forms. But spammers are inventive: Some blog comment scripts can now recognize letters and numbers in an image, so many sites that use CAPTCHAs distort the text by stretching it, or layering it with graphic random graphic elements.

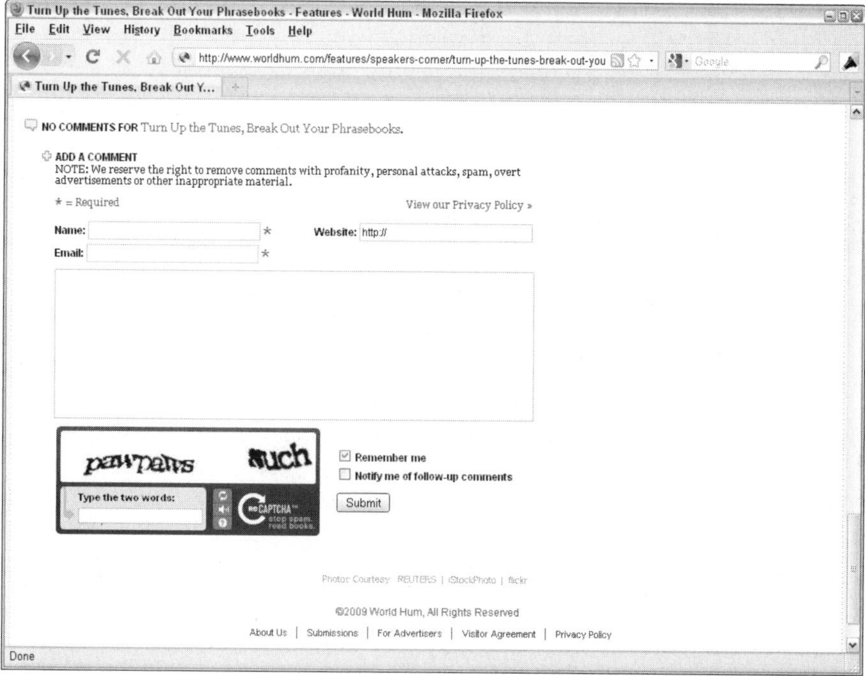

Figure 9-5: On World Hum, the visual CAPTCHA is designed to let humans leave comments and block spam scripts.

Other sites use CAPTCHA questions that are simple for humans to answer, such as trivia or mathematical questions. For example, "What color is a red balloon?" These kinds of CAPTCHAs are new and have yet to prove their effectiveness, but you might want to check into them and see for yourself how they work.

Your blog software may have CAPTCHA technology built in, or you might be able to add one by using a plug-in. Check your blog software's documentation and support tools for suggestions on installing and configuring a CAPTCHA system.

User registration

Registration is a popular option with larger communities, especially online forums. The community requests or even requires that users who want to leave comments sign up for a user account. These accounts are typically free, but to complete the registration process, you must provide a name and valid e-mail address, thereby cutting down on the number of spam scripts that can create an account and therefore post comments. Sites that require registration actually prevent anyone who isn't registered from leaving a comment; sites that simply request registration reward registering by recognizing members or by marking a registered user's comments in some highlighted way.

This setup lets you keep a record of everything that a particular poster adds to the system, easily identifying your most frequent contributors and visitors. Also, if a poster gets out of hand, or an automated spam system acquires an account and posts by using that username, you can simply close the account and stop the poster from posting again by using that account.

Blog software is increasingly offering registration, so be sure to check your documentation. If your software doesn't offer registration, look for a plug-in that does.

Screening for spam

Software that filters the incoming comments in various ways can provide a defense against spammers by identifying and removing comments that look like spam. These filters give a blogger great tools: They run all hours of the day and they don't require any effort on your part. But an automated process is never as smart as a human, so you might occasionally lose a valid comment if you use a filtering system.

A third-party software solution called Automattic Akismet (see the sidebar "Akismet," in this chapter) is the clear leader when it comes to spam filtering, though many blogging software applications have added their own internal tools, as well. Check to see whether your blog software has any of these technologies in place for you to use — you can probably find some of them available. If you don't, check `http://akismet.com/development` to see whether you can add Akismet to your blog.

Keyword filtering

Keyword filters can help you identify incoming comment spam. This kind of filtering is probably the oldest type of protection for blog comments and might not work all the time because spammers have become much smarter since this technology was first used. Spam filtering usually works by comparing incoming comments against lists of words and/or phrases associated with spam. Matches indicate spam, and the filter yanks those comments.

Keyword filters are typically updated frequently to keep up with the ploys that spammers use. Some of these lists contain Web addresses and other computer identification information, as well as keywords. Users also can submit and maintain their own lists in case custom spelling or other methods of tricking the anti-spam system come into use (for example, using `V1agra`, rather than `Viagra`).

Several services over the years have allowed different blog tools and platforms to take advantage of a central keyword listing. These lists are maintained and updated by a third-party company. Today's most popular anti-spam system, Akismet (see the sidebar "Akismet," in this chapter), falls into this category.

One problem with this kind of filter system is that some spammers leave nice messages that include bad links. These messages get past the filter because they aren't offensive and don't violate any rule that you have.

Blacklists and whitelists

A blog *blacklist* is a method of keeping spam off your Web site by preventing certain known spam systems from accessing your comment system or your Web site as a whole. By specifically identifying spammers from certain addresses, countries, or computers, or by using certain URLs, you can block those individual spammers, keeping your blog much safer.

Most blogging software comes with a blacklist system built in or a system that you can easily add by using a plug-in or third-party solution. Consult your blog software documentation to be sure that you understand how to keep your blacklist up to date and how you can contribute to the blacklist.

Whitelists perform the opposite action of a blacklist by specifically permitting certain visitors or types of visitors. A *whitelist* is a preselected list of visitors whom you know won't post spam on your blog. Bloggers use a whitelist in conjunction with a blacklist. Whitelists can allow you to accept comments from visitors who have been misidentified as spammers in the past. Essentially, you're making your blog accessible to certain people or computer networks. If you want to guarantee that your mother, for instance, can always post to your blog — or even if you want to set it up so that she doesn't have to comply with a CAPTCHA or other anti-spam techniques — add her to the whitelist so that she can post with impunity. Whitelists are uncommon, so if your blogging software doesn't offer this functionality, you probably can't find a good third-party solution.

IP banning

Similar to blacklists, IP banning prevents certain IP addresses or a range of IP networks from accessing your Web site. IP banning is probably the oldest method of protecting blogs.

An IP (Internet Protocol) address is a series of numbers that identifies a network, a computer, or any networked electronic device within a computer network. Devices such as printers, fax machines, desktop and laptop computers, and some telephones can have their own IP addresses.

Many blog software solutions offer lists of banned IP addresses that they collect from other users of the same software who have identified spammers, and you can automatically update your own list to prevent those spammers from posting to your site.

A potential problem with banning networks or certain IP addresses is that the offending poster may connect via a different IP address the next time that he or she posts something. Banning by IP address can work for known spam companies, but it's highly fallible because so many computers regularly obtain new IP addresses through their Internet Service Provider (ISP). IP banning can also affect people whom you don't actually want to block. For instance, if you block a computer on a particular network, others who use the same network but are blameless might end up using the offending IP address at some point and be blocked. Many bloggers discount IP banning, saying that it has no real usefulness in today's mobile world.

Dealing with Coverage on Other Blogs

You can't do much about negative blog posts or comments about you on other blogs, although many a blogger has stayed awake all night worrying. (It doesn't seem to help.) You can easily post a comment that responds, but you may not want to respond when you're feeling angry and emotional because you may post something you would regret.

You're taking part in a public conversation, and free speech means that people can openly express their opinions about you, your blog, your opinions, your business — you name it. You can find negative criticism hard to take, especially when you feel it's unjustified. Before you send off an angry e-mail or post a vicious comment, sit back and take a little time to consider your options. If you can be objective, try to understand exactly what the other person is criticizing and whether the critic has a point.

Here are a few ways that you can handle a case in which another blogger posts a negative statement about you or your blog:

- Point to the negative coverage on your own blog and get some other opinions on the issue without taking a position yourself.
- Ignore the post and comment about it only when someone specifically requests your opinion.
- Post respectful comments on the blog in question and constructively add to the conversation there.
- Counter the criticism, in a respectful manner, on your own blog.

Akismet

One anti-spam service is worth a special mention: Automattic Akismet (`www.akismet.com`). The Akismet service has been around since the latter half of 2005, and it's one of the best spam-filtering systems in the world. Plus, it's very easy to use. While you moderate your comments, a simple series of links and buttons helps you make quick choices about good and bad comments.

Akismet works by running your comments through a central data center. The Akismet system runs a number of tests each time a user submits a comment, and if the comment passes all the tests, Akismet automatically posts the comment to your site. It holds comments that fail the tests in a queue for your review so that you can identify any valid comments and post them. (Or you can just delete them all without going through them.)

The software updates itself and maintains the blacklist that it uses, so after you install it on your blog, you don't have to do anything to keep it up and running. Akismet is free for personal use but requires a monthly fee for commercial use. Also, some deals are available for non-profit organizations.

Whichever path you choose, make sure that you deal with the comment in a respectful manner. You can very easily escalate a conflict online because you don't have to deal with people face to face. The anonymous feeling people get when they're on the Internet can lead them to behave in ways that they wouldn't in person. Try to take the high road as much as possible, if only because an uninvolved reader is more likely to see you as right if you handle things in a better way than your critic.

In some cases, criticism of an individual or business on a blog has led to legal ramifications, from copyright violation to libel. If you feel that the negative comments about you online might fall into the legal realm, consult with a lawyer about the best course of action.

You might not be the only target of criticism — some bloggers use their blogs as a way to publish attacks on everyone, from public figures to private individuals. Some other bloggers might even attack your readers and ignore you. Deal with these kinds of situations quickly and with as much care as you can provide. Think of yourself as the referee in a situation that involves personal attacks from one member of your audience to another, and look for ways to defuse the situation and prevent future occurrences.

Part IV
Going Beyond Words

"As a blog designer I never thought I'd say this, but I don't think your blog has enough bells and whistles."

In this part . . .

If you've mastered the basics, you can have some fun! In this part, you can try some of the truly cutting-edge tricks being used by successful bloggers. They say a picture is worth a thousand words, so photo blogs are going to repay your efforts in a big way. In Chapter 10, you find out how to make the most of photos and other graphics in your blog. Or, say it by simply speaking, as I describe in Chapter 11's tour of the world of podcasting. I know you, though. You're not satisfied with words and pictures — unless they are moving! Chapter 12 tackles the challenging world of video blogging, from hardware to software, and everything in between.

Chapter 10

Working with Photos

In This Chapter

- Getting set up with a digital camera and editing software
- Making or collecting images to use on your blog
- Using Picasa to edit your photos
- Putting Flickr photos into your blog posts

It's a fact: People love photos! You can increase your readership and decrease your writing time by including photos in your blog posts or putting photo badges (code you can place on your blog that shows off your photos) into your sidebar. Many bloggers have discovered that including a photo in a blog post, even if the photo is only tangentially related to the post, ensures that more people read the post than read entries without photos.

If you already have a digital camera and photo-editing software, you have the tools at hand to start putting photos into your blog quickly. But if you're new to photography, this chapter also includes information about choosing a digital camera or software.

Putting graphics on the Web isn't incredibly hard to do, and today's wonderful photo-sharing Web sites make posting photos online both quick and easy. In fact, if you already have a Flickr account that you use to share your digital photos, you can jump right to the section "Inserting Photos into Blog Posts with Flickr," later in this chapter — you'll be pleased as punch to find out how easily you can do it.

Getting Equipped

Today, digital cameras are quite inexpensive, and using one can expedite the process of putting your photos online. Most digital cameras can take photographs in file formats that you can use on the Web with no further processing, but you can also pick up software that helps you convert your photos to the right format quite quickly. Some cameras shoot photos in particular formats, some of which are not Web-compatible, so you have to convert them into Web-friendly formats like JPG and GIF. (I cover the more nitty gritty details of Web-compatible file formats and photo editing in the section "Editing Photos," later in this chapter; if you're in the market for a camera, make sure that you know in what format or formats the camera captures pictures.)

The ingredients to getting photos onto your Web site are

- A camera, preferably a digital camera
- A way to get your photos from your camera onto your computer, such as a USB cable or scanner
- Image-editing software that can help you crop, resize, and touch up your photos
- A photo-sharing service or blog software that has file-upload tools

The following sections cover these items in detail.

Picking a digital camera

Digital cameras come in all kinds of price ranges and with tons of different features. When you take a photograph, the image is saved on a storage card or small hard drive, and many cameras have a nice preview screen that lets you see the results of your photography right away.

When you need your photos, you can remove the storage card from your camera, and then insert it into the card reader hooked to your computer, or even into a printer. You may want to have a removable storage card if you plan to take a lot of pictures because you can easily carry several cards with you, switching them out when you fill one. Some cameras can also connect directly to your computer.

Digital cameras usually come with several quality settings that determine the resolution of your image and the sizes that look good when you print your photograph. If you choose higher-quality settings, you can fit fewer images on your storage card, but the resulting files look better, print more sharply, and can be resized more easily than lower-quality images.

Today, even relatively inexpensive digital cameras can take high-quality images suitable for use in almost any medium, so the real challenge is to pick a camera that suits your picture-taking style.

Be realistic about how you plan to use the camera and how comfortable you are with it when you look at the options:

- **Digital SLRs:** If you're a professional photographer or a dedicated amateur, you likely want a high-end dSLR camera. But these cameras are quite large, which makes them awkward to carry and use unobtrusively on a day-to-day basis.
- **Low-end point-and-shoots:** If you're a photography amateur, super lightweight cameras can get a lot of admiring glances. But they might lack important features, and their tiny size might also make them hard to use and hold steady.
- **Mid-range:** If you're not a professional photographer but want more than just the basics that low-end cameras provide, look for a camera in the midprice range. These cameras come in a range of styles and sizes, and with a wide range of features designed for use by completely inexperienced to professional photographers.
- **Mobile cameras (phone cameras):** These days, most phones come with cameras built-in — convenient, but picture quality from camera phones can be quite low.

Start your search by visiting CNET (`www.cnet.com`) and looking at the product reviews written by CNET editors and readers. Reading through the reviews can really help you understand the options and features, and it can give you a feel for the price ranges that include the feature package you want.

With some CNET recommendations in mind, head for a camera or good electronics store to test-drive some cameras. You need to feel physically comfortable handling and using any camera that you purchase, regardless of how well it was reviewed online.

Another Web site I thought I should mention is DPReview (`www.dpreview.com`), which highlights a collection of digital cameras with lots of detail about different brands and models. This site shows example photos from most of the cameras along with reviews from readers.

If you're more comfortable using a film camera, rather than a digital one, you're in luck! You can still use film photos by scanning the photos to create a digital file. Or ask your film processing shop to provide you with a CD of your photographs along with prints.

Choosing photo-editing software

You need to find a program to help you edit and organize your photos. You have loads of options, at all pricing levels. In fact, your computer might have come packaged with image-editing software, or the digital camera that you purchase might include software.

When you're looking for image-editing software with the ultimate goal of getting your images online, consider these criteria:

- **File formats:** You need to be able to create images in the right format for display on the Web. These formats are JPG, GIF, and PNG. These formats also allow you compress the file size of your images for the Web.
- **Standard editing tools:** At a minimum, you need image-editing software that allows you to resize, crop, rotate, and adjust brightness and contrast in your photos. These tools should be quick and easy to use.
- **Organizing tools:** Look for software that helps you keep track of your images by using thumbnail previews, naming schemes, and search, especially if you take a lot of photos.
- **Photo sharing:** You don't need a program that integrates with the blogging tool that you use or with a photo-sharing service such as Flickr, but it can speed up the time it takes to post a photo online. I discuss inserting photos with Flickr in the section "Inserting Photos into Blog Posts with Flickr," later in this chapter.

With these ideas in mind, don't forget to think about whether you want an image editor that can do more than just get photos into shape for online publication. If you plan to print photographs, be sure you look for photo-editing software that has good tools for printing.

I cover two software programs (Picasa and iPhoto) in the following sections. Other image-editing programs also work well for touching up and formatting photographs:

- **Adobe Photoshop Elements:** Around $100; version 8 supports Windows and Mac (previous versions support only Windows); `www.adobe.com/products/photoshopelwin`. This program is suitable for users who have the patience to figure out how to use a full-featured program but don't need professional features, such as the ability to produce color separations for high-end professional printers. Photoshop Elements is a great compromise between basic and high-end software.
- **Adobe Photoshop Lightroom:** $299; Mac and Windows; `www.adobe.com/products/photoshoplightroom`. This software is intended specifically for photography, and serious amateur photographers and professionals find this program valuable for managing large collections of photographs.
- **Adobe Photoshop:** $699; Mac and Windows; `www.adobe.com/products/photoshop`. For anyone who isn't a designer or very serious photographer, Adobe Photoshop can be overkill. But this program can really make your

photos look great if you are willing to pay the premium price. Advanced editing tools and more control over the quality of the images you are utilizing for your blog puts this package heads and shoulders above Adobe Elements' more basic toolset.

- **Adobe Fireworks:** $299; Mac and Windows; `www.adobe.com/products/fireworks`. Although you can use Fireworks to process photos, it's really intended to be a Web graphics production tool. If you have it already, go ahead and use it, but if you're looking over your options, I recommend some of the other products on this list for photo editing.

Picasa

`http://picasa.google.com`

Picasa, from Google, is priced competitively (it's free) and works especially well for photographers who want to put photos online. It has highly developed organizational tools, allowing you to do everything from automatically importing and naming photos from your camera when you hook it up to your computer, to quickly labeling and tagging your photos, to rating good photos, to creating photo albums.

Picasa has good editing tools, but they sacrifice some fine control in favor of being easy to use. You can crop, straighten horizons, fix red-eye issues, adjust color and contrast, and make other edits to your photos easily.

However, the photo-sharing tools really set Picasa apart. You can use tools to e-mail photos, get them onto the Web, create online slideshows, and put photo collections onto other devices. You can also print photos quite easily.

Picasa (shown in Figure 10-1) is available for Windows, Mac OS X, and Linux.

In the section "Editing Photos," later in this chapter, I walk you through using simple editing tools in Picasa.

iPhoto

`www.apple.com/ilife/iphoto`

If you're a Mac user, you have a great image-editing program in Apple's iPhoto (see Figure 10-2). It gives you all the basic tools for cropping, straightening, adjusting color and brightness, and resizing. Plus, you can dabble with fun effects, and increase or decrease highlights and shadows in your photos.

iPhoto also comes with excellent organizing tools: You can categorize, tag, caption, and title your photos quickly and easily, and the simple search interface helps you find old photos.

Figure 10-1: Quickly import, edit, and share photos by using Picasa.

Figure 10-2: iPhoto is Apple's solution to image editing and organization tools.

If you don't want to publish photos only to your own blog, use iPhoto to publish to the MobileMe Web service, put up slideshows and albums, and share your photos with groups of friends and family.

You can also use iPhoto to print a real photo album, calendar, cards, and individual prints. iPhoto frequently comes packaged on new Macintosh computers, but if you don't have it, head to the Apple Store (`http://store.apple.com`) and buy a copy of iLife, which includes iPhoto and other digital applications.

Choosing a photo-sharing tool

When you're ready to put your photos online, regardless of whether you ultimately want to include images on your blog, you have plenty of options. Photo-sharing Web sites have become full-fledged members of the Web 2.0 movement, offering friend lists, tagging, and other sophisticated tools.

The media darling of photo-sharing sites is definitely Flickr (`www.flickr.com`). For avid photographers, Flickr has nearly replaced the need to have a blog at all because many of the best blogging tools are integrated into the Flickr service.

On Flickr, you can

- Create a list of friends whose photos you want to follow.
- Upload and organize photos by using *tags* (keywords), sets, and collections.
- Start groups around a visual theme and add your photos to other groups.
- Set privacy controls to dictate who can see your photos.
- Use your photos to create books, prints, calendars, business cards, DVDs, and stamps.
- Post photos in your account and receive comments (see Figure 10-3).
- Create slideshows of your photos.
- Browse other members' photos and leave comments.

Basic Flickr accounts are free for 100MB worth of photos each month — you can display only your most recent 200 photos, though. Pro accounts cost $24.95 a year and receive unlimited uploading and image display.

In the section "Inserting Photos into Blog Posts with Flickr," later in this chapter, I show you how to put Flickr to work for you when you want to add images to blog posts.

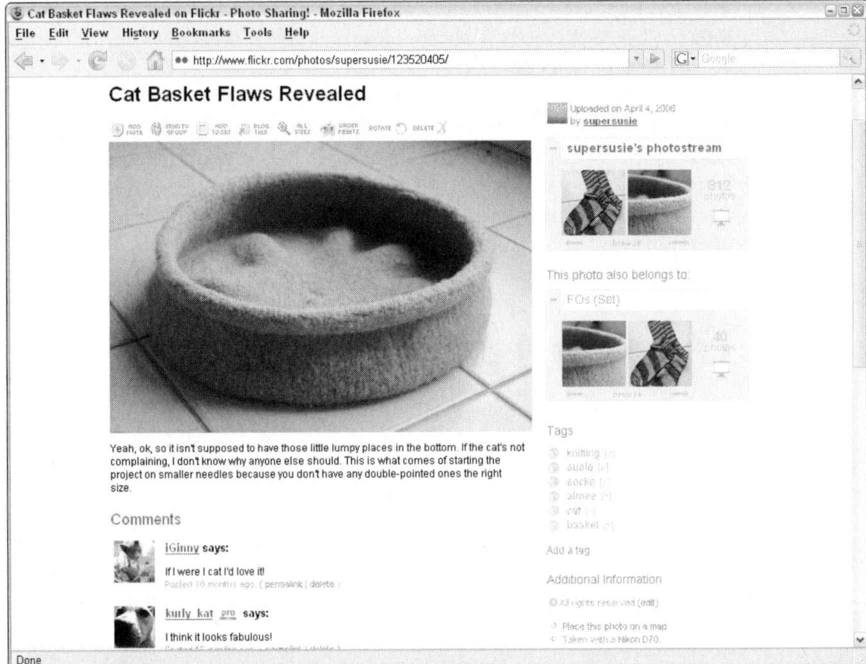

Figure 10-3: When you post photos on Flickr, your friends and other Flickr members can leave comments for you.

Flickr isn't alone in offering photo sharing online; it just happens to be my favorite. You can also upload your photos to Photobucket (`www.photobucket.com`), Shutterfly (`www.shutterfly.com`), SmugMug (`www.smugmug.com`), Snapfish (`www.snapfish.com`), and Webshots (`www.webshots.com`), among others.

Whatever service you choose, look for tools that can make your life easier when it comes to putting your photos on your blog. For example, look for services that

- Allow you to create a photo *badge* (a bit of code that displays your photos) to put in your blog's sidebar. I talk more about using Flickr for this purpose in Chapter 20.
- Let you post a photo to your blog or give you code to put the photo in your blog post.

Choosing Visuals for Your Blog

Far be it from me to tell you how to take photographs — I'm a rank amateur when it comes to photography. But I can give you tips on taking photos that you can use for a new blog post, which I do in the following sections.

Taking photos

Readers respond well to photos: Visitors are more likely to read posts that have photos than those that don't. And, most of the time, your photos and images don't have to have a strong relationship to what you're blogging about. In fact, they can go off on a tangential topic or idea.

You can't always throw unrelated images onto your blog, though. After all, if you're blogging about your new mobile phone, go with a picture of that phone. And if you're talking about your recent trip to Peru — well, you need some pictures from your trip. But if you're just pontificating or talking about a favorite book, think about adding a photograph as more of an accessory.

Bloggers often add pictures to posts that just need a little zing, as Degan Beley does in her blog (`www.ethniceats.ca`) in the post shown in Figure 10-4. When she writes food and restaurant reviews, Degan always tries to include a photo of where she's been and what she's eaten as an illustration for her text descriptions.

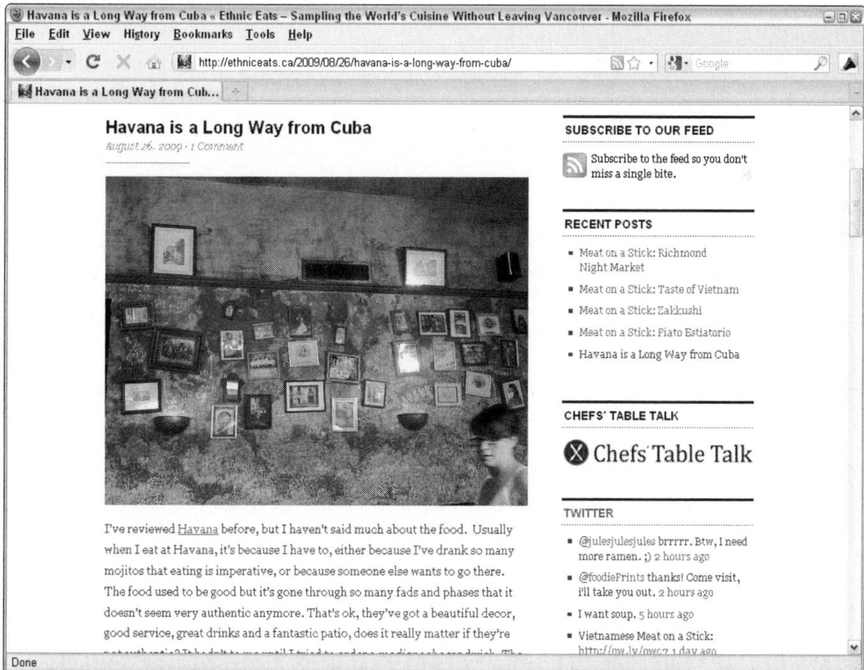

Figure 10-4: Photos are an invaluable addition to a food blog.

If you want to take photographs to put on your blog, keep your eyes open all the time for visuals that inspire or interest you. You don't have to be a rocket scientist to find good picture subjects, but you do need to be thinking about your blog and your camera more often than you might normally. In fact, some bloggers find that carrying a camera with them actually helps them find things to blog about and illustrate regular blog posts.

Here are a few tips for taking photos for your blog:

- Carry your camera with you when you leave the house, even if you're just running down to the grocery store.
- Keep fresh batteries in your camera so that when you need to use it, it isn't dead. If possible, keep a second set of batteries in your camera pouch. (By the way, digital cameras quickly suck up battery juice, so you really should buy rechargeable batteries, reducing the impact on both your pocketbook and the environment.)
- Don't worry too much about taking the perfect picture. Just take the picture!
- Take photos of the people you meet and talk to, and your friends. Be sure to ask them whether you can use their photo on your blog. Then, when you blog about going to a movie with Sam, you have a photo of Sam to include.

Using art from other sources

One nice thing about the Web: You can find tons and tons of photos, images, graphics, and visuals out there to inspire you. Some bloggers have taken advantage of this vast offering by including some of those great visuals in their blog posts. Photos attract readers' attention better than a few paragraphs of text. You may decide to use photos on your blog, as long as you have the rights to republish those images.

Here are some tips when you need images other than your own:

- **Checking the public domain:** Some materials are designated *public domain* works, which means anyone can use them for any purpose, although you must still give the author credit. If you're interested in featuring public-domain and licensed images on your blog, do a search for **public domain photos** on your favorite search engine. You can investigate a number of good resources.

  In the United States, anything published before 1923 is considered public domain, but other countries don't necessarily have the same policy.
- **Searching through Creative Commons:** By using the Creative Commons licensing tool, you can look for works that authors have licensed for republication. To find additional works that you can use, visit `http://search.creativecommons.org` and search by using keywords that

describe the material you're looking for. (Creative Commons licenses allow the author of a blog to make known their copyright wishes for the copying of their blog content.)

- **Asking for permission:** If you see something that you like and want to use, but it's protected by full copyright, consider just asking whether you can use it. Many photographers, especially those who don't make a living selling their work, are willing to let you use their work, especially if you give them credit!

Many of the photos on the Flickr photo-sharing site (`www.flickr.com`) have been licensed for use on other Web sites and blogs. When you're looking at a photo on Flickr, check the copyright information on the right side of the page.

Editing Photos

As long as you have the rights to do so, you can edit any photo. In general, you can do what you like to photos that you acquire from a public domain Web site or a picture that you take yourself. Photos that you obtain permission to use, or use under a special license, may have restrictions when it comes to making edits, so be sure you understand what you're allowed to do. In the following sections, I show you how to do some of the most common photo-editing tasks by using Picasa.

Most of the edits that you want to make most frequently include resizing, cropping, adjusting lighting and contrast, and adjusting the color of a photo. For each of the following tasks, you should have Picasa running and have a photo available to edit.

When you edit a photo in Picasa, it doesn't save any changes until you choose File⇨Save. At the same time that it saves the changes, Picasa creates a copy of the original image, so if you ever need to start fresh, you can.

Getting photos into Picasa

Before you can edit a photo, you need to get it into Picasa. Follow these steps:

1. **With Picasa installed on your computer, connect your camera to your computer.**

   You can also put your camera's storage card into a card reader or printer, if that's how you usually move photos from your camera to your computer.

   Windows displays a pop-up window, asking what program you want to use.

2. **Select Picasa from the available programs and click OK.**

   Photos begin to load in Picasa's Import Tray.

3. **Click Import All to bring the photos into Picasa.**

   The Finish Importing pop-up window opens.

4. **Create or select a folder for the photos.**

   You can use the Browse button to set a location where you want to save the photos. The default location is the My Pictures folder.

   You can also add where and when you took the photos, as well as give them a description, but this information is optional.

5. **Click Finish.**

   Picasa finishes importing the photos and returns you to the photo Library.

Cropping a photo

Cropping a photo allows you to remove unneeded or unattractive parts of an image. For example, if you take a picture of a group of friends and then want to include a photo of just one of the individuals in your blog post, you can crop out the other people in the image.

To crop a photo that you've imported into Picasa, follow these steps:

1. **Open Picasa and, in the Picasa Library, double-click the photo that you want to edit.**

   The Editing screen opens.

2. **Click the Crop button at the top of the Basic Fixes tab.**

3. **Select whether you want to crop to a preset size or crop manually.**

   If you're cropping to a preset size, simply select the size that you want to use from the menu.

4. **Use your mouse to click and drag over the area that you want to retain in your photo, as shown in Figure 10-5.**

   While you click and drag, the area that will be cropped out of your photo appears slightly grayed out, leaving the portion that will be retained at the original brightness.

   If you want to start over, click Reset to remove the cropping box that you created. If you don't want to crop after all, click the Cancel button to exit the Crop tool.

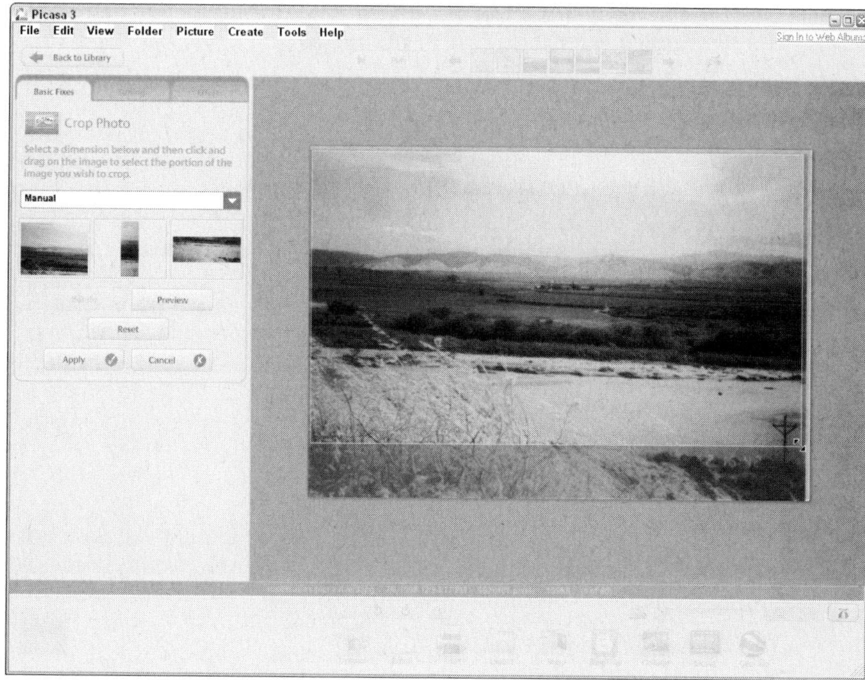

Figure 10-5: Cropping manually lets you choose a specific area that you want to keep in your photo.

5. **Click the Preview button and check out how the cropped photo will look.**
6. **Click the Apply button to crop your photo.**

   Picasa displays the cropped photo.

Adjusting brightness and contrast

Sometimes, despite your best efforts, photos end up looking too dark or too light. By using photo-editing software such Picasa, you get a second chance because you can make adjustments to brightness and contrast.

To adjust the brightness and contrast, follow these steps:

1. **Open Picasa and, in the Library, double-click the photo that you want to edit.**

   The Editing screen opens.
2. **Click the Tuning tab on the left side of the application.**

3. **On the Tuning tab, click and drag the slider bar below Highlights to adjust the brightness of the image.**

   Picasa adjusts the image being displayed while you move the bar.

   If you're lightening the photo, watch the brightest parts of your photo to make sure that they don't get too bright, losing information you want in the photo. If you're bringing down lightness, watch the darker areas of your photo so that you don't end up with too much black in your photo. Let your eyes be the judge of a well-adjusted image.

You can have Picasa make an educated guess about the brightness settings that you need by clicking the Auto Contrast button in the Basic Fixes tab. Click the Undo Auto Contrast button if you don't like the results.

Adjusting color

Color in photos frequently needs a little adjusting. I've taken too many greenish photos in fluorescent lights! With a little help from photo-editing software such Picasa, I can turn my friends' skin back to their normal colors.

To adjust the color of a photo, follow these steps:

1. **Open Picasa and, in the Library, double-click the photo that you want to edit.**

   The Editing screen opens.

2. **Click the Tuning tab on the left side of the application.**
3. **On the Tuning tab, click and drag the slider bar below Color Temperature to adjust the color tone of the picture.**

   Color can be tricky to adjust. As a good rule, look for an element in the photograph that you know should be a particular color, and then adjust the overall color to make that element look right. Then, look at the overall picture and adjust, if necessary. Elements that you can use for the purpose include eye color, skin color, sky, and other consistent elements.

You can have Picasa make an educated guess about the color settings that you need by clicking the Auto Color button in the Basic Fixes tab. Click the Undo Auto Color button if you don't like the results.

Optimizing a photo for the Web

Digital cameras commonly store photos as high-resolution files suitable for print, but that high-resolution is more than you need for display on a blog or Web site. And you probably don't want to make your blog visitors download a great big image when they don't need to. Usually, you compress the file size of your image when you plan to put it on your blog.

If you plan to upload your image to Flickr, don't worry about compressing the image when you export. Flickr can handle large files and can resize the photo for you.

You may also need to change the image's dimensions in order to fit it into your blog layout, or even create a thumbnail version.

In Picasa, compressing — also called setting the image quality — and resizing a photo actually occur when you export the image, so you don't need to deal with these issues until after you do all your other edits. When you export, you're creating a file that you can upload to your blog, so don't skip this step!

To resize and export an image, select the photo in Picasa that you want to export and follow these steps:

1. **Click the Export button at the bottom of the Picasa window.**

   The Export to Folder dialog box opens, as shown in Figure 10-6.

2. **Click the Browse button and select the location on your computer where you want to save the file that you're exporting.**

3. **To resize your image, click the Resize To radio button below Image Size Options and enter a pixel width that you want to use for your new image in the text box below Resize To.**

   You may need to experiment to find the right pixel width for your particular blog design, but a good rule is to choose a pixel width of 400 pixels because many blog templates tend to hover around this width.

   You can also use the slider bar to the right of the pixel text box to change the width.

4. **Select an Image Quality setting from the Image Quality drop-down list.**

   For Web graphics, Normal is a good setting to choose because it has a good balance between image size and file size.

5. **Click OK.**

   Picasa exports your image to the folder you chose in Step 2.

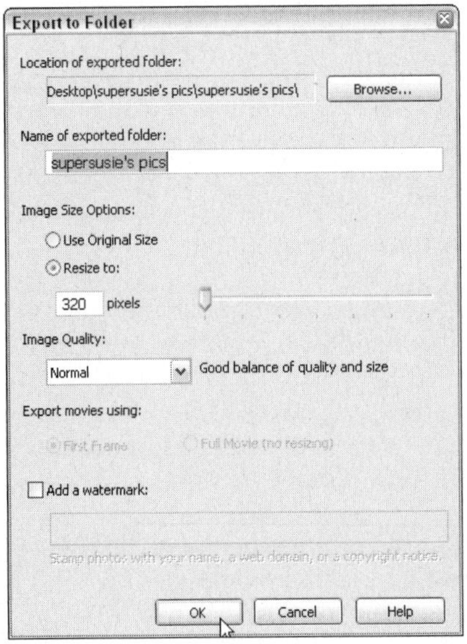

Figure 10-6: Export and resize an image in one step by using Picasa.

Inserting Photos into Blog Posts with Flickr

If you have a photo prepared for use on your blog, you're ready to upload it to the Web. You can take two approaches to get your image online:

- **Uploading directly to your blog:** If your blog software supports it, you might be able to upload your image directly into your blog post. In Blogger, for instance, you can use the Image Upload button in the New Post interface to upload an image. You can read more about this process in Blogger in Chapter 4.
- **Other online sharing sites:** If your blog software doesn't include an image-uploading tool, you can upload your photos to an online sharing site, such as Flickr. You can then add your photo to your post from that site.

Follow these steps to add photos to Flickr:

1. **Log in to your Flickr account and select Upload Photos & Video on the home page.**

   Alternatively, click the arrow next to the You navigation button and select Upload Photos and Videos from the menu that appears.

   The Upload to Flickr page appears.

2. **Click the Choose photos and videos link.**

   A Select File dialog box opens, showing files on your computer.

3. **Navigate to the location of the photo that you want to upload, select the photo, and click Open.**

   Your photo goes into an upload queue on the Flickr page.

   If you want to upload more photos, click the Add More link and add those photos to the queue, as well.

4. **Make sure that your Privacy setting is Public so that readers can view your photo when you put it on your blog.**

5. **Click the Upload Photos and Videos button.**

   Flickr displays a progress bar and notifies you when it has fully uploaded your photo.

6. **Click the Add a Description link.**

   The images you've just uploaded will appear and you can now enter in tags, descriptions, and titles.

7. **Give your photo a title, description, and tags that describe it in the text boxes provided.**

8. **Click the Save button.**

   Flickr adds your new photo(s) to your photo page. After you've completed your upload, you are sent back to your main photostream.

9. **On your photo page, click the photo that you just uploaded.**

10. **Click the All Sizes icon above the photo, as shown in Figure 10-7.**

   To post your photos directly from Flickr onto your blog and skip the rest of the steps, click the Blog This icon to the left of the All Sizes icon. Flickr shows you the starting point for configuring the connection between Flickr and your blog. Have the Web address for your blog's publishing interface, your username, and password ready.

Flickr uploading tools

You have four ways to upload your photos to Flickr: You can use the method described in this chapter, download the Flickr Uploadr tool and install it on your computer, use a plug-in for iPhoto, or upload via e-mail. If you upload via e-mail, don't forget that you can use your mobile phone to e-mail pictures directly onto your Flickr photostream.

To find out more about the Flickr uploading tools, go to `www.flickr.com/tools`.

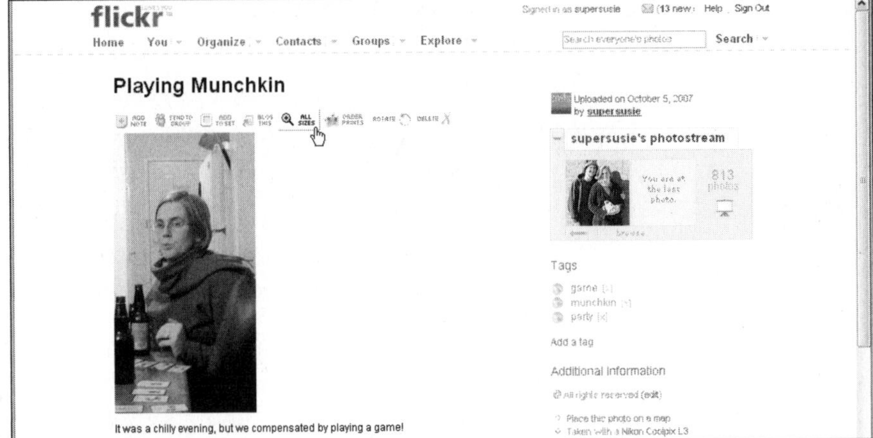

Figure 10-7: Clicking the All Sizes icon gives you access to the HTML code for your photo.

11. **Scroll down the page to find the HTML code for your photo, click in the code box, and copy that code into your Clipboard by pressing Ctrl+V (⌘+V on a Mac) or choosing Edit➪Copy.**
12. **Go to your blogging software and start a new post.**
13. **Paste the code from Flickr into your post entry field.**

    After the Flickr code, type your post like you normally would.
14. **Publish your post.**

    Be sure to check how it looks on the blog.

Chapter 11

Starting a Podcast

In This Chapter

- Figuring out whether you want to create podcasts
- Evaluating the equipment and tools needed for podcasting
- Finding fun audio files to include in your podcast
- Getting your podcast onto the Web and promoting it

By adding *podcasts* — either video or audio files that you publish on the Internet for people to download and listen to or view — to your blog, you reach a wider audience and reach your audience in different locations: People might listen to you while they drive or commute, or they might watch your videos on their television or their hand-held iPod.

The production process for a podcast is (in theory) simple: You go out into the world, record a video or some audio, edit it on your computer, and then upload the files to your blog for release onto the Internet. Your blog's readers then download the files, and they can still leave comments and interact with your blog in the usual way.

Intrigued? Podcasts are attracting a whole new audience to the blogosphere. With the creation of improved software and portable hardware units that can consume these kinds of media, you might want to seriously consider adding podcasting to your blog.

If you want to become the coolest podcaster in your neck of the woods, check out *Podcasting For Dummies,* by Tee Morris, Chuck Tomasi, Evo Terra, and Kreg Steppe.

Deciding to Podcast

Podcasts come in all flavors. You can find personal podcasts, technical podcasts, sports reports, music samples, recorded social gatherings, previously recorded radio broadcasts, book reviews, and audio books. If you can think of a topic, you can probably find a podcast for it.

Knit Picks (`www.knitpicks.com`) is a knitting yarn and supplies company that offers a regular podcast about knitting activities, techniques, books, and guest interviews in an informative and entertaining mix. The Knit Picks podcast page (`http://community.knitpicks.com/profile/knitpickspodcast`) is shown in Figure 11-1.

Blogs and podcasts can look very similar; the main difference is that a podcast entry contains a media file that the consumer can download, either by directly accessing the Web site or by subscribing to a syndicated *blog feed* (also known as the RSS feed). See the section "Delivering your podcasts," later in this chapter, for more information about your options.

Many bloggers who want to podcast don't because of the learning curve to build and maintain a podcast. As wonderful as podcasts can be, writing, recording, uploading, hosting, and promoting one requires a higher level of technical proficiency than written blog posts do. However, you may find figuring out how to work podcasts worth it if you think they can help grow your audience, enhance your blog content, or improve and expand your blogging skills. In the following sections, you can take a closer look at the advantages of podcasting and figure out how to choose between audio and video podcasts.

Figure 11-1: Get knitting tips and tricks from the Knit Picks podcast.

Podcasting in ancient times

In 2003, a number of bloggers thought it would be interesting to record their thoughts out loud and then publish the audio, usually as MP3 files, through their blogs. Some of those bloggers started releasing audio blog entries on a regular basis. What happened next was a bit of a surprise. Because of the rising popularity of MP3 players, such as Apple's iPod, the audience for these podcasts grew extremely quickly. And thanks to RSS feeds, listeners could easily retrieve and download the latest recordings. People from all over the world started listening, recording, and publishing their own audio blogs. Several audio blogs became popular enough to gain some notice within the mainstream media. A hidden audience had been discovered.

In fact, most people believe the word *podcast* comes from the Apple iPod device, a popular MP3 player that can store and play podcasts and music. This belief comes close, but it's not the whole truth. Podcasts arose at the same time that Apple's device came on the scene, and bloggers conceived the name *podcast* to echo the idea that people could listen to these audio files on the go by using a hand-held device. But many devices could play the files, and in fact, people listen to most podcasts on a computer, not an MP3 player. Some say the word comes from a combination of the acronym *pod* (*pod* standing for portable-on-demand) and the word *broadcast,* but this meaning evolved after the word itself, probably in response to Apple's attempts in 2005 to try to restrict the commercial use of the word *pod.*

Although some bloggers were also experimenting with video in 2003, it took until 2005 for videocasting to really start to gain traction. Two technological shifts helped make this happen: iTunes, the program most people used to subscribe to podcasts, started supporting video; and YouTube, the video-sharing site, made uploading and sharing video a much more common online activity.

Reaching a wider audience

Podcasting can help you reach a different audience. Many people like to read and enjoy taking in a well-written blog post. However, some blog readers enjoy listening to what you have to say as an audio recording. Other blog followers like to watch, rather than read, your blog post — especially if you have a compelling voice or are more photogenic than average. (I've been told I have a face for radio.)

Also, some of the things that you want to talk about on your blog might work better as an audio recording, rather than as a text post, such as interviews, soundscapes, or special events. And video is even more powerful: You can show off much more of your personality than you can by using just a text blog, and you can demonstrate things that you might find difficult or impossible to convey with just words.

Think about when and where people might play your podcast and use that knowledge to help focus and inform your entries.

Choosing between audio and video

If you're ready to take the plunge into the production of a podcast, you need to decide what format you want to use. Both audio and video require specialized skills to produce.

Your level of technical competence and comfort can determine what medium you choose. You need to consider what type of podcast fits with your blog's audience — don't use videocasting, for example, if your blog targets those who use low-bandwidth connections.

Here are a few tips that can help you decide what type of podcast to use:

- **Audio:**
  - Easier to produce than video because of a larger availability of open source software. Most software for professional video editing is expensive.
  - Easier and generally quicker to edit than video.
  - More portable than video. Fewer portable devices are designed to deal with video than with audio.
  - Less of a space hog than video, making audio files less expensive to store on a Web host than video files.
- **Video:**
  - More compelling. The visual and auditory components combined are more likely to keep a viewer from becoming distracted.
  - You can make video shorter than audio. Audiences likely feel satisfied with a 2- to 4-minute video podcast, whereas they might want a much longer audio podcast.
  - Gives you more visual elements to work with — both when you're designing your blog and in individual entries.
  - Has more related sites online where you can upload and share files.
  - Requires the viewer's attention, whereas people can listen to audio podcasts while completing other tasks. You can listen to an audio podcast while driving to work, for example.

Video and audio files can get very large. When you upload them to your Web server, you fill up your available disk space more quickly than you do if you upload only text and photos. Also, distributing audio and video requires more bandwidth. Be sure to keep an eye on your disk space and bandwidth usage so that you aren't hit with unexpected overage charges. Ask your Web host how to keep tabs on those elements, any fees that you may accrue, and whether you need more space and bandwidth.

If video is the medium of your choice, be sure to read Chapter 12 for tips and tools specific to video production.

Planning Your Podcast

To create a podcast, you first need the desire to make it the best experience for the listeners that you can. If you aren't having fun, it shows in the final result. Remember, even if you find your very first podcast a little frustrating, it gets easier.

Here are a few key ingredients that you need for a good podcast:

- **Planning what you'll say:** You can make a single podcast, like a blog entry, about anything, so have a clearly defined topic before you start. Some podcasters write a script for every podcast that they record. Although you may find a script is overkill for you, jotting down a few notes or creating an outline to follow can help you streamline the creation process. You can find a list to help you brainstorm topics and the flow of you podcast later in this section.
- **Finding your voice:** You need to establish the tone of the piece before you go forward. How will the format of your overall podcast determine how you shoot or record it? Do you want to use some kind of traditional show format, or do you want to improvise the entire program each time? Taking these kinds of questions into account when you're planning out your first podcast can help you make your program a success.
- **Timing:** Technically speaking, you can use as much or as little time as you want in your podcast, but you may find that you get a better end product when you give yourself limits, rather than chattering on about your favorite color or a funny thing your cat did when you really should be getting to the point of your recording session. Think about how much time you can reasonably expect your audience to give you, and target that length for your podcasts. In general, podcasts range from a few minutes to an hour. Also, make sure that you have enough time to record the entire podcast in the same location so that you don't have awkward changes in the background noise, which can distract your listener or viewer.

- **Recording conditions:** When you want to record anything, you need to take into account environmental considerations before you hit the Record button. Is the environment you're in quiet enough? Does the room have fans or computers that may annoy the listeners running in the background? For video, do you have sufficient lighting to produce watchable video? Try to eliminate distractions, such as phones ringing or people walking by. And if you can, do some test recording that you can listen to or watch so that you know what the quality of the final product will be before you record your entire podcast.

Blogging in writing is relatively easy in comparison to recording a podcast, and you can also more easily hide your inexperience in a text blog because you can rewrite and edit before posting. Although you can edit audio and video, removing stuttered speech or inappropriate facial expressions is harder than revising text in a blog post. The good news is that practice can help eliminate awkward moments.

If you get stuck thinking about a podcast topic or format, ask your readers for suggestions. Even if only five or ten readers respond, you can get some good ideas and direction.

Here's a short list of podcast ideas that have been successful for other podcasters. Use this list to spark your creativity to find other topics that interest you:

- **One-on-one interviews:** Fascinating people in your neighborhood are just waiting to get on your podcast — especially people involved in a cause, an organization, or a business. Discover more about your family's background or the adventures of your friends. See who in your acquaintance might fit the theme and direction of your podcast.
- **Show your expertise:** Show off what you know and share your knowledge with others — maybe even show your audience how to do something.
- **Soundscapes:** You can find fascinating sounds all around you that you can document. Record yourself walking through a forest or park. Make some observations about your surroundings, describe each sound, and explain why it's important to you. Remember, what's ordinary for you (waves at the beach, a passing train, construction noise, or a barn owl) might fascinate someone living on the other side of the country or the world.
- **Events:** A performance at your local coffee house, a city hall meeting, or a surprise party all might make for an interesting podcast. Make sure to get permission before recording or publishing a podcast of an event.
- **Discussions:** General discussions in social settings can reveal some great conversations. Take your recorder along to your next BBQ or evening social, and direct the conversation along a theme or idea.

If you take the time to plan out what things you want to share with your subscribers, you can make your podcast happen. With a recording device, a plan, and maybe someone else to talk to (although, not entirely necessary!), you can have a complete podcast episode in no time.

Assessing the Tools

Making your podcast requires a bit more than your fingers and a computer keyboard. Podcasts require recording equipment for audio and video. Here's what you're looking at:

- **Computer:** You need a computer of some kind. You can use a desktop or a laptop, although laptops are more flexible and allow you to edit on-the-go. The computer must be able to handle editing audio files and, more importantly, video files. Video is a computer-intensive medium and requires a computer with a lot of power and a lot of disk space in order to process the large files that you record. Audio files can also be fairly large.
- **Microphone:** Microphones these days are built into almost every laptop, and you can easily buy external microphones. Consider purchasing a good microphone from a professional audio store because the microphones that you get from the average computer store or on the typical laptop are poor quality. Ask a podcaster or the staff of a good audio store for advice about the best microphone for the kind of recording situation that you expect to be in. Expect to spend at least $40 for your microphone — it's not the item to economize on.
- **Sound-recording and sound-editing software:** Unless you're the sort of person who never deviates from a script or says "um," you need software to edit your audio or video. Solutions range from free to the price of a small automobile. Let your budget be your guide. You may want to start small and upgrade when you know more about podcasting and your own needs. A good starting point for audio software is the free program Audacity (`http://audacity.sourceforge.net`). Audacity (as shown in Figure 11-2) is available for Windows, Mac OS X, and Linux/Unix. It's the program of choice for many podcasters, largely because it's free and open source. Audacity is a *multi-track recording* program — which means you can have two pieces of audio, such as a voice and a piece of music, and you can mix the two at different volumes or even fade from one to the other.

  A high-end solution is Sony's Sound Forge (`www.sonycreativesoftware.com/products/soundforgefamily.asp`).

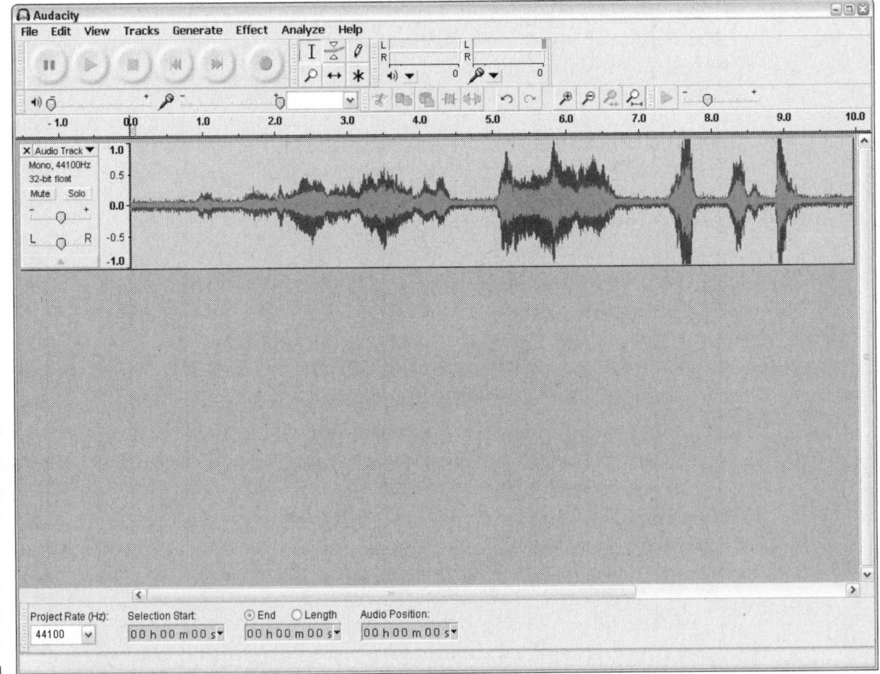

Figure 11-2: Audacity is a popular audio-editing software program.

Dressing Up Your Podcast with Music and Sound Effects

Nothing spices up a podcast like a little intro or background music. But podcasts — even if they're produced and released at no cost to the listener — aren't exempt from copyright restrictions. You need to find music and/or images that are in the public domain or licensed for republication.

Let me be clear: Even if you use only a little bit of a copyrighted song or give the performer credit, you're still violating copyright if you don't have a license or other permission to use the music. The same goes for using copyrighted images and video clips in videocasts.

But plenty of this material is available for you to use. The term *podsafe* has appeared to describe music, sounds, and other clips that are available for free unlimited use in podcasting, but no specific license exists to identify that a clip is podsafe, so be sure to read the terms and conditions before you integrate sound or audio into your productions.

Creative Commons Search

```
http://search.creativecommons.org
```

Creative Commons is an organization that has evolved a set of licenses that you can use on your own content to permit or disallow use by others. If a publisher applies a Creative Commons license that allows republication, you can search for and find that content in the Creative Commons search area, specifically requesting content that you can use for commercial purposes or modify (see Figure 11-3).

Some of the types of licenses are

- **Commercial Use:** Permits use of the content for business and revenue-generating purposes.
- **Noncommercial Use:** You may use this media only for noncommercial podcasts.
- **Attribution:** You can use the work only when you give credit to the creator.

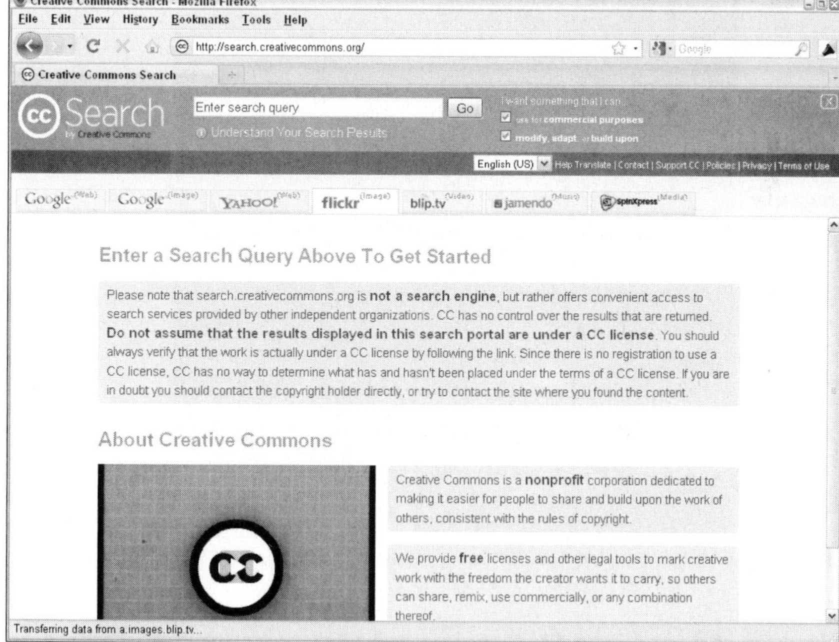

Figure 11-3: Search for licensed content to use in your podcast on Creative Commons.

- **Derivatives Allowed:** You can cut, chop, and excerpt this media to create new works.
- **No Derivatives Allowed:** You must leave the media intact and unchanged.

Magnatune

`www.magnatune.com`

Magnatune is a record label that helps artists promote and share their music, and make money doing it. The label and the artists sell their albums on CD and via download, and they split the money evenly. The music on Magnatune (shown in Figure 11-4) is available for download and purchase, as well as to noncommercial podcasters. To help promote artists, podcasters are granted a waiver to use Magnatune music without paying a royalty fee.

Figure 11-4: Magnatune is the only record label that specifically allows noncommercial podcasters to use music for free.

Music Alley

`www.musicalley.com`

Music Alley is a place where artists provide tracks from their albums for sharing and use in podcasts. Everything is released by using a Creative Commons license, and registered users can create playlists and download tracks to share on their podcasts.

The Freesound Project

```
www.freesound.org
```

Music is great, but what about sound effects? What podcast wouldn't be improved by a few barking dogs and fart noises? I'm kidding, of course. But sound effects can really add a lot of value to your production, from realistic sounds of dialing a phone to a spring breeze. The Freesound Project can help you dress up your podcast.

Use their simple search box to find Creative Commons–licensed sound. You can also contribute your own sound effects to the project by creating an account and uploading to their Web site.

Publishing Your Podcast

You can put your podcast into the blogosphere fairly simply: Write a blog post about your podcast, upload your podcast media file, and then publish it by using your blog software.

But before you do that, you have a couple of tasks: You need to add metadata to and choose a file format for your podcast.

Assigning metadata

Metadata, simply put, is data about data. In the case of podcasts, metadata is data that describes your video or audio podcast. When you publish a podcast — whether audio or video — you need to provide descriptive metadata that podcast systems such as Apple's iTunes and the RSS feed can read. After all, the computer can't listen to or watch your podcast and figure out what it contains!

Common metadata types include

- Title
- Author name

- Publication information
- Topics covered
- Type of file
- Descriptions
- Keywords

Your editing software (both video and audio software packages) asks you to enter metadata when you create your audio or video files, and software such as iTunes, which is designed to support podcasts, also offers you a chance to provide metadata.

Choosing a format

Creating video and audio for general release means that you need to choose a file format that your audience can consume.

Most audio bloggers release audio files in the MP3 format. MP3 files are easy to create and play on a variety of devices. Most computer users are familiar with the format, and both browsers and preinstalled audio players have good built-in support for MP3s.

Other options are available, such as OOG, an open format, and AAC, a format popular on Apple computers. Windows users can play AAC files, too, if they install QuickTime. The Apple iPod can't play OOG files, which is a significant issue for most audiences. AAC has some nice features, such as audio bookmarks.

Storing your podcasts

When you have a podcast ready for primetime, you need to figure out where to put it online. Posting your podcast poses two problems:

- **Storage:** You need a place to put the actual file. Audio and video files are larger than text files, so you may run into an issue with disk space when you store them.
- **Bandwidth (the amount of data your audiences downloads):** You have to account for the additional bandwidth required for your audience to download those files. It takes more bandwidth to deliver audio or video to your audience than it does text or images.

You have two options for getting the storage and bandwidth you need: your Web-hosting server (the one that hosts your blog) or a free storage Web site.

Putting your files on your own Web-hosting server

Check with your Web host to find out how much disk space you have available and what it costs to increase your allotment. Be aware that if you keep podcasting, you'll eventually run out of disk space, even if you start off with quite a bit. If you're a video podcaster, you want a hosting package that has several gigabytes of storage space. If you stick with only audio, you need a few gigabytes to start. While your podcasts grow in number, you'll require more and more space, so keep that in mind. I talk about choosing a Web host in Chapter 3.

You also need to consider bandwidth when you choose your hosting service. Most Web-hosting packages offer a standard amount of bandwidth, and you're charged if you and your audience use more than that. Most Web hosts have pretty reasonable fees, unless your podcast becomes the hottest thing on the Web and your traffic becomes astronomical.

To give you a better idea about how file sizes can affect your Web-hosting costs, I show you some reasonable working numbers and you can compare these to your hosting package bandwidth:

- **1MB (megabyte) audio file:** If you have 100 subscribers and you post one audio file a week, your estimated bandwidth for that file is about 100MB.
- **10MB (megabyte) video file:** If you have 100 subscribers and you post one video file a week, your estimated bandwidth for that file is 1000MB or 1GB.

From these numbers, you can see how your bandwidth needs may skyrocket. Thinking about these almost hidden costs is very important because you could get stuck with a hosting bill you weren't expecting.

Bandwidth can be a confusing concept especially when dealing with a podcast. Web sites like Podtopeia (`http://www.podtopia.net`) have tools that let you generate estimates on how much it could cost you to host your own files.

Most hosting packages come with a finite amount of disk space and bandwidth. You most likely can post only a certain number of podcasts before your hosting package runs out of space. Unless you have the dollars to spend, you probably need to find an alternative for storing your files.

Using a free storage and sharing Web site

Luckily for podcasters, a great service called Archive.org (`www.archive.org`) is the home of the Internet Archive, a nonprofit organization founded in 1996 to build an Internet library in which researchers, historians, and the general public can store and access text, audio, moving images, software, and a vast collection of archived Web pages.

You can upload your podcasts to the Internet Archive for free, as long as you comply with its guidelines and describe your content. The system also provides and converts your video or audio format into other formats for increased accessibility.

You can find other podcast storage options, too. If you haven't seen a You Tube video on a blog or Web site lately, you must be living under a rock. YouTube (www.youtube.com) has soared in popularity. When you upload a video to YouTube, your video is listed on the site, where visitors can view and comment on it. But you can also grab the code for the file and embed it directly into your Web site or blog post. Files that you upload to YouTube are reformatted into Flash video. They must be shorter than ten minutes and less than 1GB in size.

Delivering your podcasts

After you have your audio and video online and your blog post created, you need to make sure that your blog has an RSS Web feed. Podcasts are typically delivered to playback software (such as Apple iTunes) through a subscription to your blog's RSS feed. I talk extensively about setting up and using RSS in Chapter 13.

Suffice it to say that you need an RSS feed so that your viewers and listeners can subscribe to it themselves, but also so that you can promote your podcast by using some of the handy podcast promotional directories and software out there. (See the following section for the promotion details.)

If you already subscribe to a number of blogs, you know that a syndicated blog feed contains information such as the title of the post, the main content, and maybe some author information. A podcast feed, in addition to the typical entry information, contains a link to a media file. If a consumer subscribes to a podcast feed by using an RSS reader, most modern readers automatically download the files so that the user can listen or watch at his or her convenience.

Promoting Your Podcast

Publishing your podcast on your Web site can help you publicize it, but you can get the word out in more effective ways. If you already have a good promotional system built into your site and a decent-sized audience, you can get users to subscribe to your podcast without too much additional marketing, but if you need a little more promotion, you can use a number of strategies.

Adding your podcast to FeedBurner

FeedBurner (`http://feedburner.google.com`) provides custom tracking and customization of podcast feeds. If you submit your podcast to Feed Burner's service, you can implement good promotion tools to help your podcast get more play.

Now a Google company, FeedBurner has a lot to offer bloggers and podcasters. You can use FeedBurner to do the following:

- Add metadata to your files.
- Make your feeds compatible with every RSS reader available.
- Add your podcast to the major podcast directories, making sure that people can find your podcast.
- Track the number of subscribers to your feed.
- Keep track of which podcasts visitors actually download.

To use FeedBurner, you must already have an RSS feed. If you're using blog software, it probably offers you a feed. Check your documentation for more information and jump to Chapter 13 for more about RSS feeds.

Follow these steps to create a feed with FeedBurner:

1. **Go to `http://feedburner.com`.**
2. **Create an account on FeedBurner if you don't already have one.**
3. **On the FeedBurner main page (shown in Figure 11-5), paste the Web address (URL) of your RSS feed into the Burn a Feed Right This Instant field.**
4. **Check the I Am a Podcaster! box.**
5. **Click the Next button.**

   FeedBurner verifies that the feed is working and loads the Welcome screen.
6. **Give your feed a title, if it doesn't already have one, by entering it in the Field Title text box.**

   You can also customize the feed address in the Feed Address text box, if desired.
7. **Click the Activate Feed button.**

   FeedBurner creates your new feed and loads a screen that displays the Web address of your feed.

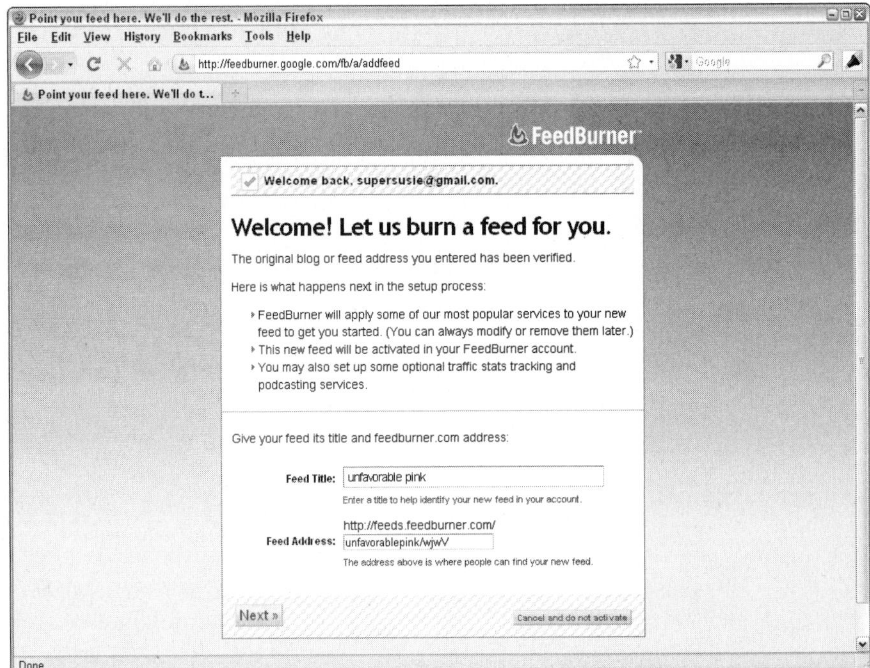

Figure 11-5: Get a podcast feed going with Google's FeedBurner.

8. **Click the Next button.**

   FeedBurner loads the podcast configuration screen.

9. **Fill out the configuration screen.**

   FeedBurner offers these configuration options:

   - *Create Podcast Enclosures from Links To:* Select the kinds of files that you want to include in your podcast — any, audio, video, or images.
   - *Include iTunes Podcasting Elements:* Deselect this check box if you don't want your podcast listed in Apple's iTunes Store.
   - *Category:* Select a category from the drop-down list. You can also select a subcategory in the text field that appears.
   - *Podcast Image Location:* If you created a graphic for your audio or video podcast, paste the Web address of the graphic into this field. This graphic is like an album cover for your podcast. iTunes uses it to fill in the album artwork.
   - *Podcast Subtitle:* Expand on your title in this field.
   - *Podcast Summary:* Provide a short description of your podcast.

- *Podcast Search Keywords:* Provide descriptive keywords for your podcast.
- *Podcast Author E-Mail Address:* Enter your e-mail address.
- *Include "Media RSS" Information and Add Podcast to Yahoo! Search:* Deselect this check box if you don't want to be included in Yahoo! Search.
- *Contains Explicit Content:* Select the Yes, No, or Yes (Cleaned) radio button. Click the Information icon if you want help understanding how FeedBurner defines explicit content.
- *Copyright Message*: Provide a short copyright message.
- *Podcast Author*: Fill in your name.

10. **Click the Next button.**

    FeedBurner loads the traffic statistics screen.

11. **Fill out the Feed Traffic Statistics screen.**

    These options appear on this screen:

    - *Click-throughs:* Select this checkbox if you want to know when subscribers use your feed to come to your Web site.
    - *Item Enclosure Downloads:* Select this checkbox if you want to know which podcast entries your subscribers actually download.

12. **Click the Next button.**

    FeedBurner finishes burning your feed. You can begin monitoring subscriptions and activity on your feed by using FeedBurner.

After you create a feed by using FeedBurner, head to your site, put the link to your new feed on your blog, and urge your blog visitors to subscribe.

By using FeedBurner, you can actually keep track of how many subscribers your feed has and how they're using your podcast, which is useful information if you plan to pursue funding or sponsorship. Once you have set up a podcast with FeedBurner, log in and select it in order to view traffic information in the Analyze section of the site.

Adding your podcast to iTunes

Due to the overwhelming popularity of Apple's iTunes software as the main podcast viewer, you absolutely must submit your podcast to its service — unless, for some reason, you don't want people to find your podcast.

Before you submit your podcast to iTunes, you need to do the following:

- **Sign up for an Apple ID.** Each submission is associated with a user account. If you have iTunes installed on your computer and have purchased songs or other media from the iTunes store, you already have an Apple ID. To get an ID, download iTunes, which you find at `www.itunes.com`; after you install the software, click the iTunes Store option on the left of the main screen to begin setting up your ID.
- **Set up an RSS feed.** If you're using blog software, you likely already have a feed. Check your documentation for more information, and jump to Chapter 13 for more about RSS feeds.
- **Have a few entries in your feed and make sure that the feed is working.** You can test your feed by making sure your own feed reader (like Google Reader) can subscribe to your feed. If you see your posts in your reader, the feed should be working fine. Refer to Chapter 13 for information on subscribing to feeds in Google Reader.

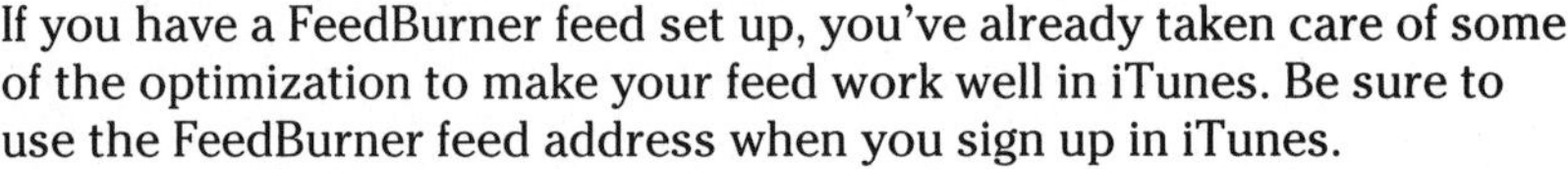

If you have a FeedBurner feed set up, you've already taken care of some of the optimization to make your feed work well in iTunes. Be sure to use the FeedBurner feed address when you sign up in iTunes.

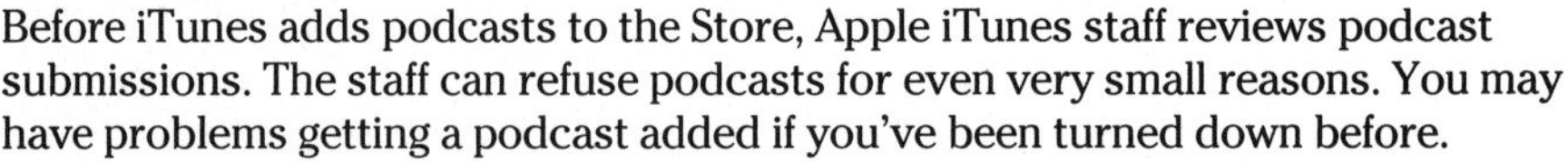

Before iTunes adds podcasts to the Store, Apple iTunes staff reviews podcast submissions. The staff can refuse podcasts for even very small reasons. You may have problems getting a podcast added if you've been turned down before.

If you have the iTunes software installed on your computer, you can submit your podcast by using the iTunes interface. In order to get your podcast into the iTunes Store, follow these steps:

1. **Start your iTunes software.**
2. **Click the iTunes Store navigation item in the left column.**

   This will open the iTunes store interface.
3. **Select the Podcasts link from the iTunes Store menu on the top of the screen.**

   The Podcasts page appears.
4. **Click the Submit a Podcast menu item located in the top-right of the page.**

   iTunes loads the Submit Podcasts page.
5. **Enter the RSS feed of your podcast in the Podcast Feed URL field and click the Continue button.**

   If you're not logged in to the iTunes Store, you're prompted to log in at this point.

   iTunes submits your feed for review by Apple staff.

After you submit your podcast, it might take several days or even weeks until your feed shows up in the iTunes library of podcasts. If your podcast is rejected for any reason, you receive an e-mail from Apple. (Unfortunately, they don't provide reasons for rejections.)

Getting listed in podcast directories

Podcast directories help would-be listeners and viewers find known podcasts. Getting listed in these directories is an easy step to letting people know about your podcast. Most directories are organized by topic, and many of them offer subscription features that allow people to quickly sign up for your podcast. Listing your podcast in these directories can most certainly provide you with new traffic to your blog and podcast.

Here's where you should get your podcast listed:

- **Podcast Alley** (`www.podcastalley.com`): This site contains a podcast directory, as well as news and information about podcasting.
- **Podcast.com** (`www.podcast.com`): Podcasts are organized by category (for example, entertainment or sports), and the home page displays a list of recently updated podcasts.
- **Odeo** (`www.odeo.com`): Plans are underway to turn this excellent directory site into a resource for finding information and Web sites for podcasting tools and functionality.
- **Podcast Pickle** (`www.podcastpickle.com`): One of the older podcast directories, Podcast Pickle offers visitors organization tools for the podcasts to which they subscribe.
- **PodNova** (`www.podnova.com`): More than just a directory. You can subscribe, listen, view, read, and maintain your feeds online by using PodNova.
- **PodBean** (`www.podbean.com`): Another directory where you can publish and host your podcast. You and your audience can listen and view your podcasts and share them on other Web sites like Facebook.

And if you don't want to put your podcast on any of the sites in the preceding list, check out Robin Good's extensive list of podcast directories at `www.masternewmedia.org/podcast_directory`.

Chapter 12

Working with Videos

In This Chapter

- Choosing a video camera and editing software
- Shooting and editing videos
- Getting your video on the Web

Like photos, videos add a new element to your blog that keeps people coming back more often. When you record and share a video online, you get to show off the real you in full color! Using video on your blog can increase your readership and viewership dramatically in ways that text-only blogs can't achieve. Combining videos and text together in a single blog post is one of the more interesting ways to cover both sides of the Web readership battle: You can attract a broader audience to your Web site by using both video and text.

Of course, to use video, you need a video camera and the knowledge to transfer that recorded gold from your camera to video software on your computer, and then to your Web site. Editing video can be an art in itself, and if you do it well, your videos can increase traffic to your blog.

Fortunately for you, the explosion of video tools and sharing services has made it easier than ever to put your video online and display it on your Web site. In this chapter, you can find tips for choosing your tools, recording and editing video, and hosting the videos that you create.

Getting Equipped

Today's video cameras are a far cry from the equipment of the same name only a few years ago. At that time, most video cameras used Hi8 digital tape and MiniDV as the recordable medium. You could find options for MiniDVD cameras as well, but they weren't as popular. But that was then, and this is now. The video camera landscape has changed, and I mean, *it has changed!*

The days of having to purchase video tapes and recordable media are nearly gone.

A quick walk around any consumer electronics store proves my point: Most of the latest and greatest cameras come equipped with hard drives and Flash memory. For the average blogger who wants to get into some video blogging, you can shoot video more quickly and put that video online and onto your blog much, much more quickly than ever before.

To fast track your career in video blogging, you need the following:

- A digital video camera that has a USB or FireWire connection to get your video from the camera to your computer
- Video-editing software that can help you review, edit, and add any special effects that you may want
- A video-sharing service or blog package that lets you share video files easily

Doing your research

Plenty of great consumer review Web sites and blogs offer all kinds of advice about what cameras on the market today can do and what kinds of recording they're suited for. CNET is one of my favorites (`http://reviews.cnet.com/camcorders`). Many traditional camera stores also train staff about all the video options of traditional cameras, so don't hesitate to ask for help from a real person who has expertise.

Ultimately, the type of video blogging that you want to do determines what camera you need. Most video cameras are quite small and portable, others are designed for hand-held shooting, and still others for tripods and external microphones. Some cellular phones have video cameras built into them, and the quality from those phones is high enough to post online. Or a large camera that has better lenses and more recording options (such as night shooting and motion stabilization) rather than lower end cameras may appeal to you. Here's the breakdown of what's available:

- **Low-end point-and-shoot digital cameras:** Many digital still cameras and mobile phones also enable you to capture short videos. The cameras are cheap, and you can retrieve video as easily as still photographs. For amateur video artists who are focusing on very short video clips, a digital still camera that has limited video capabilities is the best choice because of the lower cost. You can also check out portable HD pocket cameras.

You may not get the best quality on a cheap digital still camera, but if you just want to experiment with video, getting this kind of inexpensive camera may do the trick. The latest digital still cameras can shoot video in high definition and have single-click or push-button uploading to a YouTube account. If you're interested in both a still and video camera, an all-in-one solution works well, as long as you plan to produce only very short videos.

- **Midrange:** If you're looking for more video options and a higher quality picture than you can get with a low-end point-and-shoot camera, or if you're planning to record segments of more than a couple minutes, a midrange digital video camera is more than ample. Such a camera gives you the flexibility to use it for everything from sit-down interviews to shots from atop your bike. The following section introduces the different kinds of midrange cameras that you can find on the market.
- **High-end:** Most video bloggers have no need for professional-level video cameras, which are typically priced in the thousands of dollars. For one thing, the video quality that they can record is likely wasted on a Web audience, and frankly, most consumer-level computers don't have the hard drive space or processers to handle the humongous files generated by these machines. High-end cameras are also so large that they're not all that portable.

Exploring camera options

Do as much research as you can about the type of filming that you want to do. Video cameras traditionally are more expensive than digital still cameras, so hobbyists who want to record quick videos for their blogs may not want to make the investment. This higher price point means that you need to research features; the most feature-loaded camera may not be the best one for your budget or needs. If you're looking to experiment with video, consider renting a video camera or borrowing one from your best friend (who's quite understanding!), and then see how you like it.

Flash memory cameras

Flash memory is the most common storage medium for digital still cameras, and video cameras have adopted the same technology for a majority of the low-cost camcorders. Flash memory cameras come in two flavors: removable cards or built-in nonremovable memory. Cameras that have nonremovable Flash memory cards (or sticks) usually come with a USB cable that you can connect to your computer so that you can move your video from the camera to the computer (and thence on to your Web site). Some cameras even come with a button that you can press — after doing a little configuration — to upload anything that you record directly to YouTube.

A quick note about single-click uploading: Some manufacturers of video cameras have chosen YouTube as the de facto single-click video service. If you don't use YouTube to host your videos, having a camera with this feature doesn't do you much good and certainly isn't worth paying extra. Check around and do your research. Video recorder companies may latch on to other services in the next few years. And if you do end up with one of these cameras and don't want to use YouTube, you can still access your videos on your camera in other ways. It isn't the end of your video career if your camera doesn't talk to your video-hosting provider.

If your camera has a removable card, you need the means to read the card by using your computer, either with a USB card drive or through a built-in card reader in your computer or printer.

Hard drive cameras

Hard drive cameras are usually relatively high-end cameras and tend to cost more than Flash drive or tape cameras. However, if technology trends in the video camera market continue (and there's no reason to think that they won't), many of the hard drive cameras will continue to drop in price and become affordable even to the hobbyist video bloggers.

This level of camera usually has both a higher quality of construction and quality of picture than cheaper cameras. Good-quality lenses and long recording times are also the norm for the more expensive recorders. Unlike some of the less pricey cameras, hard drive cameras don't have removable media that you can plug into your computer. To get video from your camera to your computer, you need to plug your camera into your computer and then copy files over, much like you do with any external hard drive. Some cameras require you to install a software package to facilitate this process.

Webcams

In the past, I've played with recording video by using a Webcam (specifically, on YouTube). If you have a Webcam attached to your computer, you can record video quickly and (when you tie that Webcam into YouTube) upload it while you record, which means you don't need to store it locally. I think Webcams provide a perfect way to record and post quick video commentaries.

Webcams tend to be of a decent but not wonderful quality, and if you upload directly, you clearly can't use any editing or special effects. If you're comfortable going live while you record, a Webcam absolutely gives you the fastest way to create video and get it to your audience. Most consumer electronics stores carry a good selection of Webcams, and many computers (particularly laptops) come with one already installed.

Choosing video-editing software

Software that you use to process video images is a little more challenging than the software that you use to edit still images, such as Picasa or iPhoto. For starters, video-editing software can be a little more demanding on your computer's resources; the file sizes alone are probably bigger than most digital documents that you deal with regularly. Add in a few special effects, and the RAM (random access memory) that is needed can really tax your trusty old desktop machine.

Having said that, you can find good video-editing software options for all levels of videographers. Microsoft Windows and Apple OS X both come with video-recording and video-editing software built in, and this software easily meets the needs of beginners and light hobbyists. If you decide that you need a little more editing flexibility and a few more options, the software that you need is more complex to use and can get a bit expensive.

When you're looking for video-editing software, you need to pay attention to options such as file types and special effects:

- **File formats:** Video requires certain codec functionality, and you have many kinds to choose from. Computers and the Web tend to recognize only a couple of formats, but most software can work with all kinds of formats. The most common formats for video on the Web include WMV, MOV, AVI, and MPEG.

  Make sure that your video-editing software enables you to import the file format in which your camera records video and can convert your edited video into a Web-friendly format. (Or see the sidebar "Dealing with video formats," in this chapter, for details about conversion software.)
- **Standard editing tools:** Most video-editing software provides you with the editing tools that you need. You ultimately want nonlinear editing software — which enables you to divide your video recording into clips and arrange them in whatever sequence you want — because editing in this way is much faster. If you can get a few additional options in your software, such as transitions and minor special effects, you should be good to go.
- **Video sharing:** You don't need a program that integrates with the blogging tool you use or with a video-sharing service such as YouTube, but such a program can really help you speed up the amount of time it takes you to get video online.

If you've purchased a digital video camera recently, be sure to check two things. First, did your camera come with any software for editing video? More and more, cameras are coming packaged with video-editing software, which are sometimes "light" or trial versions that you can upgrade for additional features. Also, check whether the camera comes with software recommendations that the manufacturer knows are compatible with the camera's video formats.

Dealing with video formats

Worst case scenario: You have a digital video camera and software for editing digital video, but the software can't read the file format of your camera's video. Before you run out and replace either your camera or your software, look into a solution that's likely to be a little less pricey — conversion software. Sure, it adds an extra step to the whole process, but if money is tight, you may prefer to spend time, rather than dollars.

You can find some free software packages available that allow you to convert your existing video files into the format of your choice. Find out what formats your software can accept, and then set up conversion software to convert the format your camera produces to the format your software can read, and then save it or export it as a new file.

Software such as Prism Video Converter (`www.nchsoftware.com/prism`) or AVS Video Converter (`www.avs4you.com/AVS-Video-converter.aspx`) are good starting points if you have to deal with this issue.

Editing video does require a bit of practice, and as always, not all video packages are created equal. Here are a few of the most common video-editing packages available:

- **Windows Live Movie Maker:** Free; Windows only; `http://download.live.com/moviemaker`. Available for Windows users whose computers run Vista or Windows 7, this free tool gives you basic editing functionality in a quick and easy interface. See more about Windows Live Movie Maker in the following section.
- **iMovie:** Free; Mac only; `www.apple.com/ilife/imovie`. Import, edit, and organize video in one tool. You can easily use the editing tools, which use the much-vaunted Mac plug-and-play interface. You find a section devoted to iMovie later in this chapter.
- **Adobe Premiere Elements:** $99; Windows only; `www.adobe.com/products/premiereel`. This program is the top-selling consumer video editor, and it has a decent level of power and an easy-to-use configuration. If you're new to video editing, check out *Premiere Elements 8 For Dummies,* by Keith Underdahl, for help in how to use this program.
- **Adobe Premiere Pro:** $799; Mac and Windows; `www.adobe.com/products/premiere`. This software is for those who really want to become professional video editors. It's overkill for most folks, but if you want professional results and have money to burn, you can get access to some incredibly flexible tools by choosing this great suite.
- **Final Cut Express:** $199; Mac only; `www.apple.com/finalcutexpress`. If you want to get into the Final Cut world but can't afford the price of the Pro level, Final Cut Express — a sold, flexible editing tool — may suit your needs.

- **Final Cut Pro:** $999; Mac only; `www.apple.com/finalcutstudio/finalcutpro`. Like the Adobe Premiere Pro package, Final Cut Pro is over the top for most Web bloggers — a tool for serious videographers who have serious budgets.

Windows Live Movie Maker

`http://download.live.com/moviemaker`

Microsoft Windows comes with Windows Movie Maker 2 installed; the newest release of the Movie Maker program is called Windows Live Movie Maker (see Figure 12-1). It's available online for free.

The editing suite has been redesigned with ease of use in mind. It comes with all the basic video-editing tools. You can figure out how to use the program reasonably easily, and the interface is consistent with the Microsoft Office 2007 applications.

By using Windows Live Movie Maker, you can edit, clip, and add some minor special effects. In addition, you can upload directly from the program to YouTube.

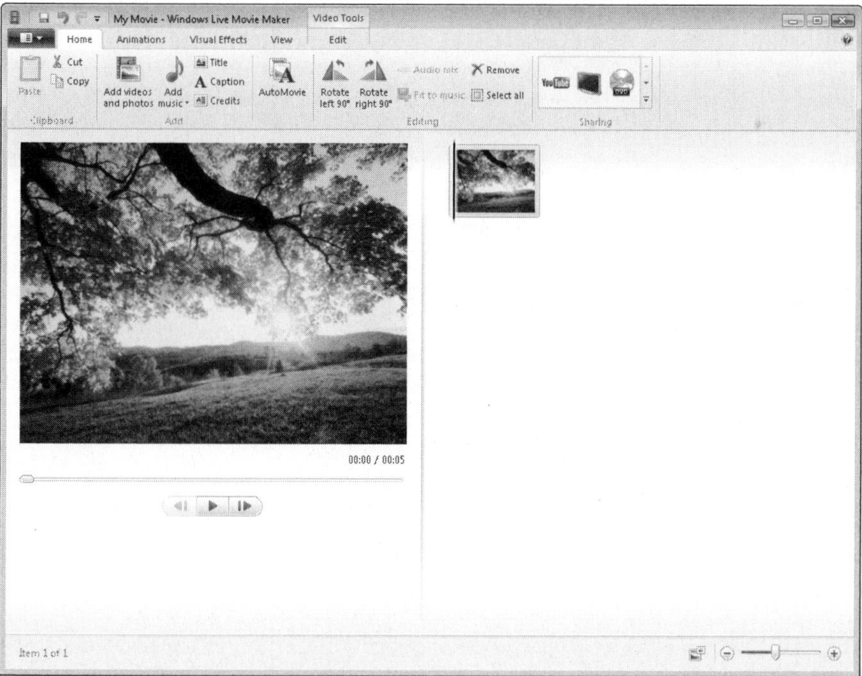

Figure 12-1: Windows Live Movie Maker offers a suite of useful video-editing tools.

iMovie

`www.apple.com/ilife/imovie`

Apple's iMovie is part of the suite of tools that comes with iLife, usually pre-installed when you purchase an Apple computer. If you don't have iLife, $79 gets you iPhoto, iMovie, GarageBand, iWeb, and iDVD.

iMovie — see Figure 12-2 — is the most affordable editor that you can get for Mac OS X. The software provides you with all the basic tools for editing videos: inserting clips, adjusting the quality of the picture, adding minor special effects, and then exporting them in formats that you can post on the Web.

The latest version has adopted much of the interface from iPhoto, letting you organize and sort your videos like you do with still photographs.

Figure 12-2: Get iMovie by installing Apple's iLife.

Choosing a video host

Storing video files and then serving them to your Web visitors can be costly. Web hosts typically charge for disk space and bandwidth used, and that means the more videos you put online and the more popular they are, the more Web hosting costs you. So, consider using a video-sharing service that takes care of storage and bandwidth for you, and still lets you embed the files in your Web site or blog. Social-network video-sharing services, such as YouTube, Blip.tv, Vimeo, and others, have become the de facto way of sharing video with your viewers.

YouTube (`www.youtube.com`) is the most popular of all the video services. Since it was purchased by Google in 2006, its popularity hit the mainstream, and now even traditional media outlets use YouTube to post their own clips of shows and newscasts that they produce. You can see all kinds of video on the site, and I recommend trying YouTube as your first sharing service. (You can always post your videos on other services, as well.)

On YouTube, you can

- Upload and organize videos by using *tags* (keywords), create playlists, and add your videos to groups.
- Post videos and receive comments (see Figure 12-3).
- View other members' videos and leave comments. You can also leave video responses!
- Choose to make some or all of your videos private, or share them with a select group.

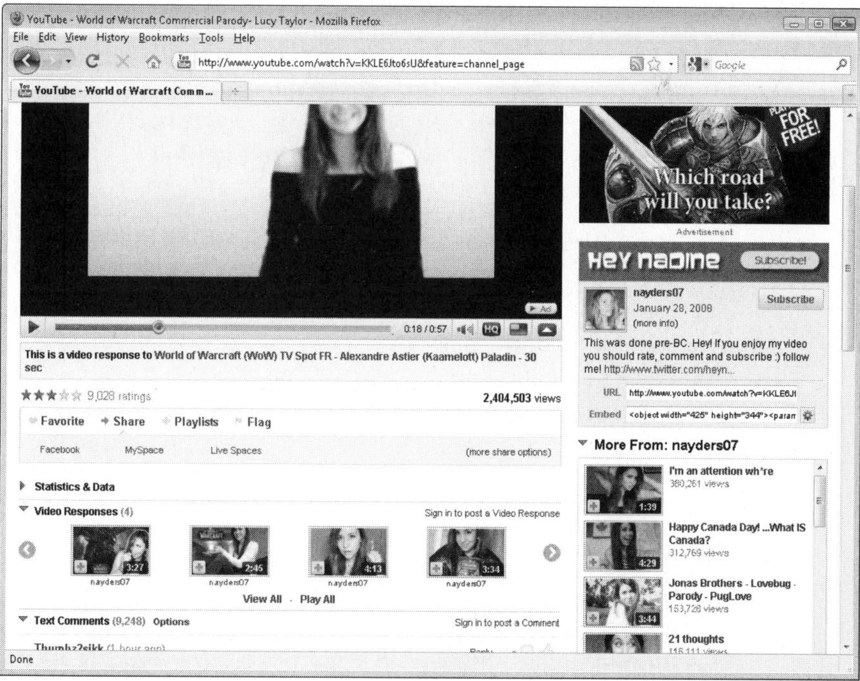

Figure 12-3: You can leave comments and video responses on YouTube.

YouTube accounts are free, and you can upload as many videos as you want. However, an individual video file that you upload can't exceed 1GB in size and must be less than ten minutes long.

If your videos are much longer and you don't think you can make them any shorter, you may want to consider other video services. Services such as the following are alternatives to YouTube on which you can upload and post videos:

- Blip.tv (`www.blip.tv`)
- Dailymotion (`www.dailymotion.com`)
- Yahoo! Video (`http://video.yahoo.com/explore/videos/categories/video+blogs`)
- Metacafe (`www.metacafe.com`)
- Revver (`www.revver.com`)
- Vimeo (`www.vimeo.com`)

Each has a slightly different set of features, but all do the basics: allow you to upload videos and share them with others.

Many of the popular video bloggers share their videos on three or four of the most popular video-sharing services, although these bloggers usually use only one service to share the files on their own blogs. The purpose of putting the video on several video-sharing services is to tap into the communities on each, building up views and traffic.

Whatever service you choose, look for features that simplify uploading and sharing videos on your blog, such as the following:

- ***Embedding* a video (adding a bit of code that displays your video):** Some services make embedding very easy, but others may be a bit more technical.
- **Tracking views of your video:** See at a glance which of your videos are popular (and which aren't).
- **Subscribing to your video stream:** When visitors can subscribe, they know about your new content right away and are more likely to view your video.

Creating a Video

I don't have enough space in this book to give you in-depth advice about shooting video and editing it, so in the following sections, I give you the basics. However, I recommend that if this topic interests you, look into *Digital Video For Dummies,* 4th Edition, by Keith Underdahl, and *Videoblogging*

For Dummies, by Stephanie Cottrell Bryant. Those books together give you a crash course in how to shoot, edit, and post video to the Web in much greater detail than this book can cover.

Shooting video

Video is probably the hardest thing to capture for your blog because video cameras can be bulky, and sometimes, taking a video camera with you just isn't convenient.

Here are a few tips for shooting video for your blog:

- **Always take your camera with you.** If you're heading out to the corner store or visiting family, find a way to have your camera with you so that it isn't annoying to carry. I can guarantee that if you don't make a habit of having your camera with you, you'll miss good stuff.
- **Keep your camera charged and make sure to have extra charged batteries in your camera bag.** Some devices have built-in batteries and require you to plug them into your computer to charge them. All video cameras have custom rechargeable batteries, so try to maintain a charged state in the batteries — you never know when you'll need to shoot something.
- **The higher quality of video in newer cameras means that you don't need to worry about shooting the perfect video.** You can shoot from the hip, even with a video camera. Remember, having a poor-quality piece of video is still better than not having any video at all.
- **You may find a tripod really helpful, especially in situations in which you're taping long pieces of video.** For one thing, you don't have to hold the camera the whole time. For another, handheld video shots can look shaky, making them hard for your visitors to watch.
- **Not everyone wants to appear in videos, especially videos that go online for anyone to see.** Before you shoot, get the permission of your subjects, and be specific about how you plan to use the footage. You might also want to get some of these permissions documented in writing to cover yourself, legally.
- **Practice, practice, practice.** Your videos get better the more effort and time you put into them, so don't get too discouraged if your first efforts don't come out the way you imagined. You'll get there.

Of course, not all video bloggers shoot video of things around them in their life, of events, or of whatever they run into. Many video bloggers choose to talk to their camera directly or have personal conversations with their audience. These kinds of videos are very popular and garner quite a number of comments and responses from people who view them. The most interesting blogs can do both styles of video recording and still maintain large audiences.

Try different styles and see what your readers like best. Do they like you talking to the camera, or do they prefer when you're out shooting in the wild? Get creative with your video style and figure out what you like to shoot. Keep it fun for yourself — that enthusiasm shows through in the videos you post.

Editing video

After you shoot some video, you can edit it by using your video-editing software.

The most common edits to make involve trimming a video, selecting the parts that you want to show, and adding text and transitions between the cuts that you make. You really get to decide how creative you want to be. You don't need to use transitions or even edit your video at all. Remember, just because you can add a barn-door transition effect doesn't mean you must! Go with what feels right for the tone of your video and with your audience. Here are a few of the most common editing methods video bloggers use to make their videos more appealing:

- **Cuts and trims:** A lot of amateur online video is actually only a single shot. For example, a video blogger who uses a Webcam typically just sits in front of the camera and talks. The camera viewpoint doesn't change. However, most professional video is actually made up of several different shots, played one after the other (a shot of the exterior of a building, then your subject's office, then the interview of the person, for example). Taking multiple shots means that you likely need to cut out unwanted material, or even to rearrange the order of the clips that you have.
- **Transitions:** *Transitions* are edit points between different video clips. Many videographers like to make those points flow smoothly and not jar the person watching the video between cuts. They add effects such as fades, wipes, or peels, or they insert a shape or black screen in between the clips.

  Software that allows you to add transitions typically offers you the ability to customize a transition by changing its length or appearance.
- **Text and credits:** You can add three types of text bits to your videos:
  - *Title:* You typically show titles at the beginning of your video.
  - *Caption:* A *caption* is text that sits on top of your video clip to identify who's talking, or to provide additional information.
  - *Credits:* The credits are scrolling text, much like movie credits.
- **Audio:** Audio tracks, such as music or voice overlays, can add value to your videos. Audio transitions can smooth the flow from one clip to another, and you can adjust the volume and add fades at the beginning and end of your video or each scene.

Putting Video Online

After you create your video masterpiece, you need somewhere to upload it. In the following sections, I show you how you can upload your video to YouTube. You use a similar process with most other video-sharing services. Regardless of which service you choose, look for the uploading instructions if you need help.

Uploading to YouTube

Uploading your videos is straightforward: Grab your video file, upload the file, add a few tags, and you're done! Just follow these steps:

1. **Open your browser to YouTube (**`www.youtube.com`**) and sign in.**

   The main YouTube account page opens.

   If you don't already have a YouTube account, you have to sign up for one before you can upload a video.

2. **Click the yellow Upload button at the top-right of the screen.**

   The uploader interface appears.

3. **Click Upload Video (another yellow button) in the center of the screen and select the video file you're uploading from your local hard drive.**

   The Video File Upload screen opens.

4. **While your video is uploading, you can enter the video title, a description of the video, and some tags in the appropriate text boxes, and select which category the video belongs in from the drop-down list (see Figure 12-4). You can also select which privacy setting you want if you want to restrict your video to a select group of other YouTube users.**

5. **Click Save Changes.**

   Your video page loads, displaying your file. It may take a little while for YouTube to fully process the video (depending on the size of the file that you uploaded).

Uploading to YouTube via your Webcam

You can upload a video directly to YouTube by using your Webcam. If you have a Webcam and want to try this direct upload, follow these steps:

1. **Open your browser to YouTube (**`www.youtube.com`**) and sign in.**

   If you don't already have a YouTube account, you have to sign up for one before you can upload a video.

2. **Click the yellow Upload button at the top-right of the screen.**

   The uploader interface appears.

3. **Click the Record from Webcam button.**

   A page opens, where you need to authorize your browser to connect to your Webcam.

4. **Click Authorize so that you can start recording.**

5. **Record your video (see Figure 12-5).**

   You can also preview your video or re-record if you don't like what you just did.

6. **Click Publish.**

   After you publish your video, it may take a few minutes to show up online. While you're waiting, you can fill in the description and title on the video page.

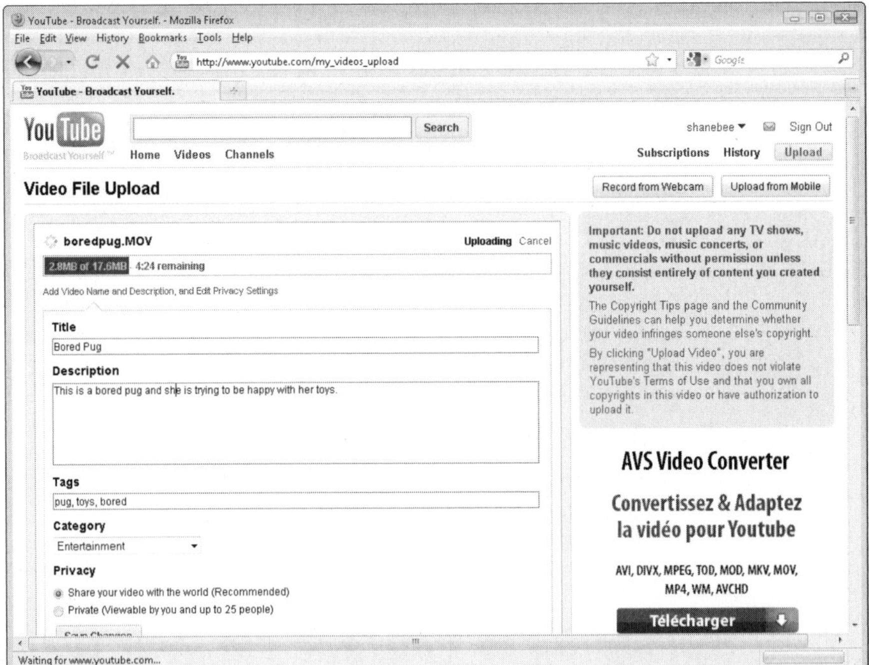

Figure 12-4: Uploading your video files to YouTube.

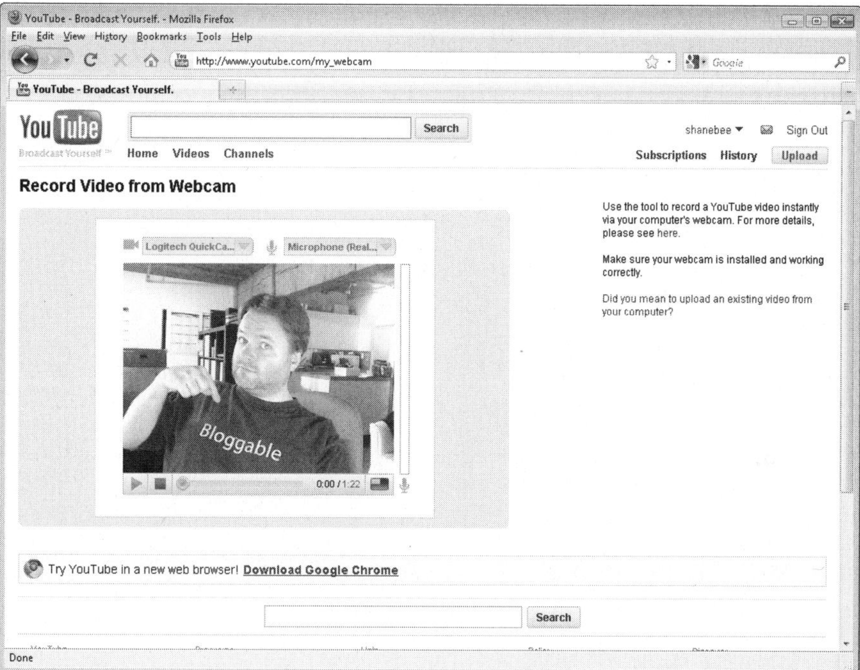

Figure 12-5: Uploading video in real-time via a Webcam.

Inserting a YouTube video in a blog post

You can add your videos to your blog via YouTube quite simply. You need to copy a little bit of code called the *embed code* from your video on YouTube and paste it into your blog post. Follow these steps:

1. **Open your browser to the YouTube page of the video that you want to embed.**

   Most videos on YouTube offer embed code. The code is located on the top-right side of the video page, where it says Embed.

2. **Copy the Embed code from the YouTube page.**

   Click the code to select it and press Ctrl+C (⌘+C on the Mac).

3. **Start a new blog post in your blogging software and paste the code into the appropriate spot by pressing Ctrl+V (⌘+V on the Mac).**
4. **Save and/or Publish your blog post.**
5. **Check your blog and try playing the video, just to make sure it all works.**

Part V
Marketing and Promoting Your Blog

"I'm sorry. I'm answering email right now. And since when does the Taco Bell Chihuahua have a blog anyway?"

In this part . . .

Undecipherable acronyms become your friend in Chapter 13 when you find out how to handle all the flavors of RSS feeds, syndicating your content across the Web and on other blogs. Your friends are doing it, your kids are doing it; it's time to find out what this Twitter thing is all about. Chapter 14 walks you through starting an account and the etiquette of *tweeting*. And if that isn't enough, you can really enter the realm of hipness by reading through Chapter 15, which is all about the world of social networking. Chapter 16 makes it real, with tips on installing and understanding Web statistics tools for tracking your traffic.

Chapter 13

Reaching Out with RSS

In This Chapter

- Figuring out what RSS really is
- Signing up for an RSS feed
- Putting RSS to work for your blog

No fashionable blog would be caught dead without a Web feed — it's essential for both accessibility and promotion of your blog. RSS (Really Simple Syndication) feeds, or Web feeds, give you an easy way to distribute your content, such as blog posts and podcasts, to your Web audience.

But what is RSS, really? In this chapter, I explain what an RSS feed is, how to create your blog feed (it's easy), how to subscribe to feeds, and more.

Getting the Goods on Web Feeds

RSS is one of the hottest technologies on the Internet today. Since 2003 — which is when blogs truly reached mainstream awareness — blogs and other technologies have adopted RSS at an exponential rate. Companies such as Mozilla, Microsoft, IBM, and many others are finding new and interesting ways to use RSS feeds to share information, both through their Web sites and through internal communication processes.

Put simply, when you syndicate your blog by using a Web feed, software reads your blog posts, which it formats by using XML (eXtensible Markup Language). XML is an Internet standard and marks your prose so that software applications can understand and display it properly for readers who subscribe to your blog.

Why is RSS a good thing? Well, it means that code can be used to easily display your blog's feed on other Web sites, from blogs to search engines. Sites that pull in news from multiple sources use RSS feeds to do so, and being syndicated in this way can earn you traffic from those sites back to your blog.

But more importantly, newsreader software that any visitor to your site might use can read RSS feeds, and visitors can then access your blog quickly and easily. By subscribing to a blog via an RSS feed, visitors don't have to bookmark hundreds of blogs and check them every 20 minutes to see whether the bloggers have updated them; a user can simply log in to his or her newsreader software to see in one window all the feeds to which he or she subscribes.

On the Web, several different terms describe the subject of this chapter: *RSS, Atom, Web feed,* and *news feed* are a few. Web site developers use all these terms interchangeably, but the most accurate one is *Web feed.* RSS is simply a type of Web feed. Even though Web feed is the most accurate name, I usually refer to RSS feeds because that's how most blogs and bloggers refer to them.

If you want to find out more about RSS than I can provide in this chapter, either to give your blog visibility in the world or to pull other blog content into your own blog or site, consider reading *Syndicating Web Sites with RSS Feeds For Dummies,* by Ellen Finkelstein.

Breaking it down further

Essentially, RSS gives your blog the ability to break down its content into a basic text file. Software creates this text file in a special XML format that makes up the feed. Blog software then distributes this plain-text version of your blog content to other Web sites, search engines, and blogosphere tracking services. Figure 13-1 shows the code behind an RSS feed.

CP Home › Templates › Edit Template

View Rendered Template

Template Name weblog/rss_2.0

View Revision History View

```
<?xml version="1.0" encoding="{encoding}"?>
<rss version="2.0"
   xmlns:dc="http://purl.org/dc/elements/1.1/"
   xmlns:sy="http://purl.org/rss/1.0/modules/syndication/"
   xmlns:admin="http://webns.net/mvcb/"
   xmlns:rdf="http://www.w3.org/1999/02/22-rdf-syntax-ns#"
   xmlns:content="http://purl.org/rss/1.0/modules/content/">

   <channel>

   <title>{exp:xml_encode}{weblog_name}{/exp:xml_encode}</title>
   <link>{weblog_url}</link>
   <description>{weblog_description}</description>
   <dc:language>{weblog_language}</dc:language>
   <dc:creator>{email}</dc:creator>
   <dc:rights>Copyright {gmt_date format="%Y"}</dc:rights>
   <dc:date>{gmt_date format="%Y-%m-%dT%H:%i:%s%Q"}</dc:date>
   <admin:generatorAgent rdf:resource="http://www.pmachine.com/" />

{exp:weblog:entries weblog="{master_weblog_name}" limit="10" rdf="off" dynamic_start="on"}
   <item>
```

Template Notes

Figure 13-1: Web feeds aren't very pretty for humans to look at.

A few acronyms for RSS are floating around out on the Internet. Here are the acronyms you're most likely to see, and if you want to talk about RSS with your blog readers, you can use any of them (but the first one tends to be the most popular):

- Really Simple Syndication
- RDF Site Summary
- Real Simple Syndication
- Rich Site Summary

You can use RSS to syndicate content on your blog, but most mainstream news agencies also use RSS to make their news information more accessible. News services such as Reuters, CBC, CNN, and the Washington Post use RSS technology to spread their articles beyond their own Web sites.

Many Web browsers use XML to handle displaying RSS feeds in a more attractive format for humans. If you click an RSS feed link and find that the content that loads looks rather user friendly, you're probably using a browser that understands and formats XML nicely.

For a really excellent short video that describes just what RSS is and how it works, visit the Common Craft blog at `www.commoncraft.com/rss_plain_english`. This video uses simple graphics and words to get across the concepts that make RSS so groundbreaking.

Confused? Well, don't worry, because nearly all blog software automatically builds your RSS feed and helps you advertise it to your blog visitors. So, you're most likely covered, in any case — but if you know a little bit about RSS and why it's important to your blog, you can ensure your blog content reaches a wider audience.

Generating Web traffic

Some bloggers have a tendency to limit the distribution of their content and keep it off other sites. The reasoning goes that you worked hard to create that content, so why should other sites and software get to display it for free?

Actually, because of its ease of use, RSS can help you gain more users. Your Web site can travel farther than ever because you can distribute RSS feeds with little to no effort on your part. Because syndication of your content includes links back to your blog, people who are exposed to your RSS feed probably click those links and come to your blog.

So, because the RSS feed is only text, it doesn't have to stay in one place. Any number of Web sites and blogs can pick it up and display it.

Creating a feed for your blog

Unless you really want to mess around in the code of your own RSS files, you shouldn't need to do anything special to get started with RSS. Most blog software already includes an RSS feed that pulls together and syndicates your blog. At most, you might have to turn on the option to have an RSS feed.

Then, just blog normally and ignore the feed — your users can find it and subscribe, and your blog content flows automatically into the feed.

Chances are that your blog software already has RSS capability. Be sure to check your administrative settings and documentation. If it doesn't, you might also be able to add the functionality by using a plug-in.

If you don't have software that creates an RSS feed, you have a couple of options. If you're a programmer or coder, you can probably pick up enough XML to hand-code an RSS feed yourself. But an even better option is to use some of the third-party feed creation tools available today:

- **FeedYes** (`www.feedyes.com`): Use this simple tool to create an RSS feed from any Web site or blog. You can create multiple feeds and, with an account, edit and manage them. FeedYes is free.
- **Feedfire** (`www.feedfire.com`): This service lets you create RSS feeds for any Web site that doesn't already have one, and it promises to let you do it without *any* programming (although none of these tools have a high technical bar). You can get started for free.
- **Feed43** (`www.feed43.com`): Set up a feed for your blog quickly and for free. Increase the frequency with which your feed is updated by buying a higher level of feed, starting at $29 a year.
- **FeedForAll** (`www.feedforall.com`): You can use this tool to create and edit RSS feeds for your blog or podcast. You must be able to install software on your Web host to use this tool. Pricing starts at $39.95.

When a feed exists, you don't need to do anything else. Search engines and software tools automatically find it when they index your blog, and your readers can subscribe to your feed when and if they choose to do so.

Subscribing to an RSS Feed

I'm sure you read at least a few favorite blogs regularly. Do you visit them every day or maybe even several times a day? Are you ever frustrated because the site hasn't been updated yet? Do you ever miss a post by a few minutes, and then read it hours or days later, and miss out on the conversation? The solution to this problem is RSS.

Follow these basic steps to get set up with your favorite blog's RSS feed:

1. **Choose a newsreader and sign up to begin using it.**

   You can find tons out there, and I tell you about a few of my favorites in the sections "Finding a Web-based newsreader" or "Choosing a desktop-based reader," later in this chapter.

2. **Subscribe to an RSS feed.**

   Don't worry — you can subscribe to an RSS feed even more easily (and cheaply) than you can subscribe to a newspaper or magazine, although the idea is similar. The newsreader software you chose and signed up to use provides specific instructions on subscribing.

3. **Check your newsreader.**

   When you subscribe to an RSS feed, new blog posts appear in your newsreader every time the blogger posts a new entry to his or her blog. When the blogger publishes a new post, the RSS feed is updated a few minutes later, and the newsreader checks the feed and alerts you to the new posts.

4. **Click, read, and *voilà!***

   No more boring bookmarking and refreshing a blog over and over. You go to the blog only when it has new content, so you never miss anything.

You can subscribe to as many (or as few) feeds as you want, potentially keeping track of hundreds of sites, all in one place.

Browser newsreaders

Some browsers have built-in newsreaders that you can use to subscribe to feeds and then read them. On a PC, Internet Explorer 7 and higher allows you to read, subscribe to, and manage feed subscriptions right inside the browser. Mac and PC users of the Firefox Web browser, you can install a plug-in called Sage (`https://addons.mozilla.org/en-US/firefox/addon/77`) to add news-reading capabilities to the browser.

On the Mac, you can use the built-in newsreader in the Safari browser to subscribe to and read feeds.

Finding a Web-based newsreader

Web-based newsreaders are online services that allow you to aggregate your favorite feeds into a simple interface where you can read your subscriptions. These online services are usually free.

The big advantage to using a Web-based newsreader is that you can log in to the service from any computer, even if you're traveling, at the library, or using your son's laptop. In most cases, however, you need to have Internet access in order to read the blog posts because you have to be online. Google Reader, Bloglines, and NewsGator, introduced in the following sections, are three popular Web-based newsreaders.

Google Reader

`www.google.com/reader`

Google Reader is a great Web-based feed aggregator. If you already registered with Gmail or other Google services, getting started with Reader is as simple as signing in at `www.google.com/reader`. If you don't have a Google account already, click the Create an Account Now link.

Google Reader's interface is similar to the other Google Web products, and it features feed searching, RSS feed sharing, mobile access, and offline reading. Google Reader is shown in Figure 13-2.

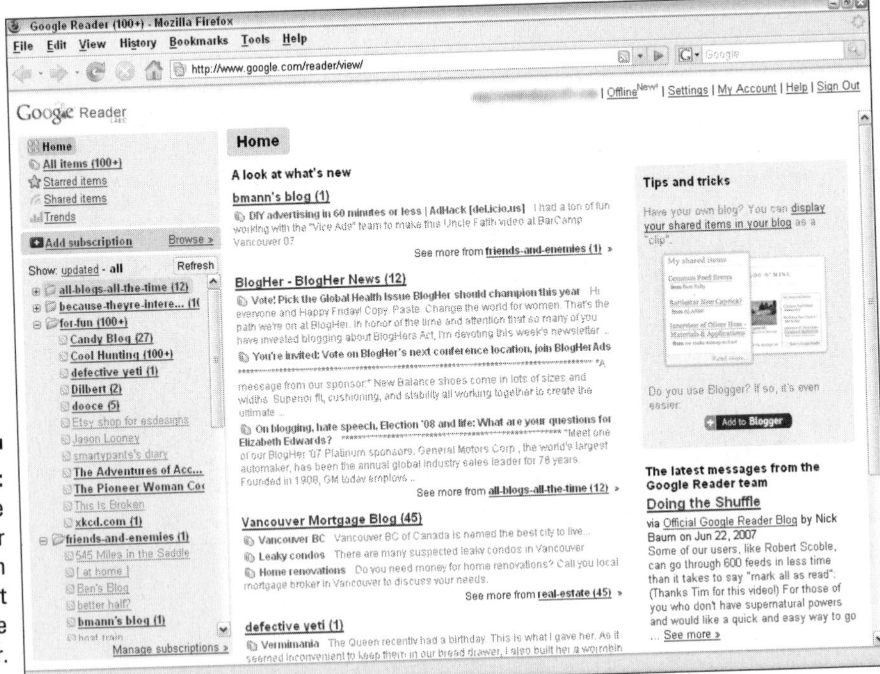

Figure 13-2: Google Reader is an excellent online newsreader.

Bloglines

```
www.bloglines.com
```

The Web-based application Bloglines is super-simple to use, with quick tools for adding a subscription and sorting your subscriptions into categories. One of the fun features of Bloglines is that you can produce a blogroll — a list of links to blogs — to put in your blog's sidebar, sharing the blogs to which you're subscribed with your readers. Bloglines even carries over the categorization when it displays your blog subscriptions. You can mark some feeds as private if you prefer not to share them with the world.

NewsGator

```
www.newsgator.com
```

Like Bloglines and Google Reader, NewsGator is a handy online newsreader that you can use for free. In NewsGator, you can quickly subscribe to blog feeds, sort them into categories that you choose, and tell at a glance which sites have new content. NewsGator also gives you some handy tools next to each post to let you e-mail the post to a friend, send the post via an instant messenger program, or save it in a Clippings file for later use.

When you sign up for NewsGator, you can pre-populate your newsreader with popular blogs in categories such as Sports, Technology, or Top Blogs. If you're new to blogging, you can use this feature to find some interesting blogs to read to help figure out this whole blogging thing.

Choosing a desktop-based reader

Desktop readers are a little different than online newsreaders. You install desktop readers directly on your computer (so they don't use any Web-based tools), which gives you a bit more control over when the reader checks and updates your feeds. Best of all, a desktop reader actually downloads the feeds to your machine, so you can read blogs even when you don't have Internet access — perhaps while making a commute or on an airplane.

Some people believe that a major drawback of desktop readers is that they cause your computer to run slower than it normally would, especially when it has to check a large number of feeds. Because computers have so many differences, I can't predict whether a desktop reader may slow down your computer, but definitely watch out for this problem.

FeedDemon (Windows)

```
www.newsgator.com/individuals/feeddemon/default.aspx
```

FeedDemon is a free RSS reader client that you can install locally on your computer. It downloads updates from your feeds on a regular basis (which you can configure), and it features many great organizational tools that keep your feeds updated and easy to peruse.

FeedDemon, available from the folks at NewsGator, also downloads and stores any podcasts to which you subscribe, and it transfers those podcasts to your portable audio player. As if that isn't enough, you can also set up custom news watches to keep track of topics or events that you want to know more about.

FeedDemon is available only for Windows.

NetNewsWire (Mac)

```
www.newsgator.com/individuals/netnewswire/default.aspx
```

NewsGator's Mac newsreader solution is NetNewsWire, a free program that takes advantage of preinstalled Apple software on the Mac. As with FeedDemon, you can use NetNewsWire to read and organize feeds, as well as save them for later reference or send them via e-mail or instant messenger to a friend.

NetNewsWire automatically downloads podcasts and transfers them to Apple's iTunes software, and you can even use NetNewsWire with iCal and Address Book.

NewsGator also makes a newsreader for the Apple iPhone, which you can download via the iPhone App Store. The premium version, at $1.99, ensures that your reading experience is ad-free.

AmphetaDesk

```
www.disobey.com/amphetadesk
```

AmphetaDesk is a free, open source, cross-platform newsreader that should satisfy the truly geeky. Its code is highly customizable, so if you care to do so, you can change the interface's look and feel, as well as its functionality.

Signing up for a feed

After you select a newsreader, you can subscribe to a feed and start reading! This task has two steps: visiting a blog that you enjoy reading and then subscribing.

Somewhere on the blog page, you might see a small orange icon, sometimes with the acronym RSS or XML in it. Or you might just see a small text link to the feed.

Look closely — RSS feeds can be hard to find on the page. Because you need to use the link only once, bloggers tend to downplay them in the design.

Alternet (`www.alternet.org`) offers several different RSS feeds, so you can choose between getting front page news stories, video stories, columns, and so on. Check out all the flavors at `www.alternet.org/webfeeds`.

When you find the RSS link or icon, click it. If you're using a Web-based newsreader, you might be subscribed automatically, or you might see an icon for subscribing using one of the most common newsreaders.

If you don't see a link or an icon to an RSS feed, copy the URL from the address bar of the browser. Return to your newsreader and follow your newsreader's instructions for adding a new subscription.

Follow these steps to subscribe to an RSS feed in Google Reader:

1. **Visit a blog or Web site to which you want to subscribe and locate the feed link or icon.**
2. **Click the link.**

   The browser displays the feed.
3. **Copy the URL from the address bar.**

   You can also simply right-click the feed link or icon and select Copy Link Location or Copy Shortcut from the pop-up menu that appears.
4. **In Google Reader, click the Add Subscription link in the left column.**

   A small dialog box opens, as shown in Figure 13-3.

Figure 13-3: Subscribing to a feed is quick and easy in Google Reader.

5. **Paste the URL into the box and click Add.**

   If Google Reader finds the feed, that feed appears in the right column. If it doesn't find the feed, Google Reader notifies you.

6. **Repeat as desired!**

Making the Most of RSS

You can use RSS in all sorts of ways. Industries as diverse as financial sectors and breaking news stories have adopted RSS because it's so flexible and generates Web site traffic, attracting new readers from search engines and news aggregators. But that's not all you can use RSS for:

- **Syndicating content:** In the blogosphere, *syndication* means that you publish your information on the Web so that newsreaders and other Web sites can display it.
- **Aggregating news:** Do you like other blogs that deal with similar topics as your own? You can use their RSS feeds to include their content on your Web site. You can link directly to it or, if your blog software has such functionality, display other blog content on your own blog.
- **Replacing e-mail newsletters:** Some RSS advocates make astounding claims that RSS will be the death of e-mail. Although this dire prediction hasn't yet come to pass, RSS definitely has many advantages over e-mail newsletters. The most important is that you can avoid spam. How? You can simply choose to read an RSS feed, rather than receive more e-mail; by not giving away your e-mail address, you don't put it at risk for being sold to a spammer.
- **Keeping communities updated:** RSS feeds are terrific for keeping people updated. Some feeds merely post information, such as sports scores — as fast as a goal is scored, an RSS feed can be updated. Here are a few of the kinds of things you can share that people might want to know as soon as possible:
  - Security bulletins
  - Classified listings for apartments
  - Emergency weather changes
  - Changes to bids on eBay or Amazon
  - Product availability at retail stores

Because of the simplicity of using RSS technology (yes, the actual building of RSS feeds might still be too geeky for most bloggers), you can use it in many ways to augment the communication channels of your blog or within your community that you haven't quite figured out yet. Get creative!

Chapter 14

Joining the Twitterverse

In This Chapter

- Taking the measure of Twitter
- Using Twitter
- Customizing your account
- Using your phone to tweet
- Bringing Twitter and your blog together

While I was watching a well-known sitcom on TV the other day, a character mentioned Twitter. If that's not mainstream, I don't know what is! But just because Hollywood knows about Twitter doesn't mean that you don't have questions, so this chapter gets down to brass tacks.

Twitter (`www.twitter.com`) is a free social network used for *micro blogging,* which is essentially blogging, but in very short updates. How short? Well, on Twitter, your posts are limited to 140 characters — barely enough for a couple of sentences. (I introduce micro blogging in Chapter 6.) If you use Facebook, you may be surprised to know that you're already familiar with micro blogging.

Although you can post only up to 140 characters of text at a time on Twitter, you can use it to share photographs and links, even videos. Many businesses have jumped onto the Twitter bandwagon and use the tool to tell their customers about sales, specials, and other news.

If this chapter whets your appetite for even more Twitter tidbits, be sure to check out *Twitter For Dummies,* by Laura Fitton, Michael Gruen, and Leslie Poston.

Understanding Twitter

Twitter started in 2006 and grew slowly into the phenomenon it is today. It's fundamentally difficult to explain both its popularity and its purpose; as with blogs themselves, some very logical and common-sense questions jump to mind for most people:

- Who's going to read this stuff, anyway?
- What am I supposed to talk about on Twitter?
- Why do people use Twitter?
- Isn't Twitter a huge waste of time?
- Just how do the creators of Twitter make money?

And in the case of people who already have a blog, the big question is, "Do I really need Twitter, as well?"

I hope you can forgive my answer to these questions: It's up to you! People are using Twitter for all kinds of reasons — I've seen Twitter accounts devoted to spiritual guidance, sports, sex, marketing, Web development, and diaries. You name it, and someone is using Twitter to talk about it. So, explaining why you should use Twitter, and what you might get out of it, is pretty hard to do!

For example, food blogger Degan Beley has a Twitter account set up using the same name as her blog (Ethnic Eats, which is online at `www.ethniceats.ca`), and uses Twitter to let her readers know short tidbits about what she's doing or planning next. In Figure 14-1, you can see her Twitter profile page (`www.twitter.com/ethniceats`).

Degan also displays her Twitter updates on her blog, ensuring that the audiences for both her main blog and Twitter micro blog know what's going on in each place. The goal of having both a blog and a Twitter account is pretty simple: Get more readers by producing different kinds of content in different Web formats.

For most Twitter users, the first goal is communication, quickly followed by reaching out to more people in a format that they can use easily (and for free), which reaches people very quickly.

Here are just a few ways in which individuals and businesses are putting Twitter to work:

- **Restaurants:** Advertise specials, let customers know about available tables, and offer coupons.
- **Pundits:** Post links and resources to support their viewpoints.

- **Friends:** Coordinate get-togethers and even arrange dates.
- **Conference organizers:** Remind potential attendees of sign-up deadlines and early-bird pricing specials.
- **Conference attendees:** Let other attendees know about good speakers (and snacks) and keep those who aren't attending up to date.
- **Celebrities:** Extend their personal brand and identity by talking about their projects.
- **Characters from popular television shows:** Carry on dialogue with viewers between episodes — written by the show's writers, actors, or marketing folks.
- **Political candidates:** Update voters about their policies and appearances.
- **Emergency services:** Update followers about operations. In 2009, the Australian County Fire Authority used Twitter to send out alerts and updates about the Black Saturday bushfires that killed 173 people and injured more than 400.

Figure 14-1: Ethnic Eats blogger Degan Beley uses Twitter for updates too minor to deserve a whole blog post.

Twitter updates have a lot of potential to inform and entertain. To get a sense of the mechanics of using Twitter, follow these basic steps:

1. **Sign up for a Twitter account and choose a nickname.**

   When you set up your account, you can choose to share your updates — called *tweets* — with anyone (meaning the public) or to restrict access to only the people you choose to follow.

2. **Customize your icon and profile page to make it reflect your personality or brand.**

3. **Run your contact list through Twitter to see if any of your friends, family, and colleagues are on Twitter.**

   If any of them are on Twitter, decide whether you want to follow their updates.

4. **Post updates.**

   You can tweet about anything, from news about your plans, your thoughts, or activities.

   People who follow you on Twitter see your updates. On the Web, updates appear right when you post them to Twitter. Followers who have their phones configured to do so get your updates as text messages and can respond to them by sending a text message to a number provided by Twitter.

Following people on Twitter is equivalent to making them into a friend or contact on other social networks; Twitter simply calls those folks that read your updates *followers.* Like with other social networks, the number of followers you have indicates your popularity, and a lot of people really focus on getting those numbers high.

The really neat thing about Twitter is that you can participate without ever visiting the Twitter Web site. Twitter's designed so that you can handle the whole thing by mobile phone text messaging, keeping you updated with a device that you probably already have close to hand.

Getting Started

I'm a big fan of learning by doing, so in the following sections, I walk you through signing up for Twitter and getting started. I get the easy job — getting you started with Twitter. You have the hard job of figuring out what to tweet about!

Signing up for an account

Follow these steps to set up a Twitter account:

1. **Point your Web browser to** `www.twitter.com`**.**

   The Twitter home page opens.

2. **Click the Sign Up Now button on the home page.**

   Twitter loads the Create an Account page.

3. **Enter your first and last name in the Full Name field.**

   You're limited to 20 characters in this field.

4. **Choose a Twitter username and type it in the Username field.**

   Unlike some social networks, you can change your username later.

   Your username is limited to 15 characters, and while you type in your desired username, Twitter checks to see whether it's available. If you don't get a green OK message (see Figure 14-2), try again until you find an available username.

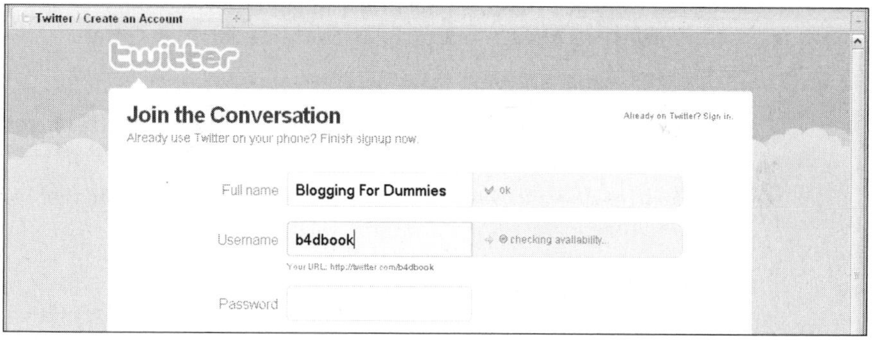

Figure 14-2: You can sign up for Twitter quickly (and for free).

5. **Type a password that you can remember in the Password field.**

   A status message indicates whether your password meets the Twitter requirements and is likely to be secure.

6. **Type your e-mail address in the Email field.**

   Select the checkbox below the Email text box if you want to subscribe to the Twitter e-mail newsletter.

7. **Type the words shown in the visual CAPTCHA area.**

   This feature is designed to ensure that only real people (not automated software) can sign up for accounts.

8. **Click Create My Account.**

   Twitter creates your new account and loads the Find People You Know on Twitter page. You also receive an e-mail that contains your new account information at the address you used to sign up.

Finding friends to follow

After you set up your account, you can let Twitter help you find friends, family, and colleagues who are also Twitter users by giving the service access to your contact lists in Gmail, Yahoo!, or AOL. If you don't have contact lists with any of these tools, click the Skip This Step link at the bottom of this screen.

To let Twitter access your contact list in an online e-mail tool and find people to follow, just follow these steps:

1. **On the Find People You Know page, click the name of the service that you use to keep track of your contacts, such as Gmail.**

   Twitter loads a login information screen.

2. **Provide your login information for the service to which you want to give Twitter access, such as your e-mail address and password.**

   Twitter doesn't keep this information; you're granting the company only one-time access to your contact list.

3. **Click Continue.**

   Twitter connects to the service and loads your contact information, matching the e-mail addresses from your list against the e-mail addresses of other Twitter users.

   A list of your contacts who have Twitter accounts appears.

4. **Deselect the check boxes next to the contacts whom you *don't* want to follow on Twitter.**

   You can always unfollow people later.

5. **Click Continue.**

   Twitter subscribes you to your contacts' updates and loads the Why Not Invite Some Friends page, which shows contacts in your contact list who don't have Twitter accounts.

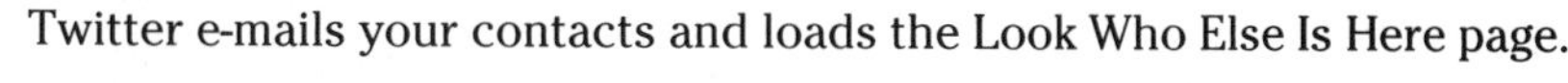

6. **Select the checkbox beside the name of any contact you want to invite to use Twitter and click Invite.**

   Twitter e-mails your contacts and loads the Look Who Else Is Here page.

   Don't invite everyone you know to use Twitter; people often perceive participation invitations as spam. If you'd prefer not to invite anyone, click the Skip This Step link at the bottom of the page.

7. **Select anyone from the Look Who Else Is Here page whom you want to follow and click Finish.**

   If you prefer not to follow any of these popular Twitter users, simply click Finish without selecting any of them.

   Twitter loads your personal home page, which displays messages from all the people you're following.

If you'd prefer not to run your contact list through Twitter, you can easily search for individual users by clicking the Find People link that appears in the navigation area at the top of all Twitter pages and then using the search tools provided.

Twittering

After you sign up for a Twitter account, it's time for the fun part — your first tweet! You can send a tweet pretty darn easily from the Web site. Follow these steps:

1. **Point your browser to** `www.twitter.com` **and log in to Twitter if you aren't already logged in.**

   Twitter loads your personal home page, which displays messages from all the people you're following.

2. **Type your tweet into the What Are You Doing field at the top of the page.**

   While you type, watch the number at the top-right of the field; it tells you the number of characters still available.

3. **Click Update (see Figure 14-3).**

   Twitter posts your tweet into your message stream, where your followers can read and respond to it. If any of them subscribe to your updates with their phones, they receive a text message that contains your tweet.

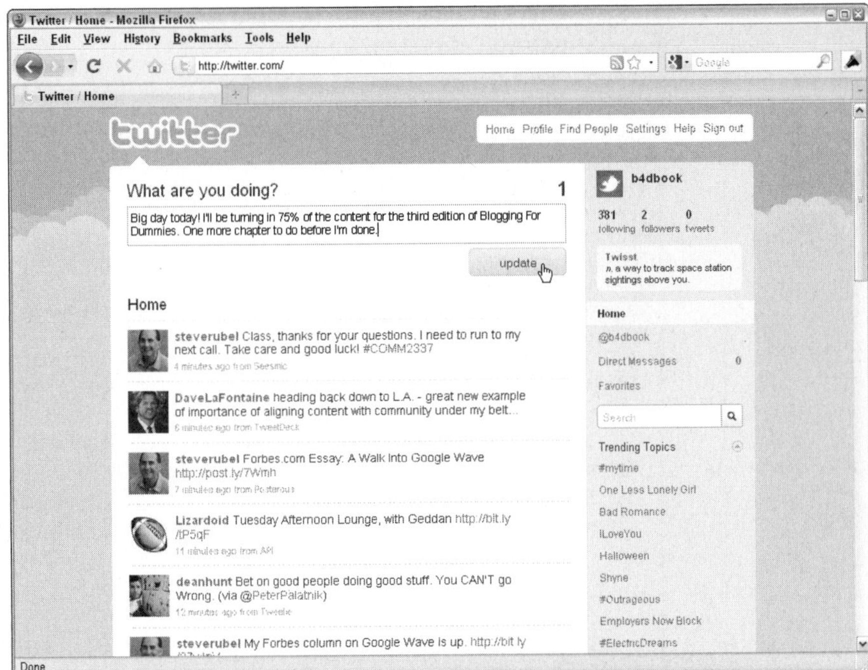

Figure 14-3: You can post a tweet on Twitter very quickly.

Posting a tweet is just the beginning. Other kinds of messages include the following:

- **@ messages:** When you want to direct a message to a specific person, but still include it in your main message stream (which means all your followers, and possibly the public, can see it), start your message with the `@` symbol followed by the username of the person. For example

```
@b4dbook i'm reading your chapter on Twitter right now!
```

  To view these messages quickly, click the *@username* link in the right navigation of your Twitter page, as shown in Figure 14-4.

- **Direct messages:** You send direct messages to only a specific Twitter user, and they don't appear in the general message stream. To send a direct message, visit the user's profile page and choose Message *Username* from the right navigation. Or preface your message in the What Are You Doing field with a `d` and the username. For example

```
d hopstudios thanks!
```

  Be careful sending direct messages — you can too easily post things publicly that you meant to be private!

- **Retweets:** Do you see a tweet in your stream that you want to rebroadcast to all your followers? That's called retweeting, and you simply have to copy the full message and paste it into the What Are You Doing field, prefaced by the characters `RT`. For example

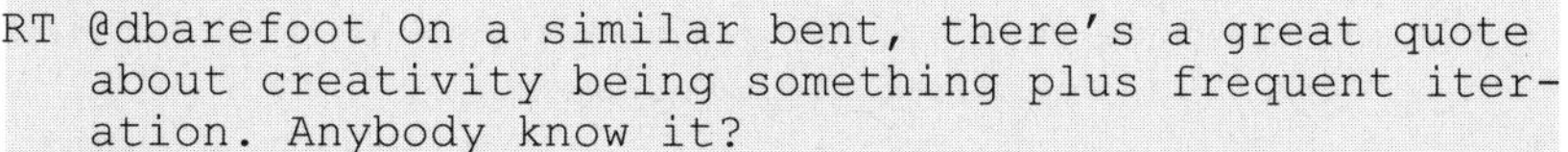

```
RT @dbarefoot On a similar bent, there's a great quote
   about creativity being something plus frequent iter-
   ation. Anybody know it?
```

It's considered good form to include the username of the person you're retweeting.

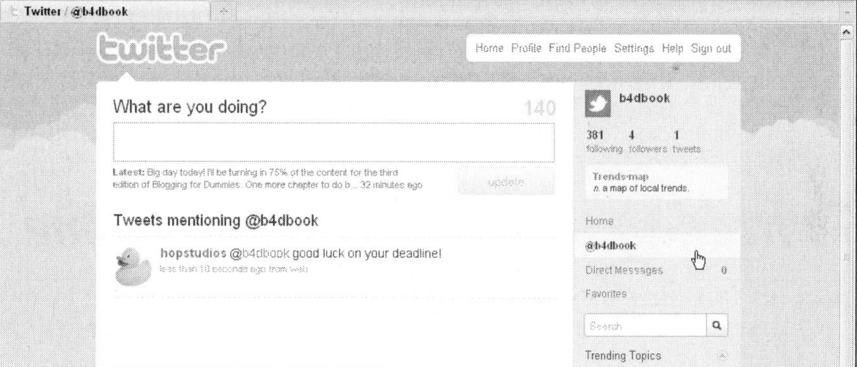

Figure 14-4: View public messages directed at you by clicking the *@username* navigation item.

Exploring the Settings

You can personalize your Twitter home and profile pages in a lot of ways, and of course, you can also update your account information, change your username and password, and so on. You can make all these changes on the Setting page, which you access by clicking the Settings link on the top-right of any Twitter page. The Settings page includes the following areas:

- **Account settings:** Change the e-mail address at which Twitter contacts you and your username. You can also customize the following:
  - *Time Zone:* Make sure Twitter knows your time zone.
  - *More Info URL:* Your profile displays this URL, so you can send people to your home page quickly.
  - *One Line Bio:* Give people a little bit of background about who you are.
  - *Location:* Specify your geographic location to let followers know more about you.
  - *Protect My Tweets:* Change this setting if you want to close your tweets down from public view.

- **Password:** Change your password. You need to know your current password in order to change it.
- **Devices:** Set up your phone to receive tweets from Twitter. I cover this setup fully in the following section.
- **Notices:** Decide whether you want to receive e-mail messages when you get a new follower, receive a direct message, or subscribe to the Twitter e-mail newsletter.
- **Picture:** Customize your Twitter icon by uploading a photo or other graphic. Businesses often choose to display a logo as their icon.
- **Design:** Select a new theme for the look and feel of your Twitter pages, upload your own custom background image, or even change the background, text, and link colors.

Twittering with Your Mobile Phone

Twitter is intended for use with your mobile phone, either by receiving and sending tweets as text messages or by using one of the device-specific pieces of software that interface with Twitter.

Tweeting from your phone

When you want to use your mobile phone to tweet, you first need to let Twitter know about your phone by setting it up on the Settings page. Follow these steps:

1. **Point your Web browser to** `www.twitter.com`**, sign in if you need to, and click the Settings link in the top-right of the page.**

   The Settings page loads.

2. **Select the Mobile tab from the Settings menu at the top of the page.**
3. **Fill in your mobile phone number and select the checkbox labeled It's Okay for Twitter to Send Txt Messages to My Phone. Then, click Save.**
4. **Click OK on the notification drop-down menu that Twitter displays, offering information about texting rates.**

   Remember, depending on your mobile phone plan, it may cost money for you to receive and/or send text messages on your phone. Check with your service provider to see what is and isn't included in your plan! If you don't have an unlimited text message plan, be sparing with the number of Twitter feeds sent to your phone.

   Twitter displays a confirmation code and phone number.

5. **From your phone, send a text message to the number provided, making the text of the message the confirmation code on the Twitter site.**

   If you send this text correctly, you receive a text message from Twitter, confirming that you've signed up.

6. **Refresh the devices page on the Twitter Web site and customize what kinds of text messages you want and the hours you want to receive them.**

From this point on, you can post tweets from your phone. Simply text the same number to which you sent your confirmation code. In the U.S., the number is 40404. When you send a text message to that number, the text message is posted as a tweet on your account, and your followers can read it.

Receiving selected tweets on your phone

You can request to receive the tweets of people you're following as text messages. I recommend you be selective about this option! For example, I follow several hundred people by using Twitter, but I want to hear from only a handful of friends and family at the moment they tweet and as a text message.

To get someone's tweets on your phone, follow these steps:

1. **Point your Web browser to** `www.twitter.com` **and sign in, if you need to.**

   Twitter loads your personal home page.

2. **Click the Following link in the right navigation area.**

   Twitter displays a list of all the users you're following on Twitter.

3. **Find a user whose tweets you want to receive as text messages and click the tiny phone icon to the right of his or her information.**

   The icon turns green — you've just turned on text message updates from that user.

   To turn off text message updates, repeat these steps, but click the green icons.

Tying Your Blog into Twitter

Some bloggers have set up a system that automatically tweets about their blog posts. If you might want to use this system, I suggest you explore Twitterfeed (`www.twitterfeed.com`).

Setting up such a system is pretty simple, really. If your blog has an RSS feed (see Chapter 13), you simply point Twitterfeed at both the feed and your Twitter account, and whenever you post a new blog update, a tweet containing the blog post title and URL is added to your Twitter feed.

Tweeting about your blog posts can really help to drive traffic to your blog, but some users find the impersonality of this kind of message irritating. Be aware of what you audience is looking for if you decide to go this route.

You can also display your tweets on your blog by using the Twitter Widget. I cover how to use this widget in Chapter 20.

Chapter 15

Diving in to Social Networking

In This Chapter

- Adding value to your blogging efforts by sharing and networking
- Getting to know popular social-networking Web sites

Ever Facebooked? Done any tweeting lately? What about endorsing someone on LinkedIn? Is this all gibberish to you? Welcome to the world of social networking, the hottest topic online in the last few years.

At first glance, social networking can look overwhelming and difficult to understand because it uses a lot of jargon, and so many players are in the field. Never fear, however. Social networking is a very simple concept: You can meet others online by using an online Web site or service. At the very heart of it, social networking is the simple process of finding people you want to hang out with, or connecting online with people you already hang out with.

The Web has opened the door to meeting people who share your interests, but whom geography or professional careers — to name just a couple of possibilities — made it unlikely you would ever meet in "real" life. Social-networking Web sites are designed to bring together people who share hobbies, careers, friends, geographic regions, and other interests, and then encourage communication and sharing. And believe me, social-networking sites exist for everything under the sun!

In this chapter, I introduce you to some of the most popular social-networking tools being used today and show you how they can tie into your blogging efforts.

Thinking Strategically

Social networks allow you to connect with current friends and make new ones while sharing photos, videos, text, and more. They've exploded in popularity in the last few years, and many social networks have even added blogging tools. From MySpace to Facebook, these tools are proliferating, and their quality is improving. Social networking can build:

- **Friendships:** You can form long-lasting bonds with people you meet online. By building your social network, you inevitably find others who share your interests.
- **Communities:** Connecting with other people is one of the greatest ways to improve your blogging experience. Other bloggers are using social networks to connect with those who share their interests and passions.
- **Audience:** Bring more eyeballs to your blog. The fact that these eyeballs belong to folks you already have things in common with — well, that's just a bonus!

In general, social networks that have blogging tools are good for, well, social networking. If you're starting a business or professional blog, these blogging tools are probably too unprofessional and may appear amateurish — unless you're trying to appeal to a very young, hip audience.

Many blogs include a feature on each post that allows you to share the post and a link to it on many social networks. You can add this feature to your own blog if your blog software has these tools built in, or by implementing the ShareThis service (`www.sharethis.com`). I cover ShareThis in detail in Chapter 20.

Because this book talks about blogging, I focus mainly on how social networks can benefit your blog. You may forget that, sometimes, you also need to select social networks that work for you, overall. The following sections give you some tips on choosing a network or networks.

Connecting with your audience

The key is to know your audience and to choose what information to share. The more information you share among the social networks you use, the more attention you can bring to your blog. You must take the time to identify your audience and choose networks where that audience is active. Be sure that the social networks where you spend time are those that likely can repay that effort.

You can tie your blog and your social networks together, letting blog readers know about your actions on social networks and vice versa. The payoff? More readers and, hopefully, more readers from the audience that you're trying to attract.

Essentially, if you participate in a social-networking site that has something to do with the topic of your blog, the friends you make on that network naturally fit into your target audience. And the readers of your blog are also likely to want to join your social network, bringing along with them their groups of friends, family, and colleagues, who may in turn be interested in what you blog about. That's the idea, anyway!

These sites can attract huge audiences, and you greatly increase your ability to filter content through to groups who are most interested in what you have to say on your blog. The friends and contacts you make through social networks may very well be hungry for good blogs to read.

Selecting networks

Integrating social networks into your online activities and your blog does require some planning. With so many options, how do you determine which networks to spend time in? You could just dive in and sign up for a bunch of social networks, then see where the chips fall, but if you want your time spent using social networks to pay off, consider the following questions:

- What do you want to accomplish with your online efforts?
- What networks does your current readership use? What about your friends and family?

  If you're unsure what networks you have to choose from, the section "Getting Familiar with Social Networks," later in this chapter, introduces you to a variety of popular networks.

- Which networks have the coolest designs and best functionalities?
- How active is your audience on social networks? What do they seem to be getting out of that interaction?
- Is your blog content subject-appropriate for any particular social networks? On the flip side, is your blog inappropriate for any of them?
- Does your audience want to know about you in ways that a social-networking tool might fulfill?
- How much time do you want to spend playing around with social networks?

You need to consider these types of questions when you're looking to fit a social network into your blogging life. Take a look at where your readers are coming from and, using the analytics information that you should be collecting for your blog (see Chapter 16), find out what attracts visitors to your site.

Post a question on your blog about a social-networking Web site, and solicit responses and advice.

The social-networking online realm is a bit of a Wild West scenario: Everyone's experimenting to find out what works and what doesn't. So, jump in the saddle, pardner!

Protecting your privacy online

You may worry about the security of your identity online if you're jumping headlong into the social-networking world.

Be smart. Don't post information on any social-networking Web site that you feel is inappropriate. You want to keep certain bits of information private. If a social-networking Web site asks you to provide information that you're not comfortable sharing, don't share it. If the Web site insists you share that information, don't use that service. It's as simple as that.

If you're at all concerned about your security online, make sure you check regularly with your bank and any credit card company you deal with. Some financial institutions are taking new and additional precautions to make sure that your security and identity remain private.

Social networks often feel safer than the Internet at large because they require membership and logins, and of course, profiles of your new friends often include photos and other elements that look convincingly real. However, remember that these sites offer very little barrier to creating an account — the accounts are free, the services don't require identity verification, and the social networks can't prevent people from including misleading information or outright lying about who they are.

So, remain vigilant. If you're aware of what information you place online, you should be able to protect yourself without much of a concern. Just like writing on your blog, consider using this guideline: If you wouldn't blog it, don't social network it.

Getting Familiar with Social Networks

Almost any interest group and almost any method of sharing has a social network. Deciding which ones to try out depends on what you want to get out of the social networking. If you're a photographer, social Web sites such as Flickr (which allows you to share photos) may be your cup of tea. If you like to read books and talk about them, LibraryThing and Goodreads may be the places to hang out.

In the following sections, I show you some of the most popular (and some of my favorites) so that you can get familiar with social-networking sites and decide where to get started.

You can find many more sites that I don't have the space to cover in this book, so make this chapter a starting point while you explore social networks.

Friend-based networks

Social networks are never really all that general, but the most popular social networks allow their users to share almost anything, from photos to friends to games. Social networks such as Facebook simply try to throw everything and the kitchen sink into the mix; others, such as Twitter, go with a more minimal approach.

Here are a few all-purpose social networks:

- **Facebook** (`www.facebook.com`): Facebook is one of the most popular social-networking platforms and boasts a user base of over 300 million — and that number gets bigger every day. Started in 2004 by Mark Zuckerberg, Facebook was initially intended to be a communication tool for university students but quickly grew beyond that audience.

  The service allows users to share photos, audio, and video; install apps, such as games and horoscopes; and friend others. *Friending* is the method of identifying people you want in your network. On most social networks, Facebook included, friends are entitled to see more of your shared information than other members of the network.

  For more information about Facebook security settings, why not check out *Facebook For Dummies* written by Carolyn Abram and Leah Pearlman.

  Not surprisingly, you can also post messages and short status updates, and you can set up your profile to let others know when you post to your blog. You can install widgets on your blog that automatically post a Facebook update when you create a new post (see Figure 15-1).

- **MySpace** (`www.myspace.com`): At its height, MySpace was the king of the hill in terms of social-networking Web sites. It's currently ranked in second place overall, which (given the number of users that place represents) is nothing to sneeze at. MySpace is targeted to people who are friends or share interests, and it's an especially popular way for musicians and other performers to make connections with listeners.

Most interestingly, MySpace includes an integrated blogging tool, so you don't need to tie your blog and social network together; they're already in the same network, which makes promotion pretty darn easy.

Like with Facebook, you can have fun on MySpace by finding friends who are also active on the site, and then sharing information with them.

- **Twitter** (`www.twitter.com`): Micro blogging is all the rage on today's World Wide Web, particularly as mobile-phone technology has really taken off in North America. Twitter is a micro-blogging tool that allows you to post small bursts of text, called *tweets,* about your plans, thoughts, and activities. Following other people's Twitter feeds means that you can stay abreast of their activities, as well. You can handle the whole Twitter experience by mobile phone text messaging, keeping you updated by using a device that you probably already have close at hand.

  Though you can post up to only 140 characters of text at a time, you can use Twitter to share photographs, links, and even videos. Many businesses have jumped onto the Twitter bandwagon and use the tool to let their customers know about sales, specials, and other news. I cover Twitter in detail in Chapter 14.

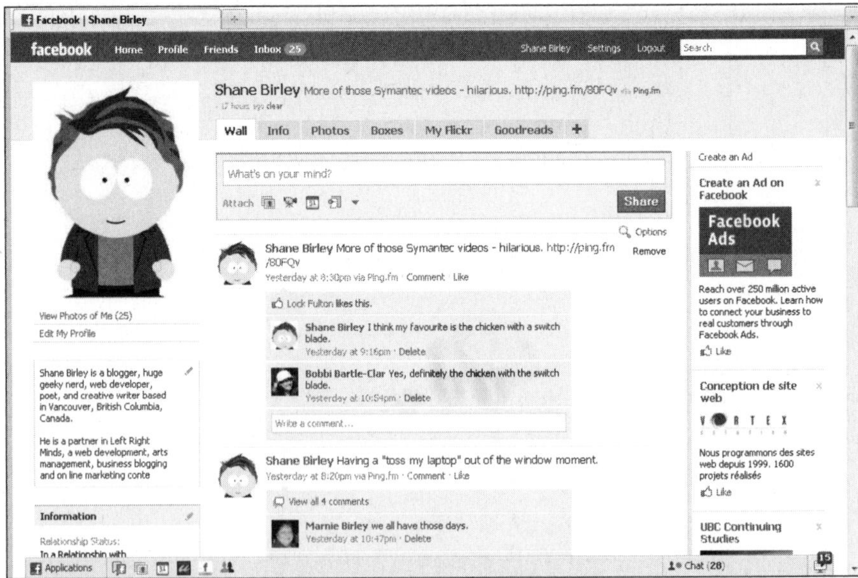

Figure 15-1: Facebook allows you to communicate with millions of potential friends.

Hobby-based networks

If you're a bookworm like me, hold onto your hat. A number of social-networking sites are designed specifically to let you catalog your bookshelves, find cool books to read, and chat with other book lovers.

The same is true of music lovers; you can share your musical tastes with others online and get suggestions for new music that you may like. Some services even allow you to listen to full tracks of music, or you can listen to bite-sized chunks.

The fun doesn't stop there, either. If you have a hobby that you share with a large enough group, you can probably find a social network out there designed just for you. Here are a few of my favorites:

- **LibraryThing** (`www.librarything.com`): A great Web site that allows you to share books that you're reading. You can catalog your collection and find information about your books by using a variety of libraries, such as Amazon.com or the Library of Congress.

  The tie-in with your blog? Widgets let you share what you're reading and have read with your blog visitors.

  See Chapter 20 for details about connecting picks in networks like LibraryThing or Last.fm, discussed in an upcoming bullet, to your blog via widgets.

- **Goodreads** (`www.goodreads.com`): Goodreads is another social book-cataloging Web site that allows you to build virtual bookshelves of books that you've read or want to read. You can recommend books to others, compare what you're reading with others in the forums, and even run a book club.

  Some of my friends who share my taste in books find the site useful for choosing what to read next, by keeping track of the ratings others post for books they've read. I really like using it to keep track of the books I want to read next, so that I don't have to keep all that information in my head. And, of course, there are widgets for your blog (not to mention for Facebook and MySpace).

- **Last.fm** (`www.last.fm`): Founded in 2002, Last.fm (shown in Figure 15-2) is a social-networking site that allows you share your musical tastes. You can track the music you're listening to and share what types of music you enjoy with others. If you install Last.fm's *audioscrobbling* widget, it records automatically whatever music you play on your computer, phone, or MP3 player. It then posts this information on your profile on the Web site.

Over time, you can see what music you listen to most often, and then the Web site and the community can make suggestions about what other music you may want to check out. You can tie Last.fm widgets to your blog so that your readers can subscribe to your music playlist and also be your listeners.

- **Blip.fm** (www.blip.fm): Blip.fm is another, and very recent, addition to the music social-networking realm. This tool is tied closely to Twitter, so users of the one social network get the benefit of the other.

  Blip.fm allows you to sign up, identify your friends, search the Web for music that you want to recommend (or just listen to), and then build a playlist based on the results. Do you have a friend who has impeccable musical taste? Get him or her signed up for Blip.fm, and then listen to his or her playlist. This site also allows you to give *props* — praise — to users who *blip* — post @md a song you like, giving feedback about what you want more of.

  You can even link your Last.fm account to Blip.fm and let your computer do all the work of blipping songs for you.

- **Ravelry** (www.ravelry.com): This chapter wouldn't be complete without a mention of my favorite social network of all time, Ravelry. I admit, it may not be your favorite! Ravelry is a social network designed for knitters to share information about what they're making or thinking of making, how they did it, and other such conversation. You can add friends and send messages, and of course, if you have a knitting blog, you can pull your blog posts into Ravelry and get your friends from Ravelry over to your blog.

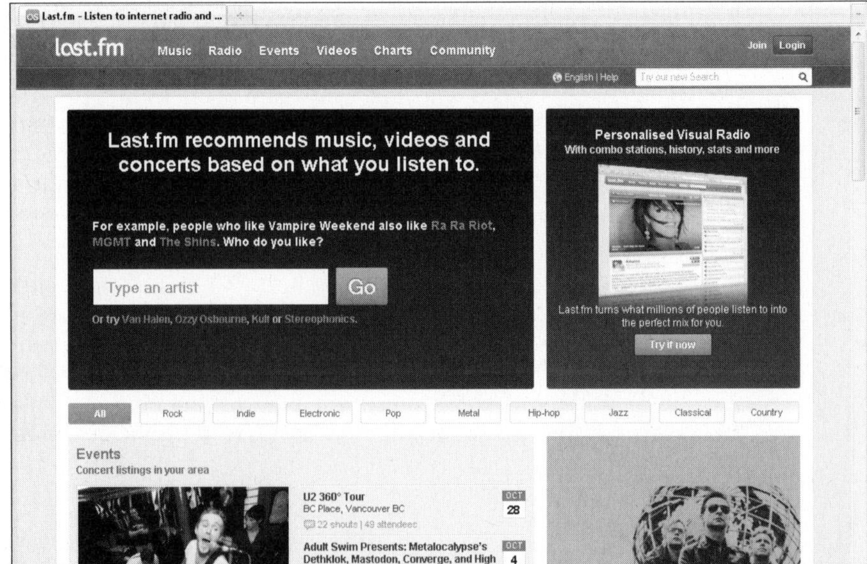

Figure 15-2: Last.fm shares what music you play and recommends music that you may like.

Professional networks

The business world has latched onto social networking, as well. Many businesses are using social-networking tools to find new clients, build more creative advertising, and create a conversation with the public. Many of them use the existing popular social networks, from Facebook to Twitter, but the big player in business-related social networking is LinkedIn.

LinkedIn (`www.linkedin.com`) claims to have more than 45 million users, and it targets its service to your professional life. Looking to find a new employee or a new job? LinkedIn can put you in touch with others in your industry, recommend partners, help you locate contractors, and generally get the lowdown on those you work with.

One of the most useful features of LinkedIn is that your profile looks much like a résumé, so you can refer people you want to work with to your LinkedIn profile. You can also connect with past and present colleagues, and make use of their network so that you can make connections with people they interact with. The business world can become a surprisingly small place, thanks to these connections. In fact, I used LinkedIn to make contact with many of the businesses that I discuss in this book by putting my own network to use.

Media-sharing networks

The Web has allowed all of us to share more than just text — you can easily display video, audio, and photos online, and a number of social-networking sites let you do just that, regardless of whether you have a Web site or blog. Here are the big hitters:

- **Flickr** (`www.flickr.com`): Flickr is one of the most successful social networks going. Flickr allows you to post and store your photographs — and recently, videos — online. You can share these photos and videos with the community at large, as well as your friends and family. Viewers can mark each photo as a favorite, and they can also leave comments and feedback for you.

  You can use Flickr to build albums and galleries of your photos, and even slideshows. Best of all, you can place your photos online with Flickr, and then quickly and easily embed those photos into your blog posts (see Chapter 10).

- **YouTube** (`www.youtube.com`): For those video bloggers out there, YouTube is probably the most popular social-networking video platform online today. People from all over the world record, edit, and post videos, and then share them with the YouTube community. You can post these videos and also embed them into your Web site or blog.

Informational networks

Initially, social bookmarking was just an online service that allowed you to save all your bookmarks without worrying about whether you'd lose them. While social networking became more popular, social-bookmarking Web sites got into the act and began to offer all kinds of ways in which you can share your bookmarks with others or discover new and interesting Web sites to visit. Use these sites to organize your bookmarks, recommend Web sites, and Web surf:

- **Delicious** (`www.delicious.com`): Early on in the life of the Web, someone realized that we all spent a lot of time e-mailing each other links ("You *have* to see this; it's hilarious!") and that a more efficient way to share that kind of information probably existed. Enter Delicious.

  Delicious (see Figure 15-3) enables you to record and tag links for later retrieval. You no longer have to be at the same computer to remember what Web sites you've visited or bookmarked. You can make your bookmarks private or share them with the public. This incredibly easy-to-use social-bookmarking service is also incredibly powerful. You can share your bookmarks by using the built-in RSS feeds and by sharing your bookmarks with your personal network of other users.

  Social bookmarking is a little different than creating bookmarks of sites that you go to often, which you probably already do with your browser. I use Delicious to keep track of research around a particular topic — for example, looking up activities to do on my next trip to Asia.

- **StumbleUpon** (`www.stumbleupon.com`): Many people have called StumbleUpon one of the biggest time wasters online today. But that's not actually a bad thing. Web surfing is a time-honored way of negotiating the World Wide Web, and StumbleUpon simply acknowledges that fact, and then gives you some outstanding tools for more efficiently and intelligently surfing.

  With StumbleUpon, users post and recommend interesting things that they find on the Web, and others view those recommendations and add their own endorsement, effectively creating a snapshot of the most interesting and compelling links on the Web. You can imagine how useful sharing becomes when you create a community on StumbleUpon of your friends and colleagues; if you combine their recommendations with the personalization options that StumbleUpon provides, it's like reading a personalized (albeit somewhat eccentric) newspaper.

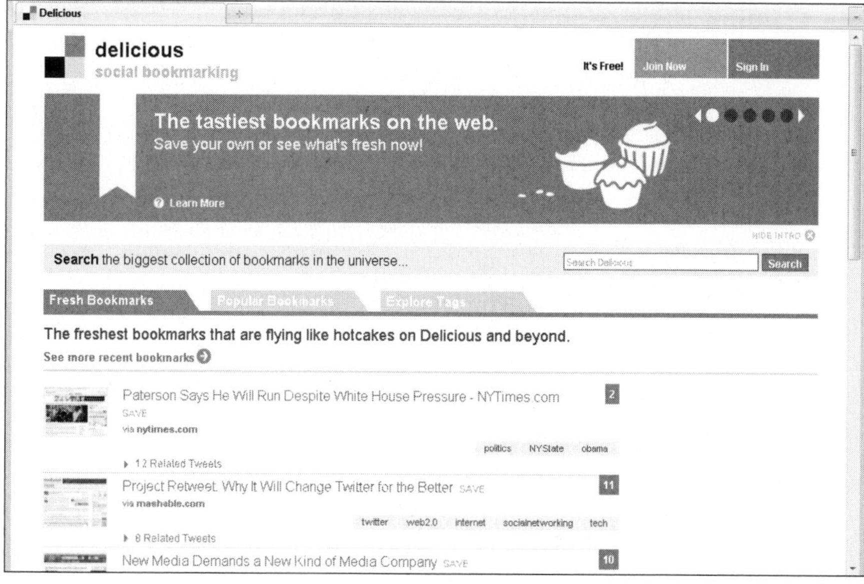

Figure 15-3: Sharing your bookmarks with Delicious lets you share links with others.

Location-based networks

A bunch of networks allow you to post your location on a map or track your (and your friends') geographic whereabouts. Typically, these kind of social-networking applications need a little forethought before you use them. Do you really want your colleagues to know where you are at all times? I didn't think so. But these kinds of programs can help you create impromptu coffee meetings or figure out whether someone you want to see is nearby. Many location-based networks also give you information based your current location for nearby great places to eat, shop, or visit.

These services are really designed for mobile phone users who have signed up for data plans.

Try these networks on for size:

- **foursquare** (`www.foursquare.com`): This is the newest kid on the location block. foursquare allows you to use your phone as a GPS device — it tracks your location, checks you in at the places you visit, and awards points for everywhere you go. If you're the most frequent visitor to a location in a 30-day period, foursquare declares you the mayor of that location, and you can also earn badges. Foursquare has some handy apps for different types of phones as well as a mobile phone Web site version.

Some businesses are rewarding users with freebies and recognition. You can link your foursquare account with your Twitter and Facebook updates.

- **Brightkite** (`www.brightkite.com`): Brightkite is a popular location-based social-networking Web site. It offers applications for iPhone, BlackBerry, and Android mobile devices. You can rate different locations and also post your location on Twitter. A very cool section of the Brightkite Web site lets you build a visualization of all the Brightkite activity in a certain location, by keyword, or of everything going on in the Brightkite universe.
- **Google Latitude** (`www.google.com/latitude`): Google Latitude (see Figure 15-4) is another location-aware mobile application that allows you to share your current location and keeps track of places you've been. You can have this application automatically update with your whereabouts, or you can manually add your check-in points. The application plots your updates on a Google Map for your friends to view. The application is available for many mobile platforms, including iPhones and BlackBerries.

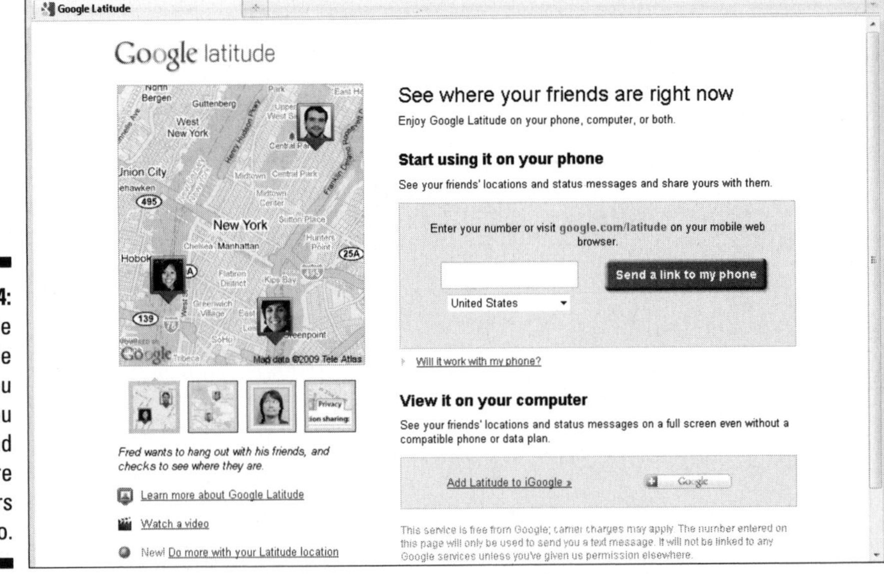

Figure 15-4: Google Latitude shows you where you are and where others are, too.

Chapter 16

Measuring Blog Presence

In This Chapter

- Figuring out what Web statistics tell you
- Checking out good statistics-tracking tools
- Tracking the blogosphere for keywords and topics

For a moment, picture your new blog running just the way you want it. The graphics are pretty, you're blogging every day, and comments are rolling in. Everything looks perfect, and you seem to be well on your way to a successful blogging career. But wait! For no real reason, over a few weeks, the number of comments left on your blog each day starts to decrease. Your visitor numbers are down. You don't find an obvious explanation, and you can't imagine why your readership is disappearing so quickly!

If you ever find yourself in this type of situation, you may start to ask yourself questions such as, "How many visitors do I have every day, anyway?" or "How many of my visitors have been here before?"

It's time to understand your Web traffic statistics. You, as a blogger, may find Web stats especially important because your audience numbers are affected each time you post.

You must pay attention to how your blog is performing on the Internet, but it can be confusing and boring. Spending an afternoon peering at Web stats, especially if you don't know what you're looking for, can be a tedious experience. It's like . . . well, it's like watching paint dry. But it doesn't have to be as painful as it sounds. Web statistics are very geeky, but these days, you can choose from services available to bloggers (and Webmasters, in general) that allow you to track your blog's success in interesting and informative ways by using a friendly interface.

For more help with Web analytics, check out *Web Analytics For Dummies,* by Pedro Sostre and Jennifer LeClaire.

Exploring the Power of Statistics

Even if you like the way your blog is performing, you should take a look at your blog stats once in a while. Some bloggers look at them daily to see what kinds of visitors appeared on their blogging radar overnight; some bloggers check their stats once a week or once a month. Whichever pattern you choose, keep a good handle on your statistics — knowing how many visitors you have can help you improve your blog in the future, making it even more popular.

For an example of what a typical Web-stats tool looks like, check out StatCounter's measurement of the Find-A-Sweetheart Web site (`www.find-a-sweetheart.com`) in Figure 16-1. (You have to be logged in if you want to view stats on StatCounter.)

Using Web statistics, you can track

- What countries your Web visitors are surfing from
- How long visitors stay
- How many visitors check out your site for the first time
- How many visitors have been to your blog before

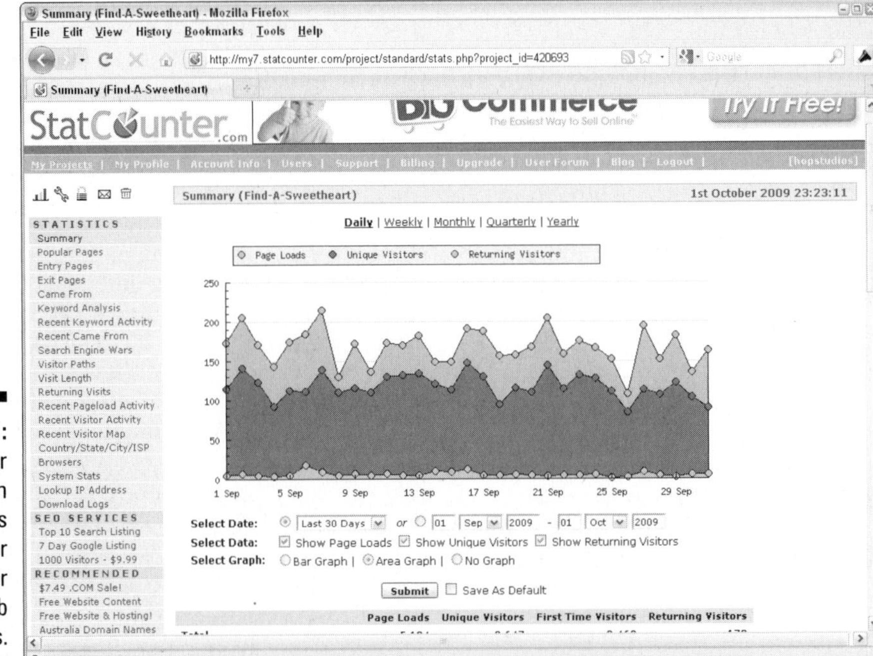

Figure 16-1: Blogger Kathryn Lord uses StatCounter to track her site's Web stats.

- What pages your visitors start their visit on
- What pages visitors end their visit on
- What sites send visitors to you
- What search words visitors use to find your site
- What browsers your visitors use
- What kind of computers your visitors use to surf the Web
- What screen resolutions your visitors set their monitors to

With some of the more advanced Web analytics software, you can see what pages are the least popular, find out how search engines handle your blog, and even see what errors or missing pages your visitors get when they try to access parts of your site. (If you have removed an old blog post or renamed a posting, you will be able to tell from your statistics which pages are missing.) A lot of bloggers especially want to know what Web sites are sending visitors to their blogs so that they can figure out where to invest time and energy in comments and discussion forums.

Knowing even a little bit about your traffic can help you make all kinds of strategic decisions about your blog, from what kind of design to use to the subject of a post.

Blog stats become even more useful when you begin analyzing them. *Web analytics* are the trends that your statistical or log software shows you. Some traffic software helps break down these trends for you, but the most basic software simply displays the raw data about how visitors use your site and lets you draw the conclusions. When people talk about Web analytics, they're referring to the process that you undertake when you're looking through those stats and logs to figure out what visitors are doing on your Web site. Commonly, you look for trends about what content the visitors view, how often they visit, and what other sites direct traffic your way.

Pay close attention to your Web site logs so that you can chart what your users are doing over time. You can see what your site visitors are reading and what keeps them coming back for more. You can then use this information for a variety of purposes (such as deciding what to blog about). The following examples illustrate how gathering your blog's statistics and interpreting them can be useful:

- **You notice that a large bunch of readers are coming from a particular country (see Figure 16-2), and you don't live in that country.** In this case, you should see what pages those visitors are viewing — and determine why they're coming to your site. You can then write more to attract additional visitors who have similar tastes. In fact, noticing a trend such as this one might help you really focus on a core audience that you didn't even know about. You can even redefine what you do with your blog in the future.

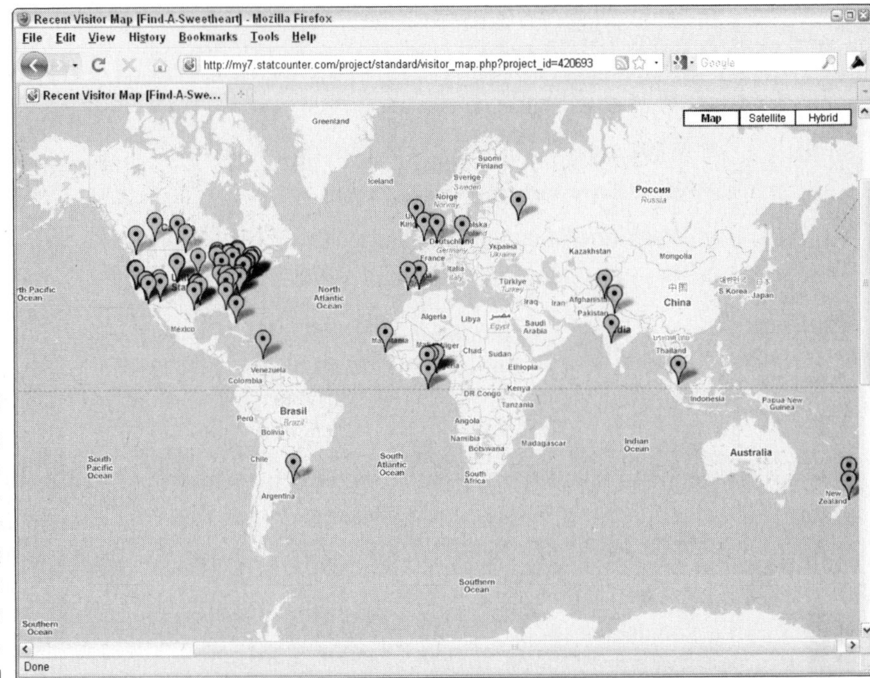

Figure 16-2: Track where your visitors live by using a stat program such as StatCounter.

- **You have ads on your blog (see Chapter 17), and more people are clicking a certain type of advertisement.** If you take the time, you can see what kinds of visitors are clicking advertisements on your site (if you have any ads, of course). You can use information about what ads your visitors click to sell ad space to certain advertisers.

You may have trouble staying away from your blog's Web stats, and you might want to check them daily. But don't forget that you have a blog to run, which requires that you focus on the quality of the content you produce for your community. Try to avoid an obsession over your Web statistics because no amount of tinkering with Web analytics can make your blog popular. Your content is the only thing that can accomplish that feat.

Knowing What the Statistics Mean

To understand what you're looking at when you scan your Web statistics or server logs, you need to know a series of terms. Most Web analytics software use these terms, but you should always check to see how the software's creators define measurements — Web analytics software tends to use these terms in the same way, but not always. I cover the most vital terms in the following sections.

You'll run into more terms than the ones I cover in this chapter, but the most important ones for bloggers are *page views, unique visitors,* and *repeat visitors.* Together, these three statistics give you the most accurate picture of how many visitors your blog receives and what they do while they visit.

I also introduce you to what the term *hits* means, which new bloggers often find misleading, and how statistics can help you resolve errors on your blog.

Hits

A *hit* is an official request from a Web browser for a file from the Web server. The file can be an HTML file or a movie file. Essentially, accessing any file available on a Web server to the surfing public counts as a hit.

Any given Web page causes *multiple* hits on the server when it loads, even though it's only one page. Multiple files are actually called to display the page: the HTML file, any associated style documents, and all the image files. If an HTML file has five images, it counts as six hits — one for the HTML file and five for each individual image.

A lot of people think that hits indicate the number of Web site visitors or even the number of pages viewed, but hits don't even come close to measuring those kinds of figures. Hits are pretty meaningless if you're trying to understand how many visitors you have, but they can help you get a feel for the traffic load that your site puts on the Web server.

Page views

A *page view* is normally defined as a page within a Web server log; if the Web browser requests an HTML file, the log records that as a single request, even if the server needs several files to display the page. Each time the Web browser loads a page of your site, it counts as a page view. Page views are a valuable measurement because you can get a better understanding of how people actually use your site.

In Figure 16-3, you can see the page views for September 30, 2009.

Advertisers are often very interested in the number of page views on a Web site (more is better), and most bloggers consider a high page-view number something to brag about.

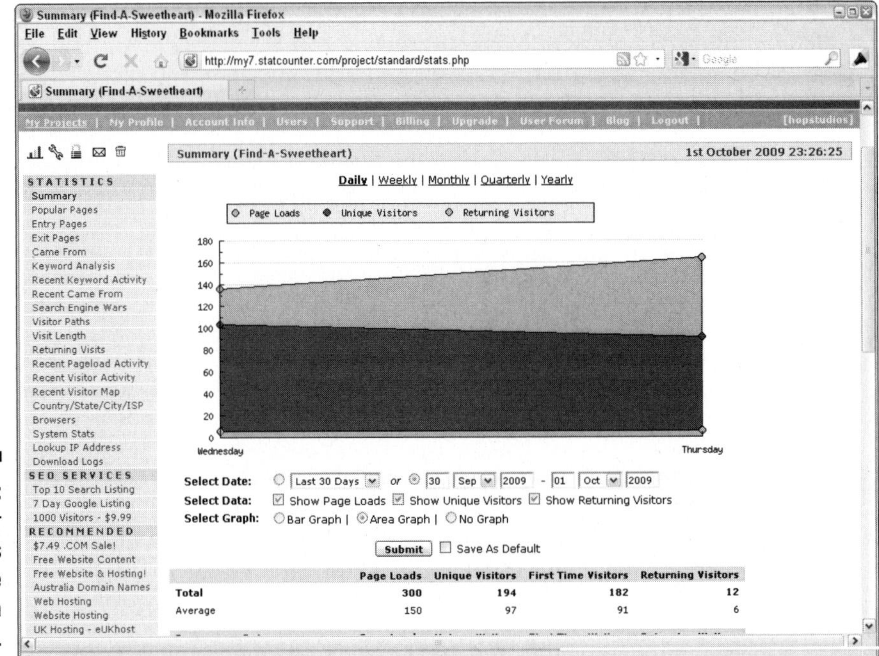

Figure 16-3: StatCounter breaks down page loads for a given day.

Unique visitors

Unique visitors are just what they sound like — individual visitors who come to your Web site. The analytics software counts them only once, no matter how many pages they view or how many times they visit. When you're looking at the number of unique visitors your blog gets, take a look at what time period the analytics software refers to. Fifty unique visitors in one day, for example, is a much bigger deal than 50 unique visitors in a month.

Repeat visitors

Repeat visitors are blog readers who visit your site on more than one occasion and, usually, visit multiple pages. Pay attention, just as with unique visitors, to the time period this repeat-visitor number covers.

In Figure 16-4, you can see a graph that breaks down the percentages of first-time visitors to repeat visitors on the Web statistics tool StatCounter.

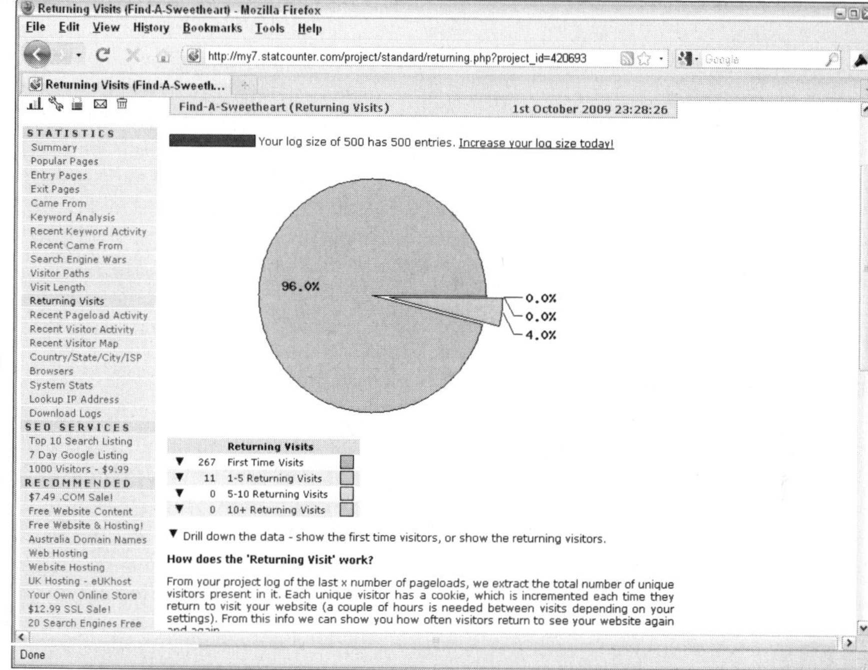

Figure 16-4: Keep tabs on how much of your traffic is new and how much is repeat visits.

Errors

Most stat software tracks *errors,* instances when your visitors get an actual error message when they try to do something on your site or when they try to view a page that doesn't exist anymore (or never did).

Track your error logs to find out where visitors are having problems — and be sure to fix the errors.

A lack of standards

Currently, no official standards govern the world of server logs and Web statistics. No large corporations tell anyone how to do capture their traffic numbers, what terminology to use, or how to analyze the statistics. The world of Web stats has, more or less, grown organically, and a set of rules around the analysis of server logs has emerged from the community.

The various software tools have a lot of inconsistency in what and how they measure statistics. As a result, I commonly use two different programs to measure unique visitors on my own blog, and the two software programs rarely agree about what that number is. It's a frustrating fact of life. (Between you and me, I tend to use the bigger number.)

(continued)

(continued)

Knowing about this inconsistency, you might want to consider using at least a couple of Web statistics tools (I talk about the options in the section "Getting Web Stats," in this chapter) and comparing the results that you get. Different Web analytics software treat server logs differently, and some software is certainly better than others. Most often, users prefer packages that create charts and graphs, which represent their data visually, making the numbers easier to understand quickly. Because no hard and fast rules exist, you're free to do research into what packages can work best for you.

Getting Web Stats

You can find many statistics software applications that track Web traffic available for installation on your blog. But before you get too carried away, check to see whether your blog host offers Web traffic–tracking software or gives you access to your server logs.

If your Web host offers stats software, be sure to review the offering carefully. You might not need any additional tools, or you might want to supplement the preinstalled tool with one of those discussed in the following sections, if only to check the accuracy of the numbers you're seeing. Keep in mind that different applications can measure statistics differently, so the numbers may not be exactly the same.

Some bloggers like to look at the server logs for their sites. *Server logs* are simple text files that Web servers generate in order to keep track of information about who visits a Web server, when, using what kind of browser, when errors occur, and so on.

Most Web hosts provide access to stat software and server logs through an administrative control panel.

In the following sections, I cover the different services and software available. You should be able to find a service that fits your Web-stat needs.

Choosing hosted statistics software

Like hosted blog software, the company that creates the hosted Web statistics software package also manages that software. Typically, you install the software by adding a chunk of HTML code to your pages, which communicates with the hosted software.

Because you must be able to place some HTML code into your blog software templates so that it appears on every page that you want to track, blog software that doesn't give you the ability to add code will rule out using a hosted statistics solution.

Google Analytics

`www.google.com/analytics`

In 2005, Google purchased a software package known as Urchin, created by a Web statistics company. Google has since released Urchin as the online stats system Google Analytics.

Google Analytics has a great interface with many options that you can customize and use to analyze stats to your heart's content. Google Analytics can calculate how many page views and number of visits your blog or site has received. The Google Analytics system (shown in Figure 16-5) is free, but it requires a registered Google Account (which is free, as well).

StatCounter

`www.statcounter.com`

StatCounter is a free hosted statistics tracker, and new users can figure it out easily, thanks to good organization and explanation in the control panel.

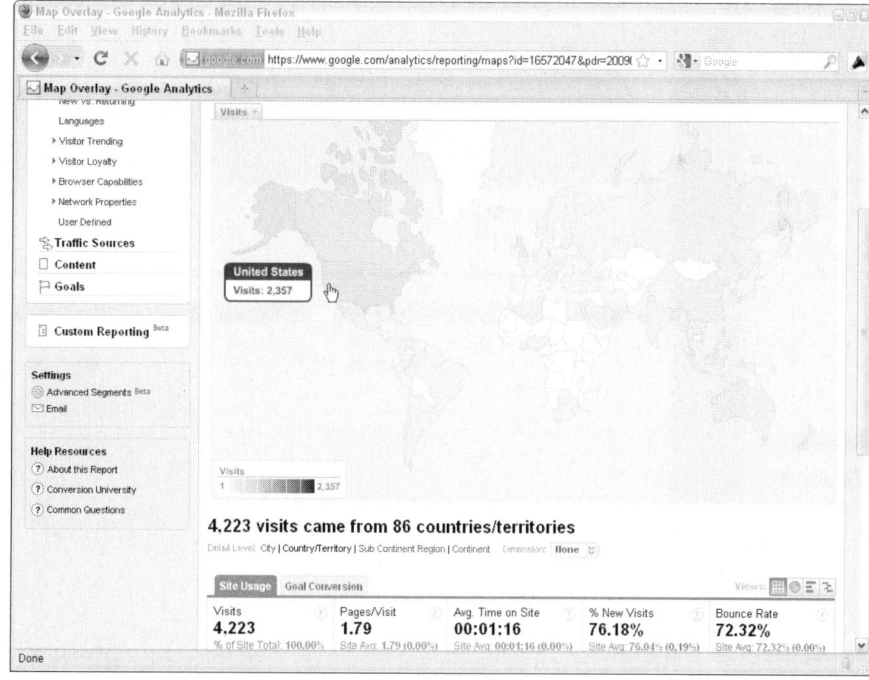

Figure 16-5: Use Google Analytics to check out where your Web site's traffic comes from.

After setting up your site in StatCounter, you must insert StatCounter HTML code into your blog templates so that it can track every page. StatCounter measures page views and hits, of course, but also what terms your readers use in search engines to a Google Maps interface of where your traffic originates.

Site Meter

```
www.sitemeter.com
```

Site Meter has been around since the beginning of stat tracking on the Web. This tool provides you with basic details about each visitor who comes to your blog and shows you what the visitor does while he or she is there, even down to what page he or she is on before leaving.

Site Meter (see Figure 16-6) has two levels of service: the free Basic edition and the Premium edition. The Premium edition provides more information than the Basic setup and grants access to a longer history of your statistics, but the free edition is a good starting point for new bloggers. The professional edition starts at $6.95 a month.

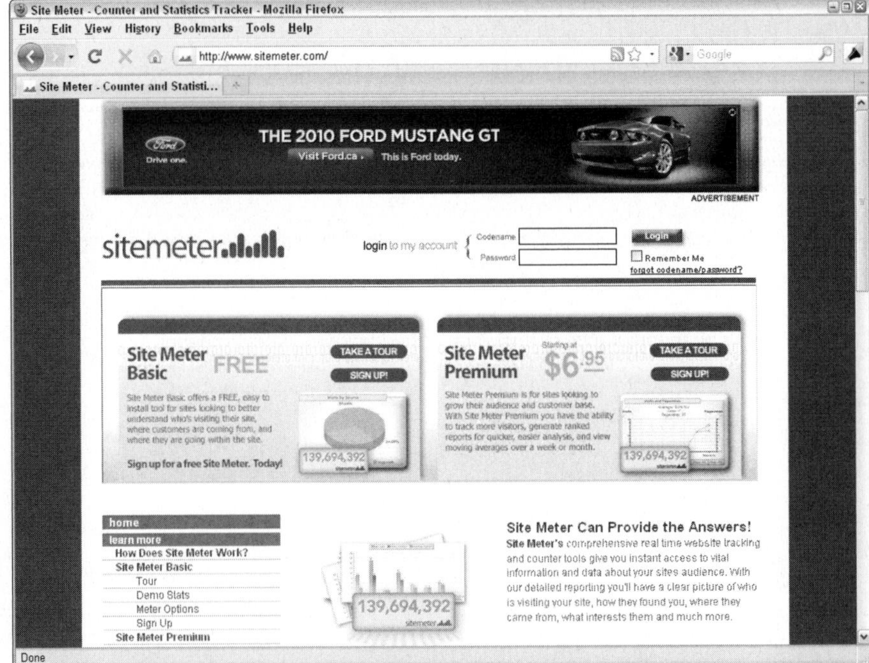

Figure 16-6: Site Meter offers two levels of statistics tracking.

Choosing installable statistics software

Web analytics software that you can install on your Web server and manage on your own is called *installable* software. If you want to use a specific analytics package that your Web host doesn't normally provide, look into whether you can install software on your server. Some hosts can give you suggestions and may even assist you when you install analytics software.

Installed software usually measures the same metrics as hosted statistics software, but it does so by analyzing log files stored on your Web site, rather than gathering information when a visitor hits your site. Some Web developers feel that installed software therefore provides more accurate numbers than hosted software, but many Web developers and bloggers hotly debate that opinion.

When you sign up for a Web-hosting package, the Web host probably has some kind of Web statistics available to you. These packages can range from open source software to custom, home-grown solutions.

Be sure to check the technical requirements for the package that you want to install to be sure that your server works with it.

The Webalizer

`www.mrunix.net/webalizer`

The Webalizer is an open source application that you install on your server. Because it's free to use, many Web hosts offer it as part of their standard Web hosting packages. Originally created in 1997, the Webalizer lets you track hits, page views, geographical origin of your traffic, and other data.

The Webalizer generates easy-to-read pages that show traffic to your site broken down by month, but you can also see traffic figures by day and even by hour. It offers all the usual suspects, from page views to unique visitors to the top referring sites.

AWStats

`http://awstats.sourceforge.net`

AWStats is a popular Web statistics analyzer that you can install on your Web server. Its features enable you to track not only visitors, but also streaming media, e-mail, and FTP transactions on your server. AWStats requires that you have the Perl programming language installed on your Web server to operate. (Most Web servers support this requirement.)

AWStats generates graphs and other visual indicators about the activity of your visitors month by month, letting you see the region and cities where traffic originates, as well as the operating systems and browsers that your visitors use, among many other measurements.

Mint

`www.haveamint.com`

Mint, which began in 2004 as a basic Web site tracking tool, has matured into a great service. Mint's installable software offers the usual suspects: new and returning visitors, the sites from which they get to your site, search terms that they use to find you, and so on. Mint also looks really cool: It produces fun graphs and charts.

A Mint license costs $30 per site.

Finding Out What Others Are Saying

With Web analytics software, you can watch the behavior of your site's visitors but you can also find out a lot by monitoring mentions of you, your blog, and your topic on the Web (especially on your competitor's blogs!) on other Web sites. Watching what's going on within the blogosphere is a huge task. You could spend hundreds of dollars to have others do it for you, or you could check out some of the simple tools available on the Web.

Among the simple blogosphere tools available to you are the following:

- **E-mail notifications:** Receive updates via e-mail about content or topics that you want to keep up with.
- **RSS watch lists:** Keep current on topics by using your favorite newsreader software. (Read more about RSS in Chapter 13.)

You can use these tools in a variety of ways by doing random manual searches and installing software designed to display Web information on your desktop.

The power of RSS and the syndication of news and blog feeds become apparent when you start trying to monitor certain phrases and keywords. RSS is one of the best ways to track what people are saying about your blog and about topics that you're interested in.

Google Alerts

`www.google.com/alerts`

Google Alerts (see Figure 16-7) provides you with e-mail notifications that it sends to you based on keyword searches of Google's search system. Sign up for an account, and then create an alert by entering keywords about which you want Google Alerts to notify you.

In order to receive any e-mail from the Google Alerts system, you need to enter some keywords. Follow these steps:

1. **Go to** `www.google.com/alerts`**.**
2. **Enter the keywords that you want to be notified about in the Search Terms text box.**
3. **Select the type of Web content that you want included in your search from the Type drop-down list.**

   Your options are News, Blogs, Web, Comprehensive, Video, and Groups.
4. **Select how often you want to be notified from the How Often drop-down list.**

   You can select As-It-Happens, Once a Day, or Once a Week.
5. **Type your e-mail address into the Your Email field.**
6. **Click Create Alert.**

   Google begins to track your search and sends you the e-mails that you requested at the rate you want them.

When a keyword gets a hit, you get an e-mail that includes a link to the Web page. Google Alerts can do automatic keyword searches for all kinds of Web sites, including blogs.

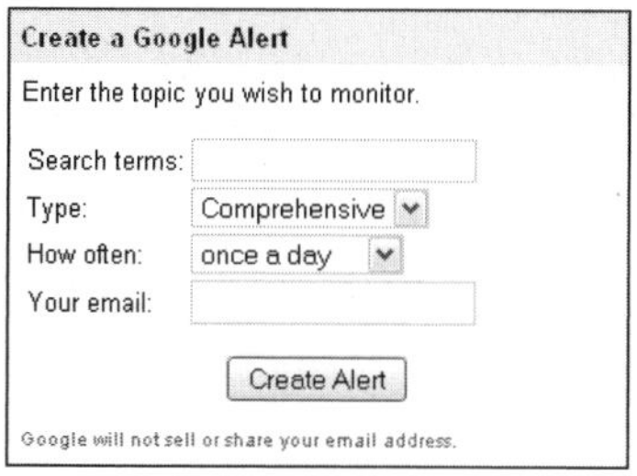

Create a Google Alert
Enter the topic you wish to monitor.
Search terms:
Type: Comprehensive
How often: once a day
Your email:
Create Alert
Google will not sell or share your email address.

Figure 16-7: Google Alerts sends you e-mail if it hits your keywords in searches.

These alerts work best when you create a specific and detailed search. Think about how you can refine your search to keep your results to a manageable number. For instance, if you want to track a particular news topic, use several keywords, rather than just one. For example, use `knitting sock yarn hand-dyed`, not just `socks`.

Set Google Alerts to search for your name, your blog name, and any keywords that you want to be aware of. Use these alerts to find out when people are talking about you, your blog, or the topics you're covering.

Twitter

`www.twitter.com`

Twitter is a social-networking service that allows you to post online messages known as *tweets*. People can then watch your tweets, and you can watch theirs. Your tweets can be anything from short messages, links to Web sites, or conversations with others. You can also use Twitter to track what people are talking about by searching for keywords and *hashtags* (Twitter users sometimes mark keywords in their tweets with a # to set them off and make it easier to search for them). You can search using the Twitter search engine (`http://search.twitter.com`). For instance, after Michael Jackson's death, Twitter users posting about the pop star used the hashtag `#mj`. You can read more about Twitter in Chapter 14.

Technorati

`www.technorati.com`

Technorati is a search engine that focuses its energy on blogs — and does it very well. Technorati publishes information periodically that gives people who use its service a status of the blogosphere. Technorati can update you on the following:

- The number of blogs that are tracked
- Ongoing trends in conversations throughout a given time period
- The growth rate of blog technology adoptions
- Up-to-the minute search results from blog posts

Part VI
Getting Business-y with It

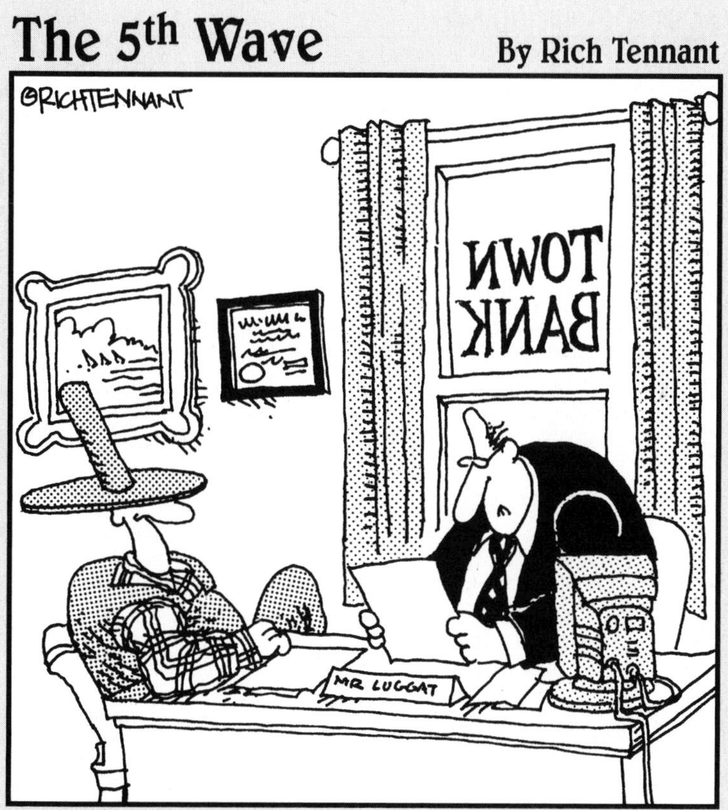

"We have no problem funding your blog, Frank. Of all the chicken farmers operating blogs, yours has the most impressive cluck-through rates."

In this part . . .

Blogs aren't just for the hobbyist, as you discover in this business-oriented part of the book. If you have a business idea up your sleeve or want to put ads on your blog, get the lowdown on using blog advertising programs and tools in Chapter 17. Some bloggers make a little money, and some make a whole lot! Businesses and non-profit organizations aren't left out, either. Chapter 18 describes how today's companies are making use of blogs to reach customers and critics alike, and even using the technology internally to foster communication.

Chapter 17

Making Mad Mad Money

In This Chapter

- Checking out the advertising options
- Blogging for money
- Putting products on your blog with affiliate programs and gifts
- Looking for a blog sponsor

Advertising on your blog has never been easier. Many different advertising systems offer bloggers a free way to place ads on their blogs, and businesses have picked up on the fact that blog advertising can really work. Putting an ad or two on your blog can help you easily earn a little money doing something you enjoy. Many bloggers turn a pretty penny, and some even earn a living, from advertising.

Ever since Web sites came into existence, you could find online advertisements. From the first Web banners of the early Internet to today's contextual advertising systems, ads have run the gamut from wildly successful to a waste of precious bandwidth.

In some cases, the effectiveness of ads has more to do with the readers than anything else — on the blog for some topics, blog readers willingly look at ads and even click them, but audiences on other blogs just don't have the patience to wade through advertisements that clutter their reading pleasure. So, you need to know what your audience can tolerate before you make a big play with ads!

Turning your blog into a retirement savings plan won't happen overnight, and don't take the addition of advertisements to the average blog lightly. It all requires planning, patience, and faith and trust in your readership. Depending on your audience, you might even need to request input from them about the advertisements that you choose to deploy on your blog.

Finding Out How Advertising Works

Banner ads (rectangular ads usually placed along the top of a site) used to dominate ad slots on the Web but have become less important because people often just tune them out. Then, pop-up, animated, and blinking advertisements generated a few clicks and ultimately managed to generate a massive backlash. Many of these moving, beeping, and blinking ads just irritated users, instead of successfully advertising.

Today's contextual advertising tools are actually intelligent; ads are matched by subject to the words and phrases that you use on your blog. Generally, this approach gives you ads that better suit your readers' interests, making those readers more likely to click the ads.

First, decide whether your blog is meant for an advertising campaign. Many blogs can benefit greatly from advertisements. However, you should think about a few things before diving in:

- Does your blog have a design that's ready for ads?
- Does your blog software support the advertising system you choose?
- Will advertising earn you any money?
- Will your audience put up with ads?

Answering these questions isn't easy; in fact, you might find it impossible unless you jump in — try using some advertising and observe the results.

Planning for advertising

You can use several kinds of advertising methods to turn a blog into a place where you can make a tidy profit. The last few years have seen an explosion of companies that want a piece of the action in the blogosphere, and these companies have come up with creative ways to make ads easy to use, simple to implement, and appealing to your readers.

If you're a new blogger or just new to advertising programs, you can easily latch onto the first advertising system that you find and commit to using it. Although this system may serve your needs well, you might want to take a look at some of the different ad systems available and find out about how advertising tends to work in the blogosphere before you start using ads.

While you do your research, keep in mind that if you decide to make that leap into monetizing your blog, you should choose software that allows you to control your advertising so that it doesn't overwhelm the blog audience that you worked so hard to build.

A multitude of advertising companies offer bloggers simple solutions to monetize Web sites. Most of these programs work in similar ways but have unique delivery methods. Advertising programs range from text-only ads to flashy animations, and even full-page advertisements that really get your readers' attention! As a blogger, choosing an advertising program that works for your audience can make the difference between an increase in readers and turning off your existing traffic.

Looking at the formats

You can deliver ads to a blog audience in four different ways. Additional methods are available, but most don't work very well in a blog. The most popular advertisement formats for blogs are

- **Text-based ads:** These ads are text-only and feature a link or links to the advertiser's Web site or service. Each ad is very plain, and most advertising systems limit your ability to customize their look and feel.
- **Graphical banner and button ads:** Banner and button ads can be static or animated images. These ads usually have preset sizes, but you can customize them to fit your blog design.
- **RSS ads:** Ads are a new addition to RSS feeds; while the format has taken off with the public, advertisers have jumped on the bandwagon. Such ads can include text or images, and they're linked to the advertiser's Web site straight from your RSS feed. See how this kind of advertising looks when someone views the RSS feed in a newsreader, shown in Figure 17-1. If you want to find out more about RSS, see Chapter 13.
- **Pop-up ads:** Pop-ups tend to be everyone's least favorite type of ad, but oddly enough, pop-up ads that open in a new window are still quite successful at getting people to click an advertiser's Web site. The readers might be fairly irritated by the time they get to the site, but they do click.

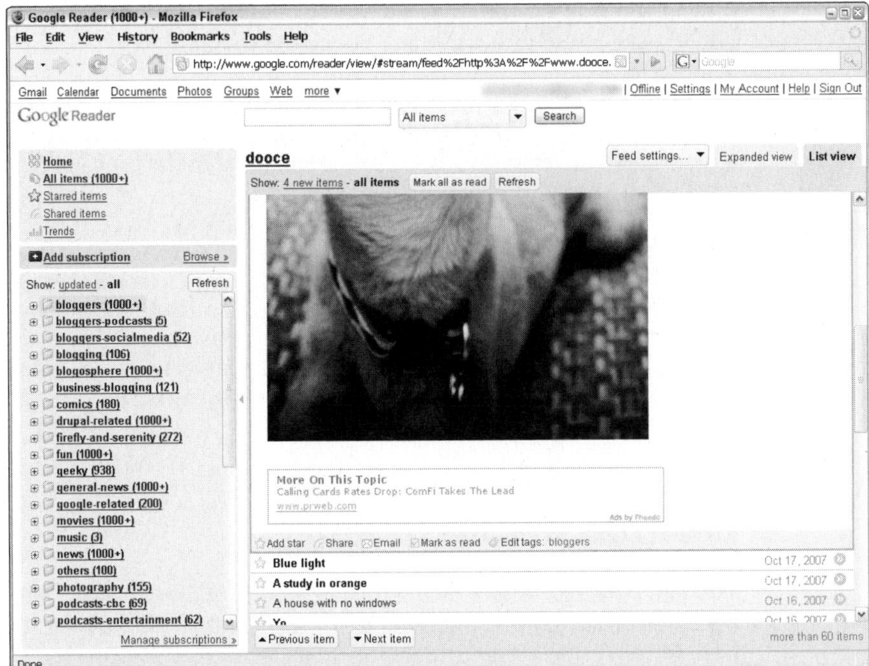

Figure 17-1: Place ads directly into your RSS feed.

The Interactive Advertising Bureau makes recommendations each year about ad sizes and standards. You might find the recommendations useful in planning for ads. Visit `www.iab.net/standards/adunits.asp` to see the options.

Most ad programs today — with the exception of sponsorships — use *contextual advertising,* which coordinates ad display with related editorial content. So, a blog post about skiing might include ads for ski shops and resorts. A blogger who posts about blogging, for example, ends up with ads for blog software and tools. (I speak from experience here.)

Contextual ad systems search your blog for keywords that match products the advertisers have in their inventory. These ads then appear beside the topic keywords and, in theory, apply in the context of the Web page on which they appear.

Contextual ads about blog polling tools appear on the left side of the Smiley Cat Web Design blog, as shown in Figure 17-2.

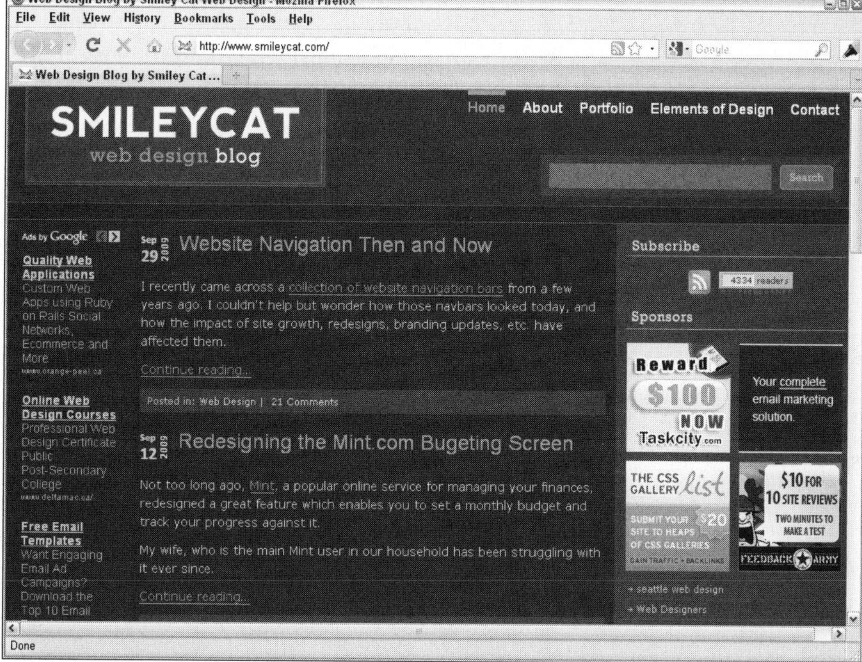

Figure 17-2: Contextual advertising puts blogging tool ads next to a post on the same subject.

Courtesy of Christian Watson www.smileycat.com

Assessing business models

Money can flow from the advertiser to the blogger in different ways. Always read the terms of service for an ad program because each advertising company has a different idea about how to compensate bloggers. The usual business models for online ads are

- **Cost per impression:** In this model, advertisers pay for the number of times a computer loads a page that displays the ad. The advertiser might prefer that a reader click its ad, but it recognizes that simply appearing on a blog that users access also has value.
- **Cost per click or pay per click:** The blogger makes money only when a reader clicks an ad and goes to the advertiser's Web site. This type of ad is very common in contextual ad programs, as well as on search engines in the sponsored results section.

- **Cost per action:** The advertiser pays only when the reader actually takes action after he or she views and clicks the ad on the blog. This required action can include anything from signing up to receive more information to actually purchasing a product.
- **Sponsorships:** When an advertiser wants to be actively associated with the content of your blog, it might offer to sponsor the blog or some part of the blog. A sponsorship usually includes premium advertisements and exclusive ad placement, and the blogger sometimes even thanks the sponsor in the editorial content of the site. See "Seeing Sponsorships" later in this chapter.

A lot of bloggers have had the same great idea about the ads on their blogs: "I'll just click these myself and send my cost-per-click rates through the roof! I'll make millions!" Unfortunately, the advertising companies have figured out this little scheme, and they refer to it as *click fraud.* Advertisers spend good money to have their ads displayed, and companies that run advertisement programs go out of their way to make sure that clicks on those ads are good clicks. Make sure you that understand what happens if you click ads on your own blog before you do it — some programs penalize or even ban bloggers that engage in click fraud.

Getting Advertising Going

Most bloggers choose to incorporate advertising programs by signing up with a company that serves as a middle man between the blogger and the advertiser. This company typically negotiates rates with the advertiser, tracks ad performance, and pays the blogger for advertising placement.

Although you can cut out the middle man and sell your own ad space, many bloggers find that they don't really want to spend their time dealing with the negotiation, tracking, and technical overhead.

But even the most time-pressed blogger can likely find the strength to listen when an advertiser contacts that blogger directly and offers to sponsor the blog. These arrangements are typically more lucrative for the blogger (and the advertiser, presumably), and the two parties negotiate this relationship on a case-by-case basis, depending on the audience, product, blog traffic, and other factors.

After you decide on formats, placement, and business models, it's time to put ads on your blog. The good — and bad — news is that you have dozens of options to choose from. In the following sections, I show you a few well-regarded advertising programs to consider.

Google AdSense

www.google.com/adsense

AdSense is Google's contextual advertising program, and it's really the biggest player in the contextual advertising arena. When you sign up for Google AdSense, you choose what kinds of ads you want on your blog, from text to images to videos. You can see examples of the Google AdSense formats in Figure 17-3.

Advertisers pay Google money when your blog visitors click the advertisements displayed beside your content, and you receive a portion of those payments. Successful bloggers who have a lot of traffic can earn a living from Google AdSense, but income varies greatly, depending on the size of your audience and how well your blog topics match the advertisers who contract with Google.

Figure 17-3: Google AdSense puts advertisers on your blog and money in your pocket.

Yahoo! Publisher Network Content Match

`http://publisher.yahoo.com/sell/ContentMatch.php`

Yahoo! Publisher Network's Content Match program (shown in Figure 17-4) is another advertising system that displays ads in a contextual manner. You can customize the look of the ads that appear on your blog so that they blend in with your blog itself by selecting color, size, and layout options. Content Match also allows you to filter out ads from potential competitors so that they don't appear on your site.

Text Link Ads

`www.text-link-ads.com`

Based in New York, Text Link Ads is one of the most popular and recognizable advertising systems that bloggers use. Designed with blogs in mind, these ads are a slightly different option than contextual advertising programs

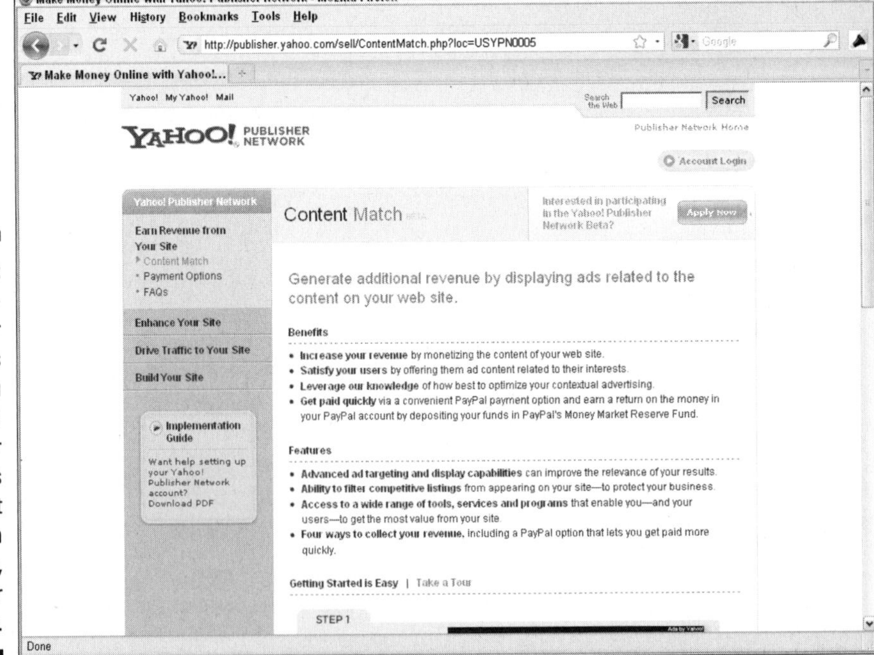

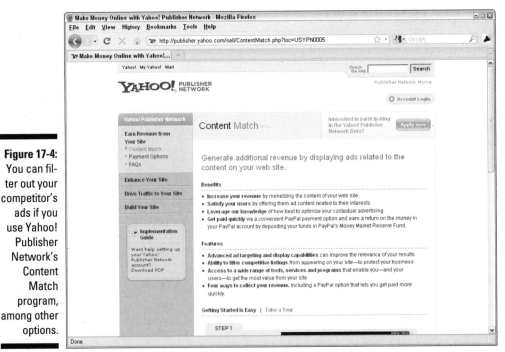

Figure 17-4: You can filter out your competitor's ads if you use Yahoo! Publisher Network's Content Match program, among other options.

that try to relate ads specifically to your content. Instead, you get only simple links that you preapprove, which are related but much lower-key in look and feel than contextual ads.

You can display Text Link Ads on the same page with Google AdSense, Yahoo! Publisher Network, and other contextually served ads.

AdBrite

```
www.adbrite.com
```

AdBrite is an advertising marketplace similar to the others mentioned in the preceding sections. Bloggers can choose between text, banner ads, full-page *interstitials* (splash pages containing a full-page advertisement), inline ads, and image ads. Interstitials are high-paying ads that take over the entire browser window when a user clicks to move from one page of your Web site to another; they usually feature a Skip This Ad link or button.

Putting Ads on Your Blog

To get these ads onto your Web site, most often, the programs you sign up for provide you with a bit of code that you insert into your Web site templates. Some programs have step-by-step instructions for popular blog software packages, but be aware that you might also need to consult your blog's documentation for help with putting your ads where you want them.

First, decide just where you want the ads on your page. The best thing to do when you're thinking about introducing ads into your blog design is to make sure the ads aren't overpowering.

Don't damage your reputation or credibility by overloading the site with ads or by associating ads too closely with your blog posts and content. Aside from pop-up ads, nothing is more annoying than having a blog design that's created around ads rather than a blog that's designed to include ads.

At the same time, you need to place ads in spots where readers can see them. Bloggers have discovered a few truths about ads, although your results might differ:

- **Ads at the top and bottom of each page do poorly.** Readers often ignore and rarely view advertisements along the top or the bottom of a blog because the site content usually appears in the middle of the screen. While users scroll their windows to view site content, they may never see these top and bottom advertisements at all.
- **Ads in the sidebars perform well but might interfere with navigation.** The left side of the Web site is a traditional place for ads. However, it's also a prime place for navigation tools, and your Web site design might require that you locate such tools higher than the ads you want people to view. As for the right side, not only are navigation tools sometimes placed here, but the bulk of blog content tends be aligned to the left side of the screen, which means that some users might cover the right with other windows and miss these right-side advertisements entirely.
- **Ads within the content itself get clicked.** Some blogs have their ads placed within their content, and therefore visitors don't miss the ads. But you need to be careful when you use advertising within your content. Remember that you want to make the content king, not the ad.

Try out ads in different places on your blog and see how your audience reacts, as well as how your earnings do. You might need to try several different locations before you find one that balances your readers' needs with your advertisers'.

Putting Ads in Your RSS Feeds

Active bloggers debate about whether RSS feeds should contain ads. Traditionally, bloggers have used RSS as a way to share information, and only recently has it become a place to put advertisements. You might want to consider using RSS ads because many of your blog readers might use RSS readers to consume the content of your blog.

RSS ads are simply banner or text advertisements that appear below or above the content displayed in your RSS reading program. The ads are usually smaller than typical banner ads on the average Web site because they're meant to fit within the RSS feed. If you want to monetize your RSS feed, consider these services:

- **Pheedo (`www.pheedo.com`):** Pheedo is the pioneering company that began the feed advertising industry. In 2003, Pheedo's creators thought up an idea to place advertisements in RSS feeds and started Pheedo. Their business has grown into one of the largest advertising networks for RSS.

- **Feedvertising** (`www.text-link-ads.com/feedvertising`): Feedvertising is a department of Text Link Ads that places ads within the RSS feed of your Web site. For its RSS feed ads, Feedvertising uses a similar system to Text Link Ads' site-based ads.
- **Google FeedBurner ads for blogs and feeds** (`www.feedburner.com/fb/a/advertising`): FeedBurner, a Google-owned company, is full of feed experts. They have a program called FeedBurner for Blogs and Feeds that allows you to control the ads that go onto your blog and blog feeds. They have established a significant ad network.

Getting Paid to Post

Being paid to post can mean a couple of different things. For many bloggers, it means receiving money or products to post a review or mention a company on a personal blog. But blogging for money can also lead you down the path of the professional blogger, where you write posts for other blogs.

Placing products on your blog

Some bloggers believe that getting paid to post about products or companies is a bad thing. However, blogging is hard work. Would it be so terrible to get paid to talk about a product every once in a while?

Some bloggers fear that the influence of advertisers might take over the traditionally independent voice of the blogosphere. When advertisers offer money to bloggers to praise their products and services in a blog, it might not result in an honest review of the business. So, if you're paid to post information about someone else, make sure that you retain your ability to post your own honest opinion. You might even want to consider starting an additional blog to showcase content that you're being paid to produce, as opposed to the content contained in your original blog.

Above all, let your readers know what products companies have paid you to mention or review, or sent you for free in hopes that you review them. You can head off accusations of deception by disclosing the terms of how you came to talk about a product or a post that some company has paid you for.

You can either set up your own system or find a service that allows you to connect with companies that want to have their products or services advertised on blogs.

SponsoredReviews.com

`www.sponsoredreviews.com`

SponsoredReviews.com is a company that connects advertisers with bloggers who are willing to write reviews about the advertisers' products and services. This company is forthright with the expectation that you, as a blogger, will offer an honest opinion and even give constructive criticism about the products that its advertisers create.

PayPerPost

`www.payperpost.com`

PayPerPost is a company that helps bloggers get paid for creating and publishing advertiser-sponsored content. The theory behind the company is that if you're a blogger, you'll inevitably write about some products that you've used in the past or are currently using. PayPerPost believes you should be paid for those kinds of posts.

PayPerPost works somewhat like a job board, where you accept bids to write about a certain product or service. The advertiser and the amount of traffic you report determine the amount of money you receive.

Blogging professionally

You can offer your blogging services to those who might want them by making a small business for yourself as a professional blogger. Believe me; companies are often looking for competent writers they can hire to contribute content to their blogs. This decision might take time away from your personal blog, but hopefully, additional practice can help you to become a better blogger!

To offer up your service, check the blogger-wanted ads on job boards and see whether you're interested in writing about any topic. Also, be sure to post about your availability on your own blog's sidebar and in your blog itself.

Two job sites where you can start your search for blogging jobs are

- **Jobs.Problogger (**`http://jobs.problogger.net`**):** A popular Web site that provides help to bloggers so that they can monetize their Web sites. The job board is highly active, and blogger jobs often appear here.
- **Performancing (**`www.performancing.com`**):** A Web resource that was established as "a home for professional bloggers." If you want to find job postings for new bloggers, you can check out their job posting forums.

When you begin blogging professionally, you need to keep track of any progress you make. Typically, this tracking includes either the number of posts that you create or the number of site visitors over a period of time. You can organize this information in various ways, but the tracking needs to prove that some interaction occurred between you and your readers.

Tying in Affiliate Marketing

If you ever blogged about a product that you really like and just knew that you were helping the company who makes the product make a sale, you can now make some money from that sale with affiliate marketing.

Popular retailers have set up affiliate marketing programs, most notably Amazon. You sign up with an affiliate program, and when you blog about one of its products, you include a piece of identifying information that the company gives you. You earn cash when readers of your blog click the product and buy it.

If you find yourself blogging about items that others might buy as a result of your recommendation, check to see whether the company that makes the product has an affiliate program and sign yourself up.

In short order, your blog can contain links to books, DVDs, or other products that provide you with a commission on each product bought through a link from your Web site.

Amazon Associates Program

`www.amazon.com/associates`

Amazon is the most recognized affiliate program available, and it's arguably one that you likely benefit from using because many bloggers mention books and DVDs that they've enjoyed.

Amazon Associates works by letting you create specially formatted links that you can use on your blog to drive traffic to the Amazon Web site. Anything that a visitor who clicks your link purchases earns you a percentage of the sale as a referral fee.

LinkShare

```
www.linkshare.com/affiliates/affiliates.shtml
```

LinkShare is another affiliate program that calls itself a pay-per-action marketing network. You can place both text and graphical ads on your blog and make money from any sales that come from readers' purchases.

Seeking Sponsorships

Sponsorships are advertisements by companies that have either requested to be an advertiser or whom you seek out to advertise on your site. Such sponsorship can mean one of two things:

- Sponsors might pay you to put their ads on your Web site.
- Sponsors might simply provide you with free goods or services in return for advertising on your Web site.

You need to think carefully about whether to take on a sponsor because not all sponsorships are equal:

- **Prominent placement or exclusivity:** A sponsor is different from the usual ad on your Web site because sponsors like a prominent placement on your blog — possibly including the exclusive right to advertise on your blog.
- **Acknowledgment:** A sponsor might ask you to use the phrase "This blog sponsored by . . . " or some variation of it to let your readers know that a specific company is funding your blog. You may also want to thank your sponsor occasionally to generate extra good will.
- **Time commitment:** Sponsorships often run for a set length of time, usually much longer than a standard ad runs. Sponsorships of several months to a year aren't unheard of.

Getting sponsors interested in your blog is probably the hardest advertising strategy, though it's also the most lucrative. To find a sponsor, you need to "sell" your blog, from the design to the content. Make the sponsor want to post its advertisements on your site — not someone else's. When you're seeking sponsors, keep your blog dynamic, on topic, and well written.

One of the best things sponsors do for your blog is legitimize your work. Many bloggers might be viewed by the public as "just another blogger" within the static of the Internet. But, if you have sponsors that believe in what you're doing, you can attract other professional relationships, such as speaking engagements or press interviews. If you're regarded as an authority, you can build a stronger brand.

Real Baking with Rose (`http://www.realbakingwithrose.com`) is an example of a sponsored blog. Written by cookbook author Rose Levy Beranbaum for cooks who are interested in baking, the blog is "brought to you by" Gold Medal Flour, which gets top billing in the blog's header.

Negotiating a sponsorship experience

Sponsors can be demanding advertisers. Unlike developing your own monetization plan, sponsorships can change the way you advertise on your site. Some sponsors demand *exclusivity* — which means they're the only business of that type that advertises on your site, and you might have to turn away other potential sponsors. Others might demand that you always write about their product or services in a positive way. Dealing with sponsors can be a true balancing act. But the rewards can be worth the work.

Here's my recipe for a successful sponsor/blogger relationship:

- **Be clear on your topic.** Know who you are and what you're writing about. If you have a blog that isn't clear about its subject, when you're seeking sponsorship, potential sponsors may be unable to understand why they are a good match for your blog. Sponsors want a very clear idea about the content you're creating and about what you can do for them.

  Keeping your blog on topic is especially important when sponsors are actively using their brand identities on your site. Make sure that they're aware of everything you might write about so that they don't have any surprises or objections to editorial content.
- **Be clear about what you're promising.** Be sure both you and your sponsor understand exactly what influence and control — if any — the partnership offers the advertiser. Thoroughly outline how you'll handle both content and advertising placement of the sponsor; the advertiser should be upfront about its expectations of you.
- **Know your audience.** Educate yourself on your audience if you're seeking paying sponsors for your blog. With increased sponsorship, you absolutely must address the question of who your audience is. You need to document the activity in your community, track your comments, and analyze the information from your Web statistics. (Check Chapter 16 for information on Web statistics and traffic software.)

Create a report of your statistics to prove to any sponsors that you have the numbers that you claim you do. Don't use any guesswork when creating this report — your sponsors want to see solid numbers and data to back up your claims. Sponsorship arrangements often require you to create statistics reports; the simple fact is that if you want to make money, you have to gather data.

You can collect data from your audience in the form of contests, polls, and other interactive experiences. Ask your audience members who they are — and if you approach it in a professional manner, they might be happy to reveal a little bit about themselves.

- **Banner placement and visual cues.** If you've been placing advertising on your blog for awhile, you already have a good idea where ads appear to good effect on your site, and you probably also know what types of ads work best. So, you can demonstrate the benefits of placement and ad types to any potential sponsors.

  However, if you've never had ads on your site when you first seek a sponsor, be prepared to offer ideas and suggestions for adequately highlighting the sponsor's ads and branding. You can even provide a design mock-up or some kind of visual representation. Or you might even consider creating a demo Web site that actually shows the ads in the positions and formats that you think can work.

- **Limit other monetization methods.** Some bloggers find that if they use other advertising systems at the same time as a sponsor, it dilutes the effectiveness of the sponsorships. Many sponsors ask to be the exclusive advertiser on your site or that you limit what other kinds of advertising and advertisers you use while they sponsor you. This request isn't unreasonable, especially if you have a lucrative sponsorship agreement that compensates you for the loss of those ad spots.

Setting boundaries

Jumping to the professional level in the blogging world poses a few potential pitfalls and requires ongoing reinvention on your part. Set up and keep to a few simple rules about what your professional limits and intentions are, and don't be afraid to write those rules down in a document that you share with sponsors and your readers.

Also, be ready to say no. Some sponsors might want more than you're willing to give. Yes, you may be able to earn some money from your blog, but don't forget the reason you're blogging in the first place. Your blog is your territory, not your sponsor's. You're renting the sponsor space on your site, giving them access to your audience. You aren't signing up for someone to tell you what to do. You already have parents for that!

Don't jump at every offer that comes in the door. You may find this advice difficult to follow when you're seeking your first sponsor, but you need to maintain a high level of professionalism — not just for yourself, but also for your audience. In the same way that you protect your audience from nasty comments and spam, you need to be sure that you give them an appropriate experience with your sponsors and advertisers. Protect the integrity of your blog and avoid sponsors that demand more time, editorial control, or space on your blog than you're willing to give.

Accepting Gifts, Not Obligations

Many companies offer news media access to products and services in order to generate press attention, and increasingly, bloggers are being offered the same goodies. After all, some blog topics are so specific that companies absolutely know that the blog's readers will be interested in their products. For example, a blogger who writes about cell phones might be targeted by a mobile phone company, and offered a free product or money in exchange for some kind of online review or feedback.

This kind of exchange can be a tricky situation because some bloggers regard the gift as some kind of bribe or obligation to write something positive about the product in question.

In fact, that perception isn't correct. I know bloggers who accept products for review on the condition that they say what they really think about it, and most companies are perfectly satisfied with this kind of arrangement. In addition, most bloggers who do these kinds of reviews are very upfront with their readers about how they obtained the product in question and what agreement they have with the company that provided it.

If you're getting these offers, you can probably benefit from establishing such a policy. Most bloggers don't want to be seen as taking bribes or favors from companies that just want the bloggers to say nice things about them. Your policy needs to lay out how you plan to deal with such situations.

Here are a few things to consider when you start to get product-review offers:

- **Be clear about what you'll do with the product.** Tell the product maker that you won't write a positive review if the product doesn't deserve it. Make sure that you're very specific about what you'll provide in return for the gift (if anything).
- **Be prepared to return gifts.** A lot of bloggers, especially the incredibly geeky ones, would love to receive a gift from a company that has the latest and hottest product. However, if the company has unreasonable demands or demands that don't match the blogger's vision, the blogger might choose to simply return the gift.
- **Donate what you receive.** You can avoid an ugly scene with your audience or any sponsors of your blog by taking the gifts you receive, writing your review, and then giving the items away. You can send them to your favorite charity or hold a contest for your audience. Donating your freebies generates all kinds of goodwill from your community while avoiding any accusations of bias.

Keep to the core of what makes your blog great. If you get an offer of a free product, think about it first — don't accept it right away. You can even go to your community members and see what they think if you require advice. Whether you accept ads or sponsorships, and how you implement them, really depends on you.

Chapter 18

Blogging for Companies

In This Chapter

- Making blogs work for your business or organization
- Establishing a plan for blogging success
- Exploring the technological bells and whistles
- Advertising on blogs

As a business owner or entrepreneur, you're probably wondering whether blogging can help you be more financially successful or allow you to promote your company in some way. Many of today's technically savvy businesses have started blogs and found them to be terrific tools for reaching out to customers, generating buzz about a service or product, building goodwill, or just informing customers about what they're up to.

If you're thinking about adding a blog to your outreach efforts but aren't entirely confident that it'll be worth the time and effort, you're not alone. Many companies have difficulty seeing the value in blogging. Some professionals worry about diverting time away from more crucial workplace tasks, whereas others worry about opening themselves up for public criticism.

And the truth is that even though blogging can provide a business with a really incredible tool, it isn't right for *every* business. Nonetheless, in this chapter, I do my best to persuade you that blogging can work for you and your company, whether you're a lone-wolf entrepreneur just starting out or a Fortune 500 executive with more marketing staff than you know what to do with.

If this chapter piques your interest, check out my book *Buzz Marketing with Blogs For Dummies,* which covers in depth what I can cover only briefly in this chapter.

Putting Blogs to Work for Your Business

A stigma still lingers around blogs. Many people still think of a blogger as a pimple-faced teenager who sits in his pajamas all day writing excruciatingly boring diary posts about what he had for breakfast. Blogs, for a lot of folks, equate with the worst kind of narcissistic navel-gazing. Those kinds of blogs do exist, of course, but in reality, the blogosphere contains so much more than that. Hundreds of nonprofit organizations, small-business owners, consultants, newspapers, and schools have moved into the blogosphere.

Why? Blogs are simple to set up, easy to publish, and have a proven track record for increasing search engine traffic to a Web site. For a company in which time is of the essence and accessibility is a necessity — show me a company where these things aren't a priority, and I'll eat my hat — blogs are a low-investment way to accomplish a lot. Don't believe me? Then perhaps you'll believe General Motors, McDonald's, Microsoft, Amazon, *The New York Times,* and Southwest Airlines; all these companies have added blogs to their business practices.

Considering the benefits of a business blog

For a business or organization, you can use blog software to release company public-relations documents to the public, or you can go further and introduce blogs as part of your external communications to your customers and potential customers. Some companies use blogs internally to coordinate work teams or communicate across distances. Here are a few of the ways businesses are using blogs:

- Generating conversation and buzz about the company, its products, or services in the online space
- Reaching out with information and support to current customers, even resolving issues traditionally handled by phone-based customer service
- Creating new pathways to interact with the public about an industry or issue, including gathering feedback and input to guide future product development
- Defusing negative criticism or press by publicly addressing problems
- Demonstrating expertise and experience to potential customers
- Directly driving sales or action
- Collaborating across teams, branches, regions, or staggered shifts

When it comes to business, the main thing that a business blogger should consider is that blog software, implemented properly, can allow companies to improve their communications and organization with very little overhead. In some cases, blogs have even saved businesses money by delivering documents and data online that were previously delivered via snail mail.

Businesses haven't been the only beneficiaries, either. Customers have benefited from increased access to news, information, support, and dialog with companies that have blogs.

Making blogs work for you can be simple if you have a communication strategy that's flexible and can evolve when your blog takes off. Blogs can generate sales and establish strong communication directly with customers, and marketing experts believe blogs are a friendly method of making customers happy.

Checking out businesses that blog

You know blogging is important. You already know that it gives you a very good way to generate talk about your company. Do you need a little more convincing? Well, the following sections discuss how some other companies are blogging.

Hewlett-Packard

```
www.hp.com/hpinfo/blogs
```

You've probably owned a Hewlett-Packard product at some point in your computing life. Hewlett-Packard has built computers, printers, cameras, and high-end computer servers for years, building up incredible expertise across a range of consumer products. You can see that knowledge in the HP blogs, which claim to convey the "unvarnished thoughts of HP employees." Topics range from computers to the Cannes Film Festival to gaming, and the bloggers come from all areas of the company's structure.

Wells Fargo

```
http://blog.wellsfargo.com
```

What could a bank possibly blog about, you ask? Apparently, banks can discuss a whole lot with their customers. Student loans, small business, and stock markets are all topics discussed on the Wells Fargo Blogs site. Wells Fargo Blogs gives multiple contributors a public voice in a variety of blogs, from The Student LoanDown to Guided by History.

Microsoft Community

`www.microsoft.com/communities/blogs`

The Microsoft Community Blogs (shown in Figure 18-1) are one way that Microsoft reaches out to customers and potential customers. These blogs, written by software and hardware developers, give interested readers a behind-the-scenes peek at their favorite products and a way to interact with the developers.

Sun Microsystems

`http://blogs.sun.com`

Sun Microsystems also reaches out to customers by using developer blogs. On the blogs, customers can seek out and talk directly to the people involved in the making of a product, giving customers a feeling of involvement and direct access not available from traditional marketing efforts.

It's pretty ingenious, when you think about it — put your engineers and programmers to work helping you promote your products and services, rather than just creating them!

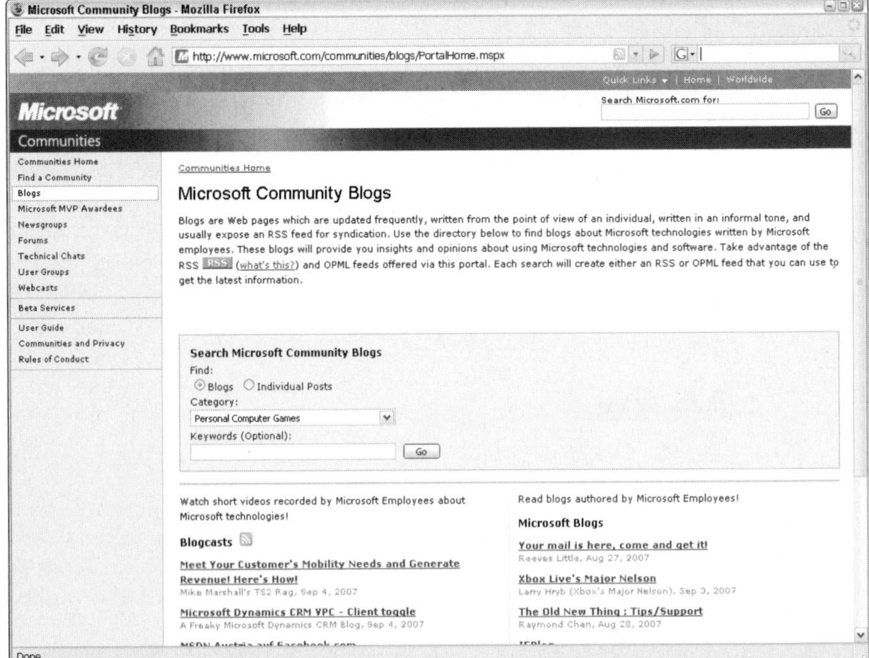

Figure 18-1: Microsoft's software coders talk about their work to customers and other employees.

Deciding whether to blog

Blogging for business reasons is a sensitive topic both in and out of the blogosphere. Old-school bloggers don't like seeing blogging turned from a personal outlet into a professional one, and many businesses worry that the informality of a blog looks unprofessional. And that's not all — some businesses also have concerns about employees who have personal blogs on which they might talk about their work or appear to be representing the company.

Blogging isn't for every corporate culture. If your company has traditionally had an open hand with communication and outreach, blogging is going to be a great tool for you. But if you have a reserved corporate culture, blogging might be too much of a stretch beyond business as usual. Many companies that might seem an odd fit for blogs for marketing or outreach have been happily surprised at the results they've obtained.

Businesses that need to keep information or trade practices confidential, or that stand to lose by having an open-door policy, probably shouldn't blog. For instance, some government agencies and law firms are limited by the very nature of their business in what they can communicate. You know best whether your corporate culture or industry can't benefit from the use of a blog.

At the very least, however, track your company and what's said about it in the blogosphere. Just because you ignore blogs, that doesn't mean they ignore you! Chapter 16 explains how you can keep tabs on what others say about your business online.

If you're still on the fence about starting a blog, try one with a set endpoint, for an event or a product launch. After the event occurs, you can end the blog's lifespan gracefully and have some real data to use in assessing whether blogging was a worthwhile endeavor for you. Also, take a look at your competitors — are any of them blogging? If so, does the blog appear to be reaching visitors effectively? Are readers leaving comments? Watch how these competitors are making use of a blog and give some thought to whether you might be able to do something similar (but more effectively).

Top five reasons why blogs work for businesses

Here are the most important reasons that blogs work so well as a business and marketing tool in today's Internet-enabled world:

- **Cost:** A lot of blogging software packages are open source and available at no cost, but even those that have licensing fees are very reasonably priced. Hosted services can also provide you with an inexpensive platform to begin business blogging.
- **Communication:** A blog allows you to communicate with potential and current clients in a direct and informal way. You can chat and communicate about your product or service without pressuring your client. You use a business blog to make sure that your potential or existing clients get the facts about your product without a heavy-handed sales pitch.
- **Research:** Many companies want to break into new markets and new demographics. Blogging allows for collaborative discussion that can help you gather valuable information about how to position products and services.
- **Feedback:** Find out what you're doing right and wrong in your business or with your products by just asking outright on your blog. Discover how to improve what you're currently doing or how you can deal with existing problems — and get points for effort while you do.
- **Reputation:** Do away with that corporate-giant personality most companies can't help but convey. Blogs can put a human, personal face on what has usually been a monolithic surface. If you let the public see how you respect and regard them, you reap the benefits of being honest and open. Smaller businesses and consultancies benefit from the publicity around their name and opinion.

Planning for Business Blog Success

Blogging for a business comes down to planning. Don't let the easiness of getting started with the technical side of blogging seduce you into jumping in without preparing. You need to decide what your goals are, figure out who you want to actually blog, map out the topics that you plan to discuss, and plan how you might integrate direct action or sales.

Setting goals

Before you jump into blogging for your business, you need to set goals that define how you can know whether your blog is successful after you launch it. Decide what you want the blog to help you accomplish. Do you want to replace some of your existing customer service efforts with the blog? Are you launching a new product that needs publicity? Whatever your direction, plan your purpose prior to launching the blog.

So many things could go into a blog, but you also have a business to run. Decide how much time you want to devote to writing and maintaining your blog. Blogging is part of your business, but it can't take away from time you need to devote to other tasks.

You might choose to define success by

- Increasing traffic to your Web site
- Reaching a certain number of blog comments on a daily basis
- Seeing more conversation about your company/products/services in the media or on other blogs
- Earning money from product sales or blog advertising

You might want to define success for your blog in other ways, so don't think you have to use any of these suggestions. A blog is such a flexible medium that yours might accomplish a goal I can't even imagine!

Choosing a blogger

Businesses have developed two approaches to company blogs: blogs written by one person and those written by multiple people from all over the organization. Either approach is valid, as long as everyone posting to the blog has a clear idea of the goals, ideas, and style of the blog.

If you create a blog that has multiple contributors, put a single individual in charge of content on a regular basis and encourage others from the organization to chime in when they have something to say. The responsibility for the blog is in one person's hands, but the door is open for wide participation.

Occasional writers are welcome, but don't suddenly give employees brand-new job duties that they can't meet. Having multiple voices in a blog can also help you to convey the culture of your company overall, giving readers a taste of what people at all levels of the organization think about and do.

If you spread the writing around, you might be able to create a blog that has a huge amount of content and satisfies a very large readership. The multiple-voice perspective might also awaken ideas in the other writers and generate internal conversations.

No matter who blogs, you must decide internally whether someone needs to vet posts before actually posting them, and who should do the vetting. It's a good idea to have someone who isn't blogging keep an eye on things, just to get a second opinion.

When you're considering just who should blog on behalf of the company, give some thought to

- **Writing ability:** You need a blogger who's an effective writer and who also *likes* to write.
- **Position within the company:** Who's the right person to reach out to the public? CEOs offer one perspective, and so do those on the factory floor. Try to match the goals and style of your blog with the right people within your company, and don't be afraid to give unexpected staffers a try. You might be surprised at how interesting readers find a behind-the-curtain approach.
- **Knowledge and expertise:** Be sure to choose a person who has sufficient knowledge and expertise to be interesting and engaging on the subjects the blog discusses. Preferably, you want people who really know what they're talking about and have information to share.
- **Time commitments:** Choose a blogger who has the time to put into the site. Don't overload already busy staff with this new job requirement.

After you choose a blogger, you have a few more folks to identify. Don't forget to plan who you want to review comments, deal with spam, and fix technical issues.

Deciding what to write

While you think about topics for the blog, consider how informal or personal you want to make your blog style. Although the occasional personal post can help to humanize your blog, don't be tempted down the journaling path: You're creating a business blog, so look for creative ways of covering your industry.

The goal of many business blogs is to establish (or maybe reestablish) the business as a leader in its industry. Think about how to demonstrate expertise while staying interesting and readable: You need to show that you know your stuff without becoming a stuffed shirt! Use the blog to persuade people that they should trust you without coming right out and telling people, "I'm trustworthy!"

Whoever blogs for your business needs to have a keen understanding of the goals and culture of the company, as well as know how much information to put on the blog without going too far. Many companies set up rules about topics that are appropriate for the blog, as well as define what information they want to keep confidential.

Here are some general guidelines to keep in mind for your blog content:

- **Keep it true.** Double-check blog posts for accuracy before making them live. Like a newspaper or any other publisher, follow a process to make sure you're publishing facts and not fiction. You can include opinions on your business's blog as long as you label them as just that.
- **Keep it relevant and real.** Be as open and honest as you can in your blog. This approach to transparency can make some in your company nervous (hi, corporate lawyer!), but the more successful business blogs provide insight or communication from real people. Some even give the public access to the viewpoints and words of high-level staff the readers would normally never meet or talk to. Furthermore, whoever blogs should stay on topic and keep posts related to the subject of the blog, no matter how interesting that TV show was last night.
- **Keep it informative and educational.** One problem that many companies encounter when they start to blog is the fact that their blog is (ahem) boring. You might have great information, but if people don't also find it interesting to read about, you can't get readers to stick around long. Try to write posts that educate with a light-hearted manner and that focus on information and news that's useful to those reading it.
- **Keep it positive.** Steer away from discussing your competition in your blog. If you can say something nice about another company, don't hesitate, but you probably don't want to point out just what other companies are doing wrong. That kind of approach can turn your blog into a giant argument, scaring off less-opinionated customers who might otherwise be interested in your products and services.
- **Keep using keywords.** Part of the plan of a business-related blog is to make sure the blog is useful to readers, but for that plan to work, you have to get readers from the search engine to your blog. Use your knowledge of your industry and topical news to use keywords that people are likely to use in search engines when they look for the subject of your blog or your business.

Pay special attention to the words that you use in the titles of your blog posts: Search engines often weight these words most heavily, so hit the highpoints in your titles. Informative is better than cutesy!

- **Keep linking.** Business blogs should also link to related articles and Web sites. You can link to resources on your business's own Web site, but don't hesitate to point folks to good information that isn't on your Web site. If you're a source for information that they need or can get them to the information they need effectively, you don't lose them for long.

  Also, look for chances to link the blog to itself! A lot of bloggers are clever about linking to old posts on their own blogs so that new readers know where to go deep within the blog archives. This kind of linking can increase traffic and also inform and educate your readers.

- **Keep posting.** Post on a regular basis and don't stop. Don't worry about an absolutely right number of posts per week, but most experts agree that two to three posts a week is enough to keep your blog active and useful without overwhelming your readers. Other bloggers post less frequently, and others post multiple times a day. Do what works for you and for your readers, but be consistent so that your readers know what to expect from you. If your blog has long silences followed by short bursts of posting, you create a recipe for low readership numbers.

Generating sales or action

Asking potential customers to check out your services after they read something on your blog can turn those readers into actual customers. If you see a logical link to a product or service that you offer, it only makes sense to let people know. But you need to do more than simply push sales. You tread a fine line between a blog that points out possible purchases, along with providing content, and one that isn't anything more than a big ad.

Keep one idea in mind: Meet the needs of your readers. If you can put yourself in the shoes of a blog visitor, you might be able to successfully discriminate between a reasonable link to a product sale and one that's too blatant.

Some blogs don't try hard to get people to pull out their wallets. Instead, the blog's purpose might be to gather feedback and get people to participate in an event or contest. Again, try to be genuine and inviting, rather than pushy. Get readers involved and invested in your goal.

The GreenView blog (`www.greenviewblog.com`) successfully negotiates between information and sales. This blog, shown in Figure 18-2, keeps readers up to date on news and information about lawn care, tracking the seasons, the environment, and other issues that impact lawns and gardens. When warranted, the blog links to some of the fertilizer products of GreenView Fertilizer, the Pennsylvania-based company that runs the blog.

Figure 18-2: Get lawn care advice and opportunities to buy fertilizer on the GreenView blog.

Delivering with Technology

You might be thinking about how you, as a blogger, can make connections with potential customers by using your blog. Words are a great start, but technology can also be your friend! A lot of the standard blog bells and whistles are designed to get people involved or to make it easy for them to consume your blog.

Use the tools in the following sections to get readers to return to your blog again and again.

Enabling comments

Comments are a double-edged sword for companies that start blogs. On the one hand, they do a great job of starting conversation and interaction. On the other hand, they can be a source of a lot of work because you have to keep them free of spam or inappropriate conversation. Many businesses are tempted to start a blog and keep comments turned off, but that cuts out a huge part of the benefit of a blog: hearing from your readers and interacting directly with them.

My advice? Turn on the comments! But take precautions by setting up a good policy about what kinds of comments are acceptable and implement some of the very good spam-fighting tools discussed in Chapter 9.

Creating RSS/Web feeds

Before the advent of Web feeds, blog readers had to remember to visit the blog periodically to see whether the blogger had posted a new entry. This dangerous method made it easy for people to forget to visit. Web feeds, or RSS feeds, give you a way to let people know quickly, easily, and automatically that you have new content available on your blog. Blog visitors simply subscribe to the feed by using a newsreader, which tracks the feed and updates it every time you update the blog, giving instant notification to the reader.

Users can set up Web feeds, usually formatted as RSS (Really Simple Syndication), quickly and easily. In fact, most blog software packages automatically include an RSS tool, so you can set it up once and never think about it again.

I talk more about Web feeds in Chapter 13.

Podcasting

Podcasting is a relative newcomer to the blogosphere, but it's proving to be a powerful blog ally. *Podcasting,* the recording and distribution of audio and video files to subscribers, has a tremendous potential to give your business blog a boost by providing multimedia presentations to your readers. You can add personality and a face to your blog. Posting interviews, discoveries, tutorials, and other adventures that your company has had can boost your visibility higher than a text-only blog can.

HBO produces podcasts to accompany many of its top shows (`www.hbo.com/podcasts`). A quick run through the selection reveals interviews with directors, stars, on-set interviews, episode clips, and more.

You can read more about creating a podcast in Chapter 11.

Starting a wiki

Wikis are collaboratively built Web sites, which any visitor can edit. Businesses and organizations have found that wikis can complement blog sites nicely. Blogs allow for comments, but a wiki can provide a little more flexibility because visitors can both post pages and leave updates in a wiki, contributing to everything from documentation to news coverage.

Wikis are terrific collaborative tools, and if you've been trying to figure out a good way to share knowledge within an organization, you might want to use this approach. Many companies have found wikis useful for group learning purposes, such as building documentation or setting up procedural tasks. One of the most well-known examples of a successful wiki is Wikipedia (`www.wikipedia.org`), an online encyclopedia to which anyone can contribute content or edit existing content. You can even find it available in multiple languages.

The Northern Voice blogging conference (`www.northernvoice.ca`) used a wiki to allow attendees of a self-organized event called Moose Camp to create its own event schedule. Figure 18-3 shows the wiki.

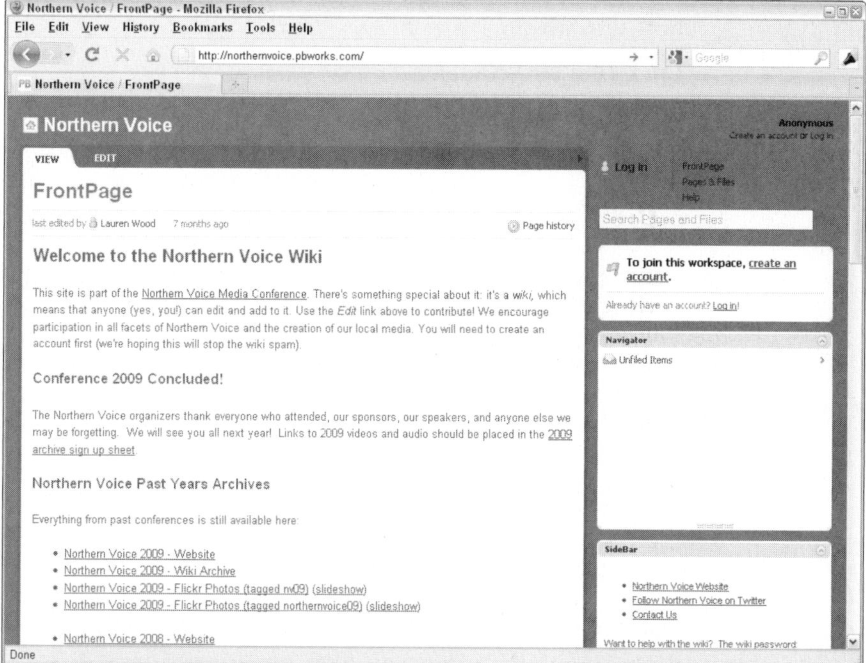

Figure 18-3: The attendees of the Northern Voice Conference organized sessions by using a wiki.

Joining a social network

Adding your company to a variety of social networks can also help to boost your visibility in the blogosphere. Businesses tend to shy away from social networking as a valid form of online advertising, but using these mediums properly can add a viral component to your communication strategy. (*Viral* marketing is advertising that consumers actually spread themselves. For example, when you forward a funny video created by a company, you've spread the "virus.")

A lot of social networks exist, so be sure to choose those that are most pertinent for your industry and approach, not those frequented by 14-year-old girls (unless that suits your business!). LinkedIn (`www.linkedin.com`) and XING (`www.xing.com`) are good places to get started.

To get started with LinkedIn, follow these steps:

1. **Use your Web browser to go to** `www.linkedin.com`.
2. **Fill out the registration form and click the Join Now button.**

   LinkedIn loads the signup continuation screen.
3. **Fill out the required fields, including your name, business information, and where you went to school.**
4. **Click Join LinkedIn.**

   LinkedIn creates an account for you.

   After you're a LinkedIn member, be sure to click the Expand Your Network button at the top-right of any page in order to invite colleagues or see who in your e-mail address book already uses LinkedIn.

I introduce social networks and what they're all about in Chapter 15.

Advertising on Blogs

Traditional marketing strategies include advertising, and blogs are no exception. But these aren't your father's ads: Blog advertising runs the gamut of everything from text links to full sponsorships.

In the past, taking out a typical advertisement meant that you'd go to the local newspaper, select an ad size, and choose a section in which you wanted your ad to appear. Maybe people saw the ad, maybe they didn't, but you got charged by how many newspapers were printed, not how many sales you made.

Online advertising offers more accountability to the advertiser: Because of the way Web sites work, you can track how many times readers' computers load an ad, when a reader clicks it, and what the person does after he or she clicks that ad. Because advertisers like this kind of measure of effectiveness, printed material has seen a significant decline in the purchase of ad space, whereas online advertising has grown hugely. You can use several methods to get your name or even your blog URL seen on other Web sites and blogs.

Going contextual

Contextual advertising is the practice in which an ad-serving tool matches the advertisements based on the content that appears in the blog. For example, a blog about candy would have ads for candy, and a blog about movies would show ads for upcoming films. If the Web site visitors are interested in the content of the Web site, they're likely also interested in goods and services related to the topic of the Web site, and thus they're more likely to click the ads.

The first major player in the contextual advertising game was Google AdSense. The program was popular from the start, and after a few rocky periods of users abusing the system, it has proven to be quite a moneymaker for successful bloggers. Many professional bloggers make their living almost entirely on the income received from Google AdSense revenue. Search-engine marketer Alexandre Brabant uses Google AdSense on his company Web site, eMarketing 101 (`www.emarketing101.net`). The Google AdSense program ads appear below the navigation bar of his site, as shown in Figure 18-4.

Here are two ways that you can get involved with Google's contextual advertising tools:

- **Sign up to put ads on your blog or Web site.** Use the Google AdSense program (`www.google.com/adsense`). Chapter 17 introduces this program.
- **Submit your blog or Web site for display.** The Google AdWords program (`http://adwords.google.com`) lets you present your blog or Web site in the ads displayed on other Web sites.

If you want to find out more about leveraging Google AdSense for your blog or business, check out *Building Your Business with Google For Dummies,* by Brad Hill; *Pay Per Click Search Engine Marketing For Dummies,* by Peter Kent; or *Google AdWords For Dummies,* by Howie Jacobson.

Yahoo! and several other companies also have contextual advertising programs — do a Web search for **contextual advertising programs** to see what's on offer.

Figure 18-4: Put ads on your site quickly by using Google AdSense, like on this site.

You can add contextual advertising to your Web (RSS) feed or put yourself into other Web feeds by using the FeedBurner Ad Network (`http://feedburner.google.com`).

Advertising via ad networks

A number of advertising middlemen can help successful bloggers put ads on their blogs. In most cases, you can choose between text and graphic ads in a set of standard Web-advertising sizes. You create the ad, the ad network serves it up, the blogger posts new content, and his or her visitors see your ad.

If you want to advertise on some of the most successful blogs around, check out one or more of these ad networks:

- **b5media (`www.b5media.com`):** Offers ad placement on more than 290 blogs reaching more than 10 million readers; bloggers can sign up to be paid for blogging on the b5media blog network.

- **Blogads (`www.blogads.com`):** Offers ad placement on 1,500 blogs and allows you to choose an audience to target (for example, parents or news junkies).
- **ClickZ (`www.clickz.com`):** Offers ad placement on the ClickZ family of news, opinion, and entertainment sites.
- **Crisp Ads (`www.crispads.com`):** Offers advertising across blog categories (such as autos and food) or on specific blogs. More than 3,800 blogs are enrolled.
- **FeedBurner (`www.feedburner.com`):** Offers placement on blogs and in RSS feeds; choose from categories of blogs and/or target specific times of day or geographic regions.

Each of these services offers you an array of popular blogs and ad formats to choose from, organizes the deal, and handles the transaction. Rates are negotiated based on the level of advertising, the blogs that you're placed on, and how many times your ads are viewed or clicked.

Sponsoring a blog

For a splashy way to be seen on a blog or Web site, consider sponsoring the site. Sponsorships for popular blogs have gained a lot of notoriety in the blogosphere. Some bloggers call accepting sponsorships "selling out," but others regard it as a great way to get paid to do what they love. Sponsorships tend to get you coverage on other blogs, even if it's just speculation about the amount you paid to sponsor a blog, but as they say, "Any publicity is good publicity."

Sponsorships usually entitle you to occupy any and perhaps all advertising slots on a blog, and they often earn you mentions in the text of the blog, as well. Few blogs actually advertise that they accept sponsorships, largely because sponsored blogs are still fairly rare. If you want to sponsor a blog, contact the blogger directly with an inquiry. He or she can let you know whether the blog is open to a sponsorship, and you can go from there.

Sponsorships can be expensive to do. Be prepared to negotiate with the blogger about the length of your sponsorship and the amount of money you're willing to pay, but think bigger than you would for advertisement. In some cases, sponsors assume the operating costs of a blog, in addition to paying the blogger for his or her time and audience exposure.

As a sponsor, you're entitled to more than just a prominent ad placement (though you should get that, too!). You can consider requesting *exclusivity* — that you're the only advertiser in your industry on the blog, the only sponsor, or the only advertiser. You can request mentions in the copy of the blog, or any other arrangement you think is good for both you and the blogger. For many sponsors, having a prominent logo placement and label at the top of every blog page, and no other advertising on the blog, fills the bill.

Topics to discuss with any blogger you're considering sponsoring include the following:

- **What topics the blog covers:** Know what kinds of content the blog you're sponsoring typically has, and what kind of language it uses. Because readers associate your brand with the blog, you need to be comfortable with the way the blogger expresses him- or herself, as well as what subjects the blogger may raise.

  You might also want to discuss how you plan to handle situations in which the blogger has blogged about a topic with which you have a problem. Understand that the blogger is likely to resist giving you editorial control, and be clear about what, if any, say you want to have in the content of the site.
- **How you want the blog to acknowledge your sponsorship:** Be sure to establish how the blogger will place your brand on the page, and when and where he or she will mention your business and link to your business's Web site.
- **How other ads or monetization occur on the blog:** Talk with the blogger about other ways that he or she earns revenue and decide what, if any, of those systems can remain in place during the term of your sponsorship. Be prepared to compensate the blogger for any revenue that he or she usually earns that you request he or she remove from the site. For example, if the blogger commonly uses Google AdSense advertising that you don't want to appear on the blog when you sponsor it, ask for accounting statements showing the value of those ads to the blogger.

Part VII
The Part of Tens

"He should be all right now. I made him spend two and a half hours reading prisoner blogs on the state penitentiary web site."

In this part . . .

Bring it all together in The Part of Tens by touring some top blogs and blog technologies. Chapter 19 covers some excellent ways to grow your audience into a true community, encouraging feedback and discussion and handling dissension in the ranks. In Chapter 20, get a cool list of technologies that you shouldn't miss. This isn't the cutting edge; it's the bleeding edge! For good measure, I leave you with ten outstanding and successful blogs you must check out in Chapter 21. And, finally, don't miss the glossary, where all the technical mumbo-jumbo gets defined clearly, or my guide to the basics of HTML code.

Chapter 19

Ten Ways of Growing Community

In This Chapter

- Putting in the time to keep your community active
- Encouraging conversation and ideas
- Asking for help diagnosing problems or building interaction

Every online community needs leaders or facilitators to keep the discussions lively, upbeat, and on topic. Playing "mom" or "dad" can be the hardest job in any community, and sometimes, the rewards come slowly. Don't let this fact discourage you, though. Encouraging growth in any community requires a certain level of patience, persistence, and attention — but when it works, it really works.

This chapter offers a few simple tricks for developing your blog from your soapbox into a real community, with true interaction between you and your readers, and among the readers themselves.

If you're lucky, in the process of getting people to read and comment on your posts and on each other's comments, you even discover how to convert readers into community evangelists who can make the community larger, more fun, and more active.

Write

Get writing (or podcasting, or posting photos, or whatever it is you're doing on your blog)!

Establish a regular schedule for maintaining your blog; a schedule really helps readers know what to expect and when. A regular schedule can even build anticipation and excitement. Be open to ideas, provide a welcoming environment, and keep yourself on topic so that interested, engaged readers get what they're looking for when they visit.

Write on other Web sites, as well. See whether other blogs might need a little help with a few additional posts. Also, help keep the conversations going on other blogs that you enjoy. Each time you comment on another blog, you get exposure to a few more potential readers for your own blog and build links back to your blog (which can help boost your search engine rankings).

Reply

If someone asks you a question, either in the comments or through e-mail, make sure to reply. Acknowledge what the person says in your reply and take the time to answer properly, even if only to thank him or her for the comment. Thoughtful responses to questions and comments about your blog can do as much to build your community as original blog posts can.

Some bloggers take the attitude that reader comments aren't important or don't count as much as the blog posts. If you actually want to build a readership that interacts with you, this attitude is dead wrong. Readers want your attention and encouragement.

Keep on top of what people are saying within your blog domain and don't be a stranger to those who like what you do. Embrace their enthusiasm for your blog. Give them a reason to keep coming back. Interaction can make those who might shy away feel that they're really part of the community that you're developing.

If you reply to comments and criticism on both your blog and in other online communities, you can really attract others to your own site. Get involved as much as you would in any offline community group.

Visit and Participate

Join other communities. It's that simple. If you want to build a community around your blog, you need to participate in others. Find blogs that are related to the topic areas of your blog. Jump into the conversation by offering a different perspective, or some feedback to the blogger or to the folks who leave comments. Mentioning your site on other blogs is fine, as long as you make sure that your comments relate to the subject at hand and add to the conversation.

Also, don't just write and leave. Keep active in the communities in which you're a member and use that time to connect with others. Take what you can from the community, but also give back what you think can benefit everyone as a whole. Remember that participating in these communities might even give you ideas for your own blog, so you're likely to benefit in several ways from the time you spend on these blogs.

You can also share links between your blog community and related blogs that you want to support. Offer to set up a type of network where you can share content between sites. Anything is possible; you only need to ask.

Add Guest Bloggers

If your blog readership is up and running, and you're attracting a significant number of daily readers, you can request that members of your community help you out by guest-blogging on your site. Depending on the software you're using, you can either set up secondary blogs or allow them to post to the main blog of your site. Getting other perspectives and comments from your community "experts" is incredibly cool, and you might be able to build a series of posts from other bloggers into your site.

This kind of blogging trade-off can let you have multiple voices fill out the content on your site and provide a richer experience for your readers.

These relationships are great to have when you get sick or want to take a vacation — tap your guest-blogging community for help covering your blog while you aren't around to do it.

Try E-Mail and Newsletters

As spam-ridden as electronic mail can be, you can still use it to stay in contact with your community. Offering e-mail delivery of some or all of your blog content to your readership can attract users who aren't comfortable with some of the fancier technologies, such as RSS. Try these three tactics:

- Let your readers send a blog post to a friend who might also be interested.
- Let your users sign up for e-mail notifications when you post something new to your blog.
- Let your readers sign up for an e-mail newsletter that supplements your blog or recaps recent blog posts of interest.

Many blog software programs have built-in Tell a Friend or Email a Friend functionality. If you turn this feature on, every blog post includes a small icon or link that, when clicked, lets your reader fill out the name and e-mail address of a friend and send an e-mail notification about your blog post to that friend. It's like free marketing. Figure 19-1 shows an Email to a Friend form on the Improv Everywhere blog (`www.improveverywhere.com`).

You can easily reach users who have mastered e-mail, but aren't up on newsreaders and RSS, by setting up your blog to allow users to sign up for e-mail notifications when you post a new blog entry. Allowing them to sign up and also remove themselves from your e-mail system puts them in control of the situation, which means that you don't contribute to the spam problem. The FeedBurner site (`http://feedburner.google.com`) lets you set up an e-mail notification/subscription tool.

Taking the time to create some kind of additional e-mail newsletter can also get people interested in your Web site. You can take a little time at the end of each calendar month to pick out your best or most popular blog posts. You can include the links to your blog posting, or you can copy and paste the blog post into an e-mail and send it off.

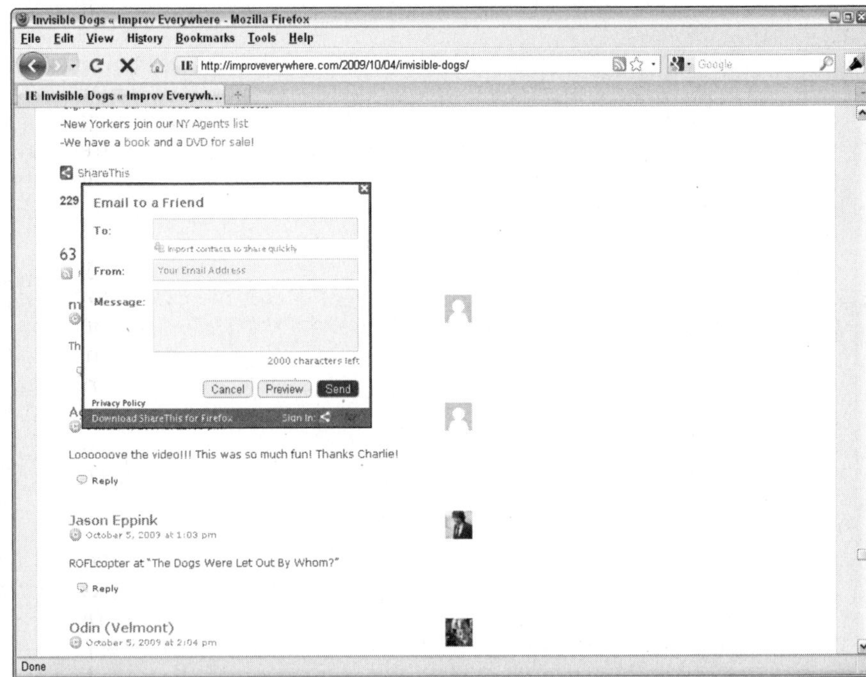

Figure 19-1: The Improv Everywhere blog offers an Email This Item feature to let you clue in friends about a great blog post.

You can create this kind of newsletter in several ways, but it's most effective if you to sign up for an e-mail service provider such as Constant Contact (`www.constantcontact.com`), Topica (`www.topica.com`), or Email Marketing Solutions (`www.lyris.com/solutions/lyris-hq/email-marketing`). These services can handle subscription requests, unsubscribe requests, and changes of e-mail addresses, all without needing you to do anything. In addition, most of them offer you the ability to track click-throughs on links in your newsletters and track whom you e-mail and when.

You can find a few free mailing-list options out there, but most of them involve a monthly fee. Shop around to find one that fits your price range.

Track and Customize

What does your community like to read? Do the members like your posts about your personal life, or are they more interested in what you're doing in your daily job? Or is it your opinion about some other topic that you've discussed?

Watch to see what element of your content is most popular and what gets the most comments and responses. Don't confuse posts that get responses with posts that people like — you want to know what people are interested in and willing to comment on, not what they like. Controversial blog posts are most likely to generate conversation and feedback.

Knowing what's popular in your blog can help you when you write later on because you can draw on this knowledge to create more posts that get responses. Keep an eye on those posts that get lots of comment and understand their appeal to your audience as you make decisions about what to post about in the future. You can learn more about understanding your audience in Chapter 9, and get some help with content in Chapter 8.

Also, pay attention to what posts are unpopular and try to refrain from covering that content again.

You can also turn this information into additional resources for your readers. TechCrunch (`www.techcrunch.com`), for instance, tracks the posts that get the most comments and displays them in an Actively Discussed Posts box, which is shown in Figure 19-2. If you assume that the blog posts with the most comments are the most interesting, readers can use this box as a shortcut to find the best content on the blog.

Figure 19-2: TechCrunch highlights the posts that get a lot of comments.

Develop Solutions

Pay attention to what's going on in your community so that you can find solutions to problems when they arise. Communities grow and change, but they don't thrive unless you resolve issues such as spam or technical problems.

I can't describe this suggestion very well because each community's problems are unique. Just know that you need to keep on top of any problems that do come up.

For instance, if your blog readers start complaining about seeing too many spam comments on your blog, you need to find and implement some spam prevention tools and techniques. If you fail to do so, you risk losing your readers who get frustrated with having to skip every other comment on your blog.

Other possible problem areas might include flame wars between overheated readers, slow Web servers, or too long a turnaround between when a reader submits a comment and when it actually appears on the site. (For the full scoop on comments and spam, see Chapter 9.)

Check Your Code and Software

Make your blog accessible to all Web users. Your HTML code needs to be flexible enough to display in the many Web browsers out there, and it must accommodate browsers used by the blind. Whether you're keeping the Website design code clean or offering RSS feeds, you're ultimately responsible in making your site work for your readers.

It's a hard fact to accept, but it's true: Your blog doesn't look the same on your monitor and in your browser as it does on other computers and in other browsers.

Test your designs and test your RSS feeds in as many places as possible. Keep checking back to see whether anything changes over time. For instance, when Microsoft upgraded the Internet Explorer from version 6 to 7, many Web sites experienced display problems that the site owners had to resolve. And of course, a blog grows, which means that the load your site puts on your Web server changes over time.

Here are some important questions to ask yourself:

- How does your site behave with 500 blog posts, versus the 10 or 20 you started with?
- Can Google's newsreader display your RSS feed? What about Bloglines? How about . . . you get the picture. Chapter 13 is dedicated to all things RSS-related.
- Does the podcast that you listed with iTunes still appear in their directory? Can someone subscribe to it? Does iTunes deliver it?
- Are the images in old blog posts still available and viewable on the site?
- Do you regularly exceed the bandwidth allowances provided by your Web host? Does your site run slowly at certain times of the day?

Changes, no matter how small, in design code or blog software programming can have unintended results. Be sure to look at your own blog on several computers every few weeks. Try leaving comments, using the search feature, clicking links, and generally kicking the tires on a regular basis.

Have Contests

Everyone loves to get free stuff! If traffic is lagging and needs a boost, try holding a giveaway or contest to spur more interaction. You could have a candy give-away or offer up that rusting Chevy in your backyard. You need to make your community members do something in order to get this free stuff that you see fit to give away.

By having contests on your blog, you can build your site traffic. You can make the contests almost anything: writing contests, reward points for different levels of activity, writing and submitting blog posts, and so on. Hold a seasonal contest, such as best costume during Halloween or most romantic date idea on Valentine's Day.

The possibilities are practically endless. Get hokey and create memorable contests. Sometimes, the sillier you get, the better the response from your readers.

If you're running a business blog, be sure that you understand the legal issues surrounding contests; legal requirements can vary state by state, and you might have to deal with national laws, as well.

Ask Your Readers

One of the best things that you can do for the community is to make sure that everyone's having the best time they can. How do you know whether your readers enjoy their time on your blog? Why not just ask?

Give people a way to let you know whether the community aspects of your site work for them by including a Contact Me page. But if you really want to hear about how things are going, try just posting a blog entry asking people for their thoughts and criticism about what you're doing.

You likely get great new ideas, as well as help identifying real problems. In fact, you can get bonus points from your readers for asking for this kind of input.

Chapter 20

Ten Cool Tricks for Making Your Blog Shine

In This Chapter

- Creating badges and widgets for your blog
- Tweaking your blog sidebar template
- Letting readers subscribe to your blog in a variety of ways

When you're committed to the blogging lifestyle, the daily grind might feel overwhelming at times — writing, tinkering with blog software, preparing images, and repeating the process over and over. Luckily for you, a slew of Web sites and software can spice things up and banish any boredom you're experiencing, all while attracting new readers to your blog.

These tools are fun to play with. Some help create more links, keep people up to date, or just add a little silliness. Others are truly useful services to add to your blog. The tools in this chapter help you share your literary and musical tastes, take polls, and make your blog look just a little bit better.

Creating Cameo Appearances

One of the really fun things about blogging is experimenting with all the great technical goodies that you can put in your blog sidebar. With a little technical know-how, you can put tons of extra doo-dads and gee-gaws in the sidebar to let your readers know more about you and your life.

All things considered, you may find these tools less than useful if you have a business-related blog. These extras are just that — information that might dress up your blog but which your readers probably don't need to have. Still, you can have some fun with these tools.

A few of my favorites include

- **Photos:** Love to take photos? Of course, you should be illustrating your blog entries with your photos, but why not put a few in your sidebar, as well?
- **Books and music:** Let your readers know what you're reading and listening to. Some tools even let you update a music feed instantly, so your readers know what you're hearing right this minute!
- **Instant updates:** Accessorize your blog with a quick update about what you're doing or where you are. A quick notice keeps your readers current, even when you don't have time to write a full blog post.
- **Surveys:** Take the pulse of your readers with a quick multiple-choice survey.
- **Avatars:** You can find some great tools for building *avatars* — visual illustrations of you — that you can then display right in your blog sidebar.

Very few blog software packages include the ability to add these kinds of elements, so in most cases, you need to know how to edit your templates in order to add them. Check your blog software to find out whether you can add sidebar elements by using a template editing tool in your software or whether you need to get into the template code of your blog.

Fiddling with templates

In general, most nonhosted blog software that you install on your own server gives you access to the templates that build your blog. Hosted blog software varies: Some offer template access, some offer it when you use a premium or paid version, and others don't offer access at all.

In most cases, adding elements to your sidebar requires that you get your hands dirty in the HTML guts of your blog software. You can make these changes easily in some blogs and with some struggle in others, and a few kinds of blog software make it impossible.

The process of adding a third-party tool — sometimes called a *badge* or a *widget* — is similar no matter what blog software you use. Just follow these basic steps:

1. **Visit the Web site of the tool that you want to implement and set up your account.**

   Contribute content as required by that Web site.

2. **Look for a link or option that allows you to add the tool to your blog.**
3. **Follow that site's directions to obtain the HTML code that you need to put the tool on your blog.**
4. **Go to your blog's administrative interface and add the HTML code to your template, or use your blog's tools for adding sidebar elements.**

5. **Go look at your blog and make sure it isn't broken!**

   Don't skip this step — you should always make sure that your blog hasn't been mangled by the new HTML code.

Most blog software runs by using a template of HTML code, so if you add your sidebar code to the template, it automatically appears on every page of your blog — assuming your software gives you access to the template and that you can figure out how to insert the code.

Don't be scared off by the gibberish of HTML, style tags, and blog software tags that you see. As long as you don't delete any of that stuff, you won't do any damage. But just to be safe, copy everything in the template into a text file and save it in a safe place on your computer so that you can go back to the original code, if necessary.

If your blog software gives you a tool to add elements to the sidebar as part of the administrative interface, you're a lucky devil. This tool makes your life a little easier while you customize your blog.

Adding elements with Blogger

Blogger (www.blogger.com) enables you to add elements to your sidebar without having to go into the template. Follow these steps:

1. **Log in to** www.blogger.com **and click the Layout link for the blog that you want to customize.**

   The Layout tab of your blog administrative panel opens.

   If you're using one of the older Blogger templates, you might see a Template link, rather than a Layout link, on the Dashboard.

2. **Select the Page Elements category.**

   The Add and Arrange Page Elements page opens.

3. **Click Add a Gadget.**

A window opens that contains a lot of page element options. Blogger offers quite a few custom sidebar tools as part of its interface, so be sure to experiment with these tools if you like adding to your sidebar. For example, Blogger has built-in tools for adding polls, photos, link lists, RSS feeds, videos, and more.

4. **Click the Add to Blog button (it looks like a plus sign) below the HTML/JavaScript header.**

   The Configure HTML/JavaScript window opens.

5. **Give your element a title in the Title field.**

6. **Paste the HTML code for the tool that you want to include into the Content field.**

   You can usually find this HTML on the Web site where you acquire the widget you're adding. I show you some specific examples of tools that work this way in the section "Finding Goodies for Your Sidebars," later in this chapter.

7. **Click Save Changes, as shown in Figure 20-1.**

   Blogger saves the element and displays it in the Layout view.

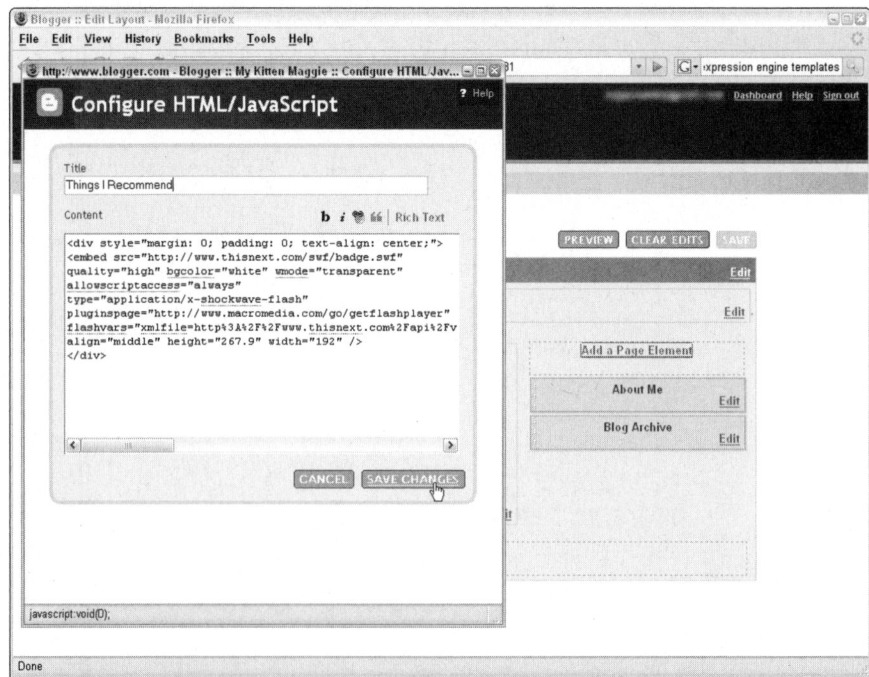

Figure 20-1: Blogger gives you an easy way to add elements to your sidebar.

8. **If you want to change the order of the elements displayed in your sidebar, click and drag the new element to a new position.**
9. **Click Save.**
10. **Click the View Blog link and admire your new sidebar element!**

Blogger's tools might have changed by the time you read this book, so you might have to take steps different than the ones I describe in this section.

If you aren't using Blogger, but you see a tool in your blog software for adding sidebar elements, you probably follow a somewhat similar process: After you choose an element, you can copy and paste HTML code and choose an order for your sidebar elements. Refer to the documentation for your blog software for help.

Rounding up the usual suspects

Sidebars usually contain a mix of meat and potatoes features and neat extras. Strike a balance on your blog that gives readers the basics and also plays up your personality. Figure 20-2 shows the sidebar for the Blissfully Aware blog written by Joshua Lane (`www.blissfullyaware.com`).

Usually, blog software comes with some content already in the sidebar, such as links to your categories, archives, and RSS feed. You can include a lot of items in your sidebar. The following list discusses common types of sidebar content:

- **About Me:** You can provide quick bits of information that describe you and what your blog is about (refer to Figure 20-2).
- **Archives and categories:** You might want to include links to category and archive pages so that your readers can quickly get to older content (refer to Figure 20-2).
- **Popular blog posts/recent comments:** Many blogs display a list of the most recent posts or a list of posts that have gotten a lot of comments. You can increase traffic on your blog by adding this information because other readers will be drawn to see what's so interesting.
- **Blogroll:** Some bloggers include a list of blogs or Web sites that they read and recommend to others, which is usually called a *blogroll,* although these lists may include Web sites that aren't blogs (refer to Figure 20-2).
- **Search:** If you have a search tool on your blog, be sure to include the Search text box and Submit button in your sidebar.

Figure 20-2: Blissfully Aware has a great design that uses two sidebars on the left of the layout.

- **Syndication links to RSS feeds:** These links let readers subscribe to your blog in their newsreaders (refer to Figure 20-2). See Chapter 11 for a lot more information about RSS feeds.
- **Navigation:** If your blog is part of a larger Web site, you can include navigation to that site's content in your sidebar.
- **Contact information:** If you want people to be able to get in touch with you, give them quick access to your e-mail address or other contact information.

Many of these elements are built in to the templates and layouts provided by your blog software. If you don't see them, check your blog software documentation to see whether you can turn them on. You may also be able to add these elements by using plug-ins.

In the next two sections, I discuss two of the more popular elements of sidebars: the About Me section and blogrolls.

Creating an About Me Section

The sidebar of a blog usually contains what you might call a 10,000-foot view of the blog and blogger — that is, a high-level look at what the blog offers and what it's about. Often, these features focus on giving readers information about the blogger, from the blogger's name to what he or she reads, eats, likes, and is doing.

When I visit a new blog, I'm always looking for a little context to understand what the blog is about and whether I'm interested in reading it, and I check the sidebar for information to help me.

I know, I know. Putting a little bit of text about you and your blog (often called the *About Me* text) doesn't seem that exciting. But it's such a great way to let your readers know more about you and why you're blogging, so I just couldn't leave it out. Frankly, I think the About Me section is the single best way to augment your site.

The blog So Misguided (`www.somisguided.com`) has a great example of a nice bit of About Me text, which is shown in Figure 20-3. Without this text you wouldn't know, for example, that blogger Monique Trottier lives in Vancouver and is a *litblogger* (someone who blogs about literature) because she doesn't mention those facts in every post. The information here, however, helps inform new readers while they try to figure out whether So Misguided appeals to them. Monique even includes a link to a longer biography for readers who just want to know more about her.

A lot of bloggers include contact information and even a photo in their About Me text, giving a quick snapshot to readers.

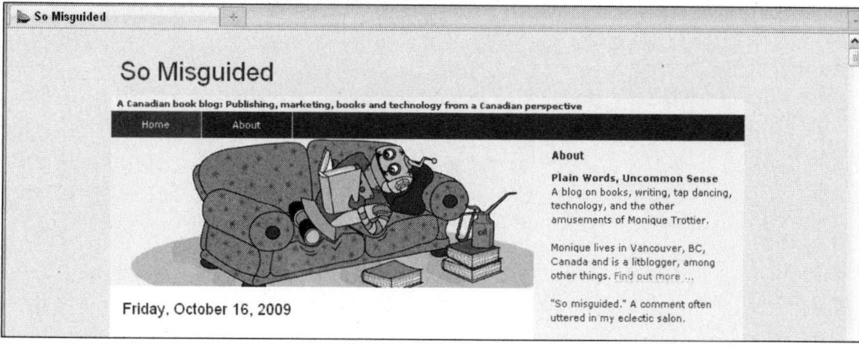

Figure 20-3: The So Misguided blog tells readers about the author and the subject in the sidebar.

Keep your About Me section short and sweet, giving readers the skinny in a few words. Save the lengthy prose for a blog post. One trick you can use is to write a long blog post that includes your bio and other blog details, and then link to that post from your sidebar About Me section.

Blogrolling

Blogrolls are common extras that you might want to put in your sidebar. A *blogroll* is a list of blogs and Web sites that you regularly read, especially those that you reference when you write your blog. Putting your blogroll in your sidebar can give your readers a sense that you aren't just making up stuff off the top of your head, especially if you have an informational blog. You may also just want to show your readers any writing that you find inspiring or entertaining.

The blogroll on the Web site for the book *Yarn Bombing* by Mandy Moore and Leanne Prain (`www.yarnbombing.com`) is shown in Figure 20-4.

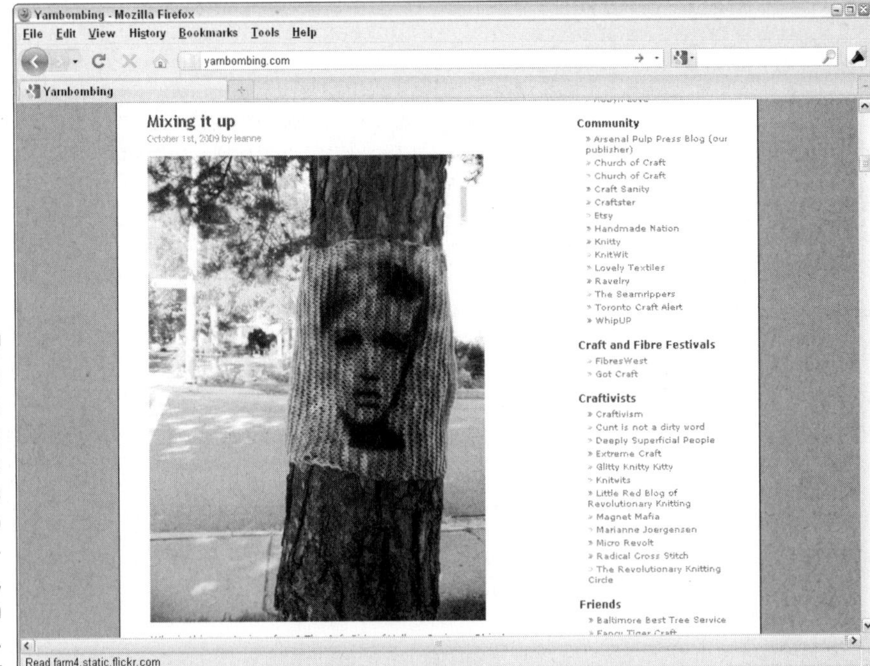

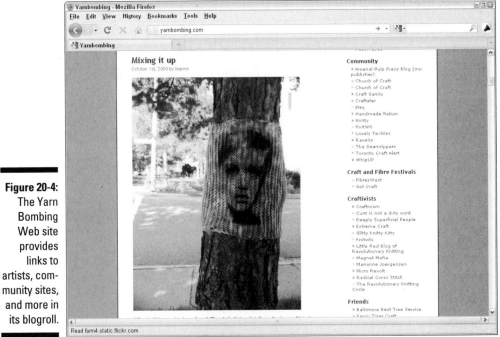

Figure 20-4: The Yarn Bombing Web site provides links to artists, community sites, and more in its blogroll.

A lot of blog software include built-in methods for adding a blogroll or building a list of links, so check whether yours already has the tools you need to add a blogroll.

Finding Goodies for Your Sidebars

Now comes the fun part — putting third-party widgets and extras into your sidebar. I'm sure you can find a widget to fit your personality and blog, and in the following sections, I show you a few of my favorites.

With each of the tools described, you generate HTML code that you need to integrate into your blog. After you obtain the code, refer to the section "Creating Cameo Appearances," earlier in this chapter, and follow the instructions for adding the code to your template or using a layout editing tool in your blog software.

Telling others about your photos

These days, everyone's a photographer, thanks in large part to the relative inexpensiveness of digital cameras and the excellent photo-sharing and -organizing services available, both for personal computers and online.

Flickr (`www.flickr.com`) is one of the best of the photo-sharing Web sites, and if you haven't already checked it out, you should do so. Pronto! I'll wait.

One of the neat tools that Flickr provides is the ability to create a badge to put in your blog sidebar. This badge shows your photos, and it automatically updates when you add more photos to your Flickr account, so you always have the latest photos on your blog. If you like to put photos in your blog posts but take many more than you can use in your entries, you can still share those photos by using the Flickr badge.

Plus, the badge includes a link to your Flickr photos, so your blog readers can jump over to Flickr and look at all your great photos, regardless of whether you decide to put them in your blog.

A small Flickr photo badge in the sidebar of Monique Trottier's So Misguided blog (`www.somisguided.com`) is shown in Figure 20-5.

Figure 20-5: Use Flickr to put your photos into your blog's sidebar.

After you create a Flickr account and upload some photos, you're ready to create a Flickr badge. Follow these steps:

1. **After logging in to Flickr, scroll to the bottom of any screen on Flickr and choose Tools from the Help navigation bar.**
2. **Click the Hey, Where Is the Badge? link in the right column of the Tools page.**

   The badge creation page loads.
3. **Select an HTML badge and click the Next: Choose Content button.**

   The choosing content page loads.

   You can also build a Flash badge.
4. **Click Yours to display your own photos on your blog.**
5. **Choose between displaying all your public photos, photos with a particular tag, or photos from one of your sets, and then click the Next: Layout button.**
6. **Select Yes or No to specify whether to display your Flickr icon and screen name in your badge.**
7. **Select how many photos you want to display in your badge from the Number of photos drop-down list.**
8. **Choose between your recent photos or a random selection.**
9. **Pick the size of the images you want to display.**

   You can select Square, Thumbnail, or Mid-Size.

10. **Select the orientation for your badge.**

    You have the options Horizontal, Vertical, or None.

    For most blog sidebars, Vertical is the best orientation to use because it creates a tall, thin badge.

11. **Click the Next: Colors button.**

    The choosing color page loads.

12. **Choose the colors that you want to use for the background, border, links, and text of your badge by clicking the item that you want to change and then selecting a color from the provided palette.**

    You can use this tool to choose colors that match your blog design.

13. **Click the Next: Preview & Get Code button.**

    Flickr shows you the badge you have created, and provides the code needed to use it on your blog.

14. **If you want to make changes to your badge, use the links across the top of the page to go back and make changes.**

15. **When you have the badge looking great, copy the code and go back to your own blog.**

    At this point, refer to the "Creating Cameo Appearances" section, earlier in this chapter, and follow the instructions for adding the code to your template or using a layout editing tool in your blog software.

If you want to find out more about using Flickr to put photos into your blog posts, be sure to read Chapter 10.

Sharing what you're reading

Are you an avid reader who always has a batch of books on the go? Do your friends constantly ask you for book recommendations or what you're reading right now? Why not share what's on your bedside table with your blog readers by using a book badge?

A number of good Web sites right now let you create a catalog of your book collection, including LibraryThing (`www.librarything.com`). On LibraryThing, after you add books, you can tag them, write reviews, rate them, even record when you started and finished the book. Also, you can see what others thought of the book. Best of all, you can also use LibraryThing to put a badge of what you're reading on your blog.

After you sign up for LibraryThing and added some books, follow these steps to create the badge, or widget, for your blog:

1. **Click the Tools navigation item at the top of any LibraryThing page.**

   In the Tools menu Put LibraryThing on Your Blog is the first item listed.

   The widget creation page loads.

2. **Click the Make a Standard Blog Widget link.**

   LibraryThing loads the configuration page for the widget.

3. **Choose a preset style by selecting one of the available layouts from the Choose a Preset drop-down list.**

   LibraryThing previews each style on the right side of the page.

   Alternatively, you can customize your widget by selecting from the many available style and advanced options.

4. **Click the Refresh button.**

   LibraryThing loads the widget into the right side of the page, as shown in Figure 20-6.

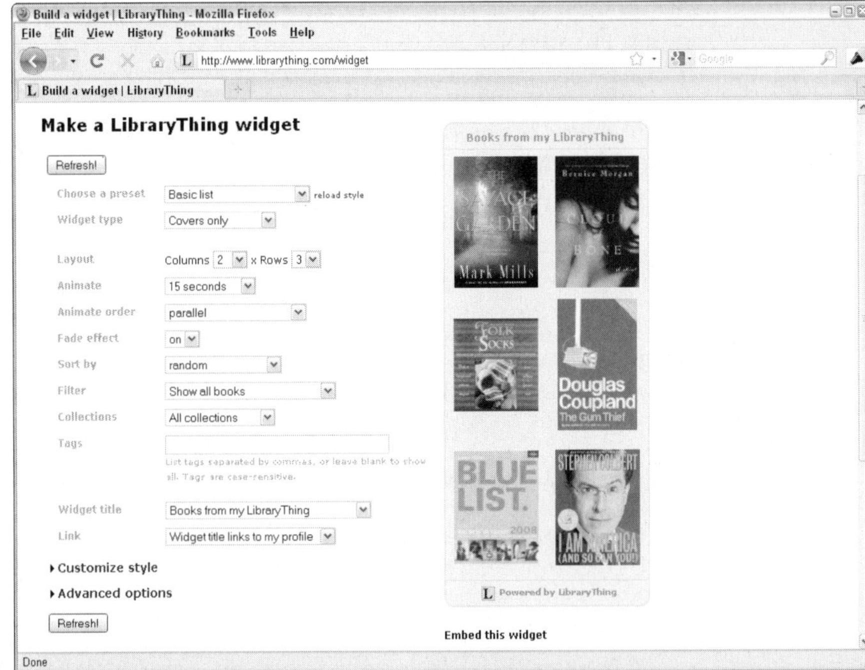

Figure 20-6: Use LibraryThing to create a book badge for your blog.

5. **Make any changes that you want to the look of your badge, clicking the Make It button to see the updates.**
6. **Copy the HTML code for your badge from the Code box on the page.**
7. **Head back to your own blog to add that code to the sidebar.**

   If you need help placing the HTML in your blog, see the section "Creating Cameo Appearances," earlier in this chapter.

You can also use the sites BookJetty (`www.bookjetty.com`) and Goodreads (`www.goodreads.com`) to catalog your existing collection, tag books with keywords, rate and review them, and share your collection.

Posting your playlists

If you like to listen to music, you can share your playlists and even the music you're listening to right now with your blog readers. Last.fm (`www.last.fm`) is a music-sharing Web site that lets you do just that.

Sign up for free, and then install a little application on your computer that tracks what you're listening to in your normal music-playing software, sharing that information with the Last.fm Web site. When you install the software, it shows a list of available audio-playing software — simply select the one that you use to listen to music. Last.fm calls this process *audioscrobbling*, or just *scrobbling*. While you build your music profile, Last.fm makes recommendations of music you might like, based on the likes of other Last.fm users who also listen to the same music.

You can also generate a personal radio station designed to play your favorite music with no advertising or DJs.

Last.fm enables you to create a badge for your blog. Follow these steps:

1. **Login or create an account with Last.fm; then choose Chart Images from the Do More menu at the bottom of the home page.**

   You see the Image charts for forums and blogs page.
2. **Choose a chart look for your badge by clicking one of the thumbnails shown.**
3. **Choose your chart style from the drop-down menu at the top right of the page.**

   Your options are My Recent Tracks, My Top Weekly Tracks, My Top Weekly Artists, My Top Tracks, Track Chart for One of My Groups, and Artist Chart for One of My Groups.

   Last.fm displays the badge on the right of the page and updates it as you make your choices, as shown in Figure 20-7.

4. **Select the number of tracks you want to display in your badge from the number drop-down menu.**

   Last.fm refreshes your badge to show the change.

5. **Copy the code from the MySpace/HTML Code box and go to your blog so you can paste it into your sidebar.**

   See the section "Creating Cameo Appearances," earlier in this chapter, to find out what to do with the code.

Showing your tweets on your blog

Twitter is a social networking tool that allows individuals (be they bloggers or not) to broadcast short messages (or *tweets*) to fellow Twitterers or to the general public. Twitter is all about keeping people updated. People can track your updates and subscribe to them through the Twitter Web site (`www.twitter.com`). They can also follow your tweets by using RSS and a newsreader. Messages can be informative, entertaining, Web links, dates, times, suggestions — just about anything if it fits into 140 characters of text. When I looked at Twitter's home page while writing this book, I found tweets about one user's plan for dinner and a link to a Web site about a missing child.

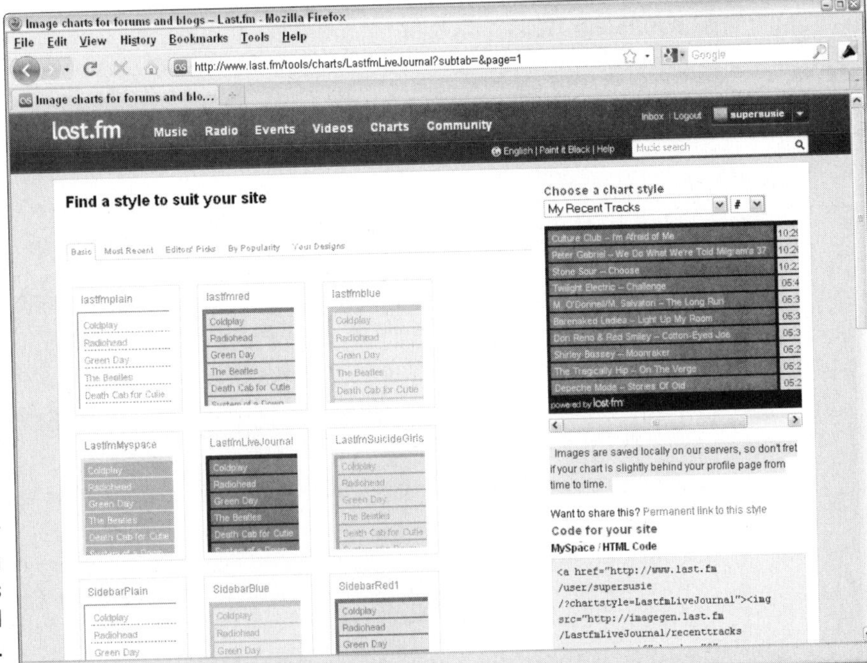

Figure 20-7: Creating a sidebar widget with Last.fm is quick and easy.

Each time you post a message on the Twitter Web site, several things happen:

- That tweet appears on the Twitter Web site at `www.twitter.com`.
- It's delivered to anyone who follows your tweets via SMS messages to a mobile phone or to an e-mail address.
- It appears in any Twitter badge that you've created and placed on your blog.

You can post a tweet to Twitter by using e-mail, many instant messenger programs, or your cell phone. When you put the Twitter badge on your blog, you can create very quick updates for your readers, even when you can't take the time for a full blog post.

For a lot more info about Twitter, see Chapter 14.

To put a badge that lists your shared posts on your blog sidebar, follow these steps:

1. **Sign in or create an account on Twitter (`www.twitter.com`) and click the Goodies navigation link at the bottom of any Twitter page.**

   Twitter loads the Goodies page.

2. **Click the Widgets item.**

   The Select Your Widget screen appears.

3. **Click My Website in the left navigation panel, and then Profile Widget from the center of the page.**

   The Customize Your Profile Widget screen opens.

4. **Customize the Preferences, Appearance, or Dimensions to suit your blog from the navigation menu on the left.**

   A preview of your badge appears on the right side of the page, as shown in Figure 20-8.

5. **Click Finish & Grab Code when your badge looks the way that you want it to.**

   Twitter displays the code for your badge.

6. **Copy the code and go to your blog so that you can paste that code into your sidebar.**

   Read the "Creating Cameo Appearances" section, earlier in this chapter, to find out how to integrate the code into your blog.

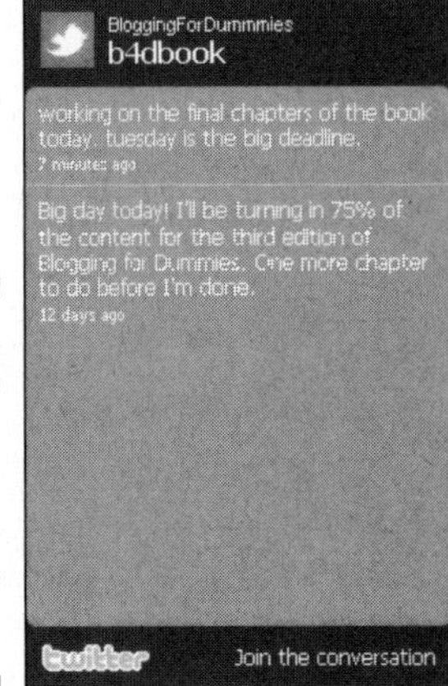

Figure 20-8: Share your thoughts and activities by using a Twitter badge.

Surveying the Field

Everybody loves to answer polls, so why not add one to your sidebar or even a post? You might be able to find out useful information about your readers that you can use in getting advertising for your blog or to inform your choices about future blog topics.

You can create a quick multiple-choice question to put in your sidebar by using a number of different polling services. Some services require you to create an account; some don't. If you use one that does require registration, you can keep track of your polls a little more easily, which is handy if you ever need to look at them later.

The term *poll* is used by scientists, media, and mathematicians to describe a sampling of a random number of people. By definition, a poll taken by only the readers of your blog can't actually be random. This type of questioning is better described as a survey. I'm just saying.

My favorite poll tool is PollDaddy (`www.polldaddy.com`). You can use PollDaddy for free, and after you create an account, you can create multiple polls for your blog or Web site, and even choose a variety of formats and styles to use with your poll.

After you create a poll, you can insert the HTML code that PollDaddy provides in your blog sidebar or in a blog entry. (See the section "Creating Cameo Appearances," earlier in this chapter, for details on how to use the code it creates.) Then, sit back and wait for the results to roll in. After your readers take the poll, they get instant results. After the reader answers the survey question, the poll screen changes to show the percentage of answers for each choice.

One especially nice feature of PollDaddy's polls is that you can create a poll widget specifically for your blog sidebar. Insert the code into your template once, and then use PollDaddy to control what poll appears in the widget, saving you from having to mess around in your template every time you want to change your poll question.

Dressing Up Comments with Avatars and Photos

Many blogs encourage visitors and content creators to set up a profile that includes basic biographical information and a photo. Some Web users see profile creation as a chance to have some fun. Rather than a photo, you can use an avatar! An *avatar* is a visual representation of yourself, often a comic or cartoon.

You can use your avatar on any Web site that lets you set an avatar or photo for use with a profile, such as Facebook, Digg, Flickr, and so on. And, of course, you can use your avatar on your own blog.

The best tool for getting set up with an avatar/photo is Gravatar (`www.gravatar.com`). Gravatar is designed to let you set up your photo and information once, and then display the photo or image on blogs all over the Internet. It all happens *automagically!*

When you create an account with Gravatar, you have the opportunity to upload an image from your computer or point Gravatar to an image that you already have online. Gravatar associates that image with an e-mail address, and from then on, when you use that e-mail address to leave comments on blogs or other Web sites that have Gravatar's tools implemented, your image automatically appears. Update your Gravatar, and the image on those sites also updates.

Many Web sites and blogs use Gravatar, but not all. If you register for a social network or blog site that lets you create an avatar, you have to follow the rules on that site for creating and using an avatar.

Sharing It All

If you spent much time online today, you've probably seen the many options that Web sites and blogs use today to get you to share their content with others. You can share online tidbits by e-mailing them, tweeting them, or posting links to the many social networks that have sprung up.

Web site publishers can build links into their stories and content pages that allow you to do this sharing with a single click. The point, of course, is two-fold: The publisher wants you to be able to tell others about interesting Web content, as well as drive additional traffic to the site.

Adding sharing tools is an easy step to take when you're trying to build up the number of visitors to a site, but unfortunately, literally dozens of sites are devoted to letting people share content, from Facebook to Twitter to Digg. Putting those links into your articles can be a big task.

ShareThis (`www.sharethis.com`) has solved the problem, however. Sign up with this free service and add the code to your site so that you can quickly and easily add all those tools to your site in a single step.

You can see the ShareThis widget implemented on the blog for this book in Figure 20-9. Clicking the ShareThis link opens a small window in the page that visitors can use to select their sharing technique.

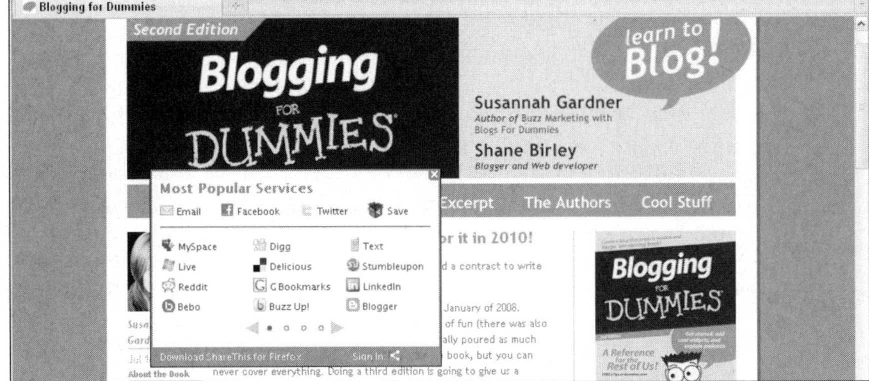

Figure 20-9: Use ShareThis as a shortcut to getting more traffic to your blog.

You can customize the ShareThis widget to match the look of your site, and you can control which sharing tools show up in the window. The neatest feature, however, is that ShareThis tracks the data of those who use the ShareThis tool on your site, so you can find out more about the ways in which people share content, as well as which stories or blog posts attract the most attention!

Chapter 21

Ten Blogs You Should Know

In This Chapter

- Blogs that talk about technical stuff and gadgets
- Blogs that discuss politics
- Blogs that help you with your blog

Because so many blogs are floating about in the blogosphere, you can't possibly read them all. In the beginning, only a handful of blogs were known well enough to attract solid audiences. A few short years later, well over 100 million different blogs exist, and each one attracts its own audience. This book has made reference to a number of blogs, but there's always room for more. This chapter includes a short list of some of the blogs that I find most interesting and useful.

Take the time to visit each of these blogs. Not only do they feature great content, but you also can discover what these bloggers do to achieve blogging success.

Engadget

```
www.engadget.com
```

In March of 2004, Peter Rojas, cofounder of the blog Gizmodo, launched Engadget. Engadget is a contributor-supported blog that has posts written by several writers; it features articles about consumer technology and boasts lively discussions in the comments section.

Engadget is one of those blogs that you can't live without. It has won a number of awards and been translated into several different languages. If you have any interest in gadgets (I know you do!) and want to find out more about them, you can't go wrong in subscribing to Engadget. And if you want to explore the podcast milieu, Engadget also hosted a podcast that ran from 2004 until 2006, which you can find by searching the site.

defective yeti

`www.defectiveyeti.com`

If you like reading funny blogs, you'll love defective yeti, written by Matthew Baldwin and "Haphazardly Spellchecked Since 2002." defective yeti is a classic personal blog — the personal diary of an amusing writer who blogs when he feels like it about whatever he wants to. Baldwin is a programmer, but he blogs frequently about his family life, games, fiction, and entertaining news stories.

Daily Kos

`www.dailykos.com`

Daily Kos is possibly the most popular political blog in the blogosphere. It discusses American politics and news, and it produces opinion pieces about the state of the United States from a liberal perspective.

Founded by Markos Moulitsas Zuniga in 2002, Daily Kos has helped small groups of like-minded individuals use discussion forums and blogs to create momentum around different causes. If you want to be a part of Daily Kos, you can create an account that allows you to post comments and also to post diaries that become part of the online community (though not usually on the front page). The main front page blog is the work of several contributors from Daily Kos; if a post from your diary is highly recommended by other readers in the community, it might be promoted to the front page.

According to the Web site, Daily Kos has about 2.5 million unique visits every month and more than 215,000 registered users.

Lifehacker

`www.lifehacker.com`

Lifehacker is a daily blog that features tips, tricks, and software downloads that can help you get things done more quickly and more efficiently. Several core writers helm the blog, devising new ways to do your day-to-day activities. They do write blog-specific tips, and many of their other posts have ideas that you can adapt for blogging.

Started in 2005, Lifehacker has produced a lot of content that's useful and may give you ideas about how you can increase your blogging success. They've also turned their blog into a couple of books!

ProBlogger

```
www.problogger.net
```

ProBlogger was founded by Darren Rowse in 2004, and it's one of the main landing spots for bloggers who want to know how to improve their blogs. The site includes tips on making money, writing solid content, and other simple tricks of the trade.

Since 2003, Darren has started many different blogs and more recently has cofounded the blog network b5media. He's the manager of many other blogs and writes daily on his ProBlogger Web site, helping bloggers find new ways of monetizing their blogs.

If you want to find out more about blog design, blogging tools and services, social media, blogging for dollars, podcasting, RSS, writing content, business blogging, advertising, blog promotion, video posts, affiliate programs, and other miscellaneous blog tips, this site is for you.

ProBlogger, shown in Figure 21-1, is a great resource — don't miss it!

Figure 21-1: ProBlogger helps you to become a better blogger and make money doing it.

TreeHugger

`www.treehugger.com`

TreeHugger is a blog about how you can make the world a better place. Many different writers submit for this blog, all with the simple goal of helping readers find ways to establish a more sustainable world. It has a great collection of green-buying guides that cover consumer products from clothing to laptops. You can submit your own tips on green living to TreeHugger. Check out its blogroll first if you need inspiration!

This comprehensive lifestyle blog features a main blog, a user-generated blog, videos, and a weekly podcast. And if you're not quite into RSS feeds yet, you can even sign up for a weekly or daily e-mail newsletter.

TMZ

`www.tmz.com`

TMZ is an entertainment blog that takes its name from the phrase "thirty mile zone," a Hollywood term from the 1960s meaning the thirty mile radius surrounding the intersection of West Beverly Boulevard and North La Cienega Boulevard in Hollywood. This is the center of the movie "studio" zone in Los Angeles. The Web site is a juicy place to go for those who want the most up-to-date information about what's going on in Hollywood.

This blog is very much a guilty pleasure because it fulfills the celebrity addiction that a lot of people have. The blog is deep in the trenches and always produces good content for people who like to keep on top of what celebrities are doing, what gossip is floating around, and how many times so-and-so goes to your local coffee shop.

I mean, who can resist a blog that has categories for Fashion Police, Celebrity Justice, Wacky and Weird, Train Wrecks, Paparazzi Video, Baby Watch, Full Throttle Fashion, Star Catcher, and Let's Get This Party Started? Not to mention the fabulous photos of your favorite stars at their *worst*.

A List Apart

`www.alistapart.com`

A List Apart is a blog and Web site that talks about nothing but how to make Web sites. This blog features articles, tutorials, and community conversation about how Web designers make Web sites, how designers feel they should create them, and tricks for readers to improve their Web development skills.

If you're a blogger who likes to get into the muck of your blog software, this site provides many techniques for making your blog accessible and friendly to both computers and human beings.

A List Apart started as a simple mailing list in 1997 and has grown into a hugely popular Web site that has spawned a conference called An Event Apart. The main topics that this blog covers include code, content, culture, design, process, and user science. When you become a blogging expert and want to contribute, you can even submit your own articles for publication on this popular blog.

Copyblogger

`www.copyblogger.com`

Copyblogger is the brainchild of Brian Clark, an Internet marketing specialist who develops content; helps people write posts that build traffic, generate comments, and attract new readers; designs online communication strategies; and is a "recovering attorney."

Brian founded Copyblogger in January of 2006 and has written hundreds of blog posts that offer concise coverage of topics ranging from copyright discussions to how you can "pimp" your blog. He blogs in a no-nonsense style and isn't afraid to tell people about the real state of writing on the Web.

This personal blog shows one person's thoughts and creativity. Brian stands out and gets noticed in the blogosphere for his forthright opinions. Read his blog to find out more about how to make yours great. Figure 21-2 shows the Copyblogger home page.

Figure 21-2: Copyblogger helps you write better copy.

Improv Everywhere

`www.improveverywhere.com`

Improv Everywhere is a blog that documents "scenes of chaos and joy" organized in New York City public spaces by Charlie Todd. Todd brings together volunteers for lighthearted "missions" that take them into public spaces to do unexpected activities.

In October 2009, Todd organized a group dog walk. More than 2,000 people made the most of the day by taking their furry friends into the streets of Brooklyn for about an hour. The catch was — the dogs were all invisible. The dog walkers carried leashes and never let on to spectators that there was anything peculiar about what was going on. Some onlookers were frustrated not to know what was happening, but others played along by asking politely about the dog's breed and petting them. Good fun!

Todd organizes these events irregularly, but they all make great, entertaining reading.

Appendix A

Glossary

aggregator: A collector of information about a topic or idea. An aggregator can be a person, blog, or Web site. Technologically speaking, RSS is an aggregation format for individual blogs. Google News is an example of a Web site that aggregates news for many sources.

audio blog: A blog consisting of audio files, or the practice of placing an audio file in a blog post.

blog: A chronological log of information kept by an individual, a group, or a business. The term *blog* is a merging of the words *Web* and *log.* On a typical blog, the most recent post appears at the top of the page, usually time-stamped. Scrolling down the page takes the reader to older posts. Each post usually offers an opportunity for readers to interact by adding their comments and might also display Trackback information about other blogs that have linked to this post. Blog content is determined entirely by the author(s) of the blog, therefore many are personal journals, but others are focused aggregations of news or commentary.

blogger: The author of a blog.

blogging: Producing blog posts. A blogger blogs on his or her blog.

blogosphere: The community of blogs and bloggers around the world.

blogroll: A collection of links used or recommended by an individual blogger. A blogroll is usually shown in a column on a blog.

buzz marketing: A no-cost or low-cost method of marketing associated with people telling other people about a company's products or services. Buzz marketing is based on people's direct experiences with specific products or on the experiences others have related to them.

comment: A piece of feedback left by a reader on a blog post.

CSS: This acronym stands for *Cascading Style Sheets,* an advanced HTML technique that permits fine control and layout of a Web site and quick changes in formats across the site.

entry: See *post.*

feed: See *RSS.*

feedreader: See *newsreader.*

follow: On Twitter, the act of subscribing to read the updates posted by another member. Unsubscribing is *unfollowing.*

friend: On Facebook and other social networks, the act of identifying another member as a part of your network; usually tied with access to information posted by that member for friends only, as well as allowing others to see who's in your group of friends.

FTP: *File Transfer Protocol* is the mechanism that allows transfer of files and data from one computer to another.

hit: A request to a Web server for a file. When the Web page (which often consists of multiple files) is downloaded from a server, the number of hits is equal to the number of files requested. Thus, one page view can often equal more than one hit, which means that counting the hits is typically an inaccurate measure of Web traffic.

HTML: HyperText Markup Language is the computer coding used by Web designers to create Web pages.

hyperlink: See *links.*

keyword: The content and/or type of meta tag included in a Web page's HTML code to help index the page. The term *keyword* also refers to terms or phrases that a user submits to a search engine when looking for content on the Internet.

links: A link, or *hyperlink,* is a navigation tool that allows a user to go from one Web location to another by clicking. They're typically underlined.

meme: Ideas that evolve virally. While bloggers post, comment on other blogs, post about posts on other blogs, and add their own thoughts, a meme spreads across the Internet, changing while it goes. Some groups spread memes consciously by participating in answering a set of questions or posting on a topic, but most memes are a natural byproduct of interesting topics.

meta tag: HTML tags used in a Web page to describe the document to search engines. Common tags are title, keyword, and description. Title and description are frequently displayed in search results; keywords are used to determine when a site should be returned as a search result.

micro blog: A blog composed of extremely brief text or multimedia posts.

moderation: The regulation of an online community; specifically, the contributions made by users to discussion forums or blog comment threads. Moderation might include removal of content if that content is deemed inappropriate.

moderator: A person granted special privileges to enforce the rules of an online community by removing or changing content from individual posts.

newsreader: Software used to subscribe to and then read blog and Web site RSS feeds.

page view: A request to load a single page of a Web site. Counting page views can help determine whether any change made to the page results in more or less visits.

permalink: Short for *permanent link.* A page of a blog that contains a single blog post and usually any comments on that post. Permalinks allow users to link directly to a single post for more accurate reference.

photoblog: A blog composed entirely of images, sometimes with caption information.

ping: A ping occurs when one computer asks another whether it's there; the second computer confirms its presence/location/status. In the blogosphere, many bloggers alert blog aggregation Web sites with a ping when posting a new entry.

podcast: A digital media file that's distributed over the Internet by using feeds with the intention for viewers to download it and play it back on portable media players and personal computers.

post: A publication to a blog, possibly containing text, images, and other media. A post can also be called an *entry.*

RSS: Stands for *Really Simple Syndication.* An XML-based feed of a blog's postings that blog aggregation sites or software pick up.

sidebar: A column to the right or left of the main content of your blog. Usually, blog software comes with some content already in the sidebar, such as links to your categories, archives, and RSS feed. Bloggers can customize sidebars with additional common and uncommon elements.

spam: Unsolicited electronic messages sent in bulk that may be commercial, nonsensical, or malicious. In addition to creating e-mail spam, spammers can target blog comments and blog forums.

syndication: See *RSS.*

tag: A relevant keyword that's associated with or assigned to a piece of information, such as an image, a blog entry, or a video clip. The content creator or online community usually chooses tags informally. Tags help give context to nontext media and organize information for easy searching.

tagging: The act of adding tags to a photo, video, audio file, or blog post.

Trackback: A mechanism that tracks references to a blog posting which occur on other blogs. Trackbacks are designed to help readers find other blogs that discuss the same topic. They also let bloggers know that another blogger has blogged about and linked to a post.

troll: A blog reader who posts offensive, personal attacks that interfere with the conversation between blogger and readers.

tweet: A post or update on the micro-blogging Web site Twitter.

unique visits: A statistic used to count the visitors to a Web site, counting each visitor only once in the timeframe of the report. The number of unique visits measures a Web site's true audience size.

video blog: A blog consisting of video files or the practice of placing a video file in a blog post.

video podcast: A digital video clip shared on the Internet that viewers can download and watch on a mobile device or personal computer.

Web content: Anything that a user can read, see, or hear as part of the experience on Web sites. Web content can include text, images, sounds, videos, and animations.

Web log: See *blog.*

WYSIWYG: An acronym for *What You See Is What You Get,* this term refers to a system in which the content during editing appears very similar to the end result.

XML: XML stands for *eXtensible Markup Language,* and it allows publishers to build their own structures into markup languages. You can use XML for any kind of structured information, and it's intended to allow information to pass to any computer system, regardless of the platform that the computer uses.

Appendix B

Basic HTML Code

On a blog, *code* can mean many things. It can refer to the complicated programming that makes up the software that runs your blog, or it can mean simple styles that make written words look cool when displayed on your blog. In this appendix, you can find out how to make the text in your blog posts look like a million bucks. (Leave the blogging software code to the experts.)

The code that you're working with affects only a given blog post; the blog software itself builds the blog pages. So, you don't have to know very many pieces of code — just the code commonly used to format text and photos, or to insert video files.

Most of the code that you need to format your blog posts is HTML (HyperText Markup Language).

Documents formatted by using HTML really consist of nothing but text, that your Internet browser can read and then display. HTML code tells your browser all kinds of things, such as how the text on the screen should be aligned and what text links to what Web page. You can easily use HTML. With a few exceptions, each bit of code, or *tag,* includes opening and closing elements, which surround the content that you want to affect. A few tags are standalone elements that you insert in only one spot. With HTML, you basically use code to mark up text, photos, and other elements.

Adding Headings, Paragraphs, and Line Breaks

You generally want to break up long blocks of text in your blog posts, maybe even throw in labels here and there. Styling headers, adding line breaks, and making sure that you divide the text of your blog into paragraphs can really improve the flow of your posts.

Headings

HTML has six levels of headings. H1 is the most important and largest, H2 is slightly less important and smaller, and so on. The final heading is H6, but people rarely use that heading level because it produces very small text. For most cases, first- and second-level headers do the job, giving you text larger than the main body text (and these headings usually are in bold). You can implement header tags by inserting code like this:

```
<h1>The most important heading ever</h1>
```

Like a light switch, the tag turns on before the first letter of your header and turns off after the last character.

You use all headers in the same way — just substitute in place of the number 1 a 2, 3, 4, 5 or 6. For example

```
<h2>The second most important heading ever</h2>
```

Figure B-1 shows each of the header tags as the browser interprets and displays them.

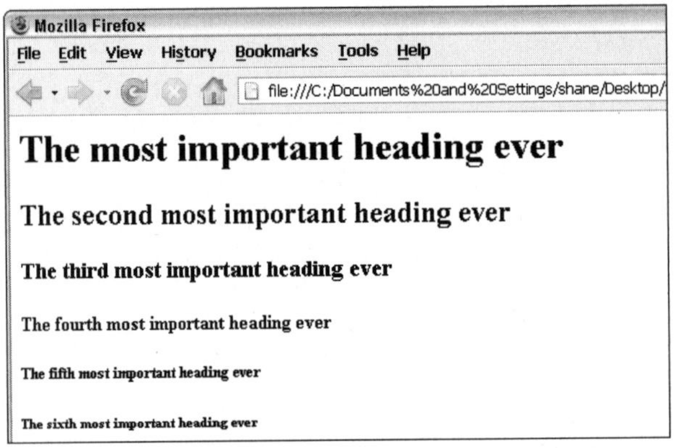

Figure B-1: Headers from the largest to the smallest.

Headers have more than just an effect on how your text looks: Search engines understand that text defined by a header tag is important, so words and phrases that you enclose in a header are marked as especially relevant to your site, and search engine results lists will place your Web site higher when search terms match words in your headers.

Paragraphs

To create paragraph breaks, you need to start the new paragraph with a <p> tag. The closing </p> is placed at the end of the paragraph after the text, like this (see Figure B-2 for how the browser displays this code):

```
<p>Paragraph one has amazing text in it.</p>
<p>Paragraph two has amazing text in it, too.</p>
<p>Paragraph three is being neglected by the first and
        second paragraphs.</p>
```

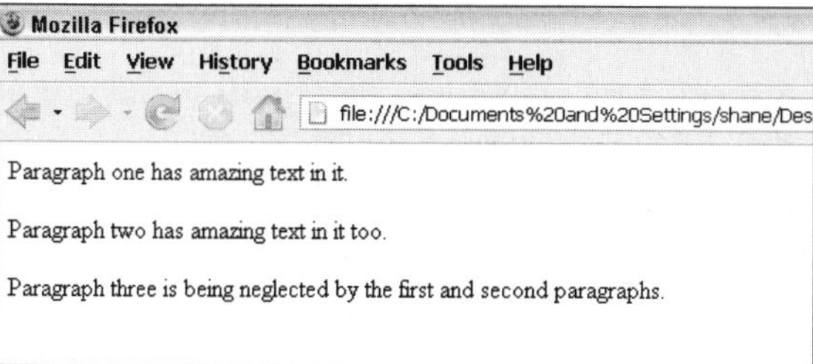

Figure B-2: Text paragraphs, displayed by a Web browser.

Most blogging software makes provision for paragraph breaks automatically, but if you ever end up looking at the code, you can recognize these fundamentally important tags. On most Web sites, paragraph breaks actually produce the effect of two line breaks, so paragraphs are spaced out from each other in the same way that they are in this book.

You can end a line of text and start the next word on a new line by using a <br> tag. You need to insert these standalone tags only once: there is no closing tag. To create a line break, here's what you do:

```
Break your line of text<br>
and start again on the next line.
```

Emphasizing Text

Dress up your text by using italics, underlining, bold, or even strikethrough code. You can add these text features by using HTML on/off tags, so you place the first tag at the start of the text that you want to affect and follow the text with the closing tag. Figure B-3 shows how each of the following code examples appears in a Web browser.

Here are the codes for each kind of text:

- **Bold:** <b> or <strong>

```
<b>Some of this text</b> is bold.
```

- *Italics:* <i> or <em>

```
<i>Some of this text</i> is italicized.
```

- Underline: <u>

```
Add punch with an <u>underline</u>.
```

- ~~Strikethrough:~~ <strike>

```
Correct an error <strike>by striking it out</strike>.
```

WARNING!

Even though the preceding list shows you how to underline text in your blog posts, I don't actually recommend that you use this style. As you know, underlining commonly indicates links online, so your readers may be very confused to see underlined text that isn't also a link.

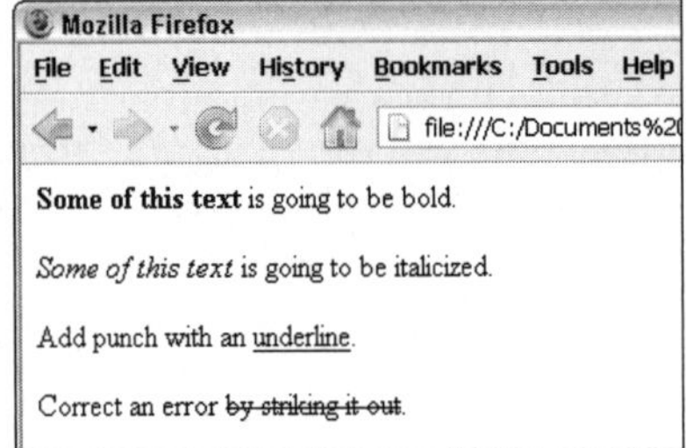
Mozilla Firefox
File Edit View History Bookmarks Tools Help
file:///C:/Documents%2
Some of this text is going to be bold.
Some of this text is going to be italicized.
Add punch with an underline.
Correct an error ~~by striking it out~~.

Figure B-3: Use bold, italics, underlining, and strike-through in your HTML to make your text pop.

Linking Up

In HTML, links are defined with the <a> tag (the *a* stands for anchor). But that's not all! This special tag also gets what's called an attribute and a value, to go along with the basic tag. The *attribute,* `href`, indicates to the browser that what comes next is a hypertext reference — in this case, a Web page. The *value* is the actual Web page that the code links to, enclosed in quotation marks. Here's how all that looks in action:

```
This link goes to <a href="http://www.google.com">Google</a>.
```

If you post the preceding line in a blog, the word *Google* appears as a clickable link that leads to the Google Web site.

Make sure that you use the full URL when you create a link — including the `http://`! Unless you include that prefix, the browser doesn't understand that it needs to find another Web site. Instead, it looks for a document on your Web site called `www.google.com`.

Also, when you turn off the tag, you need to turn off only the main tag, not the attribute or value. Those extras are turned off automatically when you use the closing `</a>` tag.

You can also use this tag around an image to make the image clickable to a Web page. Simply place the tag around your image code, like so:

```
<a href="http://www.google.com"><img src="googlelogo.gif"></a>
```

Making Lists

Lists can let people know about your favorite kinds of candy, music, or whatever. With a little help from your friendly HTML, you can create unordered lists or ordered lists. You create all lists, no matter the flavor, by using a series of HTML tags. These tags make lists a bit tricky to implement, so pay close attention to those closing tags — they're easy to forget.

An *unordered list* is a series of bulleted items. You can use this kind of list for items that don't require numbering. For example, if you want to create a list of cat breeds, you don't need to list them in any particular order. Unordered lists use the `<ul>` and `<li>` tags. Set up the code as I do in this list of kinds of chocolate:

```
<ul>
<li>Milk.</li>
<li>Dark.</li>
<li>White.</li>
</ul>
```

The `<ul>` tag stands for unordered list, and it turns on at the beginning of the list and turns off following the last item in the list. The `<li>` tag stands for list item; it turns on at the beginning of each new item and turns off at the end of that item. Figure B-4 shows an unordered list.

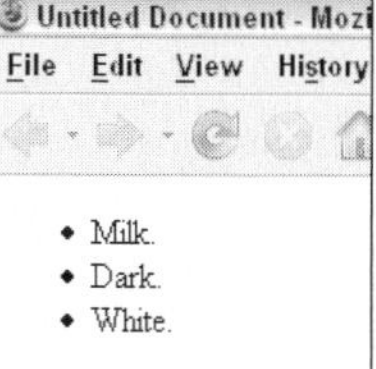

Figure B-4: Use unordered lists to create bullet items.

An ordered list contains items that use numbers instead of bullet points and are perfect for steps list or creating lists whose contents need to be ranked. Format an ordered list just the way you format an unordered list (as discussed in the preceding section), but substitute the `<ol>` tag for the `<ul>` tag (see Figure B-5):

```
<ol>
<li>Get a graham cracker.</li>
<li>Lay on a piece of chocolate.</li>
<li>Add a toasted marshmallow.</li>
<li>Add a second graham cracker on top, squish
          marshmallow, and eat.</li>
</ol>
```

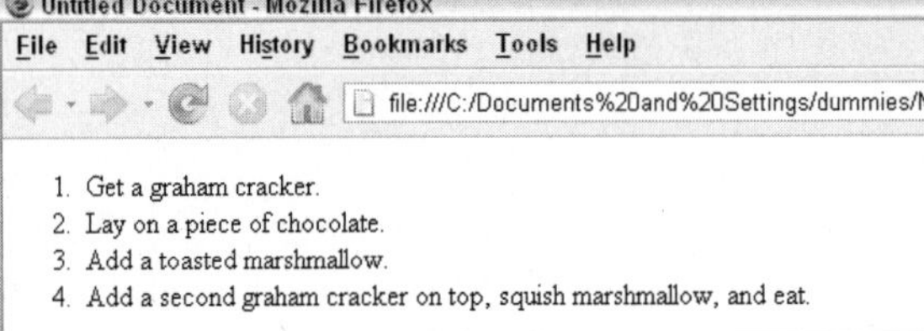

Figure: B-5: Ordered lists work well for instructions.

You can embed a list inside another list. In fact, you can even embed a different kind of list into a list. Each time you embed a new list, the Web browser creates additional indenting, giving you a nice stair-stepped look in your final page. Here's how you format the code that places an unordered sub-list inside an ordered list in a s'mores recipe:

```
<ol>
<li>Get a graham cracker.</li>
<li>Lay on a piece of chocolate. It can be:
   <ul>
   <li> Milk</li>
   <li> Dark</li>
   <li> White</li>
   </ul>
</li>
<li>Add a toasted marshmallow.</li>
<li>Add a second graham cracker on top, squish
          marshmallow, and eat.</li>
</ol>
```

Index

• Symbols •

• A •

• D •

• G •

• H •

• I •

• J •

• K •

• L •

• M •

• R •

• S •

• T •

• U •

• W •

• Z •

Business/Accounting & Bookkeeping
Bookkeeping For Dummies
978-0-7645-9848-7

eBay Business All-in-One For Dummies, 2nd Edition
978-0-470-38536-4

Job Interviews For Dummies, 3rd Edition
978-0-470-17748-8

Resumes For Dummies, 5th Edition
978-0-470-08037-5

Stock Investing For Dummies, 3rd Edition
978-0-470-40114-9

Successful Time Management For Dummies
978-0-470-29034-7

Computer Hardware
BlackBerry For Dummies, 3rd Edition
978-0-470-45762-7

Computers For Seniors For Dummies
978-0-470-24055-7

iPhone For Dummies, 2nd Edition
978-0-470-42342-4

Laptops For Dummies, 3rd Edition
978-0-470-27759-1

Macs For Dummies, 10th Edition
978-0-470-27817-8

Cooking & Entertaining
Cooking Basics For Dummies, 3rd Edition
978-0-7645-7206-7

Wine For Dummies, 4th Edition
978-0-470-04579-4

Diet & Nutrition
Dieting For Dummies, 2nd Edition
978-0-7645-4149-0

Nutrition For Dummies, 4th Edition
978-0-471-79868-2

Weight Training For Dummies, 3rd Edition
978-0-471-76845-6

Digital Photography
Digital Photography For Dummies, 6th Edition
978-0-470-25074-7

Photoshop Elements 7 For Dummies
978-0-470-39700-8

Gardening
Gardening Basics For Dummies
978-0-470-03749-2

Organic Gardening For Dummies, 2nd Edition
978-0-470-43067-5

Green/Sustainable
Green Building & Remodeling For Dummies
978-0-470-17559-0

Green Cleaning For Dummies
978-0-470-39106-8

Green IT For Dummies
978-0-470-38688-0

Health
Diabetes For Dummies, 3rd Edition
978-0-470-27086-8

Food Allergies For Dummies
978-0-470-09584-3

Living Gluten-Free For Dummies
978-0-471-77383-2

Hobbies/General
Chess For Dummies, 2nd Edition
978-0-7645-8404-6

Drawing For Dummies
978-0-7645-5476-6

Knitting For Dummies, 2nd Edition
978-0-470-28747-7

Organizing For Dummies
978-0-7645-5300-4

SuDoku For Dummies
978-0-470-01892-7

Home Improvement
Energy Efficient Homes For Dummies
978-0-470-37602-7

Home Theater For Dummies, 3rd Edition
978-0-470-41189-6

Living the Country Lifestyle All-in-One For Dummies
978-0-470-43061-3

Solar Power Your Home For Dummies
978-0-470-17569-9

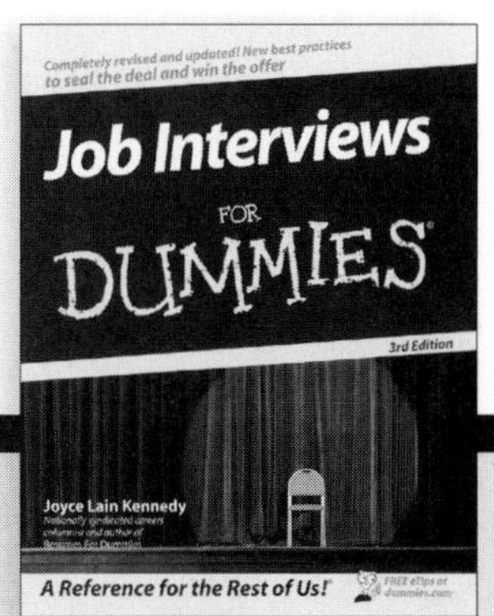

Available wherever books are sold. For more information or to order direct: U.S. customers visit www.dummies.com or call 1-877-762-2974. U.K. customers visit www.wileyeurope.com or call (0) 1243 843291. Canadian customers visit www.wiley.ca or call 1-800-567-4797.

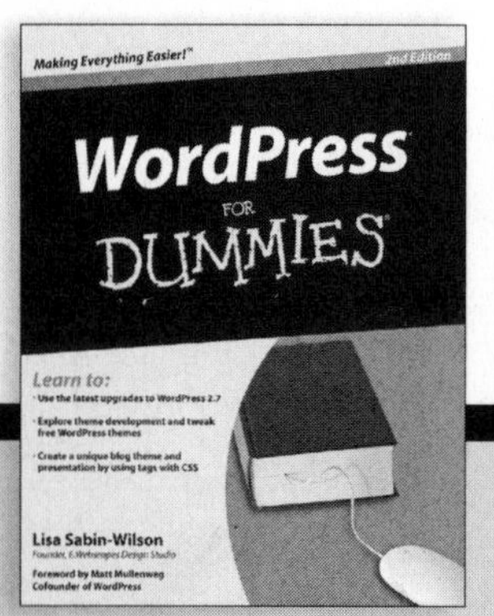

Making Everything Easier!
2nd Edition
WordPress
FOR
DUMMIES
Learn to:
Lisa Sabin-Wilson

Making Everything Easier!
2nd Edition
Web Marketing
FOR
DUMMIES
Learn to:
Jan Zimmerman

Making Everything Easier!
6th Edition
Digital Photography
FOR
DUMMIES
Learn to:
IN FULL COLOR!
Julie Adair King
Serge Timacheff

Making Everything Easier!
10th Edition
Macs
FOR
DUMMIES
Learn to:
Edward C. Baig